EXCAVATIONS AT
ST JAMES'S PRIORY, BRISTOL

Bristol and Regional Archaeological Services Monograph

EXCAVATIONS AT ST JAMES'S PRIORY, BRISTOL

by

Reg Jackson

with contributions by

Geraldine Barber, Rod Burchill, Rosie Clarke,
Peter Hardie, Sophie Lamb, Louise Loe,
Bruce Williams and David Williams

Oxbow Books

Published by
Oxbow Books, Park End Place, Oxford OX1 1HN

ISBN   978 1 84217 207 0   1 84217 207 7

A CIP record for this book is available from the British Library

This book is available direct from
Oxbow Books, Park End Place, Oxford, OX1 1HN
(Phone: 01865-241249; Fax: 01865-794449)

and

The David Brown Book Company
PO Box 511, Oakville, CT 06779, USA
(Phone: 860-945-9329; Fax: 860-945-9468)

and

via our website
www.oxbowbooks.com

Printed in Great Britain by
The Alden Press, Oxford

Contents

Summary vii
Résumé viii
Zusammenfassung ix
Acknowledgements xi

Chapter 1: Introduction 1
    Summary Contents of the Report 1
    The Background to the Archaeological Excavations 1
    Summary Phasing of Sites 1 and 2 3
    General Historical Introduction 5
    The Religious Houses to the North and West of the Medieval City 6

Chapter 2: St James's Priory 8
    Historical Background 8
    The Dissolution and After 11
    St James's Priory: Its Church, Conventual Buildings and Cemeteries 16

Chapter 3: The St James's Priory 'East End' Excavation Report (Site 1) 28
    Topography and Land Use 28
    Previous Archaeological Work 28
    Excavation Methods and Recording 29
    Report on the 1989 and 1995 Excavations 30

Chapter 4: The St James's Priory 'West Front' Excavation Report (Site 2) 57
    Topography and Land Use 57
    Previous Archaeological Work 57
    Excavation Methods and Recording 57
    Report on the Excavations 58

Chapter 5: The Burials 71
    Introduction 71
    The Archaeology of the Monastic Cemetery (Site 1) 72
    The Archaeology of the Lay/Parish Burial Ground (Sites 2 and 3) 99
    Site 2: Adjacent to the West Front of the Church 99
    Site 3: St James's Place 103
    Burials from Sites 2 and 3: Discussion 104
    Analysis of the Human Bone from Sites 1 and 2 *by Dr Louise Loe* 105
    Analysis of the Human Bone from Site 3 *by Sophie Lamb* 120

Chapter 6: The Finds 123
    The Pre-Conquest Pottery (Site 2) *by Rod Burchill* 123
    The Medieval Pottery *by Rod Burchill* 123
    The Medieval Floor Tiles (Sites 1 and 2 and Church House) *by Bruce Williams* 124
    A Note on the Petrology of Two Medieval Floor Tiles and Three Roof Tiles *by Dr David Williams* 130
    The Ceramic Roof Tiles (Site 1) *by Rod Burchill* 132
    The Clay Tobacco Pipes (Site 1) *by Reg Jackson* 133
    The Coins and Tokens (Site 1) *by Rosie Clarke* 133
    Objects of Bone and Ivory (Site 1) *by Rod Burchill* 135
    Objects of Glass (Site 1) *by Rod Burchill* 137
    Objects of Iron (Site 1) *by Rod Burchill* 138
    Objects of Copper Alloy (Site 1) *by Rod Burchill* 139
    Objects of Lead/Lead Alloy (Site 1) *by Rod Burchill* 141
    Objects of Stone and Fired Clay (Site 1) *by Rod Burchill* 142
    The Post-Medieval Pit Groups (Site 1) 142
    The Finds from Pit 1213 143
    The Finds from Pit 192 151
    The Finds from Pit 259 153
    The Finds from Pit 753 161
    The Finds from Pit 1223 169
    The Finds from Pit 586 172
    The Faunal Remains (Site 1) *by Geraldine Barber* 182

Chapter 7: Discussion 192

Bibliography and References 196
    Primary Sources 196
    Secondary Sources 196

Index 201

Summary

The Benedictine priory of St James was established in about 1129 just outside the medieval city. Two areas, one around the east end of the priory church and one adjacent to its west front, were excavated between 1989 and 1995. A watching brief was kept during landscaping work on part of the parish burial ground to the south of the church in 1997. The results of the excavations and watching brief are reported here together with a history of the priory and the post-Dissolution occupation of the area compiled from documentary, cartographic and pictorial sources and published accounts.

The area around the east end of St James's Priory church, Site 1, was excavated in 1989 and 1995. The excavations revealed a sequence of occupation on the site from at least the 12th century to the present day. The archaeological record, linked to the documentary sources, allows an understanding of the history and development of this important site.

Of particular interest was the discovery of fragmentary traces of the east end of the priory church together with a medieval monastic cemetery which yielded the remains of 245 articulated skeletons, the largest group of medieval burials excavated and studied in Bristol.

The excavations also recorded the development of the site after the Dissolution of the priory in 1540. The walls of the church were largely demolished by the end of the 16th century and pits for the extraction of sand were dug through the cemetery and then backfilled with debris from the priory.

The area remained open throughout the 17th and early 18th centuries when a number of rubbish and cess pits were dug, presumably for use by the occupants of the surrounding properties. The quality of the finds from these pits indicates the presence of quite affluent households and it is known from documentary sources that part of the priory buildings were converted into a large mansion house. A number of the pits also produced evidence of a bone-working industry in the form of bone offcuts and partly worked objects.

In the early 18th century the area of the site was developed for housing and the foundations, cellars, water tanks, rubbish pits and courtyards of those houses were recorded. Some of the houses were demolished for the construction of the Scottish Presbyterian Church and Sunday School in the mid 19th century, while the others remained in use until the National Farmers' Union offices were built on the remainder of the site in the 1960s.

An area adjacent to the west front of the priory church, Site 2, was excavated in 1994 and 1995. The excavation found evidence of the site being in use from the late Saxon period to the 20th century. During the 12th century the area was part of the lay burial ground for both the priory and the parish, the nave of the priory church probably having been in parochial use from its inception. A wall running east/west across the northern part of the site acted as a boundary between the burial ground and the approach to the west front of the church. Over the eastern part of the site burials continued until the 14th century and the remains of 33 articulated skeletons were found. However, in the latter half of the 13th century a building was constructed on the western part of the excavated area and during the 14th century burials also ceased in the remaining part of the burial ground between that building and the church. Occupation continued until the early 15th century when the building went out of use and may have been partly demolished.

There was some activity on the site during the 16th century after the Dissolution of the priory and early in the 17th century the medieval building was re-occupied and altered, the area to its east being used as a courtyard or part of an outbuilding. In the early 18th century the courtyard or outbuilding was replaced by two houses while the late 13th-century building was modified.

Alterations were made to the properties during the 19th and early 20th centuries before they were all demolished in the 1950s and 1960s.

In 1997 trenches were excavated by contractors carrying out a landscaping scheme at the entrance to the Broadmead shopping centre, Site 3. An archaeological watching brief undertaken during this work recorded seven medieval burials and a collection of disarticulated bone from an area known to have formerly been part of the St James's parish burial ground.

Résumé

Le prieuré bénédictin de St James fut établi aux environs de l'année 1129, juste en dehors de la cité médiévale. Deux sites, l'un autour de l'extrémité est du prieuré et l'autre adjacent à son côté ouest, ont été fouillés entre 1989 et 1995. Par ailleurs, un programme d'observation a été mis en place lors des travaux d'aménagement du paysage sur une partie du cimetière, au sud de l'église en 1997. Les résultats des fouilles et du programme d'observation sont consignés en cela, ainsi que l'histoire du prieuré et de l'occupation du site après Dissolution. Ces dernières ont été compilées à partir de sources documentaires, cartographiques et d'illustrations, ainsi que de compterendus publiés.

Le site autour de l'extrémité est du prieuré de St James, le Site 1, a été fouillé en 1989 et en 1995. Les fouilles ont révélé une séquence d'occupation du site, allant du 12ème siècle jusqu'à nos jours. Les archives archéologiques, associées aux sources documentaires, nous permettent de mieux comprendre l'histoire et le développement de ce site important.

Il faut noter la découverte particulièrement intéressante de traces fragmentaires de l'extrémité est du prieuré et d'un cimetière monastique moyenâgeux, qui a produit les restes de 245 squelettes articulés, le plus grand groupe d'inhumations médiévales excavées et étudiées à Bristol.

Les fouilles ont aussi noté le développement du site après la Dissolution du prieuré en 1540. Les murs de l'église étaient en grande partie démolis à la fin du 16ème siècle et des fosses pour l'extraction de sable furent creusées dans tout le cimetière, puis remplis de débris provenant du prieuré.

Le site demeura ouvert pendant tout le 17ème siècle et jusqu'au début du 18ème siècle, lorsque plusieurs fosses à détritus et à fumier furent creusées, sans doute par les occupants des propriétés alentours. Les trouvailles issues de ces fosses indiquent la présence de demeures plutôt prospères et on sait à partir de sources documentaires, qu'une partie des bâtiments du prieuré fut convertie en un grand hôtel particulier. Plusieurs fosses ont aussi produit des preuves d'industrie du travail des os, sous forme de restes d'os et d'objets en partie ouvragés.

Au début du 18ème siècle, la zone devint le site de maisons et les fondations, caves, réservoirs d'eau, fosses à détritus et cours ont été notés. Certaines des maisons furent démolies pour la construction de l'église presbytérienne écossaise et le catéchisme dans le milieu du 19ème siècle, tandis que les autres maisons restèrent en place jusqu'à la construction des bureaux du Syndicat national des agriculteurs, sur le reste du site dans les années 1960.

Une zone adjacente à la façade ouest du prieuré, le Site 2, a été fouillée en 1994 et 1995. Les fouilles ont indiqué que le site était utilisé de la fin de la période saxonne jusqu'au 20ème siècle. Pendant le 12ème siècle, le site faisait partie du cimetière pour le prieuré et la paroisse, la nef de l'église avait sûrement été utilisée par la paroisse depuis ses débuts. Un mur allant d'est en ouest, à travers la partie nord du site, servait de limite entre le cimetière et l'approche de la façade ouest de l'église. Sur la partie est du site, les enterrements continuèrent jusqu'au 14ème siècle et les restes de 33 squelettes articulés ont été trouvés. Toutefois, dans la dernière moitié du 13ème siècle, un bâtiment fut construit sur la partie ouest de la zone excavée et pendant le 14ème siècle, les enterrements cessèrent aussi dans la partie restante du cimetière, entre ce bâtiment et l'église. Cette partie continua d'être occupée jusqu'au début du 15ème siècle, au moment où le bâtiment cessa d'être utilisé et fut peut-être partiellement démoli.

Il y a eu des activités sur le site durant le 16ème siècle, après la Dissolution du prieuré et au début du 17ème siècle le bâtiment médiéval fut réoccupé et modifié, avec la zone à l'est utilisée comme cour ou comme partie d'une dépendance. Au début du 18ème siècle, la cour ou dépendance fut remplacée par deux maisons, tandis que le bâtiment de la fin du 13ème siècle était modifié.

Des modifications furent apportées aux propriétés aux 19ème siècle et au début du 20ème siècle, avant qu'elles ne soient complètement démolies dans les années 1950 et 1960.

En 1997, des tranchées furent excavées par des entrepreneurs qui réalisaient des travaux d'aménagement du paysage, à l'entrée du centre commercial de Broadmead, le Site 3. Un programme d'observation entrepris lors de ces travaux a noté sept cimetières médiévaux et une collection d'os désarticulés d'un site dont on sait qu'il faisait partie auparavant du cimetière du prieuré de St James.

Zusammenfassung

Das Benediktinerkloster St. James (zum heiligen Jakob) wurde ca. 1129 unmittelbar vor den Mauern der mittelalterlichen Stadt gegründet. In zwei Bereichen, einer am östlichen Ende der Klosterkirche und der andere neben dem Westwerk, wurden zwischen den Jahren 1989 und 1995 Ausgrabungen vorgenommen. Bei Landschaftsgestaltungsarbeiten in Teilen des Gemeindefriedhofes an der Südseite der Kirche wurden im Jahre 1997 archäologische Untersuchungen durchgeführt und die Befunde festgehalten. Dies ist ein Bericht über die Ergebnisse der Ausgrabungen sowie der archäologischen Untersuchungen, außerdem wird die Geschichte des Klosters sowie die Besiedlung des Geländes nach der Säkularisierung und Auflösung des Klosters nach dokumentarischen, kartografischen und bildlichen Quellen, sowie aus veröffentlichten Berichten beschrieben.

An der im Bereich des Ostendes der Kirche St. James liegenden Ausgrabungsstelle 1 wurden in den Jahren 1989 und 1995 archäologische Grabungen vorgenommen. Aus diesen Grabungen ging hervor, dass dieser Ort mindestens vom 12. Jahrhundert an, bis hin zum heutigen Tage besiedelt war. Aufgrund der archäologischen Funde und im Zusammenhang mit dokumentarischen Quellen war es möglich, die Geschichte und Entwicklung dieser wichtigen Ausgrabungsstelle nachzuvollziehen.

Von ganz besonderem Interesse war dabei die Entdeckung fragmentarischer Überreste von der Ostseite der Klosterkirche, sowie eines Klosterfriedhofes aus dem Mittelalter, in dem die Überreste von 245 vollständig erhaltenen Skeletten gefunden wurden, der größten Gruppe in einer mittelalterlichen Grabstätte, die jemals in Bristol ausgegraben und untersucht wurde.

Durch die Ausgrabungen konnte außerdem auch die Entwicklung des Geländes nach der Säkularisierung bzw. Auflösung des Klosters im Jahre 1540 festgehalten werden. Am Ende des 16. Jahrhunderts waren die Mauern der Kirche größtenteils zerstört, und überall auf dem Friedhof wurden Gruben zur Sandgewinnung ausgehoben, und mit Abraum aus dem Kloster wieder neu befüllt.

Das Gelände blieb während des ganzen 17. und frühen 18. Jahrhunderts offen, als eine Reihe von Abfall- und Klärgruben ausgehoben und höchstwahrscheinlich von den Bewohnern der umliegenden Anwesen benutzt wurden. Aus der Qualität der Funde aus diesen Gruben läßt sich schließen, dass sich in dieser Gegend recht wohlhabende Haushaltungen befunden haben müssen, und aus dokumentarischen Quellen geht hervor, dass ein Teil der Klostergebäude in ein großes Herrenhaus umgebaut wurde. In einer Reihe von Gruben wurden außerdem durch Knochenabschnitte und teilweise bearbeitete Gegenstände, Nachweise für eine knochenverarbeitende Industrie gefunden.

Im frühen 18. Jahrhundert wurde das Gelände zur Bebauung freigegeben, und es wurden die Grundmauern, Keller, Wasserzisternen, Abfallgruben und Hofgebäude dieser Häuser archäologisch festgehalten. Einige dieser Häuser wurden beim Bau der schottisch-presbyterianischen Kirche und Sonntagsschule in der Mitte des 19. Jahrhunderts abgerissen, während andere auch weiterhin bis zum Bau des Bürogebäudes der National Farmers' Union (dem britischen Landwirtschaftsverband) auf dem Rest des Geländes in den sechziger Jahren bestehen blieben und benutzt wurden.

In einem an das Westwerk der Klosterkirche angrenzenden Bereich, der Grabungsstelle 2, wurden 1994 und 1995 Ausgrabungen vorgenommen. In diesem Bereich wurden Nachweise für eine Benutzung seit spätsächsischer Zeit bis hin ins 20. Jahrhundert gefunden. Während des 12. Jahrhunderts war das Gelände Teil einer Laienbegräbnisstätte sowohl für das Kloster als auch die Gemeinde, wobei das Kirchenschiff des Klosterkirchengebäudes wahrscheinlich von Beginn an kirchlich genutzt wurde. Eine in west-/östlicher Richtung am nördlichen Teil des Geländes verlaufende Mauer bildete die Grenze zwischen der Begräbnisstätte und der Annäherung zum Westwerk der Kirche. Der östliche Teil des Geländes diente bis zum 14. Jahrhundert auch weiterhin als Grabesstätte; dort wurden die Überreste von 33 vollständig erhaltenen Skeletten gefunden. Jedoch wurde in der zweiten Hälfte des 13. Jahrhunderts im westlichen Teil des Ausgrabungsgeländes ein Gebäude errichtet, und im Laufe des 14. Jahrhunderts wurden die Grablegungen im verbleibenden Teil des Friedhofes zwischen diesem Gebäude und der Kirche ebenfalls eingestellt. Die Besiedlung dauerte bis zum frühen 15. Jahrhundert an, danach wurde das Gebäude nicht mehr benutzt und möglicherweise zum Teil abgerissen.

Nach der Auflösung des Klosters sind auch im 16. Jahrhundert noch Anzeichen einer Benutzung auf dem Gelände vorhanden, und zu Beginn des 17. Jahrhunderts wurde das aus dem Mittelalter stammende Gebäude neu bezogen und umgebaut, wobei das sich nach Osten daran anschließende Gelände als Hofgebäude oder als Teil eines Außengebäudes benutzt wurde. Im frühen 18. Jahrhundert wurde das Hof- oder Außengebäude durch zwei Häuser ersetzt, während das Gebäude aus dem 13. Jahrhundert umgebaut wurde.

Im 19. und frühen 20. Jahrhundert wurden Änderungen an den Gebäuden vorgenommen, bevor alles in den fünfziger und sechziger Jahren des 20. Jahrhunderts abgerissen wurde.

Im Jahre 1997 wurden Stichgrabungen an der Ausgrabungsstelle 3 vorgenommen, dies erfolgte im Rahmen eines Landschaftsgestaltungsprojektes, das von Auftragnehmern am Eingang zum Einkaufszentrum Broadmead durchgeführt wurde. Aufgrund der im Laufe dieser Arbeiten durchgeführten archäologischen Untersuchungen wurden sieben aus dem Mittelalter datierende Grabstellen sowie eine Reihe einzelner Knochen auf einem Gelände gefunden, von dem man weiß, das es einmal Teil des Gemeindefriedhofs von St. James war.

Acknowledgements

The author would like to thank:

Scottish Mutual Assurance plc and English Heritage for financing the archaeological excavations and post-excavation work on Sites 1 and 2 respectively and for jointly funding the publication of this report. Scottish Mutual generously funded the analysis of the results of the 1989 excavation at the east end of the priory church enabling them to be integrated with the 1995 excavation report on Site 1. Mr D. McKean of Scottish Mutual co-ordinated their involvement in the archaeological work.

The Little Brothers of Nazareth who helped with access to Site 2 and Stone Ecclesiastical who carried out the construction work on that site.

Ian Galbraith of Osprey Project Management, consultants to Scottish Mutual, who gave help and assistance throughout the excavation and post-excavation stages of the archaeological work.

Bruce Williams of Bristol and Region Archaeological Services for managing the project and Rosie Clarke for undertaking the administrative work.

John Bryant, who managed the Site 2 excavation, and gave much advice and assistance.

Bob Jones, Bristol City Archaeologist, for monitoring the work on behalf of the planning authority and giving advice on the results of his 1989 excavation at St James's Priory.

Ann Linge who drew all the plans and most of the finds for publication and gave much help, advice and assistance on that aspect of the report.

Davina Ware who drew some of the medieval floor tiles.

Frankie Webb for her assistance with the digital photography.

The team of archaeologists employed by Bristol and Region Archaeological Services to carry out the excavations, plan and record the archaeology and process the finds. David Wickes acted as Site Supervisor on Site 1 and ensured the accurate and detailed recording of the excavation. Lesley Cross, Georgina Finn, Peter Insole and John Turner were Area Supervisors. Tom Brogden, Rosie Clarke, Frank Coyne, Rob Curtis, Tim Longman, Richard Jones, Steve Newman and Pete Rowlstone worked as Site Assistants.

The many volunteers who gave freely of their time and energy were Frankie Webb, Robin Stiles, Chris Anderson, Julia Wilson, Jane Atkinson, Kay Ridgwell, Nic Turner, James Russell, Andy Buchan, Steve Drew, Nick Hanks, Lucy Elliott, Shaun Gibb, Dave Anderson, Martin Parsons, Christine Dalton, Mary Friend, Mike Baker, Ian Beckey, Juliet Robb, Vikki Staples, Jean Dagnall, Jennifer Pennington, Simon Burchill, Merle Wade, Julie Douglas, Virginia Pearson, Emma Jenkins, Sue Gay, John Perryman, Jennifer Roberts, Annie Marsh, Patrick Rowell, Antigone Blair, Emily Morgan, Polly Davies, Jane Strachey, Andy Clarke, Paul Harper, Peter Lennox, Rod Mansell, Virginia Rowan, John Vincent, Dennis Coote, Louise Butler, Stan Price, Claire Dieppe, Ian Lewis, John Dutton, Joanne Soppit, Tom Kavell and Andrew Loader.

The archaeology students from Bradford University who kindly gave up their holiday to assist in the work. They were Nigel Melton, Jessica Davies, Nick Harper, Belinda Simmons, Anwen Caffell and Tom Finney.

Louise Loe and Juliet Rogers who gave advice on the excavation, recording and processing of the human remains and subsequently provided the detailed specialist report on the human bones.

Geraldine Barber, Rod Burchill, Rosie Clarke, Peter Hardie, Sophia Lamb, Bruce Williams and David Williams for preparing the various finds reports.

Jon Brett for loaning relevant books and publications from his extensive library, digitising the burial plans on computer and also assisting on the excavation.

Dave Stevens for preparing the burial plans for publication.

Jeremy Hutchings for on-site conservation and Amanda Wallace who conserved and catalogued the small finds in the Bristol City Museum Conservation Section.

Roger Price for his advice on the bone syringes.

The Little Brothers of Nazareth for allowing deposition of the excavated human remains within St James's church.

The staff of the Bristol Record Office, Bristol Reference Library, Bristol University Library, Gloucestershire Record Office and The National Archive for providing facilities and advising on the documentary research. Special thanks must go to the Bristol

Record Office for allowing the publication of items from their collection.

Louise Loe would like to thank:
Dr Juliet Rogers and Dr Geraldine Barber for their supervision, Rebecca Wiggins for her advice about the non-adult skeletons, and Sadie Dunne and Dr Iain Watt from the Department of Radiology, Bristol Royal Infirmary for their help with the x-rays.

1 INTRODUCTION

Summary Contents of the Report

The first chapter of the report takes the form of a brief introduction to the nature of the archaeological work at St James's Priory, including a summary of the phasing of the remains found, together with a general historical introduction, which places the priory in the wider context of the development of Bristol in the late Saxon and post-Conquest periods and shows its relationship to other monastic foundations immediately north and west of the medieval city. Details of archaeological work undertaken on those monastic foundations is given together with published sources for their history.

That is followed by a chapter dealing with the origin and development of St James's Priory from its foundation through to the Dissolution, and the use of the site in post-medieval and modern times, obtained from documentary and published sources. An interpretation of the layout of the priory church and of the conventual buildings, including a description of the surviving remains, is then attempted using a variety of sources and through comparison with other Benedictine priories. Information on the priory derived from archaeological excavation, observations made during building work and a survey of the standing structures, some published here for the first time, is also used to help interpret its plan and history.

Chapters three and four contain reports on the large-scale archaeological excavations carried out on Sites 1 and 2 in 1989, 1994 and 1995 and describe the structures, features and sequence of occupation found on those sites. The main periods of use of the sites are described, ranging from features which may pre-date the priory through to 20th-century development. The excavation reports are accompanied by information on topography and modern land use, previous archaeological work on the sites, and the excavation and recording methods used during the excavations.

The report on the excavation of the medieval monastic and lay cemeteries is dealt with in a separate chapter. This gives details of the layout of the burial grounds, the burial types, the grouping of burial types within the cemeteries, the date of the burials and the finds from the graves. Tables summarise the information obtained from each burial and their relationship to each other. The section also records the small number of burials recovered during a watching brief carried out in 1997 within the parish burial ground at St James's Place. The skeletal remains have been examined by specialists and the full results of that examination and an analysis of the findings is given.

Chapter six contains specialist reports on the various types of artefacts found during the excavations. Only a relatively small number of medieval finds were recovered, mainly from the grave fills and the post-Dissolution destruction levels or robber trenches on Site 1, and these are reported on in full. The majority of finds from the sites were post-medieval in date including some closely dated groups of finds from 17th- and 18th-century rubbish pits on Site 1. Due to financial constraints the publication of the post-medieval finds has had to be limited to a catalogue of objects from pit groups selected for their date range and quality of finds. In an attempt to show the artefacts in use at particular times within the St James's households all the finds from the individual pits are published together.

A summary of the results of the excavations and the significance of the discoveries follows together with views on the potential for future archaeological work on St James's Priory.

A full bibliography is provided with information on the documentary and cartographic sources used.

The Background to the Archaeological Excavations

Site 1 (centred on NGR ST 58937345; Fig. 1)

In 1989 staff of the Field Archaeology section of Bristol City Museum and Art Gallery undertook the complete excavation of an area covering 140 square metres to the north-east of the National Farmers' Union Mutual Insurance (NFU) office building in St James's Parade. This work was directed by Bob Jones and was

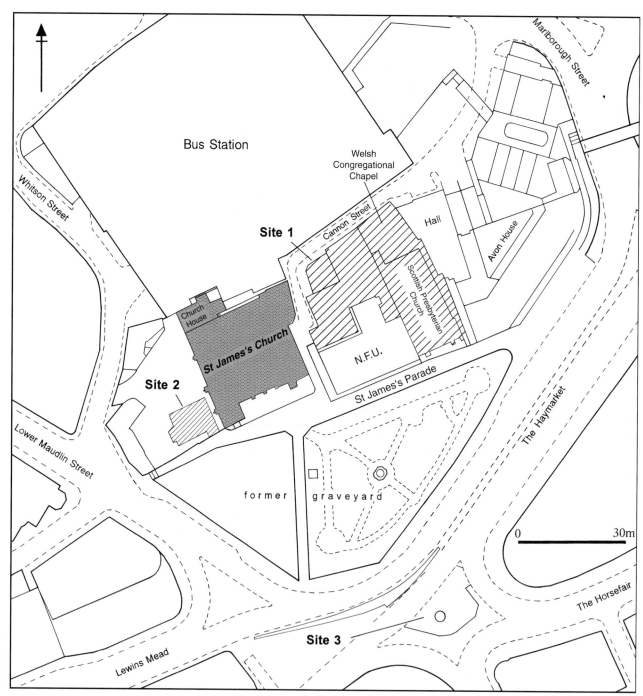

Fig. 1 Plan showing the location of St James's Priory and Sites 1, 2 and 3

occasioned by the proposed redevelopment of the site for an extension to the NFU offices. Although no priory buildings were revealed, a number of medieval burials, including distinctive body-shaped or head-niche burials, were found and interpreted as part of the monastic burial ground to the east of the priory church. The foundations of 18th-century buildings together with 17th-century rubbish pits containing fine groups of ceramics and other objects were also uncovered. An interim report on this excavation has been published (Jones 1989).

The proposed extension to the NFU building was

never constructed and the offices and adjoining land, which had been the site of the 19th-century Scottish Presbyterian Church, were eventually purchased by Scottish Mutual Assurance plc. It was intended to demolish the NFU offices and the smaller Audit Office building on the corner of Cannon Street and construct a new office block with a basement car park covering the entire area, an operation which would completely destroy the archaeological deposits lying just below the modern ground surface and which nowhere exceeded more than two metres in depth. The area proposed for redevelopment, excluding that already destroyed by the basement of the NFU building, covered approximately 1,200 square metres and included the site of the 1989 excavation.

As part of the planning process Scottish Mutual Assurance commissioned Bristol and Region Archaeological Services to carry out an archaeological desktop assessment (BaRAS 1994a) which was followed in 1994 by the excavation of five evaluation trenches (BaRAS 1994b). This assessment and evaluation work confirmed the results of the 1989 excavation and showed the medieval burial ground spreading west towards the supposed location of the east end of the priory church. It also indicated that the area occupied by the NFU car park, and possibly that occupied by the Audit Office, had been badly damaged by modern service trenches.

Under the provisions of Planning Policy Guidance Note 16 'Archaeology and Planning', planning consent was granted to Scottish Mutual Assurance subject to their funding the total excavation of the site, the cost of post-excavation work and the publication of a full report. It was agreed that their funding would also cover post-excavation work on, and the publication of, the 1989 excavation.

The main aim of the 1995 project was to recover a full history of the use of the site through the total excavation of the surviving archaeological deposits and structures before their destruction by redevelopment.

The following specific objectives were also intended to be fulfilled within the overall excavation strategy:

a)   to discover the extent and date of the pre-burial features found during the 1989 excavation

b)   to locate the east end of the priory church and any associated structures, such as chapels, to date their construction and recover a plan of those buildings

c)   to fully excavate the monastic burial ground to the east of the priory church, record its extent and, if possible, identify its period of use

d)   to recover information on the extent of the destruction of the priory after the Dissolution and determine the subsequent use of the site before its redevelopment for housing in the 18th century and

e)   to record in detail the 18th-century and later buildings and occupation.

The excavation was carried out by Bristol and Region Archaeological Services under the direction of the writer for a period of five months from early January 1995.

Site 2 (centred on NGR ST 58877344; Fig. 1)

The need for an excavation arose from a proposal by the Little Brothers of Nazareth, the present occupiers of St James's Church, to build a rehabilitation unit for drug users at the west end of the church on the site of nos. 13–16 St James's Parade. As a first response to the

planning application an archaeological desktop study was carried out which was followed by the excavation of evaluation trenches (BaRAS 1993). The trenches demonstrated that archaeological levels survived in the area and it was anticipated that the building work would cause damage to the archaeology, particularly at the eastern end of the site.

A specification for further archaeological work was drawn up by the City Archaeologist and planning permission was granted subject to an archaeological excavation on the eastern half of the site where the archaeological levels lay only 0.25m below the modern ground surface. It was considered that during building work the archaeological deposits would be severely truncated, the tops of the foundations removed and localised disturbance caused by mini piles, all of which would render meaningless any archaeological material that remained. A watching brief was to be kept on the rest of the site during groundworks connected with the development. Grant aid was provided by English Heritage due to the charitable status of the Little Brothers of Nazareth.

The objective of the archaeological work as defined in the City Archaeologist's specification was that 'a full range of data from the area under consideration should be recorded and a subsequent analysis undertaken, to allow for reasoned interpretation to be made of observed archaeological features'.

The excavation was carried out by Bristol and Region Archaeological Services under the direction of John Bryant in two phases: from February to April 1994 and from April to June 1995.

Work on the construction of the new building commenced in July 1995 and a watching brief was kept, particularly during the machine excavation of the archaeological deposits for the insertion of ground beams.

Site 3 (NGR ST 58967338; Fig. 1)

In 1997 Bristol and Region Archaeological Services were commissioned by the Planning, Transport and Development Directorate of Bristol City Council to monitor contractor's groundworks associated with the construction of a new road layout and 'gateway' to Bristol's Broadmead shopping centre to be known as St James's Place. The site lay within St James's parish burial ground and immediately south-west of a group of medieval burials recovered in 1954 during the construction of a department store. The watching brief was carried out by Rod Burchill.

Summary Phasing of Sites 1 and 2

Period 1 – Pre-priory occupation (late Saxon)
Site 1: Two U-shaped gullies which pre-dated the

earliest monastic burials, but were otherwise undated, may have been related to the late Saxon features on Site 2.

Site 2: Three shallow features contained late Saxon pottery sherds.

Period 2 – St James's Priory (c.1129 to 1540)

Period 2A (c.1129 to mid 13th century)

Site 1: Construction and use of the east end of the priory church. Establishment and use of the monastic burial ground.

Site 2: Establishment and use of the lay/parish burial ground, with an east/west wall across the northern part of the site serving as a boundary between the burial ground and the approach to the west front of the church.

Period 2B (mid to late 13th century)

Site 1: Continued use of the monastic burial ground.

Site 2: Continued use of the lay burial ground although its area was restricted by the erection of a building in the late 13th century (Building 10), which incorporated the boundary wall as its north wall. A number of pits and postholes also date to this period.

Period 2C (14th century)

Site 1: A blocking wall to the south transept of the priory church was probably constructed c. 1374. Fragments of a 14th-century occupation level survived to the north of the church. Continued use of the monastic burial ground.

Site 2: Occupation of Building 10 continued and was extended to the west and east. This ended the use of the area as part of the lay burial ground as occupation layers sealed the interments in the area between Building 10 and the church.

Period 2D (15th century to the Dissolution in 1540)

Site 1: Use of the monastic burial ground probably continued until the Dissolution.

Site 2: A large pit was dug within Building 10 after its abandonment in the 15th century.

Period 3 – Post Dissolution activity (1540 to early 17th century)

Site 1: There was evidence for the demolition of the priory walls and the robbing of their foundations. Pits were dug, probably for the extraction of sand, within the monastic cemetery. A stone-lined drain and make-up layers to the north of the church dated to the 16th century.

Site 2: Postholes, stakeholes and layers dating to the 16th and early 17th century indicate possible occupation post-dating the Dissolution.

Period 4 – Post-medieval reoccupation (early 17th century to the 1990s)

Period 4A (early 17th century to early 18th century)

Site 1: Cultivation trenches confirm the documented use of the area as gardens or agricultural land. Rubbish and cess-pits were presumably associated with the buildings outside the excavated area depicted on Millerd's map of 1673.

Site 2: Building 10, which was almost certainly one of the buildings depicted on Millerd's map to the west of the church, was altered and reoccupied and the land to its north was cultivated as gardens. The area to its east was used as a courtyard or part of an outbuilding, with a partly cobbled floor.

Period 4B (early 18th century to mid 19th century)

Site 1: The thoroughfare known initially as 'The Churchyard' and later as St James's Parade was laid out in the early 18th century and Buildings 7 and 8 (nos. 7 and 8 St James's Parade) were constructed around that time. The rear of these buildings lay within the excavated area together with their courtyards, drains, rubbish pits and water tanks.

Cannon Street was established to the north and west of the site in the 1740s and Buildings 1 to 6 were erected at that time.

Alterations were made to these buildings and their ancillary structures throughout the late 18th and early 19th centuries.

Site 2: Building 10 (no. 15 St James's Parade) continued to be occupied although it was altered internally, while in the early 18th century the courtyard or outbuilding was replaced by two houses, Buildings 11 and 12 (nos. 12 and 13 St James's Parade).

Period 4C (mid 19th century to 1940)

Site 1: Some of the 18th-century houses on the St James's Parade and Cannon Street frontages were demolished for the construction of the Scottish Presbyterian Church during the 1850s. The remaining houses continued in use.

Site 2: Buildings 10, 11 and 12 continued to be occupied with some alterations being made to the properties.

Period 4D (1940 to the 1990s)

Site 1: The Scottish Presbyterian Church was destroyed during the 1940 blitz. It was subsequently demolished and the Welsh Congregational Chapel, Sunday School and Meeting House built on part of the site in 1953. The remaining houses were occupied until they were demolished for the construction of the National Farmers' Union Mutual Insurance and Audit Office buildings in 1964. The Meeting House was demolished in 1988.

Site 2: Buildings 10, 11 and 12 were demolished between the 1950s and 1960s and replaced by a garden of remembrance and car park.

General Historical Introduction

Bristol was founded during the Saxon period in a superbly defensible and commercial position at the lowest fording or bridging point on the River Avon where it was protected on three sides by the confluence of the rivers Avon and Frome. The original Saxon burh, or fortified township, was sited at the narrowest point between the two rivers on a 20 acre ridge of Triassic sandstone which rose some 10 to 15 metres above the surrounding marsh.

Despite its strategic position, the site of the medieval town does not appear to have had an earlier, Roman origin as extensive archaeological excavations since the 1960s have failed to find any clear evidence of Roman occupation. However, traces of what was probably a Romano-British iron-working site have been found close to Upper Maudlin Street on the south facing slope leading from the River Frome to modern Kingsdown, some 800 metres north of the centre of the medieval town. That was excavated in 1973, 1976 and 1999 and found to comprise furnaces and parts of a building with stone footings within a fenced yard which overlay an earlier field boundary. The Roman occupation spanned the 2nd to the 5th centuries (Ponsford 1975; Jackson 2000).

The earliest documentary and numismatic evidence for the existence of a settlement on the central site of Bristol itself dates to the 11th century. The surviving written records contain no mention of Bristol until 1051, when it appeared in the Anglo-Saxon Chronicle as a port used by sea-going ships sailing to and from Ireland (Lobel and Carus-Wilson 1975, 3). It seems likely that coins were first minted in Bristol c.1010, in the reign of Aethelred II, although the first definite evidence is the existence of a number of silver pennies with the mint mark *Bricgstow*. All belong to Cnut's first issue and are ascribed to the years 1017–1023 (Grinsell 1986, 4; Hinton 1984, 151). The minting of coins was not allowed except in a burh so by that time Bristol probably possessed a market and some degree of trade (Loyn 1962, 137–8).

As it is clear that the Bristol area was virtually aceramic before c.940, and even after that pottery was sparse until the late 11th and 12th centuries, it is unlikely that archaeology will be able to prove the existence of a Saxon settlement at Bristol pre-dating that indicated by the documentary and numismatic evidence (Watts and Rahtz 1985, 16). However, archaeological excavation has shown that the original late Saxon settlement was concentrated close to the site of Bristol Bridge and that it spread along the crest of the natural ridge of Triassic sandstone between the present Old Market Street and at least as far west as the former Mary-le-Port Street. Excavations at the castle, Peter Street and Mary-le-Port Street have produced evidence of pre-Conquest occupation in the

form of timber buildings, fences, pits, pottery and metal and other objects of both Viking and late Saxon type (Ponsford undated, 145). Late Saxon settlement also seems to have existed in the area of Broad Street and Tower Lane, north of the centre of the medieval town, where late 10th- and early 11th-century cess-pits, postholes and rubbish pits were found during excavations between 1979 and 1980 (Boore 1984, 11).

A late Saxon origin is also suggested for the area that was later to become the site of St Augustine's Abbey to the west of the medieval town. A sculpture known as the 'Harrowing of Hell', which is believed to date from the first half of the 11th century, was found beneath the floor of the abbey's chapter house (Dickinson 1976, 121). The possibility of Saxon occupation in that area is supported by finds made during the archaeological excavations in 1983 and 1984 just to the south of St Augustine's Abbey, at the church of St Augustine the Less. There the earliest archaeological deposits were six adult burials in cist graves and another burial in a body-shaped grave with a head and shoulders profile. These were interpreted as Saxo-Norman in date (Boore 1986, 211).

Documentary sources provide some information on the development of Bristol immediately after the Norman conquest. It seems that by 1067 Bristol had become a strongly fortified burh for in that year its citizens successfully resisted an invading force from Ireland led by the sons of Harold Godwinson which had failed to take the defences (Lobel and Carus-Wilson 1975, 3). The Domesday survey suggests that in 1086 Bristol was a flourishing settlement and reveals that, while it was situated within the royal manor of Barton, it had a distinct entity with its own community of burgesses who answered for it to the King (Whitelock 1961).

During the Norman period there was a shift of emphasis in the location of the settlement due to the establishment of an eleven acre fortress on the east/west ridge, the site of part of the late Saxon settlement. This meant that the town now became largely located at the west end of the ridge on the lower ground at the confluence of the rivers Frome and Avon and during the early 12th century a stone defensive wall was built around the town (Ponsford undated, 150).

At the close of the Norman period Bristol was described as 'almost the richest city of all in the country, receiving merchandise by sailing-ships from lands near and far. It lies in the most fertile part of England and is by its very situation the most strongly fortified of all its cities' (Potter 1955, 37).

It can be seen from this description that Bristol's castle, which may have started as a ringwork and was later reinforced with a large motte and ditch, was one of the finest in Norman Britain. This was due to the extensive building work carried out in the late 11th and early 12th centuries initially by Robert FitzHamon

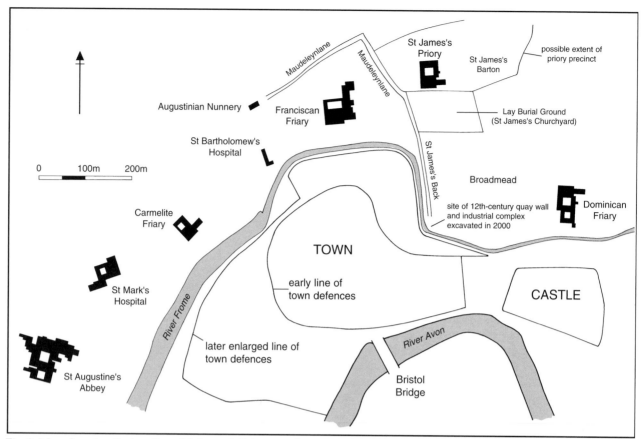

Fig. 2 Map showing the location of St James's Priory in relation to medieval Bristol and the religious houses to the north and west of the city

and afterwards by Robert, Earl of Gloucester, the bastard son of Henry I (Lobel and Carus-Wilson 1975, 4). The substantial alterations to the castle are evidence of the prominent part played by Robert, Earl of Gloucester, in the wars of Stephen's reign. By 1147 the motte had been largely superseded by Earl Robert's massive keep which was some 27 metres square and built of stone quarried at Caen in Normandy. It was said that he had set aside a tenth of the Caen stone intended for the keep of Bristol Castle towards the building of a Lady Chapel in the Benedictine priory of St James which he had founded in about 1129 (Dugdale 1823, 335). The site Earl Robert had chosen for St James's Priory was on open level land on the north bank of the River Frome and within sight of his castle (Fig. 2).

The Religious Houses to the North and West of the Medieval City

Although St James's Priory was the earliest monastic settlement in Bristol it was the forerunner of a number of other religious houses sited to the west and north of the River Frome and whose landholdings eventually

formed a continuous chain stretching for almost one and a half kilometres from St Augustine's Abbey in the west to the Dominican Friary in the east (Fig. 2). This growth in religious houses in Bristol was part of a national expansion, the Norman conquest heralding a rapid increase in the number of monastic foundations in urban areas in Britain over the following two centuries, with the establishment of two hundred urban monasteries for men, twenty nunneries and fifty colleges of canons (Butler 1993, 79).

It is necessary to provide a brief chronological review of the religious houses established just to the west and north of the medieval town, together with an outline of archaeological work carried out on the sites in order to place St James's Priory in its historic and archaeological setting.

St Augustine's Abbey: Robert FitzHarding founded an abbey for Augustinian Canons in about 1140 on a low plateau in the manor of Billeswick below what is now Park Street and Brandon Hill (Dickinson 1976, 119). Archaeological recording was carried out in 1987 during building work in the lesser cloister and on a medieval stone-built culvert below (Boore 1989, 217). An excavation was undertaken in 1992 to the south of the south-west tower on the west front of the cathedral and west of the cloister of the former abbey. The buildings found there were probably the abbot's house and the guest-house of the abbey with an adjoining workshop, replaced in the 14th century by the abbey *cellarium* (Rawes 1993, 216).

Augustinian Nunnery: A house of Augustinian Canonesses dedicated to St Mary Magdalen was founded by Eva, wife of Robert FitzHarding, possibly just before his death in 1170. It was situated at the bottom of what is now St Michael's Hill opposite St Michael's Church (Lobel and Carus-Wilson 1975, 8). Eva became the first prioress and continued in that position until her death in 1173 (Barrett 1789, 426). Excavations were carried out on part of the nunnery in 2000 when medieval walls were found together with twelve burials in part of the monastic cemetery (Longman 2003, 3–29).

Dominican Friary: This was founded in about 1227 within the parish of St James on land granted to the Dominicans by Robert FitzHarding's great grandson, Maurice de Gaunt, who was buried within the friary on his death in 1230. In 1230 the Bishop of Worcester, in spite of opposition from the priory of St James, dedicated the altar and churchyard (Leighton 1933, 152) although building apparently continued on the church and friary for over 40 years (Lobel and Carus-Wilson 1975, 8). Two of the conventual buildings, possibly the dorter and infirmary, survive in good condition as part of the Quaker's Friars complex in Broadmead (Dawson 1981, 23). Archaeological evaluation work on part of the friary complex revealed what was probably the southern precinct wall on the bank of the River Frome and walls associated with the Great Cloister and the church (BaRAS 2002).

St Mark's Hospital: Maurice de Gaunt, lord of the manor of Billeswick, founded an almonry close to St Augustine's Abbey sometime before 1230 and entrusted the administration of his charity to the monastery. The abbot and convent undertook to feed one hundred poor people in the almonry each day and to maintain a chaplain. After his death in 1230 his nephew and heir Robert de Gurnay confirmed the endowment. He made the hospital a separate foundation, independent of the abbey, with a mother and three chaplains (Graham 1907, 114). The hospital was also apparently intended to admit twelve scholars (Taylor 1878, 241). The original chapel of St Mark's Hospital survives as the Lord Mayor's Chapel on College Green.

St Bartholomew's Hospital: The hospital seems to have been founded by Sir John la Warre after 1231 but before 1243 and it apparently functioned essentially as an almshouse which also catered for visitors to the town, the community consisting of brethren and sisters (Graham 1907, 118). The site of the hospital was excavated in 1977 when extensive remains of a possible chapel and the main domestic range dating from the 13th century were found (Price with Ponsford 1998).

Franciscan Friary: The religious order of mendicant friars known variously as the Friars Minor, the Franciscans or Greyfriars, first came to England in the 1220s. Before 1234 a house of the friars was founded in Bristol at the expense of the townspeople and as the order's chief house for south Wales and the south-west of England (Dawson 1981, 23). Some time before 1250 a new site was found for the friary in Lewin's Mead on land possibly given by the Benedictine priory of St James. The site of Greyfriars was bounded by Upper Maudlin Street on the north, Lewin's Mead on the south, Lower Maudlin Street (and St James's Priory) on the east and St Bartholomew's Hospital and its lands on the west. Large-scale excavations in 1973 revealed the church, cloister, chapter house and other friary buildings (Ponsford 1975). Further archaeological excavations were carried out in Deep Street in 1989 on a 13th-century ground-floor hall interpreted as a friary lodging or guesthouse (Gaimster *et al.* 1990, 168–9).

Carmelite Friary: The Carmelites or Whitefriars established their friary in 1256 (Lobel and Carus-Wilson 1975, 8) although it is traditionally said that it was founded by Edward, Prince of Wales in about 1267 (Dawson 1981, 8). The 16th-century topographer Leland wrote that it was the fairest of all the houses of the friars in Bristol (Graham 1907, 110). When the site was cleared for the construction of the Colston Hall early in the last century fragments of the friary were noted and recorded (Pritchard 1906, 136–138).

It can be seen from the foregoing that, in addition to St James's Priory, there were seven other religious houses situated just to the west and north of the medieval city. Although extensive archaeological excavations and recording have been carried out on a number of these sites, only two of the excavations, those at St Bartholomew's Hospital and the Augustinian Nunnery, have been published in full (Price with Ponsford 1998; Longman 2003).

2   ST JAMES'S PRIORY

(This chapter draws on documentary sources in the Bristol Record Office (BRO), the Gloucestershire Record Office (GRO) and the National Archives kept in the Public Record Office (PRO)).

Historical Background

St James's Priory was built on open land just to the north of the medieval city on a low terrace of Triassic sandstone which slopes down to the west and south. It was located at a height of some 15 metres above sea level to the north of the River Frome at the foot of Kingsdown, a steeply sloping hill which rises to the north by a further 50 metres.

The early history of this religious site is obscure. Although there is no archaeological evidence for the existence of a church in the Saxon period, it has been suggested that a monastic settlement was founded there before the Norman Conquest by an English thane called Brictric, the son of Algar (Barrett 1789, 36; Seyer 1821, 261). There may be some historical basis for this tradition as we know that Brictric was a substantial landholder in the west at the time of the Conquest, his property including the manor of Tewkesbury. His lands passed first to Queen Matilda and, upon her death in 1083, to King William (Moore 1982, notes 1,39 & 1,42).

What is certain is that St James's Priory was founded as a cell to the Benedictine monastery of Tewkesbury by Robert, the son of King Henry I and Nesta the daughter of Rhees ap Tudor, Prince of South Wales. Robert, who became Earl of Gloucester, was one of the most powerful men in the kingdom, and he married Mabilia, the eldest daughter of Robert Fitzhamon. In the late 13th century Robert of Gloucester wrote that 'He [Earl Robert] reared also St James's Priory of black monks, a little on the northern side of the town ... that Convent belongs to the House of Tewkesbury' (Seyer 1821, 353–4).

It has been generally accepted that there was a concurrent building of Bristol castle and St James's Priory and that Robert put a tenth of the stone which had been brought from Normandy for building the keep of the castle towards the construction of a chapel in his new foundation (Dugdale 1823, 335). However, it was recorded that Robert gave the stone for building, not the priory itself, but the chapel of St Mary – *ad fabricam capella beata Maria virginis in dicto prioratu sancti Jacobi* – and it is possible that the chapel was built first as a kind of nucleus of the priory (Potto Hick 1932, 58). Documentary and archaeological evidence shows that temporary buildings usually preceded the building of the church and therefore it is not unlikely that a chapel dedicated to the increasingly popular cult of the Virgin might have been built before the main body of the church (Greene 1992, 58).

The precise date of the foundation of the priory is not known, but it was certainly during the period when Benedict was the abbot of Tewkesbury, which places it between 1124 and 1137. It was also at the time when earl Robert was engaged in building the great stone keep of the castle, a project which commenced in about 1120 and was sufficiently complete in 1135 to be able to withstand the assaults of King Stephen (Potto Hick 1932, 58). There is thus good reason to accept the traditional date of the foundation which was given as 1129.

A further document, a confirmation by Simon, Bishop of Worcester, to the abbot and convent of Tewkesbury, refers to the dedication of the cemetery of the church of St James but the wording makes it clear that the priory church was still in the process of being built at that time. Although the document is undated, it must belong to the period between 1125 and 1150 (GRO D293/2). While in any programme of monastic building the church was the first permanent structure to be completed, it is known from archaeological excavation and documentary research elsewhere that the construction of the remainder of the priory buildings could be spread over many years (Greene 1992, 58).

The priory church, which was dedicated to the 'honour of God, the blessed Mary, and St James the Apostle' (Evans 1816, 11, 178), was endowed with lands, liberties and possessions by Robert. After his death at Gloucester of a fever on 31 October 1147 he was buried in the middle of the choir of the priory church in a tomb of green marble or jasper, although his body was later removed to Tewkesbury Abbey (Dugdale 1823, 333). His only son, William, completed the process of endowment which was confirmed by Henry II in a charter of about 1181 (GRO D293/2). It included a tenth of the rents of the earl's mills at Newport in south Wales, of the mills at 'Rauna', 'Stapleton' and 'Seovenach', of the *vill* of Newport, and of an un-named forest. In addition he endowed it with the manor of Ashley and the profits of a fair, St James's Fair, held in Bristol in the week of Pentecost, together with all the churches of his fee in Cornwall, namely 'Eglosbrech', 'Connarton', 'Egloshale', 'Eglossant', 'Egloscrawen' with the chapel of 'Bennarton', and 'Melidan' with the chapel of 'St Germoch'; and the church of 'Escremoville' in the diocese of Bayeux in France. All the earl's 'new borough of meadow' at Bristol, situated on the north bank of the River Frome between the castle and St James's Priory, and now known as Broadmead, was given to form part of the parish of the church.

Earl William died in Bristol castle in 1183 and was buried, not in St James's Priory, but in his abbey at Keynsham which he had founded in *c*.1166 in memory of his dead son, Robert.

By a charter dated 1193, Henry, Bishop of Worcester, confirmed St James's Priory, among the other donations of earl William, to the Benedictine abbey of Tewkesbury (Barrett 1789, 381). The priors were appointed absolutely at the will of the abbot and convent of Tewkesbury and, in the absence of other evidence, it may be concluded that the monks were sent to St James's Priory to serve for a time from the mother house. The priors were usually summoned to take part in the election of the abbot and the house was subject to the visitation of the Bishop of Worcester (Graham 1907, 74).

The priory had been founded for Benedictine monks, who traced their origins back to the work of St Benedict of Nursia, an Italian monk of the early 6th century. He had described monastic life in a highly detailed and demanding set of rules which it was intended the monks would follow with total obedience (McCann 1976). St Benedict had originally prescribed these rules for his own monastery at Monte Casino, but by the Middle Ages they had become influential throughout western Europe (McAleavy 1996, 6). St Benedict had envisaged the monastery as 'a school of the Lord's service, in the setting forth of which we hope to order nothing that is harsh or rigorous'. It was to be a life in common, and one of extreme simplicity and regularity. Poverty and chastity were required of every individual. Whilst there was to be no distinction of persons in the monastery, the abbot ruled over it and was 'believed to be the representative of Christ in the monastery', and a father to his monks. His duty was to teach, love, and correct those under his charge.

The Rule of St Benedict set out how prayers should be conducted. Every hour, every minute of a monk's life was determined by the Rule, for every day of the year. Details of the round of daily prayers called the 'Opus Dei', the Work of God, were laid down, and this was the most important part of the monk's day. Benedict had stated that there should be eight services or 'offices', comprising a night service, later known as Matins, and seven daytime offices: Lauds, Prime, Terce, Sext, None, Vespers and Compline. The remainder of the day was spent in spiritual reading and in 'the labour of their hands'.

The arrangement of meals in the Rule depended on the liturgical year, and especially on the so-called temporal cycle of feasts and fasts commemorating the life, death, and Resurrection of Christ. Monks were to eat dinner every day of the year, but supper only from Easter to 13 September, and, after Pentecost, not on Wednesdays or Fridays. Flesh-meat was forbidden to all except the sick. However, by the 12th century, the consumption of fowl was regarded as permissible and gradually other meat dishes came to be eaten, if not in the refectory, the only room mentioned in the Rule, then elsewhere in the priory (Harvey 1993, 38–41).

Economically the priory was to be as self-contained as possible. 'The monastery ... ought if possible to be so constituted that all things necessary, such as water, a mill, and a garden, and the various crafts may be contained within it; so that there may be no need for the monks to wander abroad, for this is by no means expedient for their souls'. Despite the emphasis on a closed community of monks, from the earliest days monks made use of paid labour by lay servants who were not part of the monastic community. As the land holdings of the monasteries increased so did the need for lay servants to work on the estates and undertake administrative duties. It has been suggested that in some monastic houses there may have been at least two lay servants to every monk (Harvey 1993, 164).

By the time of the founding of St James's Priory in the 12th century, the majority of Benedictine houses had developed national characteristics in regard to the liturgy, and to the leading of a less enclosed life than had been proposed by St Benedict. They had acquired extensive lands and property. During the 12th century new religious orders had been established in England, and the Benedictine Order, or the Black Monks as they were termed, were now only one of several orders which attracted men to the monastic life. The Cluniacs, Cistercians, Premonstratensians and the Gilbertines were all founded in the first instance with the object of returning to the original spirit of the Rule of St Benedict. Their existence implied a criticism of the way of life then followed by the Benedictines. Certainly by the middle of the reign of Henry II, the typical Black Monk house had become a great corporation, with a vast and complex economic organisation (Lambert 1971, 50–55).

Some examples of the income being derived from various sources to support the complex life of St

James's Priory are recorded. In the charter of William, Earl of Gloucester, the priory had been granted the right to receive money from a fair or market he had established at Bristol and which was held during the week of Pentecost, beginning on the seventh Sunday after Easter; known as St James's Fair this was one of the leading markets in the south-west of England. The monks let out pitches on their land for the erection of stalls and booths, or 'standings', where the traders, who came from all over the country, could set up their wares.

Although no contemporary documents survive from the priory archives detailing these transactions, similar accounts were kept concerning the leasing of land owned by the parishioners of St James and are preserved in the parish records. For example, in January 1484 the churchwardens leased a pitch consisting of void land in the west part of the churchyard, some sixteen feet in length, to a pewterer called John White at a rent of 2s. 8d. per annum, plus the annual loan to the church of two dozen pewter vessels (BRO P/St J/F/28/15). In 1409 Richard Gladewyn, a hosier, leased a void place eighteen feet long in the south part of the parish churchyard for 1s. per annum. It was noted that the plot included a tombstone, which presumably was an inconvenience that Gladewyn had to work around when setting up his stall (BRO P/St J/F/28/15). Even parts of the inside of the church were let out to traders, especially those who were selling valuable commodities and may have required additional security. Harry Warley, a London goldsmith, leased a 'place for a standing on the two highest pews in the church' for 10s. per annum (BRO P/St J/F/28/13).

It is clear that, in addition to receiving any proportion of the profits from the fair to which it was entitled by the charter, the priory also gained an income from leasing out plots of land to traders on an annual basis and from the cost of erecting standings for which the parishioners, at least, provided the services of a carpenter.

The priory obtained income from goods shipped through Bristol and we know that the prior of St James had the full *prisage* of wines coming to the port of Bristol from twelve o'clock on the Saturday before the feast of St James to the same hour on the Saturday following. The right of prisage was granted to the King and allowed him two *tuns* of wine from every ship importing twenty *tuns* or more. The prior's right to this privilege was acknowledged by an inquisition taken in 1310, when it was found that this had been granted in the charter of William, Earl of Gloucester, and that the prior could take three pence for every hogshead imported. The findings of that inquisition were used in 1404 when a prohibition was granted by Henry IV in favour of the prior, Richard Wircestre, against Thomas Chaucer, the king's chief butler, who had challenged his privilege. The privilege was again

questioned in 1454 when the prior, William Newport, claimed prisage on the cargo of the ship 'Clement of Bayonne' and once again the king's chief butler, John Sharp, was over-ruled (Bickley 1900, 236–246).

In the later 12th century the majority of the land known as Broadmead, between the priory and the River Frome, was laid out as a suburb of Bristol in a commercial development initiated by the prior of St James. A charter by Hawisia Countess of Gloucester, of *c*.1150 to 1183, granted to St James's Church a burgage in the 'novo burgo prati ultimum, scilicet a parte orientali ....', *i.e.* in the 'new town of the broad meadow [or mead], that is on the eastern side' (Patterson 1973, 56; BRO 5139(175)). It is clear that the priory obtained income from letting out burgage plots in the new suburb.

The prior always carefully guarded the sources of income which enabled the priory to function. In 1230 the prior and monks of St James were in conflict with the Dominicans who had built an oratory within their parish. When, at the request of the Dominican friars, William of Blois, bishop of Worcester, came to dedicate their altar and burial ground, the monks of St James protested against the dedication. They petitioned that their privilege should remain intact, and that the friars should be forbidden to receive offerings or to have a burial place. Nevertheless the Annals of Tewkesbury record that the bishop went ahead with the dedicaton and the friars carried on building and taking offerings, to the 'great prejudice and loss' of the church of St James (Graham 1907, 74).

It was doubtless to attract such offerings that in 1238 the prior and convent persuaded Walter de Cantilupe, bishop of Worcester, to institute the Feast of Relics which was celebrated on the Thursday of the week of Pentecost, when Bristol was thronged with visitors to St James's Fair. He granted an indulgence of fifteen days to all who came to the church and gave alms. Probably the offerings were needed for the fabric of the priory, as some building was then proceeding, and on St Luke's Day in 1239, Cantilupe dedicated the church (Graham 1907, 74).

It seems likely that, as at Tewkesbury, the nave of the priory church had always been used by parishioners. In addition to providing a perpetual curate and other clergy to serve in St James's parish, the mother house was patron of the vicarage of the parish of SS Philip and Jacob and the rectories of Christ Church, St Ewen, St John, St Michael and St Peter within the city of Bristol (Skeeters 1993, 20, 71).

The close link between the parishioners and the monks was shown in an indenture made in 1346 between Lord John, abbot of Tewkesbury, and 'the parishioners and brethren of the fraternity of the Holy Cross of their church and priory of St James's, Bristol' in which he granted 'to the said parishioners and brethren to increase ... their devotion which they have conceived towards the image of the Saviour of all and the Holy Cross situated in the outer church, That they might repair the site and embellishment before the said Holy Cross now almost ruined, and, being so repaired, to set it up ... and make for it competent and honest steps without the door of the inner church and at their own costs to maintain that place ... And the said parishioners and brethren grant that they will build and adorn before the said Holy Cross a beautiful and dedicated altar, and at their own costs and expenses, will have there ... divine services to the honour of the image of the Saviour of all and of the Holy Cross ... So nevertheless that the prior of the said place ... shall receive the moiety of all the oblations from devotions to the said Holy Cross there coming ... The said parishioners and brethren will also grant that they will bear the cost of the repair of the whole outer church as far as the belfry, deducting three shillings and four pence which the parishioners of the said church were in times past accustomed to pay to the said prior for the repair of any part between the door of the outer church as far as the belfry' (GRO D293/2).

A further document was written in 1374 to form an agreement between Thomas, abbot of the monastery of Tewkesbury, brother Thomas de Norton, prior of St James, and the parishioners of St James's Church over the erection of a new belfry. 'That the said religious men have granted for themselves and their successors to the said parishioners that they shall have and hear daily the whole of the divine service in the said parish church to wit matins, hours, masses, vespers and complin and the other divine offices both for night and for day as well for the living as for the dead to be celebrated canonically as other parish churches are commonly wont to have lawfully throughout the diocese, with ringing of bells as often as need be at opportune times. The parishioners were to receive the moiety of the profits arising from the fixing of pales or other things penetrating or occupying the soil of the cemetery of the parish church at the fair happening yearly on the feast of St James, together with the profits from the tolling of the bells for presenting bodies for burial and for anniversaries of the dead. For which same grant the parishioners have granted to the religiousmen that they will cause to be erected a new and competently built belfry and a quadrangle of stone in the form of a tower with a sufficient roof in a fit place which within the bounds of the said priory at the proper cost of the said parishioners – the religiousmen to provide for the fabric of the belfry until its completion, freestone and other stone with sufficient earthen cement as may conveniently, without loss to the said priory, be found within the lordship of same, to be carried and wholly removed at the expense and by the labour of the parishioners. If the stone not found within the lordship then the cost to be divided equally. On completion the belfry to serve the common use of the said parties and be perpetually sustained by their common expenses and that the bells of the said parties be hung and afterwards sustained at expense in proportion to the parties' (GRO D293/2).

On 2 July 1409 there was confirmation by Thomas, Bishop of Worcester, of an agreement between the Abbey of Tewkesbury, who were acting for St James's Priory, and John Sehawe, parson of St John's, whereby the latter parish was to be permitted to have a cemetery of its own – the parishioners having until that time been buried in St James's churchyard. Nevertheless, the long-established fee paid to St James's Priory for the rights of burial were to be increased from 10s. to 13s. 4d. per annum (BRO St John's Deeds no. 99).

The documentary sources give little personal information about the priors of St James and nothing of the monks themselves. However, at least in the early 16th century, the priors seem to have been of a high calibre. In 1523 Robert Cheltenham was prior and he had Batchelor of Divinity and Doctor of Divinity degrees from Oxford. Robert Cheltenham, who became curate of St James's parish in 1540, had also served at Tewkesbury Abbey and Deerhurst Priory. Robert Circeter was prior of St James in 1535 and 1539 and he also held a Batchelor of Divinity degree from Oxford (Skeeters 1993, 228).

The Dissolution and After

In the 1530s, during the reign of Henry VIII, the life of the monastic houses came to an end. The first stage in this process was a declaration by the king that he was the Supreme Head of the Church in England and the requirement in 1534 that the monks and nuns were to take an oath accepting Henry's new status. It seems that at that time there may have been only three monks present at St James's Priory (Skeeters 1993, 12).

In 1535 a bill went through Parliament which levied an annual tax of ten percent on the income from all spiritual benefices. In order to put this tax into effect, Henry's chief minister, Thomas Cromwell, organised a valuation, the *Valor Ecclesiasticus*, of all church property, including that of the monasteries, and commissioners were sent out to undertake assessments. The valuation of St James's Priory in 1535 provides details of the income derived from various sources which was said to be worth £55 7s. 4d. per annum. This was made up mainly of rents from tenants in Bristol, the hundred of Barton, Tockington, Saltmarsh and Cattybrook, a mill in Bristol, rectories in Stapleton and Mangotsfield, the revenue from the granary of the rectory in SS Philip and Jacob parish, personal offerings and tithes at Easter in the parish of St James, income from the herbage in St James's cemetery, profits from the revenues of the town of Bristol in Pentecost week, profits from the standings at St James's Fair, and the revenue of 48 acres of pasture and 105 acres of arable land (Potto Hick 1932, 203). The *Valor Ecclesiasticus* shows that there were five 'religious' men in St James's Priory in 1535.

The Act of Suppression was passed in 1536 whereby the smaller monasteries, with an income of less than £200 a year, were closed down. The certificate of the commissioners under the terms of the Dispensations Act reveal that in 1536 there were by then only two 'religious' men in St James's Priory, apparently the prior and one brother, and that they wished to continue in religious office. In addition there were two servants. The priory's lead and bells were valued at 19s. 4d., other goods were valued at £3 12s. 10d. and the woods on the priory lands were valued at £13 6s. 8d. There were no debts owed by or to the house (Potto Hick 1932, 205)

The abbot and convent of Tewkesbury, seeing the approach of the inevitable dissolution of their abbey and its daughter houses, and perhaps fearing the early closure of St James's Priory, which had been visited briefly by the Crown commissioners in 1536, leased the priory and its lands and properties to Sir Anthony Kingston on 26 January 1539, a year before the dissolution of Tewkesbury. The lease was extremely detailed, suggesting that the monks wanted to cover anything the Crown might have wished to take possession of in regard to the priory. The property was described as the 'hoole pryorye, cell and howse of Saynte James ... with all syngular howses buyldings orcheyards gardeyns and demeane landes of the said Priorye and cell and their appurtenances .... and which Dompne Robert nowe prior of the said priory or cell hathe occupied'. By this agreement, made in the chapter house of Tewkesbury Abbey between Kingston and Abbot John, Kingston was to pay to the abbot and convent and their successors the sum of £35 7s. 8d annually (PRO E315/214 fol.106; Skeeters 1993, 79). The lease may have been intended to prevent the early confiscation of the priory by the Crown. Sir Anthony Kingston was obviously a man of some importance in Gloucestershire as in 1552 he was described as Steward of all the king's possessions in the county, a position previously held by Richard, Earl of Warwick (Baskerville 1927, 110).

Tewkesbury Abbey survived until the second Act of Suppression was passed in the spring of 1539. Then Tewkesbury with its cells, including St James's Priory, was surrendered on 9 January 1540; one of the last monasteries to be dissolved. However, it has been suggested that the monks of St James had probably already left when the mother house of Tewkesbury leased their priory to Kingston in January 1539 (Skeeters 1993, 84). At the Dissolution the monks of St James received pensions ranging from prior Robert Circeter's £13 6s. 8d. to £6 per annum for the remaining monk. Robert was still on the pensions list in 1556 (Baskerville 1927, 84).

Kingston did not surrender the lease of the priory to the Chancellor of the Court of Augmentations until 25 April 1543, the intention being that the king should grant Kingston another lease for the remainder of the 99 year term at the same annual rent. This re-grant duly took place on the provision that Kingston should find 'one sufficient and fit chaplain yearly to perform divine service and to observe the cure in the church of St James' and that he should 'well and sufficiently repair sustain and maintain all the premises in all things' (PRO E315/214 fol. 106; GRO D293/2).

In 1544 Henry Brayne, a merchant tailor of London, expressed an interest in purchasing the remaining term of the lease on St James's Priory from Anthony Kingston but before granting this change of lease particulars of the property were prepared on 16 June 1544. These show that the annual value of the former priory was £35 7s. 8d., but that this included parts of Llantony Priory near Gloucester which were valued at £1 13s. 4d. After the deduction of tithes valued at £3 14s. 1½d. there remained an annual value of £33 6s. 10½d. The purchase price of the priory and its lands was calculated on the annual value over a term of 20 years and was agreed at the then enormous amount of £666 17s. 6d., the sum of £400 to be paid immediately and the rest within three months.

In addition the trees and hedges on the priory estate, which were used for coppicing and providing timber for repairing buildings, were valued at 10s. It was recorded that 'there be growing about the situation of the said cell and divers tenements there and in the hedges inclosing the lands pertaining to the same 200 elms, oaks and ashs usually cropped and shrodde by the tenants of the same whereof 160 reserved for timber to repair the houses standing upon the site of the said cell and for stakes for hedgebote to the said fermor which he hath by covenant and for timber for 40 tenants there holding lands of the said cell part by coppie part by indenture and part at will to repair their tenements which they have been accustomed to have there, and 40 residue valued at 3d the tree' (GRO D293/2).

On 10 September 1544 Anthony Kingston assigned the residue of the term of his lease to Brayne (PRO E318/164 & 165; GRO D293/2) and on 20 December 1544 the king granted Brayne the priory, its lands and income. Besides the site of the priory, the property included 'the rectories of Stapleton and Maggersfelde, of St James beside Bristol, of St Philip and St James beside Bristol and of St Philip and St James in Bristol, with advowsons of the vicarages, annual rents out of the rectories or churches of St Peter, Holy Trinity, St John, SS Philip and James and St Andrew in Bristol, and St Michael beside Bristol and all possessions of the said cell in Stapleton, Mangotsfield, Ichyngton, Tokynton, Cadebrooke, Saltemershe and the hundred of Barton Glouc, and the City and County of Bristol and elsewhere ... Also the lands in tenure of John and Wm ap Hopkyn in Haddenocke in the lordship of

Monmouth, co Monmouth and the fishery in the river Wye, co Monmouth from Martens weir to Monmouth Bridge in tenure of Hugh Hunteley and Ric. Morgan ... which belongeth to the late monastery of Lanthonye priory beside Gloucester' (BRO P/St J/HM/7). In the Letters Patent dated 2 January 1545 confirming this grant it was made clear that the king reserved in his possession 'All the bells in the church of the said late priory and all lead in and upon the said church and the other houses and edifices within the site and precinct of the said late priory except the lead in the shutes and windows thereof' (GRO D1799/T34).

On 8 July 1545, the Crown granted a great deal more Bristol property to Brayne, including some one hundred tenements, messuages, gardens, closes, and pastures formerly belonging to various religious houses (Skeeters 1993, 80).

The destruction of the east end of the priory church must have occurred quite rapidly for in the early 1540s the topographer John Leland was able to report on St James's Priory 'that it standeth by Brode meade by northe from the Castle on a hilly ground, and the ruins of it standeth hard buttynge to the easte ende of the paroche churche' (Toulmin Smith 1910, 88).

Henry Brayne converted the conventual buildings of the priory into a large mansion house. Parallels for the conversion of former monastic buildings into urban palaces or mansions can be seen in London and elsewhere. Charterhouse Priory in London was converted into a palace by Lord North, a privy councillor, while St Bartholomew's Priory was turned into a splendid mansion by Thomas Audley and later by Thomas Howard, Duke of Norfolk. By 1545 the church of the Blackfriars in Gloucester had been converted into a substantial house, known as Bell's Place, by Thomas Bell, a wealthy tradesman (Herbert 1988, 290). Despite the restricted nature of their sites, these new urban palaces may have demonstrated current fashions in the layout of rooms (Schofield 1993, 29–33) and we know that Brayne's mansion had a great hall, long gallery and a number of bed chambers and other rooms (GRO D1799/T34).

Henry Brayne made his will on 22 August 1558 and in that he referred to his house as being called 'St James's'. He died five days later on 27 August (BRO P/St J/HM/7). An inquiry, called an Inquisition Post Mortem, was held at Wotton-under-Edge in Gloucestershire on 29 December 1558 concerning the possessions of Henry Brayne and to determine his successor. It was stated that Henry Brayne owned 16 messuages, four gardens, two water mills, 300 acres of land, 70 acres of meadow, 160 acres of pasture land and an annual rental income of £3 0s. 8d. in St James's parish. It was confirmed that Robert Brayne was Henry's son and heir (GRO D293/2).

Robert Brayne inherited the property and in his own will made on 24 March 1569 he left to his wife Goodith 'my Mannor Place of Saint James together withe all manner of buildings howsses Barnes Curtilages and edifices thereunto belonging withe all my landes lyeng to the lane leading from St James toward Horfylde till it runne to Hayles Crosse and so rounde about to Mawdelyne lane and so to the said St James againe, to her for terme of her naturall lyfe' (BRO P/St J/HM/7).

Robert died childless and his widow, Goodith, later married John Seymour. Goodith was not legally entitled to inherit the property and therefore the mansion passed to Henry Brayne's sons-in-law, George Winter and Sir Charles Somerset, the fifth son of the Earl of Worcester, who had married his daughters Emilithys and Ann. Nevertheless at the time of the division of the property in 1580 John Seymour and Goodith occupied all the mansion house.

The Deed of Partition, which formally divided the mansion house and adjoining property between George Winter and Sir Charles Somerset, was agreed by the parties on 27 January 1580 (GRO D1799/T34).

The west portion of the property was to be held by George Winter and his wife Ann. This was described in the document as 'the west part of the scite Manor place or Mansion House of St James ... viz the whole great hall from the uppermost end of the same downwards to the lower end, with the buttery adjoining to the same and all the chambers and rooms upon the west side of the same house, extending to the side of the west end of the long gallery that adjoineth to the church there, with all manner of rooms, edifices & buildings, directly under and above the same house, buttery, chambers and rooms. Also the great green court adjoining to the same the great gatehouse entering by the church yard into the said great green court together with a dwelling house adjoining to the said gatehouse. Also the great stable within the said green court, the little stable within the said green court, the brewhouse and bakehouse near unto the kitchen door. The little garden adjoining to the same brewhouse & bakehouse, & one other garden lying between the west end of the church there & the said great gatehouse. Also the little way or lane that leadeth out of the great court by the back side of the brewhouse, to the west part of the gate entering unto the way which parteth the Mountegewes and Shuters close'.

It has not been possible to determine the location of 'the Mountegewes and Shuters close' although fields called the Upper and Lower Montagues are known to have been situated on the lower slopes of Kingsdown to the north of the priory.

The east or back part of the property was allotted to Sir Charles Somerset and his wife Emilithys. This was described as 'the backer part or east side of the scite Mannor place or Mansion house of St James ... viz the rooms from the uppermost part of the hall Eastwards with the parlor the chambers in the galleries and the said galleries from the East part of the said Mannor House to the west shall be united together with all the rooms edifices, & buildings directly under & above the said rooms parlor chambers & galleries And also the little square green court that lyeth in the middest of the fore part & backer of the said Mannor House, And also all the grounds inclosed with a wall adjoining to the said plot on the east side of the said house wherein standeth a pigeon house with all the barton that extendeth from the gate in Barcs lane where unto the pound is adjoining unto the said east part, or backer part of the said Mannor house & east part of the Church, together with two great barns, the said pounds & all other houses, edifices & buildings which lyeth on both sides & within the said barton & inclosed grounds And also the little way that goeth out of the said barton to the stony stile leading to the way that divideth the Mountegewes & Shuters Close'.

On 8 April 1624 George Winter of Dyrham House in Gloucestershire passed his share of the mansion house at St James to his brother, John. The property was as described in the Deed of Partition quoted above except that there were two parts of the property excluded and they were 'one place, ground, room, edifice or building lying and being under the west end of the said gallery, commonly called the prison, forever hereafter to be used as a prison, for prisoners to be committed or kept by power of the court hereafter mentioned ... and so much of the room in the gatehouse there as the same gatehouse now standeth as hath been used heretofore for keeping a yearly court on Whitsun eve and from thence from the Saturday in Whitsun week in the afternoon' (GRO D1799/T7).

As demonstrated by research elsewhere, in the late 16th and early 17th centuries the era of the urban palaces and mansions developed on former priory sites came to an end and there was then a period of fragmentation of the precincts into several tenancies, comprising in some cases industrial premises and smaller scale housing (Schofield 1993, 29). The site of St James's Priory was no exception.

On 26 March 1639 John Winter's portion of the property was mortgaged to William Hobson and Richard Holworthy, both merchants of Bristol. The description of the property is recited again as in the Deed of Partition but it also refers to a house which had recently been built on land enclosed within walls adjoining the 'Coniger' and the 'new rooms and building which John Prigge gent hath built, with access and egress by and through the Barton adjoining the premises, now in the occupation of the said John Prigge which he holds by lease dated 15 March 1636'.

From this description it is apparent that new houses were being built in the area to the north of the church and on land formerly occupied by the priory. After its disposal by the Winter family, the property passed rapidly through a number of other hands. On 1 April 1648 Allan Corance of London sold to George Swanley of Wainsworth in Surrey 'All that divided moiety or part of the now or late site manor-place or mansion

house or late priory house of St James' (GRO D293/2). The area to the north of the church became known as Whitson Court and in 1666 Thomas Ellis purchased much of the Whitson Court complex from William Davis and John Teague of Bristol, Ellis and four associates setting up a sugar house on the site by 1667 (Hall 1944, 19). Jacobus Millerd's map of Bristol published in 1673, which is considered to be a reasonably accurate pictorial representation of the city, shows a large house and other properties to the north and north-west of the church (Fig. 3). These were certainly the mansion house and sugar house in the Whitson Court area.

Millerd depicted a house at the east end of St James's Church fronting the path along the north side of St James's churchyard. This was probably the 'two messuages' described as being east of the church in 1646 and lying within an acre of land enclosed within a stone wall (BRO P/St J/V/38). Millerd shows the building as being approximately on the site of the Lady Chapel. However, we know that the chapel still existed, albeit in a ruinous state, in 1744 (BRO P/St J/V/38/3) and the length of the parish burial ground east of the church was obviously greatly foreshortened by Millerd. Another large house is shown at the northern end of the lane (later Cannon Street) which ran north, parallel to the east end wall of the church. Apart from a group of houses further east, surrounding The Barton, the general area east of the church seemed to be open ground or gardens.

At the west end of the church Millerd shows two houses running parallel to the north side of the parish burial ground, with one of them abutting the front of the church. The distance between the west front of the church and the priory gatehouse was again foreshortened and the positioning and size of the buildings there seems to have been schematic. Nevertheless, the building furthest to the west was almost certainly what is now known as the White Hart public house, licensed since at least 1672. Photographs of the house (later no. 16 St James's Parade) adjoining the White Hart to the east show that it was of a type of construction that can be no later than 17th century in date, of two and a half storeys, with a gabled and jettied front elevation (Winstone 1970, Pl.130 and 1979, Pl.121).

During the 17th and 18th century hovels were built against the west front of the church, concealing it from view, but 'those excrescences' were cleared in 1851 (Latimer 1887, 327). At some point three similar hovels were built against the east end of the church. These may originally have been 16th or 17th century in date and were certainly shown on a plan of 1744, although they were all probably rebuilt in the 19th century (Bryant 1993, 26–28).

By the early 18th century an east/west path had been established running across the parish burial ground just to the south of the church. This became known appropriately as 'The Churchyard', and later

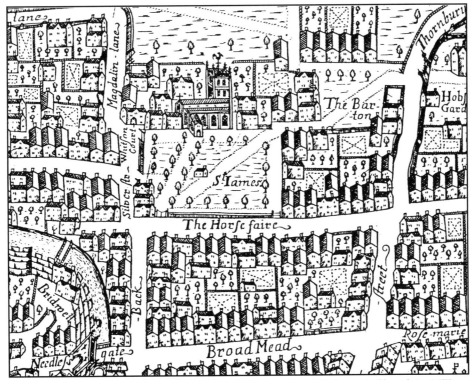

Fig. 3 Millerd's map of Bristol showing the area around St James's Church in 1673

as St James's Parade, and new houses were built along the north side of the Parade at both ends of the church (Fig. 4). These later acquired street numbers running from east to west: nos. 1 to 12a St James's Parade being to the east of the church and nos. 13 to 16 to the west. A view across the churchyard painted in watercolours by T. L. S. Rowbotham in 1826 (Bristol City Museum and Art Gallery Collection M.2839) shows nos. 13 and 14 as a pair of gabled houses of three and a half storeys next to the west end of the church and parallel to the Parade. The only record of the exterior of no. 15 St James's Parade is an undated photograph published in the *Bristol Evening Post* newspaper which shows it to have been of three storeys. The ruins of the Lady Chapel appear to have been incorporated in the houses built on the Parade to the east of the church.

The street, later known as Cannon Street, running at right angles to St James's Parade and parallel to the east end wall of the church was a cul-de-sac in 1744 (Fig. 9; BRO P/St J/V/12/4/3). However, its dog-leg continuation east of the church was described as a 'new street' on a slightly later map (BRO P/St J/12/4/6). The St James's parish rate books show that a number of houses and commercial premises, including a malt house, had been built in Cannon Street by 1760 and these gradually increased in number through the late 18th century (BRO St James's Parish Lamp Rate).

Eighteenth-century maps, including Rocque's of 1742 and Donne's of 1773, indicate that the area

around the church was fully developed, but do not provide detailed information. Plumley and Ashmead's large-scale (1:2400) map of 1828 shows that nos. 13, 14 and 15 St James's Parade were all set back from the edge of the thoroughfare and that the two nearest the church both possessed bay windows (Fig. 4). However, by the time of the next large-scale survey carried out by the City Valuer c.1855, the bay windows had been replaced by single storey shop extensions brought forward to the edge of the pavement and that was how the buildings remained until demolition.

The only major alteration in land use during the 19th century was the demolition of nos. 4 to 8 St James's Parade for the construction of the Scottish Presbyterian Church and Sunday School (Fig. 5). The construction of the church commenced in 1855 and it was opened in 1859 (BRO Building Plan Book 4 fol.176).

The twentieth century saw the destruction of the Scottish Presbyterian Church during the blitz of 1940 and its partial replacement by a Welsh Congregational Chapel in 1953, and the erection of a Bus Station in the late 1950s on all the land immediately north of St James's Church and Cannon Street. The houses in St James's Parade were demolished piecemeal during the 1950s and 1960s: no. 16 being demolished in the early 1950s, nos. 13 and 14 in 1963 and nos. 9 to 12a, together with the remaining houses in Cannon Street, in the 1960s to make way for the construction of the NFU office building and the small Audit Office.

St James's Church was declared redundant as a place of worship in the 1980s but is now occupied by

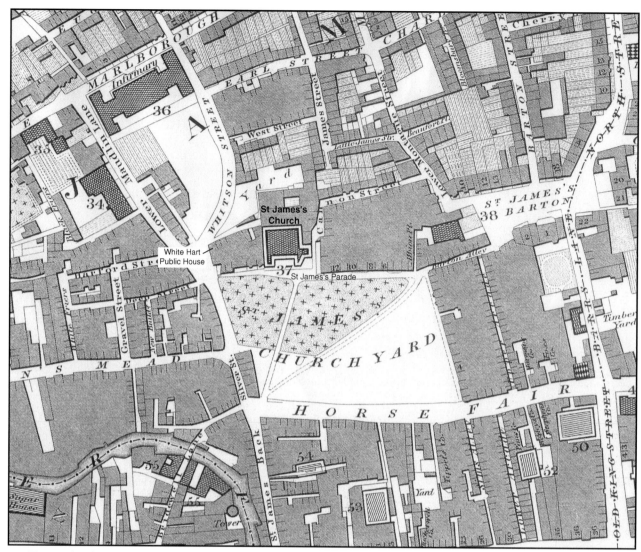

Fig. 4 Plumley and Ashmead's map of Bristol showing the area around St James's Church in 1828 (Scale 1:2400)

the Little Brothers of Nazareth, an order of Roman Catholic monks dedicated to the care of people in Bristol suffering from drug addiction.

St James's Priory: Its Church, Conventual Buildings and Cemeteries

The area occupied by St James's Priory now lies within the modern commercial centre of Bristol and as such its buildings have been subjected to demolition and disturbance since the Dissolution. Despite the importance of the site, little archaeological work had been carried out before the excavations in 1989. During the 19th century ground disturbances and the demolition of buildings were sometimes observed by antiquarians and the records of those observations published in local archaeological journals, while in the 20th century archaeological excavation and

recording work took place on a few occasions. It was unfortunate that no archaeological work was carried out during the construction of the Bus Station in the 1950s despite the destruction this must have caused to what remained of the conventual buildings to the north of the church. In the early 1960s only minor archaeological work was undertaken when parts of the east end of the priory church and the adjoining cemetery were destroyed by the construction of the NFU office building and its associated works.

Nevertheless the antiquarian, archaeological and documentary evidence permits the following tentative interpretation of the layout and extent of the priory and its conventual buildings and the production of a plan showing the possible locations of some of the monastic buildings (Fig. 6).

The Priory Church and Lady Chapel

All that now remains above ground of St James's

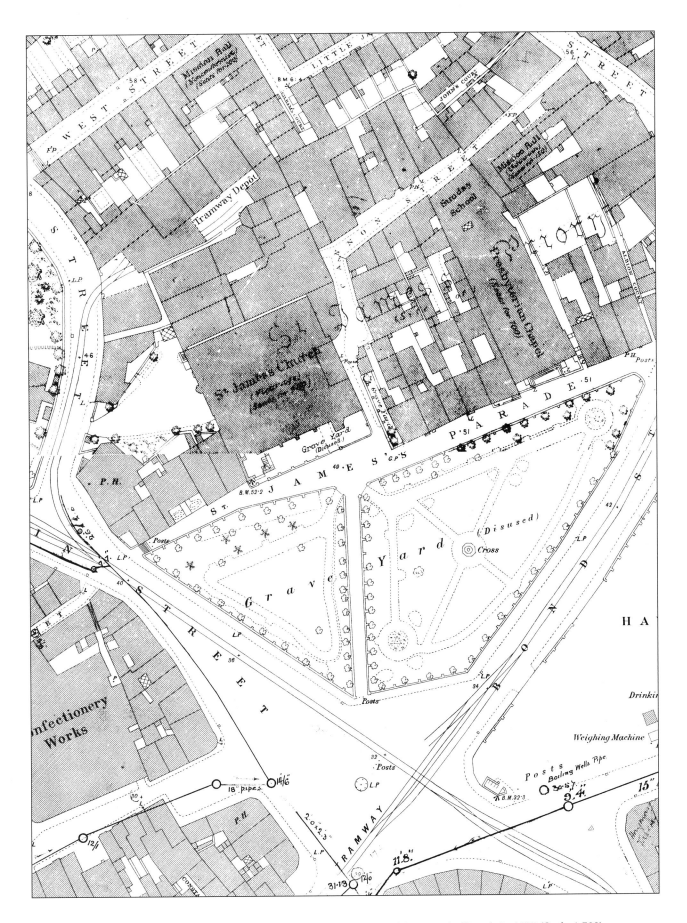

Fig. 5 The O. S. First Edition map showing the area around St James's Church in 1885 (Scale 1:500)

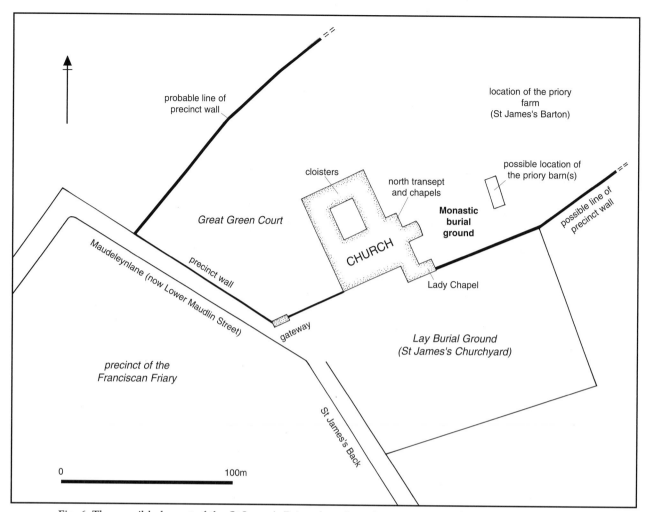

Fig. 6 The possible layout of the St James's Priory based on documentary and archaeological evidence

Priory are the nave of the former priory church and fragments of the west range of its cloisters. The latter are incorporated in the fabric of Church House which adjoins the church to the north.

The church nave owes its survival to its parochial rather than monastic use at the time of the Dissolution and it now comprises the five western bays of what was once a six-bay nave, the eastern bay of the structural nave being, behind the pulpitum wall which survives, part of the monastic church. The five remaining bays, with no triforium and with an unaltered clerestorey of simple, round-headed windows, have slender round columns, each with four attached shafts to carry the unmoulded arches and the shafts which supported the main members of a timber roof. The capitals are scalloped. The nave's more ornate architectural features were reserved for its west façade (Fig. 7). Above the central doorway, three round-headed windows are set in a row of arches with zig-zag moulding and interlaced in a way apparently not uncommon in West-Country Romanesque, which it has been thought suggest a date rather later than the 1120s. Above them is an unrestored

circular window. Although damaged by the elements it can be seen that, within a reasonably conventional zig-zag border, the circular elements of an 'early' wheel window were enclosed in an octofoil pattern of floral character (Gomme et al. 1979, 14–16).

The existing tower was added against the south side of the nave in the late 14th century and this now projects beyond the present east end of the church. In 1374 an agreement was reached between the monks and the parishioners concerning the construction of 'a new and competently built belfry and a quadrangle of stone in the form of a tower with a sufficient roof in a fit place ... within the bounds of the priory ...' (GRO D293/2). The parishioners were to pay for the cost of building the tower while the monks were to provide the 'freestone and other stone with sufficient earthen cement as may conveniently, without loss to the said priory, be found within the lordship of the same'. However, the expense and labour involved in carting the stone and cement was to be undertaken by the parishioners. The belfry was to be used jointly by the monks and the parishioners while the bells were to be maintained in proportion to their use by both parties.

Fig. 7 The west front of St James's Church showing the Norman circular window and arcading. Church House is on the far left of the photograph.

It has generally been assumed that the original south aisle of the priory church was completely removed in 1698 (Pryce 1861, 179) but recent research and architectural recording during renovation work has shown that, although the medieval aisle was largely rebuilt in the late 17th century, it was not totally destroyed or widened and has a similar width to its northern counterpart (Bryant 1993, 21). A number of fragments of the original medieval tracery of the west window of the south aisle were recovered in the early 1960s during the demolition of the adjacent houses. At that time the window jambs and sill were found *in situ* (Bryant 1993, 21). The present south porch, which is at the western end of the south aisle, was built in about 1802 and replaced a structure of similar size, shape and function.

St James's parish was a particularly populous one, and a number of measures were taken over the years in an attempt to solve the problem of overcrowding within the church. Eventually the parish was partitioned in 1794 by the creation of the new parish of St Paul. Prior to that galleries had been added inside the church. Edward Colston gave money for the installation of an organ and gallery, probably at the west end of the nave, and a north aisle gallery was added as a result of a faculty in 1753 (Bryant 1993, 23). The last extension occurred in 1864 when the north aisle was enlarged.

Documentary sources help little in establishing the size and extent of the original priory church but it is likely that it closely resembled other Benedictine priories in plan and scale and some comparisons may be made. The priory church was probably cruciform, with a central crossing, transepts which may have had chapels off their eastern sides, and a short presbytery limb. Some clues as to the layout and size of the church can be gained from an account given by the topographer, William Worcestre (Harvey 1969, 131). He visited the priory in 1478 and measured the various components of the church by pacing out the distances. The length of the nave of the priory church, which survived the Dissolution, was 22 yards (20.10 metres). The east end of the monastic, or priory church, measured a further 15.5 yards (14.20 metres) in length, giving the church a total length of 37.5 yards (34.30 metres). Adjoining the church, probably to the north, was a chapel dedicated to St Anne which measured 8 yards (7.30 metres) by 4 yards (3.65 metres).

To the south of the choir there was a large chapel, the Lady Chapel, dedicated to St Mary, and this measured 21 yards (19.20 metres) by 7 yards (6.40 metres). This chapel, which was presumably that constructed by Robert, Earl of Gloucester, survived above ground for some time after the Dissolution and was illustrated in a drawing apparently dating to *c*.1630, although the original is now lost (Fig. 8; BRO 17563 fol. 129). The view was from the parish churchyard looking north and shows the ruinous east end of the church. The building in the centre of the engraving is clearly the Lady Chapel, two storeys high with a large central doorway and with a line of Norman arcading above. To the west of the chapel are other

Fig. 8 The remains of the east end of the priory church and, in the centre, the Lady Chapel from a drawing of *c*.1630 (BRO 17563 fol. 129)

remains of the church including the south transept. Behind are other monastic structures, although these are difficult to interpret. The crenellated walls and gatehouse presumably relate to Henry Brayne's late 16th-century mansion house. Unfortunately, the accepted date of the drawing may be spurious and it is possibly a somewhat 'Romantic' representation of St James executed later than the 17th century when some of the structures shown had long been demolished.

The chapel was also depicted on a plan of 1744 where it was described as 'Old Walls Belonging to the Church' and these took the form of a rectangular building measuring 9.20 metres north to south and at least 15.20 metres from east to west (Fig. 9; BRO P/St J/V/12/4/3). The description accompanying the plan mentions that in this structure 'we find the plane marks of an Ancient Monument, against said wall, marked C and an Old Tomb, marked D, Lett into said wall about 6 inches, and an other Tomb marked E, Belonging to the Chusters family with these dates on the pannels thereof 1560 and 1641' (BRO P/St J/V/12/4/1). This building survived until at least 1753 when it was shown as a buttressed structure (Fig. 10; BRO P/St J/V/12/4/6). In the late 18th century the Bristol antiquarian, Barrett, reported that at the east end of the church the ruins of part of the priory were still to be seen, 'being a square room with niches in the wall round it, in length 24 yards, and of breadth in the

clear 8 yards .... It appears to have been vaulted with freestone, of which the side walls were built very strong. Two brick fronted houses are now built on the site of it' (Barrett 1789, 382).

In 1962 the historian Bryan Little observed the demolition of the five properties, nos. 9 to 13 St James's Parade, to make way for the construction of the NFU offices. These may well have incorporated what remained of the Lady Chapel, two of them having buttressed façades (Fig. 11) which could relate to the buttresses shown on the plan of 1753 (Fig. 10). However, the demolition revealed only two very worn corbels which were not found in their original position (BRO 35709 Box 1).

In June 1962 a small rescue excavation was carried out under the direction B. V. Arthur, partly on the site of the Lady Chapel, on behalf of Bristol City Museum with the assistance of the Bristol Archaeological Research Group. An area of approximately 330 square metres was excavated down to the natural sandstone. It was found that the entire area had been disturbed by mostly recent features such as cellars, cess-pits and an air-raid shelter. There were apparently no clear traces of priory buildings but two skeletons, both undated, were found, one of which was buried in a wooden coffin of which traces remained as stains in the soil. The other was in a stone-edged grave, with no sign of a coffin (Arthur 1962, 36–37).

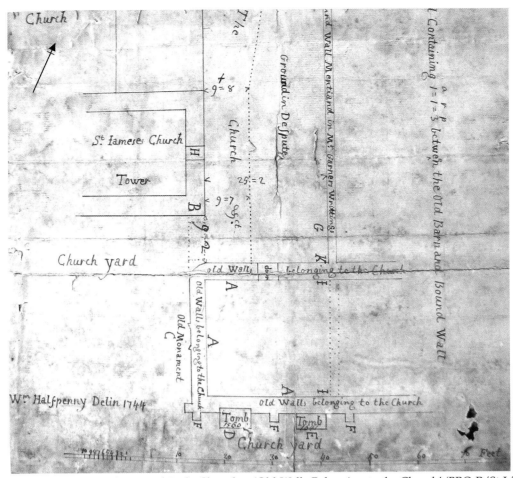

Fig. 9 A plan of 1744 showing the ruined Lady Chapel as 'Old Walls Belonging to the Church' (BRO P/St J/V/12/4/3)

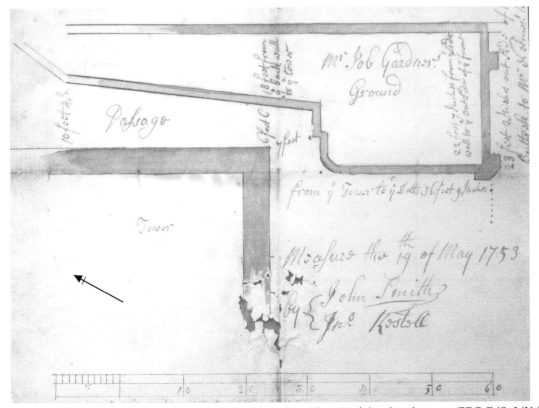

Fig. 10 A plan of 1753 showing the remains of the Lady Chapel, south-east of the church tower (BRO P/St J/V/12/4/6)

Fig. 11 Looking north-west showing the 18th-century houses fronting St James's Parade with St James's church-yard in the foreground. Note the buttresses on the front of two of the houses (arrowed) which are probably the remains of the Lady Chapel.

No foundations were excavated which Arthur considered to be earlier in date than the late 16th century. The finds, all unstratified, were described by the excavator as post-medieval although an examination of the finds by the present writer showed them to include some distinctive medieval Redcliffe-type green glazed floor tiles typical of those found during the 1995 excavations (see Chapter 6).

The Precinct Wall and Gatehouse

The area enclosed by the monastic precinct can only be approximately estimated and the course of the precinct wall is not known except along part of the western boundary.

In 1989 the foundations of the possible precinct boundary wall between the Franciscan Friary (Greyfriars) and St James's Priory were recorded in a pipe-trench excavated in Lower Maudlin Street about six metres east of its junction with Deep Street. The wall,

which was aligned on Lower Maudlin Street and built mainly of Brandon Hill Grit, was at a depth of 1.5 metres from the road surface (Boore 1990, 181–182).

Millerd's map of 1673 shows a gatehouse leading into an area of the precinct, called Whitson Court, from the south-west (Fig. 3). This gatehouse was standing until well into the 18th century and lay against the west side of the White Hart public house in Lower Maudlin Street (Fig. 12; BRO Building Plan Book A, fol. 264).

The Deed of Partition of the former priory dated 27 January 1580 refers to 'the great gatehouse entering by the church yard into the said great green court together with a dwelling house adjoining to the said gatehouse' (GRO D1799/T34). This presumably refers to the same gatehouse shown in the building plan book and the adjoining dwelling house might well have been what is now the White Hart public house.

A deed dated 8 April 1624 mentioned that George Winter, who owned the former priory, did not have the right to use 'so much of the room in the gatehouse there as the same gatehouse now standeth as hath been used heretofore for keeping a yearly court on Whitsun eve and from thence from the Saturday in Whitsun week in the afternoon'. From this we know that George Winter had to maintain the tradition of using part of the gatehouse for the Whit Sunday Court (GRO D1799/T7).

A deed dated 1 April 1648 concerning the sale of an eastern portion of the site of the former priory refers to a structure called the 'Fryers Wall' and it is tempting to suggest that this was part of the eastern precinct wall of the priory which had survived into the 17th century (GRO D293/2).

The drawing of the remains of the priory in about 1630 shows a gatehouse set within a crenellated wall running from east to west, to the east of the priory church (Fig. 8; BRO 17563 fol. 129). It is likely that this was a wall built by Henry Brayne in the late 16th century to enclose his mansion house rather than part of the precinct wall of the priory as its position does not correspond to any known precinct layout.

The Cloisters and Conventual Buildings

There are very few reliable documentary sources to help trace the layout of the priory buildings, and unfortunately there are no contemporary plans or drawings surviving which show details of the conventual buildings.

It is known that the cloisters and conventual buildings lay to the north of the priory church. Ideally cloisters were usually placed to the south of the church and it has generally been assumed that this was to achieve maximum sunlight and warmth, the cloister walk furthest from the church usually containing desks, known as 'carrels', for reading and study. Exceptions to this rule of planning can usually be

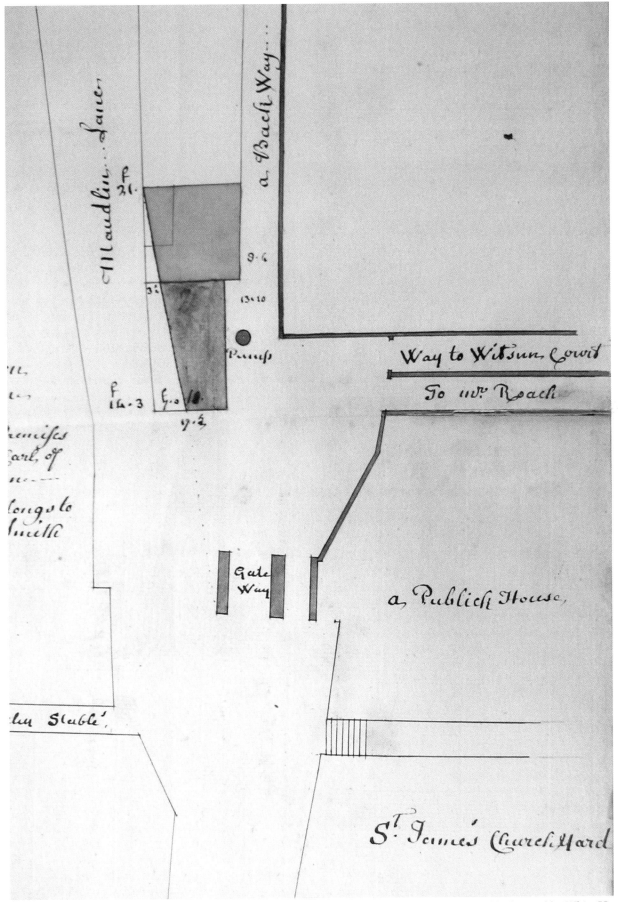

Fig. 12 The gatehouse or 'gate way' into the priory precinct shown in 'Maudlin Lane' west of a public house (the White Hart) on an 18th-century plan (BRO Building Plan Book A, fol. 264)

understood according to the functional limitations of the site. Rochester and Waltham had north cloisters due to the restricted nature of the sites while Tintern and Buildwas adopted north cloisters due to the position of their rivers (Gilchrist 1994, 129 & 131). At St James, the priory church, the most important building, was located on the crest of the slope leading up from the River Frome, in full view of the castle and medieval town, and it was therefore necessary to place the cloisters and conventual buildings on the level terrace of land to the north. This layout is paralleled at the Benedictine priory of St Mary's, Coventry, where the church occupied the hill-top site with the cloisters and conventual buildings lying on almost level ground to the north (Hobley 1971, fig. 2). Thus at St James's Priory the usual ranges of buildings, such as the chapter house, dormitory, refectory, cellarer's range, kitchens, guest quarters and infirmary were all situated around the cloisters to the north of the church.

Church House, to the north of the church, incorporates the last standing remains of the east side of the west claustral range of the priory, the rear elevation of the house including two arches of the cloister arcade (Fig. 13; Bryant 1993, 28). These arches would have been the second and third of the western arcade, the first probably having been destroyed when the church was extended in the 1860s. The south cloister arcade was most probably only three arches in length, and so a square cloister would have ended at the north end of the third arch in this arcade.

As surviving, the cloister arcade consists of the majority of two segmented pointed arches with buttresses between: the shape of these arches together with the single surviving fragment of open tracery and the arch mouldings suggesting a 14th-century date for their construction. These must have been replacements for an earlier arcade. Unlike many cloisters which had pentice roofs, the example at St James had another storey above the walk (Bryant 1993, 29). It is possible that the cloister may have been 'undershot', that is contained within the body of the range, as is found elsewhere including at the Dominican Friary in Bristol (Butler 1984, Fig. 8).

A fragment of the south cloister walk was found during limited excavation undertaken inside the church in 1974 when the Victorian north aisle was refloored. Below the set of pews on the north side of the aisle an area of about three metres by one metre was cleared of Victorian building rubble. Over half of the area had been seriously disturbed by the trench for a heating duct and holes dug to take piping, but the rest contained a consolidated deposit of building rubble, including very distinctive red mortar and fragments of painted wall plaster. Although no datable artefacts, such as pottery, were found in this rubble, its nature and the colour of the mortar strongly suggested a late medieval date. As the painted wall plaster had not been given a concealing coat of white

limewash, it seemed likely that the rubble had been deposited either immediately after or at some time before the Reformation. This rubble had been compacted around a stone foundation which was interpreted as a buttress of the south cloister walk (Dawson 1974; Dawson 1981, 19).

The only other find made in the area of the cloisters was a carved stone head discovered during groundworks for the extension of the tramway on the north side of the church in 1898. The head was unfortunately lost but was considered to be that of 'an early English queen or saint' (Pritchard 1898, 158).

The Water Supply

Urban monasteries found it especially difficult to preserve unpolluted sources of drinking water and were frequently driven to bring in a piped water supply from distant springs to serve the conventual buildings. It is thought that the priory was originally supplied from the deep well discovered in about 1940 in St James's Barton, but that this was replaced or supplemented in the 14th century by a pipe branching from the conduit which ran from a spring on the south-west side of Kingsdown to the Franciscan Friary in Lewin's Mead. Road works in 1932 and damage caused by bombing in 1941 apparently revealed sections of masonry tunnels leading towards the priory (Bond 1993, 58).

The Monastic Burial Ground

The traditional assumption is that members of monastic communities were buried in discrete areas. The head of a religious house might be buried in the choir, chapter house or cloister walk, while other monks would be buried in a graveyard to the east of the church (Greene 1992, 159).

Before the excavations in 1989 and 1995, the supposed area of the monastic cemetery had been investigated only briefly by the excavation in 1962. The two burials found then were almost certainly within the monastic burial ground at the east end of the priory church rather than being part of the parish churchyard. The results of the 1989 and 1995 excavations reported here make it clear that these two burials were part of an extensive cemetery.

The Priory Farm

An area to the east of St James's Church is known as St James's Barton and derives its name from the medieval priory farm or 'barton'.

A deed of 27 January 1580 described the 'former barton' to the east of the mansion house built by Henry Brayne on the site of the conventual buildings and at that time it still contained some of the buildings of the priory farm. It was referred to as 'all the grounds

Fig. 13 A survey of the exterior of the rear wall of Church House showing the arches and tracery of the west range of the cloisters (after J. Bryant, 1993)

inclosed with a wall adjoining to the said plot on the east side of the said house wherein standeth a pigeon house with all the barton that extendeth from the gate in Barcs lane where unto the pound is adjoining unto the said east part, or backer part of the said Mannor house & east part of the Church, together with two great barns, the said pounds & all other houses, edifices & buildings which lyeth on both sides & within the said barton & enclosed grounds ...' (GRO D1799/T34).

One of these great barns survived until the mid 18th century. In a document dated 1646 it was described as 'the Great Barn called ye Priory Barn' (BRO P/St J/V/12/4) and a plan of 1744 shows the 'Old Barn' as lying immediately to the east of the land owned by a Mr Garner which in turn was partly on the site of the former east end of the priory church (Fig. 9; BRO St J/V/12/4/3). If this was the tithe barn of the priory then it seems to have been located on the land now occupied by the Premier Travel Inn (converted from the former Avon House office block), and therefore now totally destroyed.

The 1580 deed provides some information on the extent of the lands lying within St James's parish which were almost certainly part of the priory farm. These were an un-named mead 1½ acres in extent next to Maudlin Lane, three other un-named meads one of which contained a barn, two meads called the Upper Maudlins, a mead with a pool and orchard called the Montagues, four meads called Culver House Close, Kingsdown, Galls Mead and Foxholes, two meadows called Great Earls Mead and Little Earls Mead, a quarter acre of ground adjoining the Horse Churchyard, and a mill called Baggpath (GRO D1799/T34).

A charter of 1373 defining the city boundaries names fields called 'Priourescroft', 'Priouresorchard' and 'the close of the Prior of St James' on the slopes of Kingsdown to the north of the priory (Harding 1930, 159).

St James's Back and Quay

The meadows, known as Broadmead, lying between the priory and the River Frome formed part of the priory's landholdings. Crossing these meadows was a street known as St James's Back which was probably laid out very soon after the founding of the priory in order to connect it with the river, as it seems likely that some of the materials required in the priory's construction would have been transported by ship. In Bristol the term 'Back' refers to a road laid out on or behind a quay, *e.g.* Welsh Back and St Augustine's Back.

Archaeological excavations carried out in 2000 at the southern end of this street where it adjoined the river (Fig. 2) showed that a wall had been built out into the river in the early to mid 12th century to provide a quayside against which vessels could have been moored and also confirmed that St James's Back

had been established at the same time (Jackson forthcoming). The former river-channel behind the wall was then infilled with red sand and clay which could have come from material produced during the levelling of the site of the priory. The reclaimed area behind the river-wall and the top of the original river-bank became the site of an industrial complex consisting of hearths and at least one timber building. This continued in use from at least the mid 12th century until the late 13th century when it was replaced by a substantial stone-built house.

The Lay Burial Ground and Parish Churchyard

The churchyard used by the parishioners of St James covered a large area to the south of the church on land sloping down to the River Frome. Its extent was defined by Lower Maudlin Street to the west, the Horsefair to the south and the road known as St James's Churchyard to the east. Its northern edge was crossed in the 18th century by a path originally called The Churchyard and later St James's Parade. In 1478 William Worcestre recorded the width of the churchyard as being 130 steps (Harvey 1969, 131).

Evidence for the extent of the churchyard was found in 1954 when human remains were uncovered during the construction of a department store on the site bounded by the Horsefair, Bond Street and St James's Churchyard (Mason 1957). This area was traditionally thought to have been the site of a burial pit for the victims of one of the outbreaks of plague in the 17th century. Despite the limited time available during construction work an excavation was carried out by members of the Folk House Archaeological Club. About 40 skeletons were excavated archaeologically while another 260 skeletons were removed by City Council workmen. The depth of the burials varied from a few centimetres to 1.5 metres, the bodies being laid mostly on the surface of the bedrock with apparently no graves having been cut into the bedrock. The shallow depth of some of the burials indicated that the original ground surface had been reduced at some time. The human remains were found to extend under the adjoining roads of the Horsefair, Bond Street and St James's Churchyard. However, no remains were found on the other side of St James's Churchyard which would seem to show the eastern limit of the burial ground.

The bodies were oriented east/west and laid in parallel rows, with the distance between the bodies being about 1.2 metres or less. Generally the bodies had their arms crossed over the chest with the hands resting on opposite shoulders. In a number of cases only one arm crossed, the other lying horizontally across the abdomen. There were few finds in the graves and there were no coffins or coffin fittings although some nails were found with one or two skeletons along the north-west boundary of the site.

One burial had two bronze buckles, one on each hip, which were identified as probably dating to the 14th century, and it was suggested by the excavator that all the burials generally dated to the 13th and 14th centuries.

There was certainly no evidence of the type of mass burial associated with plague victims and the regularity and spacing of the burials confirmed that the site was part of the parish churchyard.

Millerd's map of 1673 (Fig. 3) shows a building in the centre of the churchyard, which was presumably a small chapel, and a small group of buildings occupying the south-west corner of the churchyard at the junction of Silver Street and St James's Back (now Bridewell Street). Demolition in 1894 of the White Lion Inn at the junction of Bridewell Street and Silver Street led to the discovery of a tiled pavement beneath the inn (Warren 1896, 95). It was suggested by Warren that this pavement belonged to the chapel which William Worcestre had described as being in the churchyard of St James 'going towards the Franciscan Friary'. This he described as 'a fair chapel, quadrangular, all built of freestone as well as in the covering of the roof as in the windows; and it contains on either side of the chapel 18 feet square, with 8 buttresses' (Warren 1907, 196). It was postulated that it may have been a mortuary chapel in St James's churchyard. However, Warren's plan showing the location of the tiled pavement would appear to place it just outside the south-west corner of the churchyard, although the precise limits of the churchyard are not known in that area.

Whatever the use of this alleged chapel, about seventy-five medieval encaustic floor tiles were found which were of a reddish brown fabric decorated with yellow slip. These probably date to the 14th or early 15th centuries although Warren thought three of the tiles may have belonged to the 16th century. It was suggested that some of these tiles may have been manufactured at the Malvern kilns in Worcestershire. The decoration on some of these tiles took the form of Gothic windows, a shield with the lions of England and the inscription 'Fiat voluntas Dei', the Symbols of the Passion, two hearts joined with a four-leaved flower in each lobe, a crowned letter M, the initials IHC crowned within a double circle and within a border of eight inverted arches, and the shield of Edward the Confessor surrounded by foliage (Warren 1896, 96–97).

By the mid 19th century the churchyard had become very full, the ground being considerably elevated and held up on two sides with retaining walls. In 1850 the state of the churchyard was mentioned in a report to the General Board of Health (Clark 1850, 162). It was stated that 'the ground is now so full, that to make new graves, the grave-digger has often to bore the ground for a considerable time to find a free spot. The side near Lower Maudlin-street is in the worst state. Here I have seen decayed matter oozing through the wall, and many others, in warm weather, have seen ... maggots, crawl over the churchyard wall, across the street, and into the dwelling-houses of the inhabitants'.

The churchyard is now much reduced in area, having been truncated by main roads, and is used as a public park.

3 THE ST JAMES'S PRIORY 'EAST END' EXCAVATION REPORT (SITE 1)

Topography and Land Use

The site of the excavation was defined by Cannon Street to the west and north, land occupied by a meeting hall and the multi-storey office block at that time known as Avon House (now the Premier Travel Inn) to the east and St James's Parade to the south (Fig. 1). To the west of Cannon Street was the nave of the priory church, formerly used as the parish church of St James (Fig. 14), while to the north of Cannon Street was the Bus Station, built over the site of the conventual buildings of the priory in the late 1950s.

The west end of the St James's Parade frontage of the site was occupied by the NFU office building, due to be demolished as part of the redevelopment plan, while the east end of the frontage contained the tower and part of the façade of the Scottish Presbyterian Church which was to be largely retained within the development. The north-west corner of the site was covered by a small office block, the Audit Office, which was demolished during the course of the archaeological work and its footprint subsequently excavated. The remainder of the western portion of the site was laid out as surface car parks for the NFU offices while the whole of the eastern part was an area of waste land containing the partly visible remains of the foundations of the Scottish Presbyterian Church, the cellars of the demolished buildings fronting Cannon Street and the area of the 1989 archaeological excavation which had not been backfilled. The eastern end of the Cannon Street frontage retained the lower part of the Victorian façade of the Scottish Presbyterian Sunday School.

Fig. 14 Looking west showing the location of Site 1 in relation to the nave and tower of St James's Church which are towards the top of the photograph, with Cannon Street on the right and the NFU building centre left

Previous Archaeological Work

A small trial excavation was carried out during August and September 1988 by staff of the Field Archaeology section of the Bristol City Museum and Art Gallery before the proposed redevelopment of the site of the Scottish Presbyterian Church by the NFU Mutual Insurance Company.

The main objectives of this excavation were to establish the nature of the stratification, whether it had been significantly disturbed, and to determine if any medieval remains associated with the priory had survived. A trench about three metres wide was laid out, aligned north/south, and located immediately south of the 1953 church hall, within the nave of the Scottish Presbyterian Church. However, the investigation was eventually limited to three small areas within that trench. The natural subsoil was encountered at a depth of about one metre below the modern ground surface at the north end of the trench and the subsoil was noted as sloping away to the south. Over the subsoil was a layer of fine red-brown sand which, it was suggested, was either hill-wash or possibly dumped levelling material, and finds indicated it dated to the 14th or 15th centuries. One feature was interpreted as a ditch aligned east/west, which may have been cut during the later occupation of the priory but backfilled after the middle of the 17th century. A layer sealed this ditch but was cut by a series of 18th-century stone-lined drains. Substantial layers of sand and limestone fragments overlay these drains and had been laid down during the construction of the Scottish Presbyterian Church in the mid 19th century (Jones 1988a; Jones 1988b, 33).

Following the trial excavations an area of about 140 square metres was excavated in 1989 under the direction of Bob Jones. The main excavation was located to the north-east of the NFU office building and within the area previously occupied by the Scottish Presbyterian Church. A number of medieval burials, including distinctive body-shaped or head-niche burials, were found and indentified as belonging to the monastic burial ground lying to the east of the priory church. Unfortunately the human skeletal remains were generally in a very poor condition and, in some cases, showed only as stains in the soil. Some post-medieval deposits were excavated including a series of 17th-century rubbish pits containing fine groups of ceramics and other objects. Another, smaller area, was cleared close to the Cannon Street frontage on the site of an 18th-century building, although the archaeological deposits here were not fully excavated. An interim report on this excavation was published (Jones 1989).

As a result of the proposed redevelopment of the whole of the site bounded by Cannon Street, Avon House and St James's Parade, Bristol and Region Archaeological Services were requested to carry out a desk-based assessment in 1994 and this recommended an evaluation by trial trenching of the areas not excavated in 1989 (BaRAS 1994a).

The evaluation was undertaken in June 1994 by Eric Boore for Bristol and Region Archaeological Services, when four trial trenches were excavated: three beneath the car park to the north of the NFU offices and one to the east of the NFU offices within the area of the former Scottish Presbyterian Church. Two of the trenches below the car park revealed the presence of burials while the third, in the area of the supposed east end of the priory church, showed that there had been substantial disturbance of the archaeological deposits by service trenches connected with the NFU offices. The fourth trench, south of the 1989 excavation, indicated there was a good survival of archaeological deposits of the medieval and post-

medieval periods. A number of recommendations were made which involved the excavation of the whole of the area to be disturbed by the construction of the proposed office building and basement car park (BaRAS 1994b).

Excavation Methods and Recording

From the results of the archaeological excavation carried out on part of the site in 1989 and the evaluation work undertaken in 1994, it was known that the archaeological deposits in the area to be excavated were relatively shallow, especially beneath the car park of the NFU office and the Audit Office. The natural bedrock appeared to slope away to the south and the archaeology seemed to be deeper and better preserved beneath the southern part of the Scottish Presbyterian Church. The site was therefore worked as an open area excavation with relevant sections being recorded before removal.

The excavation was carried out from January to May 1995. Initially the entire area was stripped of car park surfaces, modern make-up levels and overburden using a mechanical excavator. Once archaeological deposits and structures were encountered these were cleaned and excavated by hand.

During weekdays the site was excavated by a team of professional archaeologists, assisted occasionally by archaeology students from Bristol and Bradford universities, working under the overall direction of the Project Manager, Reg Jackson, and the supervision of David Wicks. On one day each weekend the site was used as a training excavation for local archaeological societies, especially the Bristol and Avon Archaeological Society and the Clevedon and District Archaeological Society who, together with other volunteers, worked under the direction of the Project Manager.

All archaeological deposits, features and structures, including the remains of the mid-19th century Scottish Presbyterian Church, were recorded in detail. Almost the entire area was excavated to natural and the archaeological deposits removed. The exceptions were areas of the site which could not be excavated for safety reasons due to the proximity of standing walls. These were observed and recorded by means of a watching-brief during the course of the redevelopment of the site.

Adverse weather conditions during the early months of 1995, particularly extraordinarily heavy and persistent rain, caused some delay to the work and required the provision of site covers. Demolition of the Audit Office well into the period of the excavation also caused some logistical problems and the need for parts of the site to be excavated out of chronological sequence. Despite the discovery of over 150 more burials than was suggested by the pre-excavation evaluation work, and the site being less disturbed by later cellars than was anticipated, the archaeological excavation was able to be fully integrated into the developer's demolition and construction programme.

The site was divided into five areas which were given the letters A, B, C, D and E. Area B was largely that excavated in 1989, although a narrow strip of archaeology remained to be excavated in the west portion of area B. Area C was partly excavated in 1989, in particular Building 1 on the Cannon Street frontage. This area was re-excavated and recorded in 1995 and for reasons of clarity only the context numbers given in 1995 are referred to in the following report.

The archaeological features, structures, cuts, fills and layers were recorded using a continuous numbered context system. No separate feature or structure numbers were used. The contexts were numbered from 1 to 490 for the 1988/89 excavations and from 550 to 1,702 for the 1995 excavation. Context numbers 491 to 549 inclusive were not used. Context numbers placed within square brackets [ ] in the text refer to contexts recorded during the 1994 evaluation (BaRAS 1994b).

Each context number was recorded in a site register with a brief description of the location and type of context. Context Record Sheets were then fully completed by the archaeologist carrying out the excavation of that context.

Finds were cleaned and marked individually with the Bristol City Museum and Art Gallery accession number and the site context number and then bagged and boxed by find type and context for storage purposes. Finds Record Sheets were prepared giving full details of the quantity of finds from each context to aid the post-excavation work and to assist in the long-term curation of the material.

Special finds were given an individual special or 'Small Find' number and recorded in detail on a Small Find Record Form. For ease of reference the Small Find numbers in the following report are annotated with the suffix letter 'A' for the 1988/89 excavation and 'B for the 1995 excavation. Special finds were cleaned, x-rayed if appropriate, and conserved where required by Bristol and Region Archaeological Service's own in-house conservator working in the Conservation Department of Bristol City Museum and Art Gallery.

As part of the post-excavation work, analysis sheets were prepared for each context giving details of the type of context, a brief description of finds within that context, and a provisional date for the context. A site matrix of the context sequences was also prepared.

The site was planned at a scale of 1:20 using a fixed grid laid out in five metre squares. The relative heights of all layers, features and structures were related to Ordnance Survey Datum. Sections were drawn at a scale of 1:20 or 1:10.

The site was recorded photographically using 35mm colour print or slide film.

The methods of excavating and recording the burials are discussed in Chapter 5 of this report.

The excavations were ascribed Bristol City Museum and Art Gallery accession numbers: that for the 1988/89 excavations being BRSMG 62/1988 and that for the 1995 excavation BRSMG 2/1995. All the paper archive and finds for the excavations bear these accession numbers and have been deposited in the Archaeology Department of Bristol City Museum and Art Gallery, with the exception of the human remains.

Report on the 1989 and 1995 Excavations

Note on the Phase Plans: Due to the large area of Site 1 and its irregular shape it has been necessary to divide the phase plans of the site into two areas, west and east, for the purposes of publication (Fig. 15).

The Natural

The natural geology underlying the excavation was a red-brown weathered Triassic sandstone of the Mercia Mudstone Group overlaid in places with a purple-red Keuper Marl.

Period 1: The Pre-Burial Features

(Possibly late Saxon)
(Fig. 16)

The earliest evidence for human occupation of the excavated area was one shallow U-shaped gully cut into the natural sandstone (context 415). This was aligned roughly north/south and was discontinuous, having a possible terminal part way along its length. The gully was about 0.50m wide, up to 0.45m deep and contained clean orange sand. It was cut by a number of graves including one possible head-niche burial (Sk. 27; Type 1A) and one coffin burial (Sk. 15; Type 2). Another possible gully (421) was aligned roughly north-east/south-west although its width and length could not be determined due to later disturbances. The fill of this gully was cut by a head-niche burial (Sk. 12; Type 1). The fill of these gullies produced no dating evidence but they certainly pre-date the burials within the monastic burial ground and may represent boundary ditches. It is possible that they relate to the pits and gully found on Site 2 at the west end of the priory which were dated by pottery in their fills to the late Saxon period (see Chapter 4).

Period 2: St James's Priory

(c.1129 to 1540)

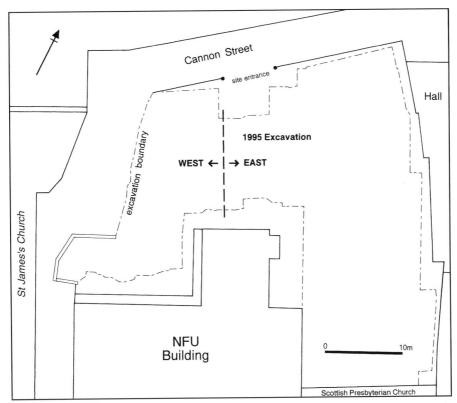

Fig. 15 Site 1: Plan showing the division of the site phase plans into two areas: west and east

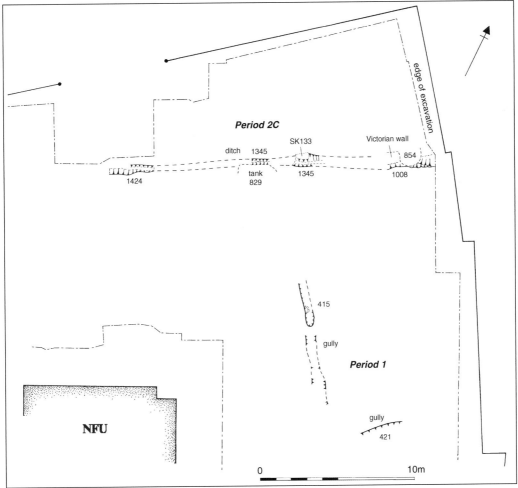

Fig. 16 Site 1: Plan of the Period 1 and 2C features

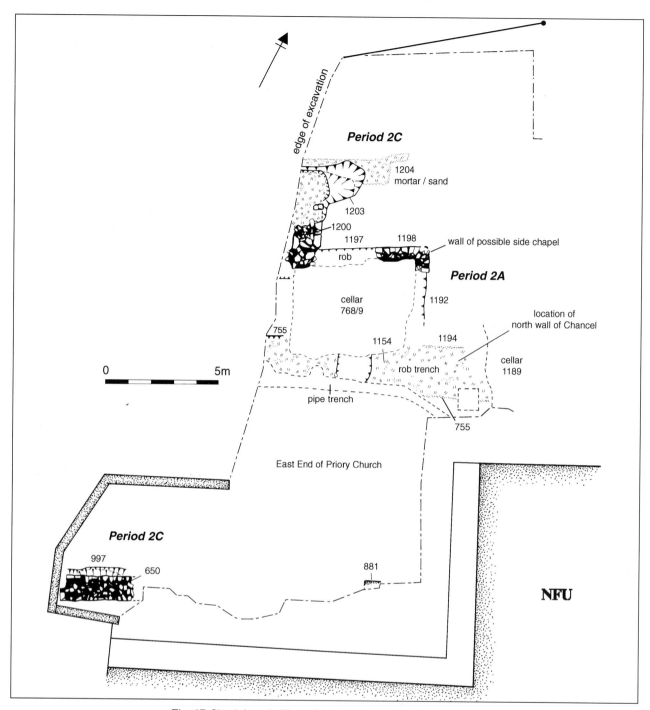

Fig. 17 Site 1 (west): Plan of the Period 2A and 2C features

Period 2A: The Monastic Burial Ground and the East End of the Priory Church

(*c.*1129 to mid 13th century)
(Fig. 17)

Documentary evidence (see Chapter 2) indicated that the east end of the priory church would lie within the area of the 1995 excavation and more particularly below the area occupied by the car park of the former NFU offices and under the Audit Office on the corner of Cannon Street. However, it seemed highly likely that the construction of the basement for the NFU offices had destroyed part of the east end of the church including the Lady Chapel.

Removal of the car park surface and modern make-up levels by machine revealed that insubstantial archaeological deposits of medieval date lay just below the modern ground surface. The archaeology that remained had been severely damaged by a number of modern service trenches and manholes and 18th- to 19th-century stone-built cellars and water tanks. The whole area of the excavation had apparently been reduced in level by up to one metre

Fig. 18 Site 1: Looking north showing the foundations and cellars of Buildings 4 and 5 (Period 4B) and the robber trench and mortar spread identifying the position of the north wall of the chancel of the priory church (Period 2A) marked by the ranging poles

prior to building work in the 18th century and during the construction of the NFU offices. Consequently all that remained of the priory church was the bottom course of the foundations, shallow robber trenches or just thin spreads of mortar. Nevertheless, sufficient traces of the east end of the church survived for a plan and a tentative identification of the structures to be made. Excavations at other monastic sites have shown that the foundation trenches and foundations of even the most important structures were often shallow and St James's Priory was apparently no exception (Greene 1992, 64).

The Burials
See Chapter 5 for a report on the burials.

The North Wall of the Chancel
An east/west wall, certainly the north wall of the chancel, was represented by a robber trench (755) and a thin spread of mortar (754) directly overlying the natural (Fig. 18). The robber trench and mortar spread were seen to continue the line of the north wall of the nave which still stands to the west of Cannon Street. Robber trench 755 had been cut into the natural to a depth of 0.18m and was at least 1.58m wide. This was filled with sandy yellow mortar and fragments of Pennant sandstone (754). It had been destroyed in places by a later pipe trench (762), a modern drain (763), an 18th-century wall (769) and two late 17th-/early 18th-century pits (772 and 783) (see Period 4A). Further east, the only evidence for the position of this

wall was a spread of yellow sandy mortar (754) some 5mm thick and at least 1.55m wide lying directly on the natural. This had been much disturbed, particularly on its northern edge, by a cut (1194) for a later wall. Between the west edge of the excavation and its destruction by cellar 1189 to the east, the north wall of the chancel could be traced for a length of some 9.8m.

There was no evidence for the north wall of the chancel continuing east of cellar 1189 so any evidence for the position of the east end wall of the chancel had been destroyed by the digging of cellar 1189 and the basement of the NFU offices.

The South Wall of the Chancel
The only evidence for the location of the south wall of the chancel was a small fragment of a robber trench (881) filled with sandy yellow mortar (880) which lay 8.4m south of robber trench 755. This was only 0.8m long by 0.2m wide and had a straight cut east/west on its north side. It had been truncated by the construction trench for the NFU building (631) and a modern pipe trench (870). However, it did appear to continue the line of the south wall of the nave, which survives to the west of Cannon Street, and also the line of wall 650 (Period 2C).

The Possible Chapel North of the Chancel
The foundations and robber trenches of one east/west and two north/south walls were revealed to the north of the chancel. The east/west wall, which ran from the west edge of the excavation for a distance of 6.2m,

Fig. 19 Site 1: Looking west showing the north-east corner and north wall of the possible chapel (Period 2A: wall 1198 and robber trench 1197), wall 1200 and robber trench 1203 (Period 2A) and stone-lined drain 1205 (Period 3)

was represented by robber trench 1197, filled with sandy yellow mortar and Pennant sandstone fragments (1196), and the bottom course of wall foundations which were bonded with a soft sandy yellow mortar (1198) (Fig. 19). Although the internal face of this wall had been destroyed by the construction of an 18th-century water tank (769), the wall was at least 0.6m thick. The north-west corner of the structure represented by wall 1198 survived and was joined to the north wall of the chancel by robber trench 1192 which was between 0.3 and 0.4m deep. The shallow remains of two postholes 0.4m in diameter, 0.04m deep and 0.72m apart (1440 and 1442) lay partly under, and on the same line as, robber trench 1197. These contained no datable material but might perhaps have been the location of posts marking out the intended position of wall 1198.

Contemporary in date with the walls represented by robber trenches 1192 and 1197 and wall 1198 was another wall 1.2m wide which ran north from wall 1197 for a distance of 3.4m and then appeared to either terminate or, more likely, turned to continue to the west. This wall comprised one course of foundations bonded with a soft sandy yellow mortar (1200) and beyond this a robber trench (1203) some 0.3m deep filled with the same mortar, Pennant sandstone fragments and sherds of floor and roof tiles (1202) (Fig. 19).

It seems likely that the structures north of the chancel were the remains of a small side chapel and possibly part of the north transept of the priory church.

There is no direct archaeological dating evidence for Period 2A as no pottery or other datable material was found within the wall foundations and foundation trenches for the construction of the walls could not be identified. However, as no burials underlie the walls this would imply that the walls were associated with one of the earliest phases of the construction of the priory perhaps shortly after its foundation. The sandy yellow mortar used in the construction of all the walls indicates that they were contemporary in date.

Period 2B: The Monastic Burial Ground

(mid to late 13th century)

This period is represented on the site by the continued use of the burial ground. See Chapter 5 for a report on the burials.

Period 2C: The Monastic Burial Ground, Blocking Wall within the Church and Occupation Level Outside the Church

(14th century)
(Figs.16 and 17)

An east/west wall, within the east end of the priory church, appeared to be a structural alteration probably associated with the re-ordering of the interior of the church for parochial use in the late 14th century. A layer to the north-east of the church was all that survived of 14th-century occupation associated with the priory.

Fig. 20 Site 1: Looking west along wall 650 (Period 2C)

The Occupation Level

Although the area to the north of the priory church had been badly disturbed by 18th- and 19th-century cellars and the foundations of the Audit Office, a small area of fine red sand with some Pennant sandstone fragments (1204) survived over an irregular area measuring approximately 4m long by, at most, 1.40m wide, and to a depth of up to 0.4m. This had been cut by the Period 3 stone-built drain (1205), a ditch (1219), a robber trench (1203) and a make-up layer (1365). Layer 1204 contained 14th-century pottery and ceramic roof tile and is interpreted as all that remains of an occupation level associated with the priory.

The Cemetery Boundary Ditch

In the later medieval period the northern limit of the monastic cemetery was defined by a ditch (1000/1008/1345/1424). This is dicussed in detail in Chapter 5.

Period 2D: The Monastic Burial Ground

(15th century to Dissolution in 1540)

Use of the monastic burial ground probably continued until the Dissolution of the priory. See Chapter 5 for a report on the burials.

Period 3: Post-Dissolution Activity

(1540 to the early 17th century)
(Figs. 21 and 22)

The excavation showed that after the Dissolution of the priory in 1540, all the walls of the priory church were comprehensively robbed for their stone leaving, at most, only the bottom course of the wall foundations remaining. Due to the levelling of the site in the 18th century and again during the construction of the NFU building, only the lowest parts of the robber trenches survived but the material used to backfill these gave some evidence of the quality of the priory buildings in the form of decorated roof and floor tiles. A number of deep pits had been dug to the east of the priory church and it is thought that these were quarry pits for the extraction of sand. Again, these were backfilled with the remains of the priory buildings including a fragment of a stone monument with painted and gilded decoration. A stone-lined drain and two postholes were situated in the area to the north of the church. A large linear feature towards the northern part of the site, filled with demolition debris from the priory buildings, may have been the remains of a path or trackway perhaps associated with Henry Brayne's mansion or another house situated outside the area of the excavation to the north.

The Burials

See Chapter 5 for a report on the burials.

The Blocking Wall

From the west edge of the excavation a wall foundation (650) ran east/west for a distance of 3.2m before it was cut by the wall of a 19th-century septic tank (641) and a modern pipe trench (654) (Fig. 20). The wall was 1m wide and built of Pennant sandstone bonded with a light pink mortar. A cut 0.3m deep and up to 0.36m wide along its north face appeared to be the remains of its shallow foundation trench (997).

There was no direct archaeological dating evidence for the date of construction of wall 650 and the fill of its foundation trench did not contain any datable finds. However, the wall was of a different construction and bonded with a different coloured mortar to the other walls of the church which implies it was of a different date to the Period 2A walls. It seems likely that the wall was constructed to block the south transept in c.1374 when documentary evidence shows that a new tower was added to the church and parts of the church were converted to parochial use (see Chapter 2).

The Robber Trenches

The location and extent of the robber trenches of the walls of the priory church (755, 1192, 1197, 1203) have already been discussed under Period 2A. The finds

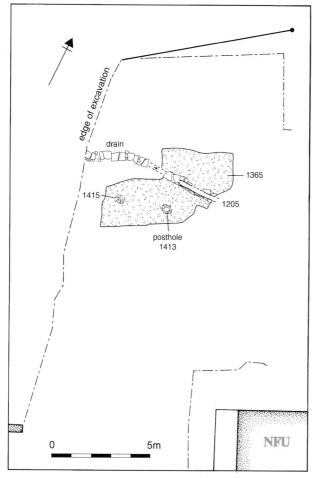

Fig. 21 Site 1 (west): Plan of the Period 3 features

The layer contained pottery, including Cistercian or black ware, dating to the late 16th or early 17th centuries. The absence of any clay tobacco pipe fragments amongst the finds would seem to indicate a late 16th-century date for this context. The mixed nature of the layer, which included Pennant sandstone and limestone fragments, pieces of 14th-century ceramic roof tile and medieval floor tile, implies that it represents disturbance associated with the demolition of the priory after the Dissolution, but before the final robbing of the foundations of the wall which it abuts. The presence of this layer immediately overlying natural and cutting the 14th-century occupation layer (1204) may be evidence for the general removal of medieval occupation levels shortly after the Dissolution.

The Stone-Built Drain

A stone-built drain (1205) (Fig. 19) ran from the west section of the excavation eastwards for a distance of 2.4m, turned to the south-east and continued for a further 4.6m before being obliterated by a modern disturbance. It was constructed of Pennant sandstone with cover slabs laid on side walls bonded with a red sandy mortar, which were in turn set on thin slabs forming the base of the drain. The drain was 0.2m wide by 0.2m deep internally and was almost completely filled with a soft brown silt containing slate fragments and lumps of pink mortar (1206). The construction trench (1207) for the drain, which was at most 0.8m wide by 0.35m deep, cut through contexts 1204 and 1365 and the fill of robber trench 1203.

The fill of drain 1205 contained pottery and decorated roof tile which all date to the late 13th/early 14th centuries. However, they must be residual as the drain-fill also contained a 16th-century Nuremberg jetton (SF 423B). The construction trench (1207) for the drain also cut through the 16th-century context 1365. The evidence indicates that the drain was constructed and in use towards the end of the 16th century.

Postholes

Two postholes (1413 and 1415) lay to the east of wall 1200. These were 1.9m apart, between 0.2 and 0.25m in diameter, were cut almost vertically through the 16th-century make-up layer 1365 and the underlying natural to a depth of 0.3m, and were packed with small fragments of Pennant sandstone, limestone and slate.

The packing (1412) of posthole 1413 contained residual sherds of early 13th-century pottery but neither posthole contained any other datable material. It seems most likely that the postholes represent a post-medieval timber structure of possible late 16th- or early 17th-century date.

Running north/south towards the eastern edge of the excavation was a line of four postholes (362, 366, 370, 361) measuring between 0.4m and 0.2m across. Three of these postholes (366, 370, 361) contained traces of post voids 0.12m square. Two cut into the

within the robber trenches were residual and could not be used to date the destruction of the walls. The robber trenches contained rubble and mortar from the walls and fragments of ceramic roof and floor tiles which represent parts of the destroyed priory buildings. However, the absence of any clay tobacco pipe fragments within the fill of the robber trenches may indicate that the robbing of the walls occurred no later than the end of the 16th century. In addition, robber trench 1203 cut through layer 1365 which appeared to date to the late 16th century.

The Make-up Layer

North of the church, a levelling or make-up layer postdating the Dissolution of the priory in 1540 had been cut by a stone-lined drain and postholes.

Although badly disturbed by later intrusions this compacted layer of red sand containing fragments of Pennant sandstone and pieces of limestone (1365) remained to the east of wall 1200 (see Period 2A). The layer, which had survived over an area of about 12 square metres, abutted the foundations of wall 1200 and had been cut by robber trenches 1197 and 1203. It was also cut by subsequent Period 3 postholes 1413 and 1415.

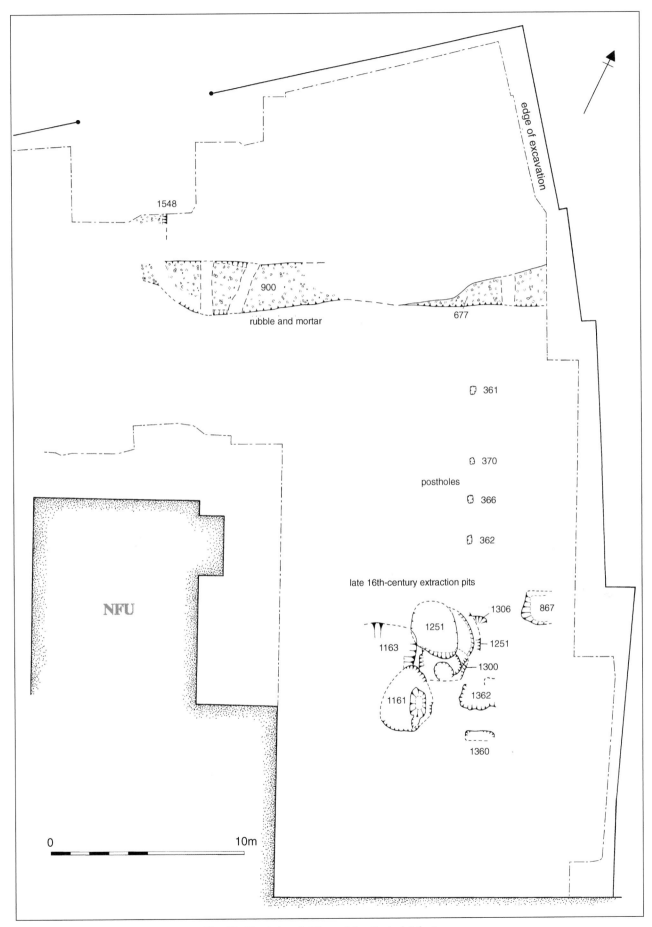

Fig. 22 Site 1 (east): Plan of the Period 3 features

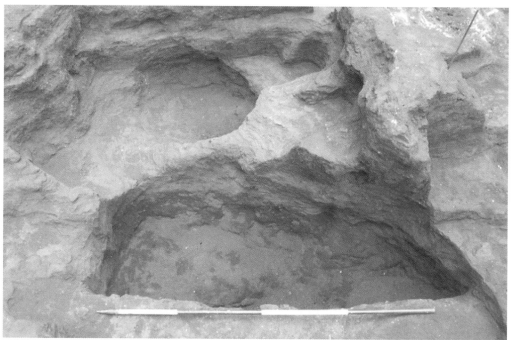

Fig. 23 Site 1: The extractions pits (Period 3), with pit 1251 half-sectioned in the foreground

fills of head-niche graves (Sks. 9 and 14). The fills of these postholes produced no finds. Probably contemporary with the postholes were two sub-circular pits (403, 444) *c.*0.9m in diameter and *c.*0.5m deep. Their function is unknown but they also cut head-niche graves. The dating of these features is problematical although they certainly post-date the head-niche burials. It was suggested by the excavator who carried out the work in 1989 that the postholes represented a boundary within the burial ground, the coffin burials all supposedly lying west of this boundary (Jones 1989, 3). However, in view of the results of the 1995 excavation, when coffin burials were found east of the postholes, this theory has to be discounted. It seems more likely that they belong to a post-Dissolution division of the property and probably date to the late 16th century.

The Extraction Pits

A number of irregularly shaped, intersecting pits (1161, 1163, 1251, 1300, 1306) were cut through the medieval graves and into the natural bedrock below to a depth of up to 1.2m (Fig. 23). The pits were revealed beneath context 1166 which was an arbitrary removal of about 0.15m of post-medieval garden soils containing cultivation trenches 912, 914 and 918 (see Period 4B). The fill of pits 1161, 1300 and 1251 contained pottery of late 15th-century date, while that of 1163 contained early 14th-century sherds. However, it is likely that these finds were of a residual nature and that the pits were excavated after the Dissolution of the priory, in the late 16th century, as they contained fragments of the demolished priory buildings such as roof and floor tiles and pieces of

worked stone. The nature of the contents of their backfill would indicate that the pits were excavated for the extraction of the underlying sand or sandstone, rather than primarily for use as rubbish pits.

Pit 1161: This was truncated by the post-medieval stone-lined pit 761 and it, in turn, cut an earlier extraction pit 1163. Its upper fill (1160) was a red-brown clayey silt containing fragments of Pennant sandstone, limestone and slate while the lower fill (1224) was a black silty deposit.

Pit 1163: This was cut by extraction pit 1161 and in turn truncated extraction pits 1251 and 1300. Its fill (1162) was similar to that of pit 1161 although it contained a number of fragments of much decayed medieval window glass.

Pit 1300: This was cut by extraction pits 1161, 1163 and 1251. Its upper fill (1299) was similar to that of pit 1161 while the lower fill (1299A) was a lens of ash, charcoal and burnt bone.

Pit 1251: This was cut by pit 1163 and cut pit 1306. It was not fully excavated for safety reasons but was sectioned at its deepest point. Its fill (1250) was a red-brown silty sand with clayey lenses and it contained oyster shells and fragments of Oolitic limestone, Pennant sandstone and slate. The fill included two lenses of rubble. The clayey nature of the fill at the bottom of the pit suggested that it was left open for a time before being backfilled.

Pit 1306: This lay to the east of pit 1251 and was cut by it. It was also cut by the 17th-century rubbish pit 753. Its fill (1305) was similar to that of pit 1161.

Pit 867: This was not completely excavated as its north edge lay below the south wall (551) of the Welsh Congregational Chapel which was left *in situ*. It was flat bottomed and just over 1.5m deep. Its upper fill (866) was a red-brown sand with flecks of pale orange mortar and charcoal and fragments of slate roof tiles. Its lower fill (868) was a red-brown silty clay containing white mortar flecks and gravel. The bottom of the pit was filled with large stones.

In addition to the deep extraction pits there were a number of shallow pits which also apparently date to the post-Dissolution period. Those pits, 1360 and 1362, were both cut by post-medieval cultivation trenches 1165 and 1304 and sealed below the garden soil 1166. They were up to 0.15m deep and had brown clayey fills (1359 and 1361) containing fragments of weathered limestone, slate, flint and sandstone lumps.

The Linear Feature

A broad, shallow linear feature was located towards the northern edge of the excavation (677, 900, 1548). This was aligned approximately east/west and its eastern end was not found as it continued beyond the limit of the excavated area in that direction. It extended west for a distance of just over 20m before it appeared to turn sharply towards the north, although here it had been badly disturbed by later buildings and pipe trenches. It had sloping sides, a maximum width of just over 3m, a maximum depth of 0.47m, and had been cut through a number of burials. Its fill (676, 899) consisted of a loose, light yellow-brown silty sand which contained large fragments of Pennant sandstone, pieces of roof slate, worked stone, lumps of pinkish coloured mortar, wall plaster, fragments of decorated floor tile and sherds of ceramic roof tile. These appeared to be parts of the demolished priory building so the feature must post-date the Dissolution of the priory. The pottery sherds from the fill date to the 16th century, although the absence of any clay tobacco pipe fragments from the feature indicated that the fill was unlikely to have been deposited later than the beginning of the 17th century.

It is difficult to interpret the purpose of this feature. It does not appear to be a robbing trench for a wall as its sides slope inwards towards the bottom and any wall it may have contained would have been founded on grave fills rather than the natural marl or sandstone bedrock. It seems possible that it was the base for a path or trackway associated with Henry Brayne's mansion house or another building situated to the north of the excavated area.

Period 4: The Post-Medieval Reoccupation

(early 17th century to the 1990s)

Period 4A: Rubbish Pits and Cultivation Trenches

(early 17th century to early 18th century)
(Figs. 24 and 25)

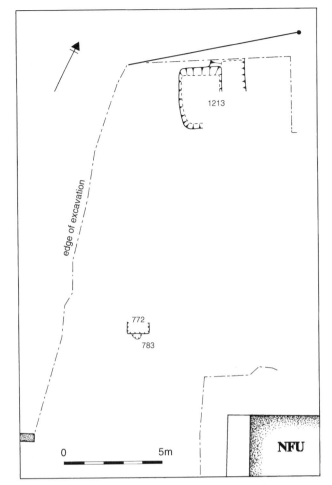

Fig. 24 Site 1 (west): Plan of the Period 4A features

Documentary sources suggest that the area of the excavation was open land from the 17th to the early 18th centuries. However, Millerd's 1673 map of Bristol shows some houses in the general area to the east of the church although their exact location, discussed in Chapter 2, is problematic. There was apparently a general levelling of the site in the early 18th century prior to the construction of the houses on Cannon Street and St James's Parade but it is unlikely that this would have removed all traces of 17th- or early 18th-century houses. Certainly no remains were found of buildings of that date in the area excavated. The rubbish and cess pits of Period 4A were apparently dug in an area of open or waste ground and were probably used by the inhabitants of the adjacent properties, for example the Brayne mansion to the north-west.

A number of the rubbish pits, 235, 318 and 335, contained off-cuts from a late 17th-century bone-working industry, although there was no evidence that the bone-working was actually being carried out within the excavated area. A discussion of the bone-working debris is contained in Chapter 6.

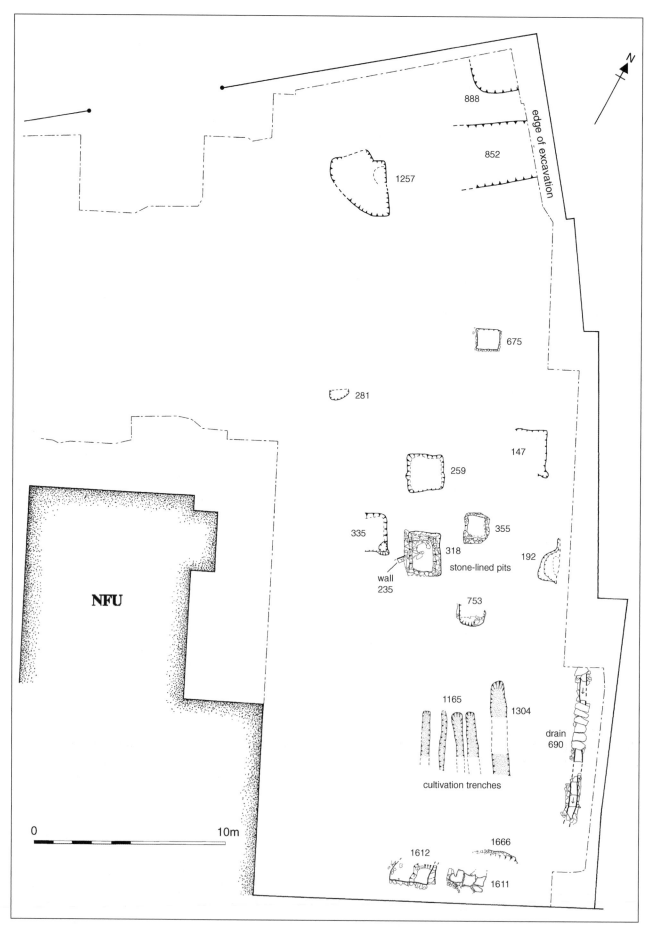

Fig. 25 Site 1 (east): Plan of the Period 4A features

The Rubbish and Cess Pits

Pit 147: A shallow pit 0.38m deep and roughly rectangular in shape, measuring 2.2m by 1.6m. The upper fill (145) was a mixed red-brown sandy loam with charcoal flecks, while the lower fill (146) was a greyish-green cess material. Both fills contained finds dating to the early 18th century.

Pit 192: A sub-circular pit in the south-east corner of the 1989 excavation. Only about half the pit could be excavated, the rest lying outside the area available for excavation. The pit had sloping sides, was at least 1.8m across from north to south, and was 1.7m deep. Its upper fill (166) was a dark brown ashy loam, the lower fill (191) being a brown loam with many large flecks of charcoal and mortar. Both fills contained finds dating to the second half of the 17th century, the occurrence of clay pipes made by Llewellin Evans indicating that the deposition of the fill could not have taken place earlier than 1661. A full report on the finds from this pit appears in Chapter 6.

Pit 235: This appeared to have been cut and largely destroyed by pit 318, only a fragment of it remaining to the south-west of pit 318. The pit was apparently lined with dry-stone walling although only a fragment 0.4m long survived. The remaining fill of the pit consisted of a mixed brown loam with fragments of plaster and charcoal (169) overlying a tip layer (214) of red-brown sandy loam containing some worked bone offcuts. The lowest fill of the pit (213) was a dump of brown loam flecked with grey mortar which contained large quantities of offcuts from bone-working including cut and worked bone, burnt bone and bone dust. The finds from the pit fill indicated a deposition date in the late 17th century, the presence of clay pipes made by Llewellin Evans from the upper fill (169) confirming that this could not have occurred before 1661.

Pit 259: This lay below the modern pit 58 and was roughly rectangular measuring 1.8m square and about 0.2m deep. The upper fill (238) was a compact rich brown loam with charcoal flecks below which was a similar layer (239) containing many lumps of pink mortar. The bottom layer of the pit (260) was filled with a green cess-like material. Both 238 and 260 contained much waste from bone-working while the fill of the pit produced finds dating to the late 17th century. A full report on the finds from this pit appears in Chapter 6.

Pit 281: The north side of this sub-circular pit had been removed by the Victorian church pillar 34 and its construction trench 73 while its east side had been cut by drain 163/164. The pit measured 1m east/west and at least 0.5m north/south and had almost vertical sides. Its upper fill (282) consisted of a very mixed sandy loam with lumps of red sandstone, cess and charcoal. Its lower fill (278 and 283) was a soft dark grey-green cess material. The finds from the fills dated to the early 18th century and the presence of a pipe

made by George Ebbery from the lowest fill showed that the backfilling could not have taken place before 1721.

Pit 296: This was a roughly rectangular cut with sloping sides measuring 1.4m square. Its fill (294, 295) consisted of red brown sand with many fragments of Lias limestone and plaster but no datable material. However, it lay beneath the remains of the 18th-century boundary wall 830 (see Period 4B) and was therefore probably late 17th- or early 18th-century in date.

Pit 318: This was at least partly sealed by a 19th-century pit (222). It was a rectangular cut (318) lined with walling of Pennant sandstone bonded with a buff coloured mortar (135, 216, 217, 220, 336). The pit measured 1.8m north/south and 1.4m east/west internally at the top, reducing to 1.5m and 1.1m respectively at the bottom. The pit was 0.62m deep and appeared to have been roughly floored with Pennant sandstone slabs. The upper fill (215) was a soft red-brown sandy loam with some charcoal flecks while the lower fill (331) was a greasy green-brown layer of cess material. Only fill 215 contained finds including a collection of worked bone offcuts and these date the fill to the late 17th century.

Pit 335: This shallow pit measured 1.9m north/south by at least 1.2m east/west, the west edge being cut by drain 164/163. The south and west sides were cut vertically to a depth of 0.32m while its north and east sides sloped inwards towards the bottom. The upper fill (237 and 293) was a dark brown loam with flecks of lime and plaster and contained worked bone offcuts. Beneath this were further fills (314 and 315) consisting of red-brown sandy loams, fill 314 being thickly flecked with plaster and charcoal, and both containing worked bone offcuts. The lower fills (323 and 332) were a soft red-brown slightly sandy loam with large fragments of plaster. The bottom of the pit contained a grey-green cessy material with fragments of Pennant sandstone. There were few finds and the only datable object was a fragment of an 'onion' shaped wine bottle indicating a late 17th- to early 18th-century date for the backfilling of the pit.

Pit 355: This rectangular pit had a drystone wall lining (375) made of Pennant sandstone and small amounts of brick, the walling being intermittent along the west and east sides. The pit measured 1.1m north/south by 0.9m east/west and was cut into the natural sandstone to a depth of 1.5m. Its fill (359) consisted of a brown loam with fragments of charcoal and Pennant sandstone. There were few datable finds from this fill but a late 17th- to early 18th-century date seems likely for the backfilling of the pit.

Pit 675: A rectangular pit measuring 1.1m by 1m internally, which had been cut into the medieval layer 704 and the underlying natural sandstone to a depth of 0.36m. Its vertical sides had been lined with a single thickness of unmortared Pennant sandstone (674),

Fig. 26 Site 1: Pit 675 looking east (Period 4A)

except along its north edge (Fig. 26). It was filled (673) with a brown sandy loam containing fragments of Pennant sandstone, brick, lumps of cream mortar and finds dating to the early 18th century.

Pit 753: This rectangular stone-lined pit could only be partly excavated as its north edge lay below the south wall (551) of the Welsh Congregational Chapel which was left *in situ*. The west, south and east edges of the pit had a drystone wall lining built mainly of Pennant sandstone (752). The pit measured 1.3m east/west and at least 0.6m north/south internally and it was 1.3m deep with a flat bottom. Its stone-lining on the south side was partly overlain by the north/south property boundary wall 747 and its robber trench 750 (see Period 4B). The fill of the pit (744) consisted mainly of a brown clayey silt with much charcoal flecking and small stones. There were clear tip lines within the pit fill which sloped down from east to west. The bottom fill of the pit contained large pieces of stone rubble. The backfilling of the pit dated to the late 17th or very early 18th century. A full report on the finds from this pit appears in Chapter 6.

Pit 772: This rectangular rubbish pit was cut by the south wall of the 18th-century cellar 769 and in turn cut pit 783 and robber trench 755. The pit measured 1.1m east/west, at least 0.64m north/south and was 1.1m deep. It was filled (771) with soft black sandy material containing late 17th-century pottery and clay pipes.

Pit 783: This small circular rubbish pit (783), 0.5m in diameter and 0.25m deep, was cut by pit 772 and had a similar fill (782) and date to pit 772.

Pit 888: This large sub-circular pit was sealed by the garden soil (886) in the north-east corner of the excavation. Only a portion of this pit lay within the excavated area and this measured at least 2.3m by 1.6m. Its sides were almost vertical and had been dug through the natural sandstone to a depth of at least 0.5m, although it could not be fully excavated for safety reasons. The fill of this pit (887), which consisted of a light brown silt with much charcoal, contained pottery and clay pipes of late 17th-century date.

Pit 1213: This large rectangular rubbish pit extended outside the northern limit of the excavation, under the pavement of Cannon Street. The pit measured at least 3.4m east/west and the same distance north/south, had vertical sides, was unlined and was up to 0.66m deep. It had been cut through medieval features into the underlying sandstone and its base sloped down from east to west. The south-east corner of the pit had been cut by a 19th-century water tank (1214) while its east edge had been cut by a modern trench filled with concrete. The fill of the pit (1212) consisted of a number of bands of interleaving ash and cinder debris containing large quantities of finds. These sloped down towards the south-west indicating that the rubbish had been dumped in from the north-east corner. The backfilling of the pit dates to the mid 17th century. A full report on the finds from this pit appears in Chapter 6.

Pit 1257/1259/1326: This sub-rectangular pit lay below the south-west corner of Building 1 fronting Cannon Street (see Period 4B). It could only be partly excavated, but measured approximately 2.8m east/

Fig. 27 Site 1: Pit 1612 looking east (Period 4A) cut by the north wall 619 of Buildings 7 and 8 on the left (Period 4B)

in its south-west corner where its depth was 0.9m below the top of the surviving stone-lining. The pit measured 2m east/west and at least 1m north/south internally. The upper fill (1613) of the pit consisted of Pennant sandstone rubble and lumps of a grey-pink mortar. The lower fill (1614) was a black organic material. Both of the fills lay below and pre-date wall 619 of Buildings 7 and 8 (see Period 4B) and produced finds of late 17th-/early 18th-century date.

The Possible Cellar Structure
This structure lay to the east of stone-lined pit 1612 and was below walls 619 and 1566 of Buildings 7 and 8 (see Period 4B). This feature was clearly earlier in date than the buildings although its relationship to stone-lined pit 1612 is unknown as this was obscured by wall 1566 which could not be removed in the time available for the excavation. The purpose of this feature, and its relationship to the rest of the site, could not be determined in view of the restricted nature of the excavation in this area which was close to the foundations of the standing walls of the Victorian church including the tower. The north edge of this feature was presumably represented by the sloping cut 1666 north of wall 619. This cut had truncated three medieval burials. The bottom of the structure was floored with with large irregular slabs of Pennant sandstone (1611) with an area of small stones, faced to the north-east, in its south-west corner. The floor of this feature was almost 1m below the contemporary occupation levels to the north. On removing the slab floor it was found to have been placed on a thin layer of black ash (1629) which directly overlay the natural red sandstone bedrock.

Stone-Lined Drain 690
A stone-lined drain bonded with brown mortar ran approximately north/south at the east edge of the excavation. This drain was 0.4m wide internally and its fill (940) contained pottery and clay pipes of late 17th-/early 18th-century date. It had been truncated by drain 932 (see Period 4B) at which time drain 690 had been abandoned. Drain 690 was also cut by a further east/west curving drain 938 (in cut 939) with fill 937 which produced 19th-century pottery and clay pipes (see Period 4B).

Cultivation Trenches
Five curving north/south cultivation trenches were found and these were sealed below the north/south boundary wall 922 and their south ends cut by the east/west drain 579 (see Period 4B). They in turn cut the earlier pits 1360 and 1362 (see Period 3). These trenches (1165A-D, 1304) were 0.4m wide by 0.15m deep and were up to 3m in length. They contained residual sherds of medieval pottery but also sherds of mid to late 17th-century pottery and clay pipes.

west and 3.2m north/south and was at least 0.8m deep with almost vertical sides cut into the sandstone natural. It had been cut by the foundations of the 18th-century walls 820 and 823, their associated construction trenches 1339 and 828, and drain 836. It had also been cut by stone-lined drain 903 and its construction trench 905. West of wall 820 the pit was sealed by 18th-century garden soils (841, 842 and 969) while east of wall 820 and north of wall 823 it was sealed below the flagstone floor (821) of the cellar. The fill of the pit (1256, 1258, 1327), which could not be completely excavated for safety reasons, was a loose red-brown silty clay containing crushed limestone, charcoal and slate. The backfilling of the pit dates to the early 18th century.

Pit 1612: This stone-lined pit lay beneath, and had been partly destroyed by, the 18th-century Buildings 7 and 8 fronting St James's Parade (see Period 4B). It had a stone-lining (1565, 1566) on its south and east sides, while its west edge (1612) was an unlined vertical cut (Fig. 27). Its north side was obscured below wall 619. The base of the pit was stepped, being deeper

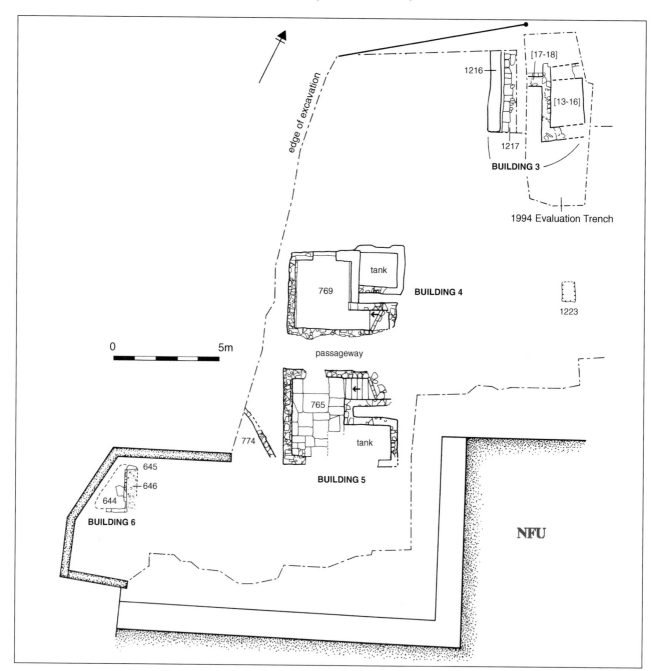

Fig. 28 Site 1 (west): Plan of the Period 4B features

Other Features

In the north-east corner of the excavation, below the 18th-/19th-century garden soil 886 (see Period 4B), was an east-west linear feature (852) 3m wide by 0.1m deep which had a dark, almost black, friable fill (687) containing finds of late 17th-/early 18th-century date. A post-pit (953) 0.4m in diameter and dug into the natural below 852 may have belonged to this period of occupation.

Period 4B: The 18th-Century Housing

(early 18th century to mid 19th century)
(Figs. 28 and 29)

A number of houses were built along the Cannon Street frontage of the site in the mid to late 18th century, the east/west length of Cannon Street to the north of the excavation being described on a map as a 'new street' shortly after 1744 (see Chapter 2). Parts of these houses lay within the area excavated although the modern pavements of Cannon Street had been extended over the front of some of these buildings after their demolition, restricting the areas of the

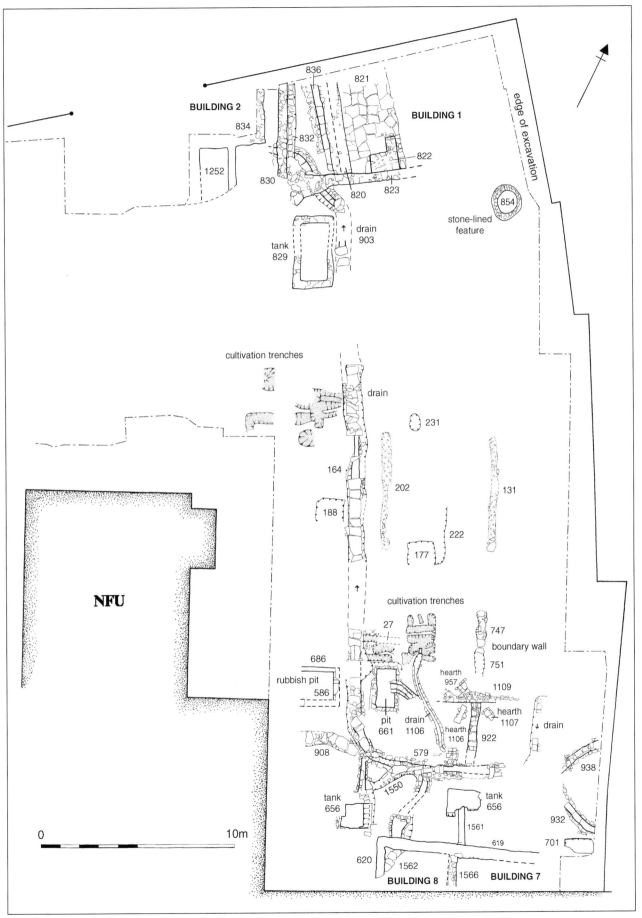

Fig. 29 Site 1 (east): Plan of the Period 4B features

buildings available for excavation. The foundations and cellars of the houses had also been damaged by later development on the site, most notably the deep service trenches connected with the NFU office building.

Houses were also built along St James's Parade, probably at a slightly earlier date than those on Cannon Street. Only a small part of one of these buildings could be excavated, the remainder lying under the tower and façade of the Scottish Presbyterian Church.

The 18th-century structures were all of similar construction. The foundations and cellar walls, which were all that survived, were built mainly of Pennant sandstone and Lias limestone bonded with a hard pink mortar with a high lime content. Brick was only occasionally used. Any variation from this type of construction is mentioned in the text.

In the following report the buildings are described as complete properties including their associated boundary walls, drains, rubbish pits, water tanks and other structures. Where features could not be ascribed to a particular property they are described separately.

Buildings 1, 2 and 3 (Cannon Street)

The remains of three late 18th-century houses – Buildings 1, 2 and 3 – were found fronting Cannon Street to the north.

The east building, Building 1, which was fully excavated, followed the present line of Cannon Street, while Buildings 2 and 3, which had been largely destroyed by modern service trenches, followed an earlier line of Cannon Street which had been obliterated by widening the road and pavement in connection with the construction of the NFU building and the Audit Office. The walls of Buildings 2 and 3 were therefore at a slightly different angle to those of Building 1. Building 1 was destroyed by the construction of the Sunday School associated with the Scottish Presbyterian Church (see Period 4C) while Buildings 2 and 3 apparently survived until they were demolished during the construction of the NFU office building in 1964.

Building 1

The remains of Building 1 consisted of a cellar cut into the natural sandstone of which only the west and south walls survived, the east part of the cellar having been destroyed by the deep, narrow boiler room of the Scottish Presbyterian Church (see Period 4C). The west wall (820) of the cellar was 0.58m wide and was butted against the south wall (823) of the building. Wall 820 had a vertical-sided construction trench (1339) 0.20m wide along its east face, although its fill (1338) did not produce any datable finds. Wall 823 was 0.5m wide although its west end (1254), which projected some 1.6m beyond the south-west corner of Building 1, was splayed out to a width of over 1m evidently in order to buttress the building which was

sinking into the 17th-century pit (1257/1259/1326) over which it had been constructed (see Period 4A). Wall 823 had a construction trench (828) up to 0.5m wide along its south face. The fill (974) of this construction trench produced mainly 18th-century pottery and some residual 17th-century material.

Against the south wall (823) of the cellar of Building 1 was the base (822) of what were presumably stone-built access steps, the cellar having been backfilled with modern demolition debris. It was floored with large slabs of Pennant sandstone set in mortar (821) and laid directly on natural. The east side of the cellar had been cut by wall 818 which formed the west side of the boiler room of the Scottish Presbyterian Church. This boiler room had removed all trace of the earlier 18th-century cellar.

Drain 836: Abutting the west face of wall 820, and running parallel to it, was a stone-lined drain (836), the southern end of which had been destroyed by a later disturbance. The side walls of this drain were built of Pennant sandstone bonded with pink mortar. The capstones of the drain did not survive but it was floored with large Pennant slabs and was 0.36m wide.

Boundary Wall 830: West of wall 820, but at right angles to Cannon Street and not parallel with wall 820, was a wall 0.5m wide which represented the property boundary between Buildings 1 and 2. This wall terminated approximately level with the south wall (823) of Building 1. It had a foundation trench (832) along its east face, which was some 0.4m wide, and whose fill (831) produced finds ranging in date from the 17th to the 19th centuries. Between drain 836 and wall 830 was an area of what appeared be garden soil (841, 842 and 969) containing 17th-, 18th- and early 19th-century finds.

Water Tank 829/901: In the garden or yard behind Building 1, 1.5m south of wall 823, was a water tank which measured 3m north/south by 1.3m east/west internally and was 0.86m deep. Its walls, which were 0.4m wide, were constructed of Pennant sandstone and limestone, and rendered internally with grey mortar. The tank had apparently remained in use throughout the occupation of Building 1 and was backfilled at the time of the construction of the Scottish Presbyterian Church when it had been cut by one of the walls (824) of the Sunday School associated with the church. The tank was positioned to respect the line of the main north/south drain 903 which ran along its east side.

Garden Area: East of Building 1 was an area of garden presumably associated with this property or the adjoining property to the east which lay outside the excavated area. The west portion of the garden had been destroyed by the construction of the boiler room of the Scottish Presbyterian Church while its eastern limit could not be determined. The garden soil (886) produced finds of late 17th- to early 18th-century date.

Fig. 30 Site 1: Stone-lined structure 854 looking north (Period 4B)

Stone-Lined Storage Pit 854: To the south-east of Building 1, cut through the garden soil 886 and sealed below a 19th-century wall 855, was a roughly circular feature with a maximum diameter of 1.8m and which was cut into the natural sandstone to a depth of 1.14m (Fig. 30). This feature was lined with a stone wall varying in width from 0.2m to almost 0.4m giving the structure an internal diameter of about 1m, while its floor was the levelled-off natural sandstone. The fill (853) of the feature included pottery and clay pipes of late 18th- to early 19th-century date. The purpose of this structure is not known. It was not deep enough to reach the water-table and so could not have been a well. The stone lining of the feature had not been rendered internally and therefore the structure would not have retained water. It seems likely that it was used as a below-ground chamber for the storage of food and drink in a cool environment.

Building 2
All that remained of Building 2 was the east wall (834) and a fragment of the south wall (834) of its cellar which had been backfilled with modern rubble (835). To the south of this was what appeared to be another cellar or water tank (1252) although this was not fully excavated. Most of structure 1252 and the rest of this building had been destroyed by large service trenches which ran from the NFU office building to Cannon Street and no attempt was made to fully excavate the area.

Building 3
It is likely that wall 1216 represented the west wall of

this house. It was between 0.46m and 0.56m wide and was 3.6m long, although its northern limit lay outside the excavated area. The late 19th-century water tank 1214 (see Period 4C, Building 9) had been built against the west side of this wall.

Drain 1217: East of wall 1216 was a north-south drain. The east side of this drain had been damaged by a service trench and its cover slabs did not survive, but its west edge was constructed of bricks bonded with a grey mortar while its base was made of Pennant sandstone slabs set in a crumbly brown mortar.

Other parts of Building 3 were found in Trench 1 of the 1994 archaeological evaluation (BaRAS 1994b, 5–6, fig. 4). These comprised a cellar or septic tank with four walls [13–16] and a Pennant sandstone slab floor [19] which had been badly damaged by a service trench connected with the NFU building. The walls were mainly constructed of Lias or Carboniferous limestone with some Pennant sandstone and brick. The mortar in these walls was a pinkish buff with black and white flecks. The building had been altered at a later date by the construction of another cellar to its north (see Period 4C).

Buildings 4 and 5 (Cannon Street)
These were two houses with identical, but mirror image, ground plans built fronting Cannon Street (Fig. 18). They dated to the mid to late 18th century and were still in use up to their demolition during the clearance of the NFU site in the early 1960s. A plan of Building 5 (no. 12 Cannon Street) shows its layout in 1952 (BRO P/St J/Pl/6a). From this it would appear that the cellar excavated was situated under the living

room towards the rear of the property and that the front of the property lies below the existing pavement of Cannon Street which was extended over part of the building at the time of the construction of the NFU building (see Period 4D).

Building 4

The remains of the northern property, Building 4, mainly comprised a cellar (769), measuring 2.5m east/ west by 2.9m north/south internally. The cellar appeared to have been constructed by excavating the area to the required size and depth and then roughly walling the sides of the hole so there was little evidence of a construction trench for the cellar wall, which had been faced internally and varied between 0.3m to 0.5m in width. The upper, inner edge of the west wall comprised a single row of bricks which might have been the remains of a brick-vaulted cellar roof. A recess in the south-east corner of the cellar, measuring 1.8m by 0.84m, contained a flight of stone- and brick-built steps which turned 90 degrees to the south at the top and led into the communal passage-way between Buildings 4 and 5. In the centre of the north wall of the cellar was an entrance 1.06m wide which had been blocked by a narrow wall at a later date. This was presumably the remains of a coal chute or sky-light into the cellar. Adjoining the cellar to the north-east, and having a common west wall with the cellar, was a water tank measuring 1.7m by 1.5m internally with walls averaging 0.3m in width. The fill of the water tank was not excavated, while the fill of the cellar (768) was partly excavated by machine. Although the cellar had been backfilled in the 1960s during the development of the NFU site, it contained a number of pieces of medieval worked stone, presumably from the priory buildings, which may have been reused in the construction of Building 4 in the mid to late 18th century. Sufficient fill of the cellar was removed to show that it was floored with flat Lias limestone slabs and was 1.25m deep from the existing top of the cellar wall. The south wall of cellar 769 cut the robber trench (755) of part of the priory church wall and also a late 17th-century pit (772) while the north walls of the cellar and water tank had damaged medieval wall 1196 (see Periods 2A and 4A).

Communal Passageway: A passageway running east-west and 1.5m wide separated Building 4 from its mirror image, Building 5, to the south.

Building 5

The southern part of this property had been badly damaged by the construction of sewers serving the NFU building but sufficient remained to show that the cellar measured 2.4m east/west by 3.4m north/ south internally. A recess in the north-east corner of the cellar contained a flight of five stone- and brick-built steps which at the top turned 90 degrees to the north to lead out into the communal passageway

separating the properties. The cellar wall (765) varied in width between 0.3m and 0.5m and the internal faces of the walls were unrendered but had been whitewashed. The south wall (767) of the cellar had been rebuilt at a later date with Pennant sandstone bonded with a hard red mortar. The inner edge of the west wall comprised a single row of bricks which might have been the remains of the brick-vaulted roof of the cellar. The cellar was 1.25m deep from the present top of the cellar wall and was floored with flat Lias limestone slabs. A water tank adjoined the cellar to the south-east but only its north and east walls remained, the rest having been damaged by modern disturbance. The tank measured 1.7m east/west and, although its north/south dimension could not be determined, it was obviously similar in size to the water tank adjoining Building 4. The cellar had been backfilled with rubble (764) during redevelopment of the NFU site in the 1960s.

A wall (774) 0.2m wide and of the same con-struction as cellar 765 ran roughly north-west/south-east to the west of cellar 765. Its north-west end lay outside the excavated area while its south-east end had been cut by pipe-trench 630. The wall was contemporary with the cellar and was obviously part of Building 5 although its purpose could not be determined.

Building 6 (Cannon Street)

To the south-west of Building 5 were the remains of another mid 18th-century building fronting Cannon Street, although this had been badly damaged by later disturbances and the majority of it lay outside the area available for excavation. The remains comprised a narrow north/south wall (645) 0.2m wide, to the west of which and abutting it, was a floor of Pennant sandstone slabs (644) laid almost directly on the natural sandstone. East of wall 645, and cut by it, was a thin layer of compact sandy orange mortar (646), possibly the make-up for the floor of an earlier building. Presumably Building 6 was served at a later date by the adjacent 19th-century septic tank (640) (see Period 4C).

Buildings 7 and 8 (Nos. 7 and 8 St James's Parade)

The back walls and the remains of the side walls of these semi-detached properties were found within the area of the excavation to the north of St James's Parade (Figs. 27, 31 and 32). Although they were formed from one building, the division between the properties was represented by a north/south wall within Building 7 and 8 and this was continued northward by a bound-ary wall within the rear garden or courtyard area. The properties had been demolished for the construction of the Scottish Presbyterian Church and their found-ations were sealed below context 575, the make-up and levelling layer for its floor (see Period 4C). The north/south walls of the buildings had been cut by

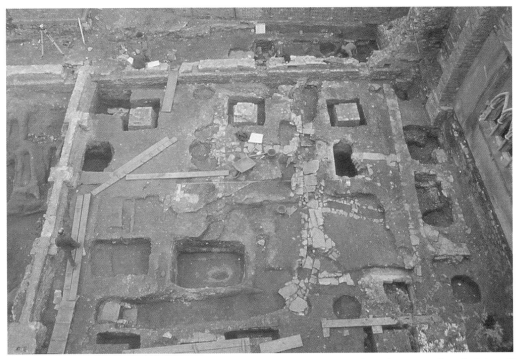

Fig. 31 Site 1: Looking east showing the excavation in progress below the Scottish Prebyterian Church (identifiable by the standing or partly standing walls and square pillar bases; Period 4C). On the right are the walls of Buildings 7 and 8 with their courtyard and garden areas to the north containing stone-lined drains, water tank 656 and boundary wall 922/747 (Period 4B)

Fig. 32 Site 1: Looking north. Water tank 656 in the foreground with the courtyard/garden boundary wall 922/747 running north beyond stone-lined drain 579 (Period 4B)

one of the main east-west walls (589) of the Victorian church. Buildings 7 and 8 had been built over and through the late 17th-/early 18th-century stone-lined pit 1612 and possible cellar structure 1611.

The structural remains of Buildings 7 and 8 comprised its west wall (620) which was 0.34m wide and had been cut by the foundation trench for wall 589 of the Victorian church; its north-west corner; its north (rear) wall (619) 0.5m wide and at least 11.2m long; the possible remains of its east wall, although this had been badly damaged by church wall 554; and an internal north/south dividing wall (1566) 0.5m wide. This building was constructed of roughly squared pieces of Pennant sandstone bonded with a fine creamy coloured mortar. The west wall (620) and north wall (619) were built over and around a stone-lined drain (1562) which passed diagonally beneath wall 620. North of wall 619 the capstones of the drain were removed and the dark grey organic fill (1671) excavated although it contained no datable finds.

Water Tank 687: This lay to the north-west of the rear of Building 8 and consisted of a rectangular stone-built structure (687) bonded with grey mortar measuring 1.2m north/south by 1m east/west. It had a brick-vaulted roof, part of which remained on the east side (580). There was evidence of a drain leading into the top of the tank in its south-west corner. The fill of the tank was not fully removed so its depth could not be determined. However, its roof had clearly been broken in and the tank back-filled in the mid 19th-century prior to the construction of the Scottish Presbyterian Church as its upper levels produced early to mid 19th-century pottery. Although this area had been badly disturbed by the construction of the Victorian church a cut for the construction trench of the tank was visible on its east and north sides (979). The tank had truncated a north/south stone-lined drain (see Period 4B) and, because of this and the type of mortar used in its construction, it was apparently an early 19th-century addition to Building 8.

Pit 761: This was a rectangular stone-lined pit to the rear of Building 8. The dry-stone walls of Pennant sandstone (661) were about 0.2m thick and the pit measured 0.9m east/west by 1.9m north/south internally and it was about 0.9m deep, the base of the pit having been cut into the natural sandstone. The upper fill of the pit (588) was a black silty material with bands of a green cess-like deposit. This overlay fill 658 which consisted of red-brown sand with slate fragments and mortar flecks. The lowest fill (840) was a thin layer of green cess on the floor of the pit. All these fills contained finds of early 19th-century date.

Structures and Features Common to Buildings 7 and 8
Property Boundaries: The internal north/south division of the building (wall 1566) was continued northwards, although not on the same alignment, through the courtyards or gardens to the rear of Buildings 7 and 8. Immediately north of the rear wall (619) of the building, the property boundary was defined by a drain (1516) consisting of a cast-iron pipe below a covering of Pennant and slate slabs which discharged into water tank 656.

The property division continued north of the tank as a wall (922) 0.4m wide made of Pennant sandstone bonded with a grey-pink mortar (Fig. 32). This wall

partly overlay the east/west drain 579. Only the bottom course of the wall survived and was covered by the destruction layer (581) associated with demolition prior to the construction of the Scottish Presbyterian Church. There was evidence of a construction trench for the wall.

Wall 922 abutted what might have been an east/west boundary wall (1109) at least 0.5m wide and bonded with a hard brown mortar, although there was scant evidence for that wall as it had been badly disturbed by a hole for scaffolding (604) associated with the construction of the Scottish Presbyterian Church and also by drain 865 to its east. It was possible that the wall pre-dated the Period 4B and 4C structures as it had been partly destroyed by a small hearth (957) which had been built over it and the course of drain 582 ignored any east/west boundary defined by wall 1109.

North of wall 1109 the north/south boundary continued as a wall (747) of similar construction to 922 but bonded with an orange-brown mortar. The north end of this wall had been robbed and its position was defined by a robber trench (751).

The positions of further north/south boundary walls may be shown by two spreads of pink mortar with some slabs of Pennant sandstone and Lias limestone (202 and 131), measuring at most 0.4m wide and in length 6m, although their southern limits were obscured by the south wall (551) of the Welsh Congregational Chapel. The mortar spreads were approximately parallel and 5m apart. The mortar type would appear to indicate an 18th-century date. Wall/mortar spread 131 lay within a construction trench (343) although this did not produce any datable finds.

Water Tank 656: This was located 1.4m north of the rear wall of Buildings 7 and 8 and straddled the apparent division between the two properties represented by the north/south boundary wall 1561. It may have served both houses. The tank (656) was stone-built, rendered internally and had part of the brick vaulted roof still surviving (Fig. 32). It measured 1.7m east/west and 1.45m north/south internally and was 1.55m deep. There was evidence of a drain emptying into its south-east corner and a possible overflow channel emptying into a stone-lined drain in its north-east corner. Its upper fill (623) consisted of stone and brick rubble while its lower fill was a grey-brown silt which contained finds of late 17th-/18th-century date. The roof of the tank was deliberately collapsed and the tank filled in prior to the construction of the Scottish Presbyterian Church.

Pit 177: This pit lay partly under wall 551 (see Period 4D) and was therefore not fully excavated. It was vertical sided and measured at least 1.4m north/south by 1.4m east/west by 1.4m deep. Its fill (176), consisting of rubble and dark grey mortar, produced finds of early 19th-century date.

Pit 188: This had been cut on its south side by

Victorian pillar base 36 and its construction trench 71 (see Period 4C). It was vertical sided, measured at least 1.1m north/south and 1.4m east/west and was 0.94m deep. Its lower fill (187) consisted of greenish cess-like material and contained finds of late 18th-century date.

Pit 222: This was a large shallow, irregularly shaped pit. It appeared to have sealed pit 318 and been partly confused with the fill of 318 (see Period 4A). However, it has been possible to differentiate the fill of both pits as pit 222 was clearly 19th-century in date. It was 3m north/south although its south, west and most of its north edge were not recorded probably due to its confusion with 318 during excavation. Its upper fill consisted of bands of red-brown sand containing charcoal flecks and lumps of plaster together with bands of cess-like material (223, 210, 212, 232, 211, 233), while the lower fill (208, 248) comprised mainly green cess-like material. The pit produced pottery of early to mid 19th-century date.

Pit 231: This sub-circular pit was 0.2m deep and contained industrial debris (230) of possible early to mid 19th-century date.

Stone-Lined Drains: A complex arrangement of stone-lined drains crossed the backyards of Buildings 7 and 8, running from east to west (579, 841, 908, 923, 932, 938, 983, 990, 1019, 1172, 1550) and then fed into a main drain which ran north across the north-west part of the site towards Cannon Street (Figs. 31 and 32). These drains had been cleaned out, blocked and re-routed on a number of occasions throughout their period of use and a detailed record of this appears in the site archive. The main north/south drain (584, 903, 164) was constructed of Pennant sandstone slabs, the side walls being bonded with a pale orange coloured mortar. The drain measured 0.8m wide internally and was approximately 0.26m deep. The north-west end of this drain curved to the west in order to avoid Building 2 which fronted Cannon Street, although its western end could not be determined due to later disturbances.

Structures and Features Relating to Building 7
Tank 701: A further water tank was situated to the east of Building 7 although this could not be fully excavated due to the proximity of the Victorian church tower and the brick wall bounding the site on the east. The stone built tank (701) was rendered internally and had a brick vaulted roof. Its size could not be determined although it measured at least 1m north/south by almost 2m east/west and was at least 0.7m deep. For safety reasons only part of the fill (678) was excavated and this was a red-brown sand and brick rubble which contained finds dating to the early 19th century as well as late 17th- and 18th-century material. The roof of the tank had been deliberately collapsed

and the tank filled in prior to the construction of the Scottish Presbyterian Church.

Hearth 1107: A small hearth had been built east of boundary wall 922 and was constructed of brick and Pennant sandstone. Its flue was 0.1m wide internally and contained soot and ash deposits.

Structures and Features Relating to Building 8
Pit 586: This pit lay to the north-west of Building 8. It was lined on its north, east and south sides with a roughly built stone wall 0.2m wide bonded with pink mortar (586/686). The wall was faced internally. The southern edge of the pit had been cut by the construction trench (568) for one of the pillar bases of the aisle of the Victorian church (see Period 4C) while the west edge of the pit lay outside the area available for excavation. The pit measured 1.4m north/south by at least 1.5m east/west internally and it was just over 0.5m deep. The upper fill of the pit (587) was a coarse black gritty deposit while the lower fill (679) was a dark grey-brown ashy silt. Both fills produced finds dating to the late 18th century. A full report on the finds from this pit appears in Chapter 6.

Hearths: A small hearth (1106) had been built west of boundary wall 922 and had brick sides with a Pennant sandstone base. Its flue was 0.1m wide internally and contained soot and ash deposits. Another hearth (957) had been constructed west of wall 922, overlying the east/west wall 1109. Again it was built of brick and Pennant sandstone. Its flue was 0.35m wide internally and contained a gritty black charcoal rich fill (956).

Cultivation Trenches: A group of shallow and generally intersecting trenches (27, 912, 913, 914, 918) aligned east/west lay within the garden to the rear of Building 8. The trenches ranged from 1.4m to 0.7m in length and were up to 0.2m deep. These were considered to be cultivation trenches and their fills (863, 889, 890) produced animal bones and clay tobacco pipe fragments.

Other Structures and Features
Pit 1223: To the east of the 19th-century cellar 1189 and cut by pipe trench 1190 were the remains of a vertical sided, flat bottomed, rectangular pit measuring 0.9m by at least 0.6m and up to 0.4m deep (1223). The pit, which was unlined and cut into the red sandstone natural, was filled with a black ashy material containing pottery, glass and clay pipes dating to c.1760–70. This pit was presumably situated in the back yard of nos. 9 or 10 St James's Parade which had been demolished for the construction of the NFU building. A full report on the finds from this pit appears in Chapter 6.

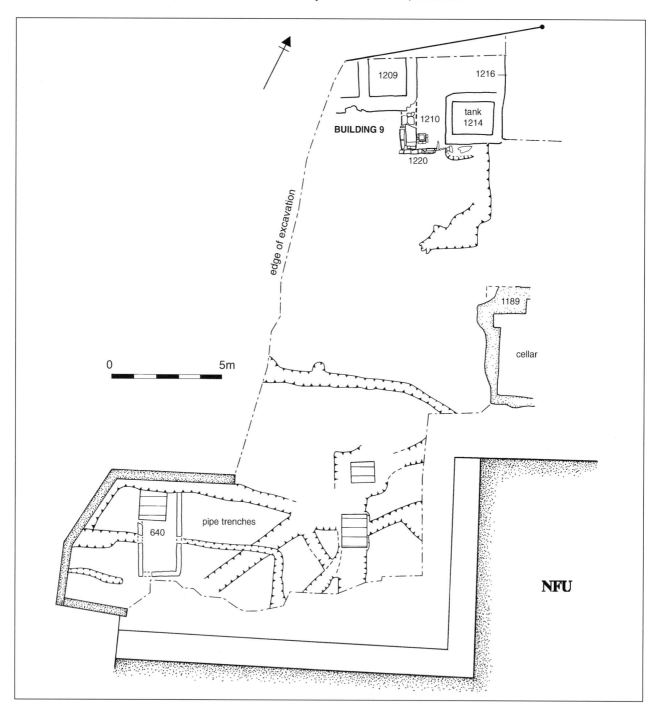

Fig. 33 Site 1 (west): Plan of the Period 4C features

Period 4C: The Scottish Presbyterian Church, Sunday School and Continuing Domestic Occupation

(mid 19th century to 1940)
(Figs. 33 and 34)

The Scottish Presbyterian Church and Sunday School
Clearance of the site and construction of the Scottish Presbyterian Church on land stretching from St James's Parade to Cannon Street began in 1855 and the church was opened in 1859. The main façade of the church faced on to St James's Parade and the church tower was located on the same street frontage. To the rear, facing Cannon Street, was the Sunday School.

The clearance of the site for the church involved the demolition of the late 18th-century Building 1 fronting Cannon Street and Buildings 7 and 8 on St James's Parade (see Period 4B). The remaining buildings on the Cannon Street and St James's Parade frontages remained in use throughout this period.

The church was destroyed by bombing during the blitz in 1940. The tower and the lower portion of the

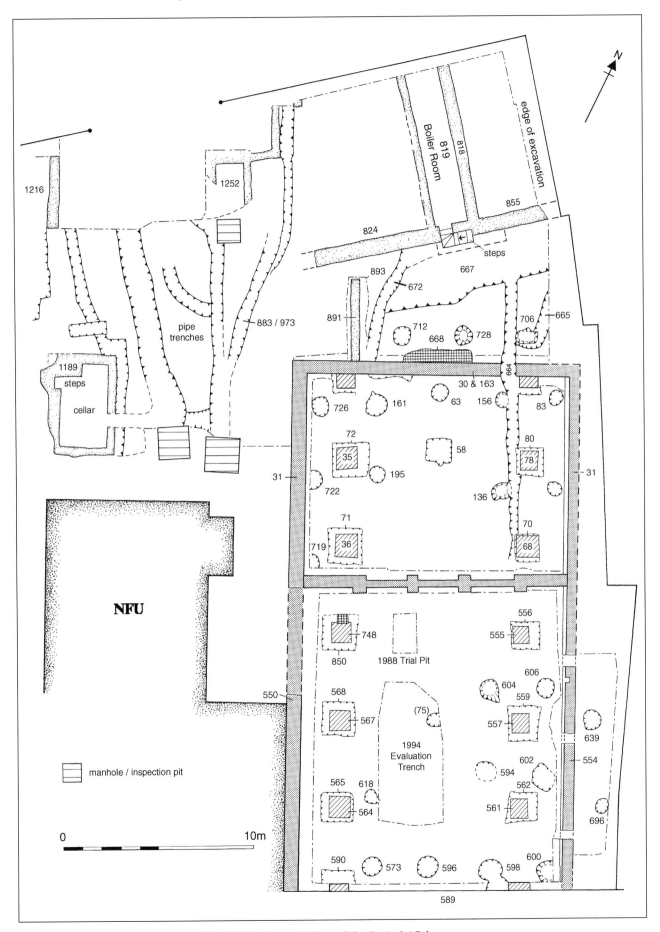

Fig. 34 Site 1 (east): Plan of the Period 4C features

façade survived the blitz and have now been incorporated in the new office development on the site.

An architectural plan (BRO Building Plan Book 4, folio 176) and a number of photographs of the Scottish Presbyterian Church survive and consequently it seems unnecessary to give a detailed description of the excavated remains of the church in this report. However, some elements of the church, such as the wall foundations and their associated construction trenches, caused considerable damage to the underlying medieval and post-medieval archaeology and it is necessary to list these here as a record of their existence and to clarify the reasons for the gaps in the earlier archaeology. In addition, evidence was found for the construction of the church in the form of circular or sub-circular holes for wooden scaffolding which had been dug down to the natural sandstone, again damaging the underlying archaeology.

The main elements of the church uncovered during the excavations may be summarised as follows (Fig. 31):

Walls and Construction Trenches
North wall of church (30 and 663): construction trench on north side of wall (709), construction trench on south side of wall at its east end (76).
West wall of church (33 and 550).
East wall of church (31 and 554): construction trench on west side of wall (76), construction trench on east side of wall (698).
South wall of church (589).

Brick Pillar Bases and Construction Trenches
West aisle from north to south:
Base 35: construction trench 72
Base 36: construction trench 71
Base 748: construction trench 850
Base 567: construction trench 568
Base 564: construction trench 565

Pillar base forming part of the south wall 589 of the church: construction trench 590.

East aisle from north to south:
Base 78: construction trench 80
Base 68: construction trench 70
Base 555: construction trench 556
Base 557: construction trench 559
Base 561: construction trench 562

Holes for Scaffolding
Within the church: 63, 83, [context 75 in 1994 evaluation Trench 4 (BaRAS 1994b, 10)], 132, 136, 156, 161, 195, 573, 594, 596, 598, 600, 602, 604, 606, 618, 719, 722, 726.
Outside the church: east side: 639, 696.
Outside the church: north side: 706, 712, 728.

Foundations for the Church Tower
An area in the south-east corner of the church had been badly disturbed and was presumably associated with the construction of the church tower. That area was left unexcavated for safety reasons.

Make-Up or Levelling Layer for the Church Floor
Overlying the destruction layer (581) associated with the demolition prior to the construction of the church was a deposit of fine red sand (575) sealing the remains of the Period 4B demolished buildings. The layer was confined to the interior of the church and was a general levelling or make-up layer for the floor of the church. Spread across the top of the layer were lumps of worked freestone and stone-dust, presumably the remains of the on-site working of the decorative stone-work required for the church. At the start of the 1995 excavation this Victorian make-up layer was removed by machine down to the underlying archaeology.

The Sunday School with Boiler Room Below
The north wall of the Sunday School on the Cannon Street frontage survived to first floor level until demolition commenced on the site in May 1995. It had been built partly on the foundations of the 18th-century Building 1 (see Period 4B). The south wall of the Sunday School was represented by foundations 824 and 855 which had been damaged during the construction of the Welsh Congregational Chapel in 1953 (see Period 4D). Where the foundations of wall 855 had been built over the late 18th-century circular feature 854, they had been reinforced with a stone arch (see Period 4B).

Beneath the Sunday School was the boiler room serving the Scottish Presbyterian Church consisting of a narrow cellar (818 and 819) which had been cut through the east side of Building 1 (see Period 4B). The boiler room was approached by a flight of brick and stone steps in its southern wall and had brick flues in the upper part of its side walls to duct hot air to the church.

Sewers
The following sewer pipe trenches appear to be Victorian: 833/973 which had been partly tunnelled (running north/south to the west of the church); 672 (running north-east/south-west to the north of church); 664 (running north/south to the north of church); 665 (running north-east/south-west to the north of church); and 667 which had been re-excavated probably at the time of the construction of the Welsh Congregational Chapel (running east/west to the north of church).

Building 3 (Cannon Street)
In the late 19th century a cellar, possibly used for storing coal, was added to the north of the earlier cellar of Building 3 (BaRAS 1994b, 5–6, fig. 4). The addition took the form of one east/west wall [17] and

a north/south wall [18], both bonded with black mortar and faced with brick (Fig. 28).

Building 9 (Cannon Street)

In the north-west corner of the excavation were the remains of a mid 19th-century building on the corner of Cannon Street. This extended outside the excavated area to the north and west. It was represented by two cellars (1209) the walls of which were constructed of Pennant sandstone blocks bonded with a grey mortar containing much lime. The southern east/west wall of the two cellars was 0.62m wide, while the two north/south walls were 0.42m wide. Only a fragment of the west cellar was uncovered while the east cellar measured 1.6m east/west by at least 1.7m north/south internally, although its northern wall lay outside the excavated area. The cellars were filled with debris containing late 19th-century transfer-printed earthenware, although the fill was not excavated for safety reasons as it lay partly below the pavement of Cannon Street. A linear disturbance (1211) 0.5m wide may have been a construction trench for the south wall of the cellar although it was not excavated.

The south-east corner of Building 9 had apparently been cut in order to key-in a later north/south wall (1210) which continued the line of the east wall of the cellar. This was constructed of Pennant sandstone bonded with white mortar and was 0.9m wide and 1.84m in length. East of wall 1210 was the stone-built base of a drain 0.5m square, possibly the remains of a water closet. A narrow east/west wall (1220), some 0.2m wide and made of Pennant blocks bonded with a brown mortar, linked wall 1210 with the south-east corner of water tank 1214. This rectangular water tank measured 1.8m by 1.4m internally. The internally rendered walls of this water tank were 0.4m wide and were of the same construction as building 1209. The tank had been cut through the 17th-century pit 1213 (see Period 4A) while its south wall had been cut through medieval levels. Most of its east wall had been built against the 18th-century west wall (1216) of Building 3 (see Period 4B). The fill of the water tank was not excavated.

Building 6 (Cannon Street)

Septic Tank: A septic tank or cess-pit (640) was uncovered immediately below the make-up layers for the NFU car park in the south-west corner of the excavation close to Cannon Street. It was cut by a manhole and gas pipe trench 628 connected with services to the NFU building. The septic tank was constructed of Pennant sandstone bonded with a hard red mortar and was rendered internally with white plaster. It measured 1.5m by at least 3.4m internally by 1.79m deep with walls 0.2m thick. A north-west/south-east drain (636) 0.22m wide and 0.17m deep with brick sides and a base of Pennant sandstone slabs emptied into the septic tank through an opening in its

east wall. The upper fill (639) of the septic tank consisted of loose rubble while the lower fill (655) was a black organic layer 0.23m thick which produced mid to late 19th-century pottery and clay pipes. It seemed likely that the septic tank served Building 6 on Cannon Street (see Period 4B) although a direct relationship could not be established.

Building 7 (No. 7 St James's Parade)

Drain 582: This was presumably associated with the installation of a water closet or privy in the courtyard or garden to the rear of Building 7. The drain had brick edging set in a clay/sand mixture, a base made of overlapping roofing slates (582) bedded in a coarse grey mortar, and was 0.1m wide internally and 0.2m deep. At the north end there was a rectangular stone feature which had formed the 'trap' of a primitive toilet 'U'-bend, while at the south there was a stone-built sluice leading into the side of drain 579. The fill of the drain (583) was a compacted deposit of mixed yellow mortar, cinders, slate and small stones containing mid 19th-century pottery.

Drain 660: This drain, which had sides of brick and a base of overlapping roof tiles, ran over the east side of pit 761 and its fill 588. The drain was 0.2m wide by 0.18m deep internally. Its fill (659) consisted of dark brown silt and dated to the mid 19th century. Its south end had been cut by Trench 4 of the 1994 archaeological evaluation (BaRAS 1994b, 10). Where the drain crossed pit 661 its side walls had been rebuilt with Pennant sandstone blocks.

Other Structures

An isolated cellar (1189), presumably associated with a substantial structure to the rear of the properties fronting St James's Parade, was uncovered immediately below the make-up for the NFU car park. It measured 2.44m north/south by 4.2m east/west internally and was 1.4m deep. The walls were of uneven thickness, varying between 0.36m to 0.6m in width and were of Pennant sandstone blocks bonded with white mortar, the internal faces of the wall being lined with brick. The cellar walls had no obvious construction trenches. Four brick-built steps led down into the cellar which was floored with well-cut slabs of Pennant sandstone. A trench (1190) 0.5m wide adjacent and parallel to the east wall of the cellar contained a sewer pipe which appeared to be contemporary with the cellar. This pipe trench cut the late 18th-century pit 1223 (see Period 4B).

Period 4D: Housing Decline, Office Expansion

(1940 to the 1990s)

The Scottish Presbyterian Church was largely destroyed during the 1940 blitz. All but the façade and tower on St James's Parade was demolished and the Welsh Congregational Chapel, Sunday School and

Meeting House were built on the northern part of the site in 1953. While the builders of the Welsh Congregational Chapel had reused some of the foundations of the Scottish Presbyterian Church, there were additional east/west and north/south walls with concrete foundations (551, 891). A construction trench (893) for wall 891 had destroyed part of the 18th-century stone-lined drain 903 (see Period 4B).

The remaining properties on the Cannon Street and St James's Parade frontages on the western half of the site continued in use until Buildings 2, 3, 4, 5 and 6 on the Cannon Street frontage (see Periods 4B and 4C) were demolished and their cellars backfilled to clear the site for the construction of the NFU office building and the smaller Audit Office building which were completed in 1964. Nos. 9 to 13 St James's Parade (outside the excavated area) were demolished at the same time.

The Welsh Congregational Chapel was demolished in 1988 and the NFU and Audit offices were occupied until shortly before their demolition in 1995.

4 THE ST JAMES'S PRIORY 'WEST FRONT' EXCAVATION REPORT (SITE 2)

Topography and Land Use

The excavation was carried out on a redevelopment site defined by the west front of St James's Church to the east, St James's Parade to the south, the White Hart public house in Lower Maudlin Street to the west and the approach to the church to the north (Fig. 1). The eastern end of the site lay on the 15 metre contour with the land sloping down to the west and south.

Until the 1950s the site was occupied by houses numbered, from east to west, 13, 14, 15 and 16 St James's Parade – no. 13 having been built against the west front of the church and no. 16 against the back of the White Hart public house. Since then the majority of the site was used as a garden of remembrance, with a paved area adjacent to the church and the remainder under grass, while the western end of the site was a car park. The site was separated from St James's Parade by a stone boundary wall which incorporated the lower portion of the façades of nos. 15 and 16. An area occupied by recent cremations, adjacent to St James's Parade, had to be left outside the excavated area.

Previous Archaeological Work

Due to the proposed development of the land as a rehabilitation centre for drug users Bristol and Region Archaeological Services carried out an archaeological evaluation in 1993 (BaRAS 1993). The footprint of the proposed building was to occupy about 225 square metres and within that area five trial trenches were excavated and an engineer's trial hole was re-excavated. The trenches were located close to the church within no.13 St James's Parade; on the east side of no. 15; within no. 16 and extending back into what had been the rear part of the White Hart public house; against the rear wall of the public house; and from no. 16 parallel to the street frontage for a distance of 5.8m to the east. The engineer's trial hole was to the rear of no. 14.

In all the trenches there were structures and stratigraphy of a fairly complex nature including medieval walls and occupation, a large 15th-century pit, 16th- and 17th-century occupation, and the cellars of 18th-century buildings. Of significance to the future of the archaeological resource was its shallow depth below the existing ground level and consequently the high probability of its destruction during the building work.

On the basis of the results of the 1993 evaluation the City Archaeologist decided that the eastern portion of the development area should be fully excavated while a watching brief should be kept on the remainder during construction work. Bristol and Region Archaeological Services were commissioned by the Little Brothers of Nazareth to carry out that work.

Excavation Methods and Recording

The excavation, covering about 103 square metres, was worked as an open area with relevant sections being recorded before removal. The work took place in two phases: from February to April 1994 and from April to June 1995. Although the western part of the development area was not excavated, the structures found in some of the evaluation trenches are referred to in this report in order to supplement the information obtained from the main excavation, particularly concerning the westward extent of the medieval and post-medieval buildings.

The site was excavated by a small team of professional archaeologists working under the direction of the Project Manager, John Bryant.

Initially the entire area was stripped of paving and modern make-up levels using a mechanical excavator. Once archaeological deposits and structures were encountered these were cleaned and excavated by hand. All archaeological deposits, features and structures, including the remains of the 19th- and 20th-century alterations to the buildings on St James's Parade, were recorded in detail. Almost the entire area was excavated to natural, the exceptions being the

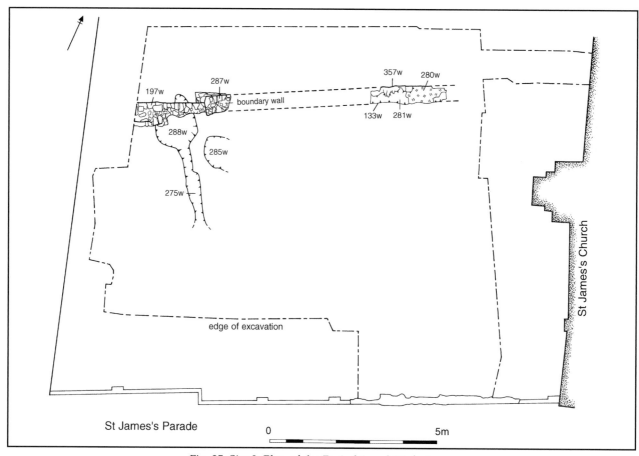

Fig. 35 Site 2: Plan of the Period 1 and 2A features

post-medieval cellars which were known to have removed all the medieval archaeology, the parts of the site which could not be excavated for safety reasons due to the proximity of standing walls and the area along the St James's Parade frontage where cremations had been buried in the garden of remembrance. Those areas were observed and the archaeology recorded by means of a watching-brief during the course of the building work.

The system used for recording the archaeology and the finds was generally the same as that for Site 1.

The contexts from the 1993 evaluation trenches were numbered from 1t to 99t while the contexts from the 1994/1995 excavation were numbered from 1w to 359w, the suffix letters 't' and 'w' being used to distinguish them from each other and from the context numbers given on Site 1.

For ease of reference the Small Find numbers in the following report carry the suffix letter 'C' to distinguish them from the small finds from Site 1.

The methods of excavating and recording the burials are discussed under Chapter 5 of this report.

The excavation was given the Bristol City Museum and Art Gallery accession number BRSMG 13/1994. All the paper archive and finds from the excavation bear that accession number and have been deposited in the Archaeology Department of Bristol City Mu-

seum and Art Gallery, with the exception of the human remains.

Report on the Excavations

The Natural

The natural geology underlying the excavation was a red-brown weathered Triassic sandstone of the Mercia Mudstone Group overlaid in places with a purple-red Keuper Marl.

Period 1: Late Saxon Features

(Fig. 35)

The fill of three shallow features, either cut into or occurring as natural depressions in the sandstone bedrock, contained a red sandy silt with flecks of charcoal and tiny fragments of pottery. A north/south gully or depression (275w) some 1.95m long, 0.3m wide and 0.27m deep terminated at its north end in a natural pit (288w) 0.66m in diameter (Figs. 36 and 37). These were sealed below the Period 2B walls and occupation layers.

To the east of the gully and pit was a circular cut

Fig. 36 Site 2: Looking east along boundary wall 197w (Period 2A), later used as the north wall of Building 10, and showing the underlying pit 288w (Period 1)

(285w), measuring at least 1.6m north/south and up to 0.18m deep, sealed below Period 2B and Period 4A walls and cut by a Period 2A burial, Sk. 254. Only its west side was exposed and excavated and the pottery came from its lowest fill (286w).

The purpose of these features is problematic although stratigraphically they were the earliest features on the site and are dated by the pottery within them to the late Saxon period. It is possible that they are contemporary with the pre-burial gullies found on Site 1, although those did not contain dating evidence.

Period 2: St James's Priory

(c.1129 to 1540)

Period 2A: The Lay Burial Ground and Boundary Wall

(c.1129 to mid 13th century)
(Figs. 35 and 38)

The Burials
See Chapter 5 for a report on the burials.

The Boundary Wall
Crossing the northern part of the site and extending west to the rear of the White Hart public house were the remains of what was probably a boundary wall, separating the lay burial ground from the approach to the west front of the church.

At the west end of the excavated area the wall was

Fig. 37 Site 2: Looking south-east. Boundary wall 197w (Period 2A) in the background with pit 288w in the foreground and gully 275w beyond (Period 1)

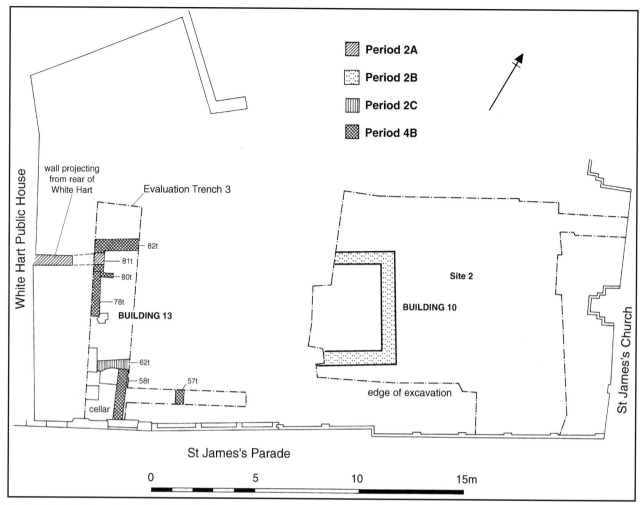

Fig. 38 Site 2: Plan of the Period 2A, 2C and 4B structures found in Evaluation Trench 3 and showing their relationship to the excavated area and Building 10 (Period 2B)

0.7m wide and was constructed using Brandon Hill Grit and the occasional piece of freestone and Pennant sandstone bonded with a distinctive orange-brown mortar (197w) (Figs. 36 and 37). Wall 197w had been partly destroyed, particularly on its south side, by 19th-century intrusions including a fireplace and alcove (see Period 4C).

To the east, a slightly narrower version of this wall was observed (280w) although there it had been largely robbed away in the 18th century, its course being defined by a robber trench (133w), filled with lumps of orange mortar in a red-brown sand (281w). A few stones bonded with orange-brown mortar (280w) at the base of the robber trench were all that remained of the wall. They had been laid in a shallow foundation trench (357w) 0.48m wide which had been cut slightly into the natural sandstone. Wall 280w and robber trench 133w had been destroyed to the west by the construction trench for the Period 4A wall 70w and to the east by the Period 4A floor 279w.

Between wall 197w and 280w was a short length (287w) of the same wall although it seemed to be wider and appeared to be slightly offset to the north of wall 197w. It is possible that 287w represented the original thickness of the wall and that the north face of 197w had been removed at a later date.

Wall 81t, found some 9m to the west in evaluation trench 3, was of the same construction and on the same alignment as wall 197w and almost certainly formed part of the boundary wall. A fragment of wall projecting from the rear of the White Hart public house was also of the same construction and on the same alignment and was probably a continuation further west of the boundary wall.

Period 2B: The Lay Burial Ground and Late 13th-Century Building

(mid to late 13th century)
(Figs. 38 and 39)

The Burials
See Chapter 5 for a report on the burials.

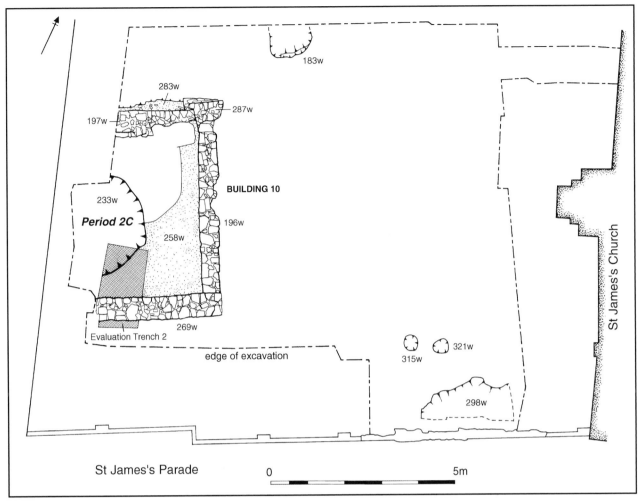

Fig. 39 Site 2: Plan of the Period 2B features

Building 10: Structure and Occupation

In the late 13th century Building 10, later known in an altered form as no. 15 St James's Parade, was built on the western part of the excavation area. Its east and south walls (196w and 269w) were constructed of Pennant sandstone bonded with a red-brown mortar with some lime inclusions, although the mortar used in 269w contained more lime and the wall itself incorporated fragments of freestone and Brandon Hill Grit (Fig. 40). The walls, which were 0.55 to 0.6m wide, survived to a height of up to 0.6m and were founded on bedrock. Building 10 incorporated the Period 2A east/west boundary wall (197w) as its north wall, while its south wall, 269w, had been rebuilt in the early 17th century (see Period 4A). Two sherds of late 13th-century pottery were found in the mortar bonding of wall 196w.

Building 10 had internal dimensions of 4.5m north/south by at least 3m east/west, its west wall lying outside the excavated area. A Period 2C wall (62t) of similar construction found 9m to the west in evaluation trench 3 appeared to continue the line of the south wall of the building (Fig. 38). Although damaged by later features wall 62t survived for a length of 1.3m and was 0.45m wide.

A possible construction or occupation layer (258w) containing two sherds of late 13th-century pottery covered the area inside, and abutted the walls of, Building 10. It was about 0.1m thick and consisted of a red sandy silt with fragments of freestone, white plaster and flecks of charcoal. A sherd of late 13th-century pottery was found in a similar layer (283w) some 0.4m thick and banked up against the outside face of wall 197w.

The construction of Building 10 prevented any further interments from taking place in that part of the burial ground, although graves continued to be dug outside it to the east and south-east.

The Pits

In the south-east corner of the site, partly underlying St James's Parade and sealed by occupation layer 295w (see Period 2C), was a pit (298w) measuring at least 2.56m east/west by 1.1m north/south and 0.4m

Fig. 40 Site 2: Looking north-west along the east wall 196w of Building 10 (Period 2B) with the west wall 71w of Building 11 (Period 4B) bonded to it along its length

deep. The pit cut grave Sk. 257 and its fill (296w) contained one sherd of late 13th-century pottery and fragments of human bone from the disturbed burial.

To the north-east of Building 10, and lying partly outside the excavated area, was a shallow pit (183w) measuring at least 0.6m north/south by 1.15m east/ west cut into the natural sandstone. Its fill (181w) of fine dark red sand contained one sherd of late 13th-century pottery.

The Postholes

Two postholes (315w and 321w), up to 0.33m deep and 0.4m in diameter were almost certainly contemporary with each other, but only 315w produced sherds of late 13th-century pottery.

Period 2C: Continued Occupation of the 13th-Century Building

(14th century)
(Figs. 38 and 41)

Building 10: Occupation

Immediately overlying the Period 2B occupation or construction layer (258w) within Building 10 were a number of patches of occupation debris (213w, 214w, 215w, 242w, 250w, 252w, 253w, 254w, 257w). One of these layers, 257w, also immediately overlay the natural sandstone. With the exception of 253w, the layers were very similar, consisting of fragments of

Pennant sandstone and weathered freestone, with flecks of white plaster and charcoal. The largest in area was 242w at 3.7 square metres and it produced over one hundred sherds of pottery dating to the period 1300 to 1350 together with pieces of floor and roof tile and two lead alloy tokens (SF96C and SF97C), the latter in circulation from c.1250 to 1350. Partly under 242w was a layer (253w) of green-brown silty clay with fragments of roof slate, floor tile and a large quantity of 14th-century pottery.

Overlying these patches of occupation debris was a large area of brown sandy silt containing abundant fragments of orange-brown mortar, Pennant sandstone fragments, white plaster and sherds of pottery dating to the first half of the 14th century (199w). The presence of the orange-brown mortar in layer 199w, identical to that bonding wall 197w, suggests that the layer was associated with a partial demolition or alteration to that wall.

An east/west wall (62t) in evaluation trench 3 may be a later continuation of the south wall of Building 10.

Layers East of Building 10

During this period the layers east of Building 10 and south of wall 280w were characterised by varying quantities of the same orange-brown mortar found in the Period 2A boundary wall 280w and were presumably debris from the partial demolition or alteration to that wall.

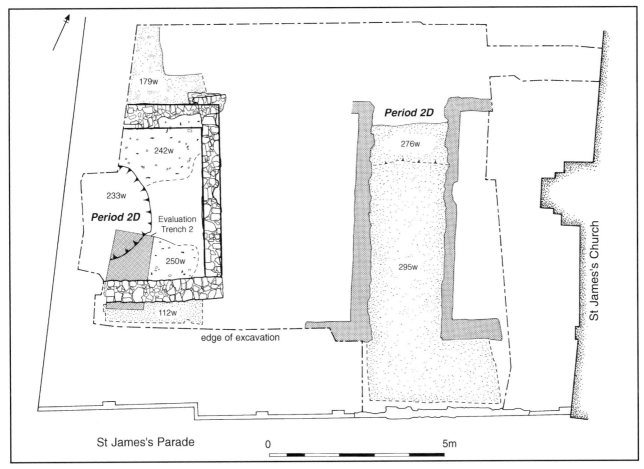

Fig. 41 Site 2: Plan of the Period 2C and 2D features

One of the layers (295w) covered a large area, was between 01.15m and 0.30m thick and consisted of red silt, fragments of freestone and lumps of orange-brown mortar. It contained pieces of slate and floor tile together with 30 sherds of 14th-century pottery and a lead alloy token (SF121C) dating to *c.*1350 to 1450. Associated with 295w was a thin layer (231w) of brown sandy soil with orange-brown mortar and sherds of 14th-century pottery.

Other Occupation Layers
South of Building 10, and cut by the construction trench 102w of drain 101w (see Period 4A), was a thin but extensive layer (112w) containing two sherds of early 14th-century pottery.

To the north of Building 10, in the north-west corner of the site, two successive layers (179w and 189w) abutted wall 197w and also contained 14th-century pottery.

Period 2D: Abandonment of the Medieval Building

(15th century to Dissolution in 1540)
(Fig. 41)

Building 10: Pit 233w
At some time during the 15th century Building 10 must have been abandoned as a pit (233w) some 1.7m deep had been cut through all the medieval occupation levels within it and into the natural below. Only the eastern portion of this pit lay within the excavated area (Fig. 42). It measured at least 2.6m north/south by 1.1m east/west and had vertical or near vertical sides. Its mainly rubble fill (216w, 232w, 234w–236w, 297w) contained layers of orange mortar, fragments of Pennant sandstone, freestone, slate, plaster and pieces of coal all in a brown sandy silt. Throughout the fill there were sherds of 15th-century pottery and the nature of the fill suggested that it derived from the collapse or partial demolition of the building during that period.

Other Evidence for Abandonment
Covering an area of about 16 square metres to the east of Building 10 and extending outside the excavated area to the south, was a 0.1m thick layer (249w) of red-brown sandy silt with flecks of off white mortar and charcoal and fragments of floor and roof tile. Immediately beneath it, and extending to the north as far as wall 280w, was a similar layer (276w), but with

Fig. 42 Site 2: Looking east with pit 233w (Period 2D) crossed by the north/south wall 198w of Building 10 (Period 4A)

some fragments of sandstone and roof slate. Together these layers produced almost one hundred sherds of 15th-century pottery and a lead alloy token (SF106C) dating to the period *c.*1380 to 1450. The nature of the debris found in the layers again point to the building's abandonment and partial demolition or collapse. Certainly by the early 17th century the south wall (269w) of Building 10 had been reduced almost to foundation level, necessitating its rebuilding at that time (see Period 4A).

Period 3: Post-Dissolution Activity

(1540 to early 17th century)
(Fig. 43)

Postholes and Stakeholes
Three postholes (244w, 246w, 272w) were found to the east of Building 10. The largest measured 0.44m deep by 0.43m across. Although the fill of only one posthole (272w) contained dating evidence in the form of late 16th- or early 17th-century pottery, it is likely that they were all contemporary. The postholes were sealed by the floors and the north/south partition belonging to the Period 4A occupation.

Twenty-two stakeholes – circular, oval and rect-angular in section – were also found east of Building 10. They varied from 0.04 to 0.17m in depth and were at most 0.1m wide. No dating evidence was found within their fills but they were all sealed below the Period 4A floors and appeared to be contemporary.

No pattern to either the postholes or stakeholes could be discerned within the small area available for excavation.

Occupation Levels
To the south of Building 10, and cut by the con-struction trench (102w) for the drain 101w (see Period 4A) was a layer (104w) of red-brown silty soil containing 16th-century pottery. This partly overlay a more extensive layer (105w) of red-brown sand with lumps of buff and dark pink mortar which also produced 16th-century pottery.

Period 4: The Post-Medieval Reoccupation

(early 17th century to the 1990s)

Period 4A: Alterations to the Medieval Building and Construction of Floors or Courtyard Surfaces

(early 17th century to early 18th century)
(Fig. 44)

Building 10: Rebuilding of South Wall and Construction of Cellar
Early in the 17th century the south wall of Building 10 was rebuilt using Pennant sandstone bonded with a red-brown mortar (195w), the medieval wall (269w) being retained as its foundation (Fig. 45). Wall 195w was 0.54m wide and was butted against the east wall

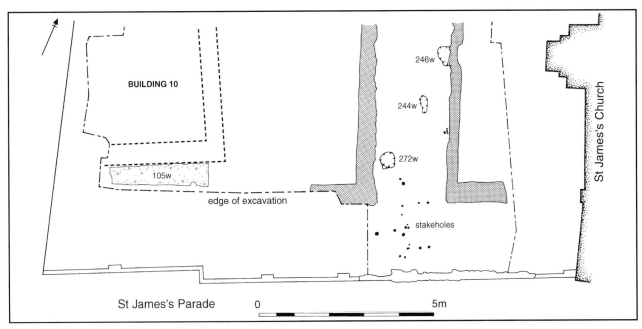

Fig. 43 Site 2: Plan of the Period 3 features

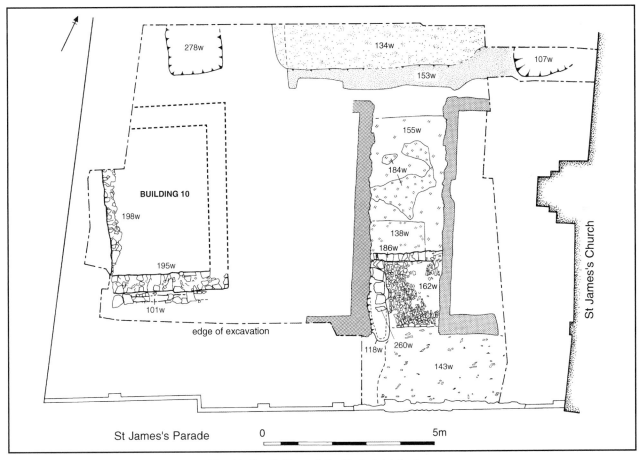

Fig. 44 Site 2: Plan of the Period 4A features

(196w) of Building 10. A stone-lined drain (101w) appeared to form an integral part of the foundations of wall 195w on its south side (Fig. 45).

A cellar was constructed below Building 10, slightly skewed to the alignment of the building. The cellar lay mainly outside the area of the excavation but its east wall (198w) was revealed (Fig. 42). That narrow wall, which had only been faced on the side seen from

Fig. 45 Site 2: Looking east showing the rebuilt south wall 195w of Building 10 with the external drain 101w to its south (Period 4A)

the cellar, was built of Pennant sandstone laid in a red-brown sandy mortar and appeared to have been bonded into the south wall (195w) of the building.

No 17th-century occupation or floor levels were found within Building 10 and those had presumably been removed during the laying of floor 85w in the 18th or 19th centuries (see Period 4B).

Floors or Courtyard Surfaces and Partitions to the East of Building 10

In the 17th century the area to the east of Building 10 appeared to have been used as a courtyard or perhaps even part of an outbuilding, although no external walls of such a structure were found. However, the area had been divided some 4.2m south of the east/west boundary wall 280w, probably by a timber partition. The insubstantial foundations of the partition (186w), aligned east/west and 0.25m wide, were of Pennant sandstone slabs set in a pink mortar with slates laid horizontally in the mortar, possibly to act as a damp-proof course (Figs. 46 and 47). The foundation had been cut to the east and west by the cellars of the Period 4B buildings and so its full extent could not be determined.

There was evidence for three successive mortar floors having been laid in the area to the north of partition 186w. All the floors were of a light grey mortar with inclusions of brick, tile, slate and plaster fragments. The earliest floor (155w) was 0.3m thick and had been patched on at least three occasions (138w, 152w, 184w). Overlying that was another floor

Fig. 46 Site 2: Looking north showing the cobbled surface 162w, the stone base of the east/west partition 186w and the later north/south slot for partition 118w/260w (Period 4A)

Fig. 47 Site 2: Looking south after the removal of cobbles 162w showing the bases for partitions 186w and 118w (Period 4A)

(129w) containing late 17th-century pottery. The latest floor (127w) had been repaired once (93w).

The floors to the south of partition 186w extended beyond the excavated area. A layer (191w) of brown ashy soil, grey clay, sand and much charcoal, contained 17th-century pottery and clay pipe stems and formed the bedding for an area of cobbles (162w) extending 1.85m to the south of partition 186w (Fig. 46). Contemporary with the cobbles, and abutting them to the south, was a floor (143w) of compacted black ash, small stones and slate fragments dated by clay pipe bowls found within it to c.1625–50. Partly overlying the cobbles 162w and floor 143w were two areas of mortar floor (137w and 126w). Sealing the cobbles 162w and floors 143w, 126w and 137w, and extending over the whole area to the south of partition 186w, was a layer (120w) of black ash, cinders and fragments of coal which contained late 17th-century clay pipes and pottery. Within 120w was a hearth (98w) made of flat slabs of Pennant sandstone edged by vertical slabs and surrounded by black ash.

In the late 17th century the area east of Building 10 was again sub-divided by the construction of a north/south partition wall running south from the east/west partition 186w for a distance of at least 3.8m. The evidence for the sub-division was a cut (118w) 0.6m wide and up to 0.3m deep, at the base of which were a number of large flat Pennant slabs (260w) laid on a thin layer of dark brown sandy silt (261w) containing late 17th-century clay pipes and pottery (Figs. 46 and

47). The slabs presumably formed the base for another timber partition.

Stone-Lined Drain

A stone-lined drain (101w) ran east/west to the south of wall 195w of Building 10, and utilised 195w as part of its own north walling (Fig. 45). To the east the drain had been cut by the Period 4B cellar and to the west it extended outside the edge of the excavation. It was built of Pennant sandstone, the walls having been bonded with red mortar. Its fill (74w) contained 17th-century clay pipes and the cover stones of the drain had been sealed by two thin layers of red-brown sandy silt (54w, 80w) which dated to the late 17th century.

Pits

Pit 278w lay to the north of Building 10 and extended outside the excavated area. Rectangular in shape, it measured 1.6m east/west, at least 1.5m north/south, was 0.85m deep and had been cut into the natural sandstone. It had probably been used as a cess-pit as the bottom layer of fill (277w) was a typical green-yellow cess-like material. The upper layers of fill (163w, 165w, 166w) contained late 17th-century clay pipes and pottery.

Pit 107w, to the north-east of Building 10, extended under the northern edge of the excavation. It measured 1.85m east/west, at least 0.7m north/south, was 0.4m deep and had been cut through a thin layer of brown sandy loam (108w), containing early 17th-

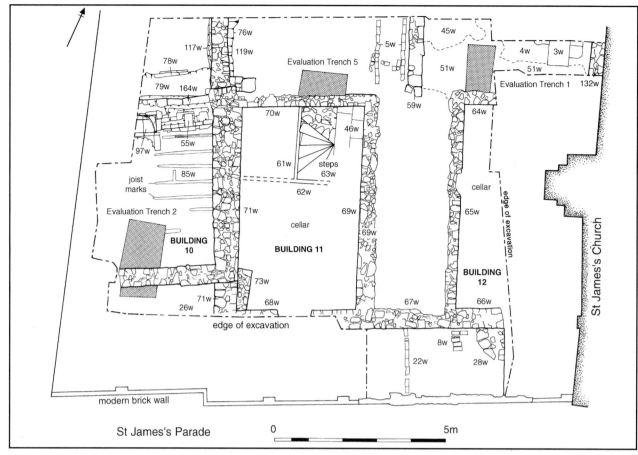

Fig. 48 Site 2: Plan of the Period 4B and 4C features

century clay pipes, into the natural sandstone. Its several layers of fill ranged from black ash and burnt stone at the top (16w) to a loose brown sandy loam at the bottom (106w) with 17th-century clay pipes and pottery.

Cultivation Soils to the North of Building 10

Large spreads and smaller patches of cultivation soils were found to the north and north-east of Building 10 and extended northwards outside the area of the excavation. They varied from areas of brown loam (134w, 153w) to grey-brown sand, coal dust or black ash (84w, 158w, 160w, 161w, 174w–176w, 168w–170w). All produced clay pipes and pottery ranging in date from the early to late 17th century.

Period 4B: The 18th-Century Houses

(early 18th century to mid 19th century)
(Figs. 38 and 48)

St James's Parade, originally known as 'The Church-yard', was established as a thoroughfare in the early 18th century. Around that time the courtyard area between Building 10 and the church was replaced by two houses (nos. 13 and 14 St James's Parade). During

the 18th century minor alterations were made to the structure of Building 10 (no. 15 St James's Parade). As no. 16 to the west of Building 10 was not fully excavated its early history is unknown, but it was certainly substantially altered in the 18th and 19th centuries.

Building 10 (no. 15 St James's Parade): Structural Alterations and Occupation (Fig. 49)

During this period the ground floor of the building was replaced by a floor on wooden joists (85w) which ran east/west across the building, supported on a 0.5m thick layer of brown silty sand and rubble (199w). At that time the earlier post-medieval floor levels seem to have been removed.

A fireplace was built into the rear wall (197w) of the building which involved cutting away the face of 197w to a depth of 0.6m and laying Pennant sand-stone slabs (97w) to form a hearth. An alcove was cut into wall 197w adjoining the fireplace to the east, and the back of the alcove was faced with stone (164w). A chute (27w) leading into the cellar was cut through the south wall of the building. A stone-lined drain (52w), probably serving a downpipe from the roof, was laid across the front garden from the south-east corner of the building.

Fig. 49 Site 2: Looking north within Building 10 during the Period 4B occupation showing walls 195w and 196w, fireplace 97w, alcove 164w, the stains of floor joists 85w and the external north/south boundary wall 119w

Building 10: Gardens

There was evidence for gardens to the north and south of the building. To the south was a layer of garden soil (26w). An oval cut (21w) measuring 1m east/west by 0.35m north/south and a rectangular cut (32w) measuring 1.4m east/west by 0.32m north/south, the latter against the outside face of the building, were probably the remains of flower beds. Another flower bed (79w) against the outside face of the building's north wall, was partly retained by a single, vertically set, slab of Pennant sandstone (78w), possibly a re-used door sill.

Buildings 10 and 11: Boundary Wall

A boundary wall (119w) separating the rear gardens or yards of the houses ran north from the north-west corner of the cellar of Building 11. The wall, about 0.5m wide and built of Pennant sandstone and freestone rubble, including a re-used medieval coffin lid, had been built in a shallow foundation trench (76w/117w).

Building 11 (no. 14 St James's Parade): Structure and Occupation

All that remained of no. 14 St James's Parade was its cellar measuring 5.7m north/south by 3.5m east/west internally and at least 1.5m deep. The cellar walls (68w–71w) were up to 0.77m wide and constructed of Pennant sandstone rubble bonded with a light pink mortar, its west wall (71w) having been built against, and bonded with, the east wall (196w) of Building 10 (Fig. 40). The cellar was plastered internally and floored with Pennant sandstone flags (46w). The entrance to the cellar was in the centre of the north wall and from there a stairway (63w) 1m wide led down into the cellar which had been divided east/west (61w) and north/south (62w) by timber and lath and plaster partitions.

Buildings 11 and 12: Boundary Walls

A wall (22w) made from a single thickness of bricks set in white mortar divided the front gardens of the buildings. The back gardens or yards were separated by a wall (59w) up to 0.4m wide made of Pennant sandstone rubble bonded with an orange-brown mortar, and bedded on a thin layer of redeposited natural sandstone (60w). Its southern end had been removed during demolition work in the 1960s.

The 2m wide gap between the front cellar walls of Buildings 11 and 12 had been linked by a wall (67w) of Pennant sandstone and Brandon Hill Grit rubble, some 0.6m wide, bedded on a layer of red-brown sand (111w).

Building 12 (no. 13 St James's Parade): Structure and Occupation

The remains of no. 13 St James's Parade mainly comprised a cellar measuring 5.7m north/south. The cellar walls (64w–66w) were up to 0.58m wide and composed of Pennant sandstone rubble bonded with a light pink mortar and had been plastered internally. Although the east side of the cellar could not be exposed or the fill of the cellar excavated due to the nearby church wall, it appeared to be a mirror image of that at no. 14 St James's Parade.

A north/south wall (132w) of the same construction as the cellar walls and built against the medieval west wall of the church, was probably part of a rear extension to the building. An area of red-brown sand (51w), which abutted wall 132w and the boundary wall 59w, probably formed a make-up layer for the mortar floor (45w) within this extension. Layer 51w sealed pit 107w (see Period 4A).

Building 13 (no. 16 St James's Parade): Structure and Occupation

This building was only partly excavated during the evaluation work on site in 1993 and consequently its early history is not known, although it may date from the 17th century. It was certainly substantially altered in the 18th century and two north/south walls (57t and 58t) found in evaluation trenches 3 and 6 date to that period (Fig. 38). They were both 0.39m wide and 2.25m apart, and constructed of Pennant sandstone rubble in a brown mortar. A number of walls (59t, 78t, 80t, 82t) were found in evaluation trench 3 but it was impossible to determine how they related to the building in the limited area available for excavation. Fragments of the flagstone floor (63t, 71t) of the property were uncovered together with a small cellar or coal-hole to the west of wall 58t.

Period 4C: Alterations to the 18th-Century Buildings

(mid 19th century to mid 20th century)
(Fig. 48)

Building 10 (no. 15 St James's Parade): Structural Alterations

The fireplace and alcove in the north wall of the building were removed, probably sometime in the early 20th century. The fireplace was infilled with stone and brick bonded in a black mortar (58w) while the alcove was blocked by a brick wall and pier base, again bonded with black mortar (55w).

Building 11 (no. 14 St James's Parade): Structural Alterations

The south-west corner of the cellar was buttressed, probably during the 19th century, by a block of stone and brick rubble bonded with grey mortar (73w). North of the north-east corner of the cellar, two parallel lines of single thickness brick laid in grey mortar (5w), 0.6m apart and each at least 2m long, probably formed the base of a staircase built in the late 19th or early 20th century.

Building 12 (no. 13 St James's Parade): Structural Alterations

At some time in the 19th century a canted bay was added to the front of the building. That projected 0.9m towards St James's Parade and was constructed of Pennant sandstone bonded in a grey mortar (28w). Documentary records show that a similar bay had been added to Building 11 but that lay outside the excavated area. Later in the 19th century a brick wall (8w), in part represented by a robber trench (9w), was built running south from the south-west corner of the cellar and may have formed part of a shop extension filling the gap between the front of the house and St James's Parade. During the 19th century the extension to the rear of the building was floored with Pennant sandstone flagstones (3w) set in grey mortar (4w).

Period 4D: Demolition of Buildings and Re-use of Land

(mid 1950s to the 1990s)

Nos. 13, 14, 15 and 16 St James's Parade were demolished in the 1950s and 1960s and layers of rubble (1w and 2w) covering the site date from that period. The houses were replaced by a garden of remembrance and a car parking area.

5   THE BURIALS

Introduction

Human remains from three sites are considered in this section. These came from:

Site 1 – inside the east end of the priory church and the monastic burial ground to its east (245 articulated skeletons)

Site 2 – the lay/parish burial ground outside the west end of the church (33 articulated skeletons)

Site 3 – St James's Place, on the site of the the parish burial ground some 88m south-east of the priory church (six articulated skeletons).

Methods of Burial Excavation and Recording

The methods adopted in excavating the burials on Sites 1 and 2 varied according to the degree of stratification present. In some cases the grave cuts, and even the skeletons themselves, lay immediately below the modern make-up levels and were exposed during removal of those deposits by machine. In other areas it was possible to excavate the burials in the sequence of their interment by the careful identification of intersecting grave cuts although, due to the nature of their compacted fills, it was sometimes difficult to distinguish them from the natural subsoil.

During the 1995 excavation of Site 1 the grave cuts and fills were each given separate context numbers, while articulated skeletons were given individual sequential skeleton (Sk.) numbers from 28 to 252 (one burial was given two Sk. numbers). At the time of the 1989 excavation of Site 1 the skeletons found had been given context numbers only and so, for ease of reference, those were also given skeleton numbers from 1 to 27, although on specialist examination the actual number of individual skeletons from that excavation was found to be twenty-one.

The excavation of Site 2 produced 33 articulated skeletons which were given individual sequential skeleton (Sk.) numbers from 253 to 285.

Five articulated skeletons were recovered, while a further skeleton was noted but not lifted for study, during the watching brief on Site 3. These were given the sequential skeleton (Sk.) numbers 286 to 291.

In the following report all numbers relating to graves and skeletons are the sequential Sk. numbers unless otherwise stated.

Each burial was recorded on a Burial Record Form supplied by the Palaeopathology Study Group. It was the responsibility of the archaeologist excavating each burial to complete that form. The work was supervised on Sites 1 and 2 by Dr Louise Loe, the human bone specialist assigned to the project, who examined the skeletons *in situ* in order to gain the maximum information available and also for evidence of pathology which might have required special attention before the skeletons were removed from the graves. She advised the excavation team on the best techniques for recording, lifting, cleaning and storage of the burials.

The graves were excavated by hand and the skeletons exposed and cleaned for recording. All the grave cuts, skeletons and disarticulated remains were planned at a scale of 1:20 and the majority of skeletons were also recorded photographically.

Once drawn and photographed, the bones were lifted, labelled and boxed, each individual articulated skeleton being boxed separately. As a rule, exposed skeletons were never left in the ground overnight, but were processed and lifted on the day of discovery. The skeletons were washed and slowly dried, either on site or in Bristol City Museum and Art Gallery after completion of the excavation, before being re-boxed and delivered to the human bone specialist for study.

Apart from coffin nails, there were few finds in the graves or associated with the skeletons. The locations of coffin nails were only planned when they occurred at the bottom of the grave and appeared to give an outline of the shape and position of the wooden coffin. Generally they were randomly distributed through the grave fills where the wooden coffin had gradually decayed and collapsed. The positions of special finds, such as coins and pewter objects, were also planned and the objects photographed *in situ*. Pottery sherds found within grave fills were not planned in position but were grouped together under the context number for each grave fill.

The human remains were excavated under the terms of Home Office Burial Licences and have now been cremated and the ashes reinterred within St James's Church.

The Archaeology of the Monastic Cemetery (Site 1)

It is generally assumed that the area of a priory precinct located immediately to the east of the church was occupied by the burial ground of the monks and other members of the monastic community. High status members of the lay community were sometimes entitled to be buried in or near the church due to their patronage of the religious house, while ordinary lay people such as servants or tenants of the abbey would be buried outside the church on the far side from the cloister.

This assumed burial pattern is confirmed by information obtained from archaeological excavations of cemeteries where an analysis of skeletal remains has been carried out, as at the Cistercian abbey of Bordesley, Hereford and Worcester (Coppack 1990, 160) and the Gilbertine priory of St. Andrew Fishergate, York (Stroud and Kemp 1993, 136). However, few monastic cemeteries have been studied in any detail and Greene (1992, 159) has pointed out that there were no hard-and-fast rules concerning burial within the monastic precincts and that they varied between orders and over time.

Before the 1995 excavation on Site 1 evidence had been found for the existence of the supposed monastic cemetery east of the church during clearance of the site for the NFU building in 1962, when two burials were uncovered, and again in 1989 when 21 skeletons were excavated.

During the 1995 excavation a further 224 skeletons were found, two of which came from within the east end of the church, making a total of 247 skeletons recovered from the monastic cemetery and church. The skeletons discovered in 1962 are no longer available for study so this section deals with the graves and human remains from the 1989 and 1995 excavations, including five graves in which the skeletal material had not survived.

The Condition of the Human Remains

Of the 245 burials found in 1989 and 1995, only 45 (18%) were undisturbed. The majority had either been cut by other burials within the cemetery or had been disturbed by post-Dissolution activity on the site. The digging of rubbish pits in the 17th and 18th centuries, the construction of houses in the later 18th century, the construction of the Scottish Presbyterian Church in the mid 19th century and the excavation of service and foundation trenches in the 20th century had all truncated the medieval burials. Consequently, in the majority of cases, the skeletons had portions of their bodies missing which led to difficulties in ageing and sexing some of the individuals (see below).

The state of preservation of the human bone varied across the site. In general it was quite good, but in some areas, notably under the Scottish Presbyterian Church, the bones had been virtually destroyed leaving either fragmentary remains or just stains in the soil. In some cases the skeleton had been eroded away completely and the grave contained no evidence of human remains. It is known that dewatering of the ground is detrimental to the survival of bone (Millard 1998, 99) and the construction of the Scottish Presbyterian Church over some of the burials would certainly have caused the drying out of the ground beneath. Nevertheless, all the skeletal remains were removed for study whatever their state of preservation.

The Cemetery Boundaries

To the west the cemetery was defined by the walls of the east end of the priory church and its chapels and no burials were found to be underlying the walls of the church (Fig. 51, page 87). Similarly there were no burials in the north-west corner of the excavation, so the western limit of the cemetery appears to continue on a line north of the church, although no structure was found defining that boundary.

To the north, the area of the site fronting Cannon Street had been badly disturbed by later buildings but some areas remained which should have contained a number of burials had the cemetery continued outside the excavated area to the north. Those areas, notably the garden between Buildings 1 and 2 and the garden to the east of Building 1 (see Chapter 3, Period 4B), contained only two graves, head-niche burial Sk. 145 and coffin burial Sk. 62. If a northern boundary existed then it appears to have been established after these burials took place. In the late medieval period a V-shaped east/west ditch (contexts 1000, 1008, 1345, 1424) (see Chapter 3, Fig. 16 and Fig. 51, page 87) probably formed the northern boundary to the cemetery and this would account for the small number of burials to its north. Although the ditch had been cut in a number of places by later structures it was found to be some 0.75m wide and at least 0.50m deep, and its backfill produced pottery sherds dating between 1350 and 1500 and some fragments of 14th-century Group 2 floor tiles (see Chapter 6). The ditch had cut a head-niche burial Sk. 144, a possible head-niche burial Sk. 197, two coffin burial Sks. 126 and 182, a simple burial Sk. 61 and a burial of uncertain type Sk. 128.

The eastern and southern boundaries of the cemetery lay outside the excavated area. In the most easterly area of the excavation one burial (Sk. 105) lay partly outside the area available for excavation while burials appeared to continue under the façade of the Scottish Presbyterian Church to the south (Fig. 54, page 90).

Jones suggested (1989, 3) that a row of four postholes found in 1989 and aligned north/south towards the eastern edge of that excavation might define the limit of the coffin burials in that direction, two of these postholes (contexts 362, 370) cutting head-niche graves Sk. 9 and Sk. 14. However, that theory must now be discounted as further excavation has shown that a number of coffin burials lie to the east of the line and it is most likely that the postholes post-date the Dissolution of the priory (see Chapter 3, Period 3).

Burials Within the Priory Church

Two coffin burials, Sk. 42 and Sk. 47, were found within the east end of the priory church, although most of Sk. 47 lay outside the area available for excavation (Fig. 51, page 87). Both burials were of adult males, that of Sk. 42 being between 35 and 45 years of age, and the grave fills contained iron coffin nails. In the case of burial Sk. 42 the coffin must have been of substantial construction as a number of unusually large coffin nails (by comparison with others from the site) lay in rows along each side of the body and across the head and feet indicating that the nails had been used to reinforce the joints between the sides and base of the coffin (Fig. 50). No other nails were found in the grave fill so the remaining joints of the coffin had presumably been pegged or dowelled. The stain of the wooden coffin could also be seen within the grave fill. The type of coffin used implies that the individual was of a high status befitting his place of burial close to the altar in the east end of the church (Greene 1992, 159). Both burials were of a late medieval date, the grave fills containing Group 2 floor tiles which date to the 14th century.

Fig. 50 Site 1: Sk. 42, within the east end of the priory church, showing the large coffin nails surrounding the skeleton (½ metre scale)

Table 1 Site 1: Analysis of burials from the monastic cemetery. Continued over the next thirteen pages.

Skeleton (Sk.) No.	Context Nos. Fill/Cut	Type of Burial	Sex: 1=M 2=F 0=?	Age	Position/ Special Features	Disturbed Yes/No	Relationship to other Contexts	Finds	Small Find No.	Date of Finds, etc
1 (333)	299/300	6	1	A						
2 (476)	404/405	1	0	A		Y	Cut by pillar & 477			
3 (477)		Not a burial			Animal bone					
4 (478)	312/313	6	0	A		Y	Cut by Sk. 27 Cuts 415 (gully)			

Sk	Context				Age	Position	Y/N	Stratigraphy	Finds	SF	Date
5 (427) (see 17)				0	33-45		N	Under 301			
6 (485)	249/250	6									
7 (486)	329/330	6	1		A						
8 (461) (see 16)			1		A						
9 (432)	418/419	1		0	17-25		N	Cut by 362 (post pit)			
10 (464) (see 18)				0	45						
11 (479)	408/409	6		0	A		Y	Cut by Sk. 18			
12 (472)	467/468	1		0	A		Y	Under 1950s wall. Cut by 474			
13 (462)											
14 (429)	297/298	1		0	33-45		Y	Cut by 370 (post pit)			
15 (428)	301/302	2		0	A		Y	Cut by 259 (pit)	Coffin nail Coffin nail Coffin nail Coffin nail Coffin nail Coffin nail Coffin nail Coffin nail Coffin nail Coffin nail	SF 675A SF 676A SF 677A SF 678A SF 679A SF 680A SF 681A SF 682A SF 683A SF 708A	
16 (461)	454/455	6									
17 (427)											
18 (464)	394/411 but confusion with 394	1A					N	Cuts Sk. 11			
19 (435)	305/306	1		0	25-35		Y	Cut by 222 (pit)	Human teeth Iron slag	SF 672A SF 684A	
20 (431)	303/304	1		0	25-35		Y	Cut by 222 (pit)			
21 (425)	376/377	6		0	A		Y	Under 338 Cut by 76			
22 (424)	265/266	2		0	A		Y	Cut by pillar	Coffin nail Coffin nail Coffin nail Coffin nail	SF 657A SF 658A SF 659A SF 660A	
23 (469)	416/417	6		0	25-35		Y	Cut by Sk. 24			
24 (475)	390/398	1		0	A		N	Cuts Sk. 23			
25 (470)	268/269	6		0	A		Y	Cut by ?pit			
26 (481)	480/482	6		0	A		Y	Cut by pillar Cuts 415 (gully)			
27 (442)	341/342	1A		0	A		N	Cut by 335 (pillar) Cuts Sk. 4 & 415 (gully)			
28	784/5	1		0	A		Y	Cut by 728, 735, 739 Under 738	2 sherds		mid-12th to early 13th century
29	794/5	4		0	A		Y	Cut by 664, 677	8 sherds		late 12th to early 13th century
30	796/7	6	?	?		R. hand (only remaining) across pelvis	Y	Cut by 664, 665, 706, 717, 739 Cuts 704	10 sherds		mid to late 12th century
31	713/4	6		0	A	Hands across pelvis	Y	Cut by 667, 677 Cuts 802	4 sherds Fe object CuAl lace end	SF 78B SF 80B	late 12th to early 13th century
32	732/3	1A		0	A		Y	Cut by 664, 709, 710			
33	790/1	6		0	45+	Arms across abdomen	Y	Cut by 667, 672 Cuts 803/4 (Sk. 41)			
34	788/9	2		0	A		Y	Cut by 667, 672, 712, 739 Cuts 802 Same cut as Sks. 35 & 36	Slag 2 coffin nails	SF 486B	

35	788/9	2	0	A		Y	Cut by 667, 672, 712, 739 Cuts 802 Same cut as Sks. 34 & 36	Coffin nails from 34, 35, 36 (marked on plan)	SF 408B	
36	788/9	2	0	A		Y	Cut by 667, 672, 712, 739 Cuts 802 Same cut as Sks. 34 & 35	Sherd Coffin nails from 34, 35, 36 (marked on plan)		mid to late 12th century
37	856/7	6	0	17-25		Y	Cut by 667, 672	1 sherd		late 12th to early 13th century
38	858/9	4	0	A	R. arm across abdomen, L. hand across pelvis	Y	Cut by 667, 672	Pottery, discarded as 20th century contam.		
39	860/1	2	0	A		Y	Cut by 664, 667, 677 Cuts 802	5 coffin nails	SF 349B	
40	792/3	6	0	A	R. arm across abdomen, L. arm across chest	Y	Cut by 667, 672	Animal bone		
41	803/4	1A	0	A	R. arm (only remaining) across abdomen	Y	Cut by 667, 672, 791 (Sk. 33) Cuts 704, 802	1 sherd Coffin nail	SF 327B	Romano-British
42	959/960	2	1	35-45	Outline stain of coffin Arms across abdomen	N	Cut by 883, 961	Floor tiles 3 coffin nails 1 coffin nail c.24 coffin nails Folded lead sheet	SF 332B SF 275B SF 616B SF 617B	14th century
43	976/7	2	1	45+	Hands across pelvis	N	Cut by 900 Cuts 986 (Sk. 44), 1025 (Sk. 49) Over 1138 (Sk. 88)	11 sherds Roof tile Slate Bone 1 coffin nail 1 coffin nail c.28 coffin nails Folded lead with iron nail through inside of fold	SF 303B SF 367B SF 620B SF 621B	early 16th (not earlier than 1500) N.B. This grave close to surface and high probability of later disturbance.
44	985/6	4	0	45+		Y	Cut by 900, 973, 977 (Sk. 43)			
45	1022/3	2	1	45+	Hands across pelvis	Y	Cut by 900 Cuts 977 (Sk. 43), 1025 (Sk. 49)	1 small nail 9 coffin nails	SF 355B SF 465B	
46	987/8 1994 trial trench 2 context 24	1	1	33-45	R. hand across pelvis, L. arm across abdomen	N		1 frag. iron/ore	SF 358B	Radiocarbon date 1120-1225 at 53% probability
47	1015/6	2	1	A		N	Under 649 Cut by 628 Cuts 997	Floor tiles 1 frag. wood 10 coffin nails	SF 369B SF 425B	14th century
48	1033/2	1A	1	45+	Stone against R. side of skull	Y	Cut by 893, 900			
49	1024/5	1	1	50-65	Hands across pelvis	Y	Cut by 900, 977 (Sk. 43), 1023 (Sk. 45)	2 sherds		mid to late 12th century
50	1050/1	2	0	9-12	R. hand (only remaining) across pelvis	N	Cut by 1053 (Sk. 60)	16+ coffin nails	SF 307B	
51	1054/5	1A	0	A		Y	Cut by pillar base & foundation trench			

52	1057/8	2	0	33-45	Hands across pelvis	N	Cut by 726, 1012 Cuts sub-circular feature (no context number)	1 coffin nail	SF 249B	
53	1059/60	1	0	25-35	Hands across pelvis	N	Cut by 1012 Either cut by or cuts 1062 (Sk. 54)			
54	1061/2	1	0	17-25	Arms across abdomen	N	Either cut by or cuts 1060 (Sk. 53)			
55	1063/4	2	0	10+/-30M		Y	Cut by pillar base Possibly cuts 1088 (Sk. 74)	7 coffin nails Lead sheet with nail	SF 393B SF 589B	
56	1065/6	2	1	17-25	Lying on right side	Y	Cut by pillar base Cuts 1096 (Sk. 67) & possibly 1094 (Sk. 72)	5/6 coffin nails	SF 511B	
57	1037/8	2	1	45+		Y	Cut by 1988 excavation Superimposed on 1089 (Sk. 71)	1 coffin nail 2/3 coffin nails	SF 435B SF 615B	
58	1067/8	2	0	A		Y	Cut by 550 Cuts 1084 (Sk. 66) & 1090 (Sk. 71)	2 coffin nails	SF 543B	
59	1039/40	2	1	45+	R. arm across abdomen, L. arm across chest	Y	Cut by 550 & 1989 excavation Cuts 1086 (Sk. 70)	Tile 1 coffin nail	SF 306B	
60	1052/3	2	2	25-35	Hands across pelvis	Y	Cuts 1051 (Sk. 50), 1081 (Sk. 68), 1128 (Sk. 83)	6 coffin nails 6 coffin nails Piece of folded lead	SF 344B SF 473B SF 283B	
61	1009/10	4	0	A	Arms across abdomen	Y	Cut by 854, 1000 = 1008 (ditch)			
62	1001/2	2	1	45+	R. hand across pelvis, L. arm by side	N	Cut by 854, 855	6 coffin nails	SF 440B	
63	1072/3	1	?	?		Y	Cut by 556, 608			
64	1101/2	2	1	30-40	Hands across pelvis 2 silver coins found, one on each shoulder Jet pendant under lower jaw	Y	Cut by 550, 663 Cuts 1132 (Sk. 85), 1134 (Sk. 86)	Silver coin (folded) Silver coin (folded) Jet pendant coffin nails 3 coffin nails 2 coffin nails	SF 193B SF 194B SF 232B SF 314B SF 492B SF 526B	1189-1199 Possibly 1189-1199
65	1078/9	6	0	A		Y	Cut by 1077 (pit)			
66	1083/4	6	0	A		Y	Cut by 550, 1068 (Sk. 58)	1 frag ashy slag	SF 571B	
67	1095/6	1	0	45+	L. arm across abdomen, lower R. arm missing	Y	Cut by pillar base, 1066 (Sk. 56)			
68	1080/1	2	1	25-35	Hands crossed on chest	N	Cut by 663, 1053 (Sk. 60) Cuts 1128 (Sk. 83), 1130 (Sk. 84), 1132 (Sk. 85), 1134 (Sk. 86)	10 coffin nails 25 coffin nails 1 coffin nail	SF 295B SF 401B SF 500B	
69	1069/70	2	1	17-25	Hands crossed on chest	Y	Cut by ? Cuts 1038 (Sk. 88), 1099	2 sherds 30+ coffin nails 6 coffin nails	SF 405B SF 575B	Romano-British

70	1085/6	4	2	A	R. hand across pelvis, L. hand missing	Y	Cut by 1040	2 coffin nails (could be from 1040)	SF 350B	
71	1089/90	1	0	A	Hands across pelvis	N	Cut by 1038 (Sk. 57), 1068 (Sk. 58)	6 coffin nails	SF 420B	
72	1093/4	1A	0	A		Y	Cut by 550 & possibly by 1066 (Sk. 56)	1 coffin nail	SF 450B	
73	1074/5	1	2	17-25	Hands across pelvis	Y	Cut by 721, 1988 excavation	Sherd roof tile		Residual
74	1087/8	6	0	1+/-4M	Disartic. bones laid on frag. lead sheet	Y	Cut by pillar base & possibly by 1064 (Sk. 55)	1 coffin nail Lead sheet	SF 555B SF 361B	
75	1099/1100	2	0	A		Y	Cut by 1070 (Sk. 69)	Coffin nails		
76	1110/11	2	0	A		Y	Cut by manhole & 1994 trial trench	1 sherd 4 coffin nails	SF 578B	1120-1170
77	1112/3	1	1	35-45	Hands across pelvis	Y	Cut by 550, 1004, 1119 (Sk. 80) Cuts 1121 (Sk. 81)			
78	1114/5	4	2	A		Y	Cut by 1117 & 1994 trial trench	1 sherd		Romano-British
79	1116/7	1A	1	33-45	Hands across pelvis	Y	Cut by 550, 1004, 1119 (Sk. 80) Cuts 1115 (Sk. 78)			
80	1118/9 Same as 1090/1	2	1	17-25	Arms across abdomen	Y	Cut by 550, 1004 Cuts 1113 (Sk. 77), 1117 (Sk. 79)	1 sherd 1 coffin nail 3 coffin nails	SF 548B SF 609B	1120-1170
81	1120/1	4	2	A		Y	Cut by 1994 trial trench & 971 Cuts 1243			
82	1143/4	1	2	A	L. hand across pelvis R. arm ?	N	Cut by 695, 932 Under 1149	1 sherd		Romano-British
83	1127/8	2	1	45+	Arms straight	N	Cut by 1053 (Sk. 60), 1081 (Sk. 68), 1138 (Sk. 83)	5 coffin nails	SF 438B	
84	1129/30	6	1	17-25	Thought to be disartic. & bagged as 1127 Long bones bagged as Sk. 84	Y	Cut by 1052, 1081 (Sk. 68), 1128 (Sk. 83)			
85	1131/2	2	1	17-25		Y	Cut by 550, 663 (wall) 1081 (Sk. 68), 1102 (Sk. 64) Cuts 1134 (Sk. 86)	3 coffin nails	SF 246B	
86	1133/4	1	0	9+/-24M	Arms across abdomen	Y	Cut by 1081 (Sk. 68), 1102 (Sk. 64) 1132 (Sk. 85)			
87	1135/6	4	1	20-30		Y	Cut by 971, 973 Cuts 1128 (Sk. 83)			
88	1137/8	2	1	A	R. arm across abdomen L. arm across chest	Y	Cut by 973 Lies below 977 (Sk. 43), 1070 (Sk. 69), 1142 (Sk. 90)	Coffin nails	SF 377B	

89	1139/40	1A	0	Juv.		Y	Cut by 973, 1142 (Sk. 90)			
90	1141/2	2	1	39-44	R. hand across pelvis L. arm missing	Y	Cut by 900, 971, 973 Cuts 1140 (Sk. 89) Overlies 1138 (Sk. 88)	1 sherd 3 coffin nails 3 coffin nails 1 coffin nail	SF 308B SF 462B SF 595B	Romano-British
91	1154/5	2	2	18-25	Arms across abdomen	Y	Cut by 900, 971, 973 Cutting 1157 (Sk. 92), 1241 (Sk. 106)	1 sherd Coffin nails	SF 354B	early 13th century
92	1156/7	1	0	Juv.		Y	Cut by 971, 1155 (Sk. 91)	2 coffin nails	SF 497B	
93	1158/9	1A	0	5-6		Y	Cut by 973	4 coffin nails (in upper fill only)	SF 439B	
94	1147/8	1	1	A	L. arm across abdomen R. arm by side?	Y	Cut by 1146 (ditch) Under 1149			
95	1179/80	6	0	A		Y	Cut by 554 (wall)			
96	1181/2	2	2	A		Y	Cut by 973, possibly by 1287 (Sk. 115) Cuts 1184 (Sk. 97)	4 sherds 4 coffin nails	SF 351B	mid to late 12th century
97	1183/4	1	1	40-50	Hands across pelvis	N	Cut by 901, 1182 (Sk. 96)	7 sherds 2 coffin nails	SF 416B	12th century
98	1185/6	2	1	A	Arms across abdomen	Y	Cut by 833 Cuts 1287 (Sk. 115)	?coffin nails 15 coffin nails 2 coffin nails	SF 305B SF 455B SF 479B	
99	1187/8	2	0	A	R. arm across abdomen L. arm by side	Y	Cut by 973 & 1994 trial trench Cuts 1276 (Sk. 117)	1 coffin nail 1 coffin nail	SF 302B SF 357B	
100	1125/6	4	1	25-35	Skull propped up by stone on L. side	Y	Cut by 973			
101	1429/30	2	1	45+	R. hand across pelvis, L. arm missing	Y	Cut by 758, 1251 (pit)	CuAl pin 12+ coffin nails 3 coffin nails	SF 453B SF 407B SF 576B	
102	1231/2	1A	0	A		Y	Wall 554 overlies grave fill			
103	1233/4	1A	0	A		Y	Wall 554 overlies grave fill			
104	1235/6	1A	0	A		Y	Cut by 554, 1146 (pit)			
105	1238/9	6	1	25-35	Observed under section only	Y				
106	1240/1	1A	1	25-35	Arms crossed on abdomen	Y	Cut by 973, 1155 (Sk. 91), 1314 (Sk. 125)	Frag. glass		
107	1400/1	2	0	33-45		Y	Cut by 604, 1397, 1407 (Sk. 147)	Coffin nails	SF 577B	
108	1244/5	2	1	35-45	Arms crossed on abdomen	Y	Cut by 1285	4 coffin nails	SF 437B	
109	1195/1262	2	1	25-35	R. arm across abdomen L. arm across chest In E-W linear feature, probably earlier grave(s)	Y	Placed on top of legs of Sk. 110 (1264)	1 sherd 1 coffin nail 6 coffin nails 1 coffin nail 1 coffin nail	SF 324B SF 371B SF 459B SF 550B	pre 1200

110	1263/4	4	1	45+	Hands across pelvis Found with one skull either side of skull In E-W linear feature, probably earlier grave(s)	Y	Cut by 1262 (Sk. 109)			
111	1599/1600	1	0	25-35		Y	Cut by 761, 848, 1161 (pit), 1249 (pit), 1602 (pit), 1621 (Sk. 227)			
112	1267/8	2	1	20-30	R. hand across pelvis	Y	Cut by 1190, 1223, 1285 Cuts 1331 (Sk. 121)	2 coffin nails 1 frag. wood	SF 549B SF 379B	
113	1294/5	1A	0	A		Y	Cut by 973, 1225	Coffin nails (NB possibly from 1225 above)	SF 343B	
114	1269/70	2	1	17-25		Y	Cut by 1285 Cuts 1335 (Sk. 119)	4 coffin nails 4 coffin nails	SF 370B SF 597B	
115	1286/7	2	0	5-6	Hands across pelvis	Y	Cut by 973, 1186 (Sk. 98) & possibly by 1182 (Sk. 96)	1 sherd 2 coffin nails 1 coffin nail	SF 373B SF 557B	early 13th century
116	1290/1	4	2	45		Y	Cut by 1285 (pipe trench)			
117	1275/6	1A	2	25-35	R. hand across pelvis, L. arm across abdomen	Y	Cut by 973, 1188 (Sk. 99)			
118	1311/2	2	0	12-15	Stone by R. side of skull	Y	Cut by 971 Cuts 1314 (Sk. 125)	4 coffin nails	SF 375B	
119	1334/5	2	1	18-19	R. hand across pelvis L. arm across chest	Y	Cut by 1190, 1270 (Sk. 114) Cuts 1337 (Sk. 131) & possibly 1333 (Sk. 120)	Coffin nails 1 coffin nail	SF 372B SF 553B	
120	1332/3	6	0	A		Y	Cut by 1190, 1331 (Sk. 121) & possibly 1335 (Sk. 119)			
121	1330/1	6	1	A	CuAl frag. under L. knee	Y	Cut by 1190, 1268 (Sk. 112) Cuts 1333 (Sk. 120)	CuAl frag. Frag. haematite Frags. CuAl object 1 coffin nail Worked flint	SF 320B SF 352B SF 353B SF 527B SF 528B	
122	1317/8	1A	0	A		Y	Cut by 1285			
123	1271/2	2	1	25-35	Hands across pelvis	Y	Cut by manhole Above 1274 (Sk. 132), 1319 (Sk. 123)	10 coffin nails 2 coffin nails	SF 374B SF 585B	
124	1315/6	1	1	20-30	Hands across pelvis	Y	Cut by 1285			
125	1313/4	1	1	25-35	R. hand across pelvis L. arm by side	Y	Cut by 971, 1312 (Sk. 118) Cuts 1241 (Sk. 106)			

126	1341/2	2	1	45+	R. arm across chest, L. arm across abdomen	Y	Cut by 973, 1000 (ditch) Cuts 1344 (Sk. 134)	3 coffin nails 2 coffin nails 3 coffin nails	SF 481B SF 517B SF 546B	
127	1279/80	1A	1	45+	Hands across pelvis	Y	Cut by 1278 (Sk. 138)			
128	1353/4	6	1	40-50	Jumble of bone	Y	Cut by 973, 1000 (ditch)			
129	1292/3	1A	0	12-15	Arms by side	N				
130	1347/8	2	2	A	R. arm across abdomen, L. arm missing	Y	Under 900 (ditch) Cut by 971, 973 Above 1350 (Sk. 135)	1 sherd 3 coffin nails	SF 536B	1120-1170
131	1336/7	1	1	A	Hands across pelvis	Y	Cut by 1190, 1270 (Sk. 114), 1335 (Sk. 119)			
132	1273/4	2	1	A	Hands across pelvis	Y	Cut by 1190, 1272 (Sk. 123)	3 coffin nails	SF 505B	
133	1375/6	2	0	Infant		Y	Cut by 1257, 1355	2 sherds Floor tile 5 coffin nails	SF 514B	1250-1325
134	1343/4	1A	0	A		Y	Cut by 971, 1342 (Sk. 126) & manhole			
135	1349/50	1	1	50+	Hands across pelvis	Y	Cut by 973 Below 1348 (Sk. 130)			
136	1388/9	2	1	45-55	Arms across abdomen	Y	Cut by 1387 (pit)	1 coffin nail	SF 365B	
137	1319/20	1	1	A		Y	Cut by 1271, 1274 Below 1271 (Sk. 123)			
138	1277/8	2	1	25-35	Hands across pelvis	Y	Cut by 550 Cuts 1280 (Sk. 127)	1 sherd 1 coffin nail coffin nails	SF 441B SF 604B	early 13th century
139	1383/4	4	2	A	Arms across abdomen	Y	Cut by 1285 Over 1386 (Sk. 140)	1 ?coffin nail	SF 523B	
140	1385/6	4	1	33-45		Y	Cut by 1285, 1384 (Sk. 139)			
141	1417/8	1	2	35-45	L. hand across pelvis R. arm across abdomen	N	Cut by 1192			
142	1377/8	4	1	45+	Hands across pelvis Pewter chalice on abdomen	Y	Cut by 971 Cuts 1380 (Sk. 143), 1382 (Sk. 158)	2 coffin nails (NB may not be from 142) Pewter chalice	SF 491B SF 300B	
143	1379/80	6	0	7-8	Skull disturbed & placed by skull of Sk. 142	Y	Cut by 971 and 1378 (Sk. 142)			
144	1371/2	1	0	A	L. hand across pelvis R. arm across abdomen	Y	Cut by 1000 (ditch)			
145	1419/20	1	1	45+	Hands across pelvis	Y	Cut by 973			
146	1402/3	2	1	45+	Arms across abdomen	N	Cut by 1362 (pit) & possibly 1304 Cuts 1405 (No skeleton)	6 coffin nails	SF 452B	
147	1406/7	2	1	17-25	Hands across chest	N	Cut by 1399 Cuts 1401 (Sk. 107), 1409 (Sk. 198)	14+ coffin nails 1 coffin nail	SF 356B SF 567B	

148	1443/4	1	1	45+	Arms across abdomen	Y	Cut by 559	1 coffin nail	SF 448B	
149	1323/4	1A	0	A		Y	Cut by 1310 (pit)			
150	1437/8	1	2	33-45	Arms across abdomen	Y	Cut by 1436 (pipe)			
151	1453/4	1	0	A		Y	Cut by 559, 865			
152	1351/2	2	1	45+	Hands across pelvis	N	Cut by 1285	Sherd 3+ coffin nails 2 coffin nails 1 nail in wood 1 coffin nail 2 frags. worked flint	SF 368B SF 426B SF 533B SF 588B SF 592B	Romano-British
153	1469/70	4	1	33-45	R. hand across chest L. arm missing	Y	Cut by 1214 (water tank) Under 1411 (pit) Cuts 1476 (Sk. 173), 1474 (Sk. 207)			
154	1445/6	2	0	33-45	Hands across pelvis	Y	Cut by 1249, 1251 (pit) Possibly cuts 1448 (Sk. 155)	3 coffin nails 1 coffin nail	SF 390B SF 560B	
155	1447/8	6	0	A		Y	Cut by 1247 Possibly cut by 1446 (Sk. 154) Cuts 1450 (no skeleton)			
156	1467/8	1	1	17-25	R. hand across pelvis, L. hand missing Pebble near jaw	N	Under 1579	Pebble by jaw	SF 468B	
157	1390/1	1A	0	A		Y	Cut by 1285	2 coffin nails	SF 359B	
158	1381/2	1	1	20-30	Arms across abdomen	Y	Cut by 971, 1378 (Sk. 142)	1 coffin nail	SF 574B	
159	1483/4	2	1	50+	Arms across abdomen Long bones & 2 disartic skulls at head end	Y	Cuts 1485 (Sk. 203), 1556 (Sk. 199), 1558 (Sk. 204)	2 sherds Lead sheet with rivets 9 coffin nails Piece folded lead	SF 346B SF 477B SF 513B	1250-1300
160	1471/2	2	2	A		Y	Cut by 1436 & E-W ditch Over 1474 (Sk. 207) Cuts 1535 (Sk. 183)	1 coffin nail	SF 603B	
161	1497/8	4	2	45+	Hands across pelvis	N	Cut by 1368 (pit)	1 sherd Tile		Romano-British
162	1461/2	2	2	A	Hands across pelvis	Y	Cut by bore hole & 579 (drain) Cuts 1464 (Sk. 167), 1466 (Sk. 168)	1 sherd 1 coffin nail Frags of metal Frags of shale bracelet	SF 573B SF 593B SF 607B	early 13th century
163 (See 186)										
164	1493/4	2	1	A		Y	Cut by 1161 (pit), 1300 (pit)	5 coffin nails	SF 510B	
165	1495/6	1	1	45+	Arms across abdomen Pewter object on stomach	N		1 sherd Pewter obj. Frag. flint	SF 383B SF 594B	12th century
166	1451/2	4	2	17-25	Hands across pelvis	N	Cut by 865, 1304	1 sherd Slag		

167	1463/4	4	1	A	L. hand across pelvis, R. hand by side	Y	Cut by 1462 (Sk. 162) & possibly by bore-hole	1 sherd Glass frag.	SF 562B	12th century
168	1465/6	1	1	30-40	L. hand across pelvis, R. arm across abdomen Strange stone in pelvis area	N	Cut by 579 (drain), 1462 (Sk. 162)	3 coffin nails	SF 447B	
169	1455/6	1	0	A	Arms by side	Y	Cut by 556, 1251, 1458 (Sk. 170)			
170	1457/8	2	1	45+	R. arm across abdomen L. arm missing	Y	Cut by 556 Cuts 1456 (Sk. 169)	9 coffin nails	SF 524B	
171	1504/5	2	1	17-25	Arms across abdomen	Y	Cuts 1486 (Sk. 203), 1508 (Sk. 177), 1511 (Sk. 184)	Folded lead 7 coffin nails 1 coffin nail	SF 551B SF 552B SF 602B	
172	1506/7	2	2	17-25	R. arm across abdomen L. arm missing	Y	Cut by 1205 (drain) Cuts 1511 (Sk. 184), 1525 (Sk. 185)	1 coffin nail Frag. wood	SF 363B SF 364B	
173	1475/6	2	0	2'-6		Y	Cut by 1470 (Sk. 153)	3 coffin nails 4 coffin nails	SF 508B SF 530B	
174	1516/7	2	2	15-25		Y	Cut by 1212? May cut 1519 (Sk. 190)	6 coffin nails 1 coffin nail	SF 400B SF 556B	
175	1512/3	2	0	6-9M		N	Cuts 1521 (Sk. 195)	1 coffin nails 2 coffin nail	SF 449B SF 569B	
176	1459/60	1	2	17-25		N	Cut by 1304, 1360 (pit)			
177	1508/9	3	1	45+	Hands across pelvis	N	Cut by 1505 (Sk. 171), 1511 (Sk. 184)			
178	1489/90	1	1	17-25	Hands across pelvis Tightly bound skeleton	N				
179	1522/3	2	1	17-25	R. hand across pelvis L. arm across abdomen	Y	Cut by 1207 (drain) Cuts 1525 (Sk. 185), 1610 (Sk. 224)	Roof tiles 4 coffin nails	SF 476B	
180	1514/5	2	1	A		Y	Cut by 1424 (ditch) Cuts 1529 (Sk. 182), 1541 (Sk. 192)?	5 coffin nails 1 coffin nail 1 ?coffin nail (Combines Sk. 18coffin nails)	SF 496B SF 522B SF 561B	
181	1530/1	2	1	50+	L. hand across pelvis R. arm missing	Y	Cuts 1533 (Sk. 194)	1 sherd 10+ coffin nails	SF 587B	early 13th century
182	1528/9	2	2	25-35	Arms across abdomen	N	Cut by 1000 (ditch), 1515 (Sk. 180) Cuts 1546 (Sk. 193)	15+ coffin nails 1 coffin nail 2 coffin nails (Combines Sk. 180 nails)	SF 509B SF 512B SF 532B	
183	1534/5	6	0	4-6		Y	Cut by 1436, 1472 (Sk. 160) Cuts 1474 (Sk. 207)			

184	1510/1	2	0	12+/ 30M		Y	Cut by 1505 (Sk. 171), 1507 (Sk. 172) Cuts 1509 (Sk. 177), 1525 (Sk. 185)	1 sherd 3 coffin nails 2 coffin nails	SF 493B SF 564B	pre-1200
185	1524/5	3	1	30-40	Arms tightly by side & legs tightly together Bound before burial?	N	Cut by 1507, (Sk. 172), 1511 (Sk. 184), 1523 (Sk. 179)			
186 (Same context as 163)	1477/8	2	1	25-35	Arms across abdomen	N	Cut by 1218 Cuts 1480 (Sk. 187)	3 coffin nails 4 coffin nails 5 coffin nails 2 coffin nails Slag	SF 519B SF 391B SF 503B SF 563B SF 534B	
187	1479/80	1A	1	A		Y	Cut by 1478 (Sk. 186), 1478 (Sk. 163)			
188	1481/2	2	1	50+	Arms across abdomen	Y	Possibly cut by 1218 May cut 1519 (Sk. 190)	1 coffin nail 4 coffin nails 6 coffin nails	SF 495B SF 518B SF 606B	
189	1633/4	6	1	A	R. arm by side, L. arm missing	N	Cut by 1994 trial trench Cuts 1636 (Sk. 231), 1638 (Sk. 202)	Frag. floor tile Piece glass		
190	1518/9	6	0	6+/ -24M		N	Possibly cut by 1482 (Sk. 188), 1517 (Sk. 174) Cuts 1574 (Sk. 212)	1 coffin nail (NB may belong to adjacent burial)	SF 501B	
191	1538/9	2	1	25-35	R. arm across abdomen L. arm by side	N	Cuts 1568 (Sk. 206), 1570 (Sk. 214)	1 coffin nail	SF 559B	
192	1540/1	1A	0	A		Y	Cut by 1285, 1515 (Sk. 180)?			
193	1546/7	6	0	Foetal		Y	Cut by 1424 (ditch), 1548 (ditch), 1529 (Sk. 182)			
194	1532/3	1A	1	50-65	Hands across pelvis	Y	Cut by 1285, 1531 (Sk. 181)			
195	1520/1	2	0	8'-10	Hands across pelvis	N	Cut by 971, 1513 (Sk. 175) Cuts 1545 (Sk. 196)	5 coffin nails	SF 502B	
196	1544/5	1	1	40-45	Arms across abdomen	Y	Cut by 971, 1521 (Sk. 195)			
197	1542/3	1A	1	A		Y	Cut by 1285, 1424 (ditch), 1548 (rob) & cellar wall			
198	1408/9	1	0	A		Y	Cut by wall, 1407 (Sk. 147)	1 sherd		Romano-British
199	1555/6	6	2	A		Y	Cut by 1436 (pit), 1484 (Sk. 159) Cuts 1554 (Sk. 200)			

200	1553/4	1	1	45+	R. hand across pelvis L. by side?	Y	Cut by 1436 (pit), 1552 (Sk. 201), 1556 (Sk. 199), 1586 (Sk. 211)	1 sherd		Romano-British
201	1551/2	1	0	10'-15	Arms by side?	Y	Cut by 1436 (pit) Cuts 1554 (Sk. 200)			
202	1637/8	1	1	25-35	Hands across pelvis	Y	Cut by 1634 (Sk. 189), 1635 (Sk. 231), 1640 (robbed grave)			
203	1485/6	2	1	35-45	R. hand across pelvis, L. arm missing	Y	Cut by 1484 (Sk. 159), 1505 (Sk. 171), possibly cut by 1558 (Sk. 204)	1 sherd (between 203 & 204) Tile Frag. of stone object/ore 1 coffin nail	SF 385B SF 516B	Roman amphora
204	1557/8	4	1	33-45	Arms across abdomen, Skull missing but stone pillow? under skull position	Y	Cut by 1207, 1484 (Sk. 159) Possibly cuts 1486 (Sk. 203) & 1488 (Sk. 205)	1 sherd (between 203 & 204)		see above
205	1487/8	1	1	25-35	Hands across pelvis 2 upright stones against edge of cut	N	Cut by 1207 (drain), 1484 (Sk. 159) Possibly cut by 1558 (Sk. 204)			
206	1567/8	2	1	25-35	L. arm across abdomen, R. arm missing	Y	Possibly cut by 1539 (Sk. 191) Cuts 1570 (Sk. 214)	6 coffin nails	SF 456B	
207	1473/4	4	1	17-25	L. hand across chest, R. arm across abdomen	Y	Cut by 1436 (pipe) Under 1470 (Sk. 153), 1472 (Sk. 160), 1535 (Sk. 183)			
208	1581/2	1	1	A		Y	Cut by 1436 (pipe), 1572 (Sk. 209)			
209	1571/2	1A	2	45+	L. hand across pelvis, R. arm missing	Y	Cut by 1436 (pipe) Cuts 1582 (Sk. 208)			
210	1583/4	6	0	45+		Y	Cut by 1436 (pipe)			
211	1585/6	2	2	A		Y	Cut by 1436 (pipe) & 1994 Trial trench Cuts 1554 (Sk. 200)	3 coffin nails	SF 412B	
212	1573/4	4	0	10-12	L. arm across abdomen R. arm by side?	Y	Cut by 1482 (Sk. 188), 1519 (Sk. 190) Cuts 1576 (Sk. 213)			
213	1575/6	3	1	45+	Clay lined burial Arms by side	N	Cut by 1574 (Sk. 212) Possibly cut by 1481 Cuts 1578 (Sk. 230) Possibly cuts 1608 (Sk. 221)	4 coffin nails	SF 535B	

214	1569/70	2	0	45+	In wide grave cut Arms across abdomen	N	Cut by 1539 (Sk. 191), 1568 (Sk. 206) Under 1605	1 sherd Slag? 5 coffin nails coffin nails	SF 384B SF 525B SF 584B	12th century
215	1591/2	2	0	A	Both femurs placed across pelvis in a cross. Hands across pelvis.	Y	Cut by 1590 (pit), 848 (drain) Cuts 1588 (Sk. 218)	2 coffin nails	SF 411B	
216	1593/4	6	0	A		Y	Cut by 1590 (pit), 848 (drain)			
217	1595/6	6	0	A	Arms by side	Y	Cut by 1590 (pit), 848 (drain)			
218	1587/8	1	1	45+	R. hand across pelvis, L. arm by side	Y	Cut by 840 (drain), 1590 (pit), 1592 (Sk. 215)			
219	1645/6	6	0	A		Y	Cut by 568 (pillar base), 848 (drain) Cuts 1598 (Sk. 223)			
220	1641/2	2	0	Juv.		Y	Cut by 848 (drain) Possibly cuts 1644 (Sk. 222)	5 coffin nails 2 coffin nails	SF 483B SF 539B	
221	1607/8	2	1	33-45	Arms across abdomen	Y	Cut by 1218 (ditch) & possibly by 1576 (Sk. 213) Cuts 1610 (Sk. 224) & possibly 1673 (Sk. 233)	1 sherd Lead sheet with iron nail Coiled length of CuAl 2 coffin nails	SF 386B SF 388B SF 488B	1120-1170
222	1643/4	6	0	A		Y	Cut by 568 (pillar base), 848 & possibly by 1642 (Sk. 220) Cuts 1650 (Sk. 234)			
223	1597/8	1A	0	A		Y	Cut by 568 (pillar base), 848 (drain), 1646 (Sk. 219)			
224	1609/10	2	1	50+	Arms by side Pewter object on abdomen	Y	Cut by 1523 (Sk. 179), 1608 (Sk. 221) Cuts 1673 (Sk. 233)	Folded lead sheet Pewter obj. Folded leed sheet Frags coffin nails	SF 387B SF 389B SF 520B SF 531B	
225	1624/5	6	0	15-25	Hands across pelvis	Y	Cut by 1190, 1436, 1622			
226	1626/7	5	1	33-45	Arms by side Limestone blocks line head of grave (1622)	Y	Cut by 1436 (drain)			
227	1620/1	2	0	A		Y	Cut by 761 (pit), 848, 1161 Cuts 1600? (Sk. 111)	4 coffin nails 5 coffin nails	SF 451B SF 466B	
228	1651/2	4	2	25-35	Arms by side	N	Cuts 1656 (Sk. 239)	1 sherd		post-1400
229	1427/8	4	1	45+	Arms by side	Y	Cut by 758, 1251 (pit) Cuts 1426 (Sk. 249), 1692 (Sk. 235)			

230	1577/8	6	0	Infant		Y	Possibly cut by 1219 (drain), 1576 (Sk. 213)			
231	1635/6	6	0	3+/-12M	Legs crossed?	Y	Cut by 1634 (Sk. 189), 1638 (Sk. 202)			
232	1653/4	2	2	17-25		Y	Cut by 579 (drain)	1 sherd coffin nail	SF 540B	post-1150 but possibly post-1200
233	1672/3	3	1	45-55	Clay lined burial Arms by side	Y	Cut by 1219 (drain), 1610 (Sk. 224) & possibly by 1608 (Sk. 221)			
234	1649/50	1	1	A		Y	Cut by 568 (pillar base) Cut by 1644 (Sk. 222)			
235	1691/2	1	0	A		Y	Cut by 1251 (pit), 1428 (Sk. 229)			
236	1659/60	4	2	45+	Hands across pelvis	Y	Cut by 657 (water tank)			
237	1661/2	2	0	4yr		Y	Cut by 657 (water tank) Possibly cut by 1698 (Sk. 248)	4 coffin nails	SF 542B	
238	1675/6	6	0	A		Y	Cut by pillar base			
239	1655/6	2	0	8+/-24M	Hands across pelvis	Y	Cut by 1652 (Sk. 228)	4 coffin nails	SF 583B	
240	1681/2	4	1	33-45	Hands across pelvis	Y	Cut by 657 (water tank)			
241	1683/4	1	1	45+	Arms by side	N	Cuts 1686 (Sk. 242)			
242	1685/6	4	1	A		Y	Cut by 1684 (Sk. 241)			
243	1687/8	1A	0	8-10	Arms by side	Y	Cut by 570 (pillar base) Cuts 1690 (Sk. 244)			
244	1689/90	1	1	35-45	Arms across abdomen	Y	Cut by 620 (cellar), 1688 (Sk. 243)			
245	1657/8	1	2	45+	Arms by side	Y	Cut by 1562 (drain)	Coffin nail	SF 541B	
246	1693/4	2	0	10+/-30M		Y	Cut by 1562 (drain)	2 coffin nails	SF 566B	
247	1695/6	1	2	17-25	Hands across pelvis	N				
248	1697/8	1	1	17-25		Y	Cut by 1680 (pit) Possibly cuts 1662 (Sk. 237)			
249	1425/6	1	0	5+/-16M		N	Cut by 848 (drain), 1428 (Sk. 229)			
250	1699/1700	1	0	A		Y	Cut by 1666 (pit) Cuts 1678 (Sk. 252)	Animal bone		
251	1701/2	1A	0	A		Y	Cut by 619 (wall), 1666 (pit)			
252	1677/8	1A	0	12-18		Y	Cut by pillar base, 1666 (pit), 1700 (Sk. 250)			

boundary ditch

Fig. 53

Fig. 54

Fig. 52

possible chapel

north wall of chancel

east end of church

42

47

Type 1 and Type 1A, head-niche and possible head-niche
Type 2, coffin
Type 3, clay filled graves
Types 4, 5 and 6, simple; burial laid on lead sheet; burials of uncertain type
Graves where no skeletal material remained

20m

0

Fig. 51 Site 1: plan showing all burials, burial types and the location of Figs. 52–54

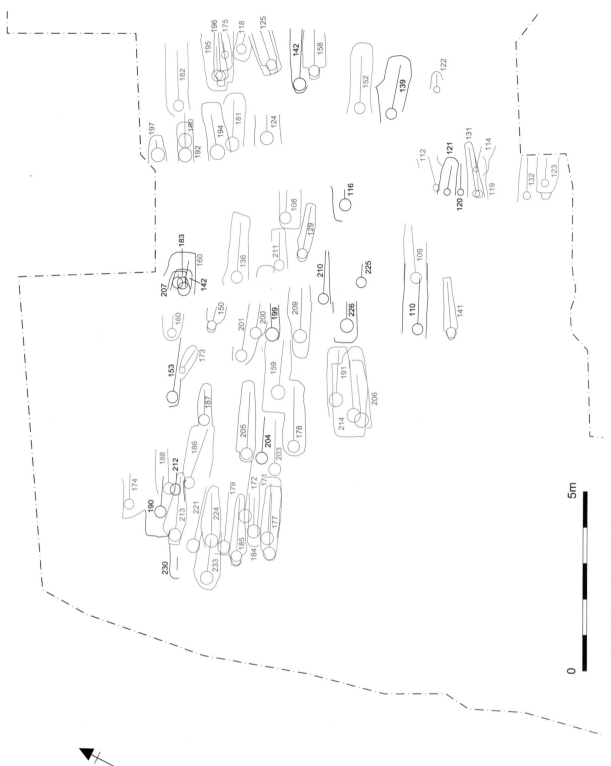

Fig. 52 Site 1: burials in the north-west part of the excavation identified by skeleton number

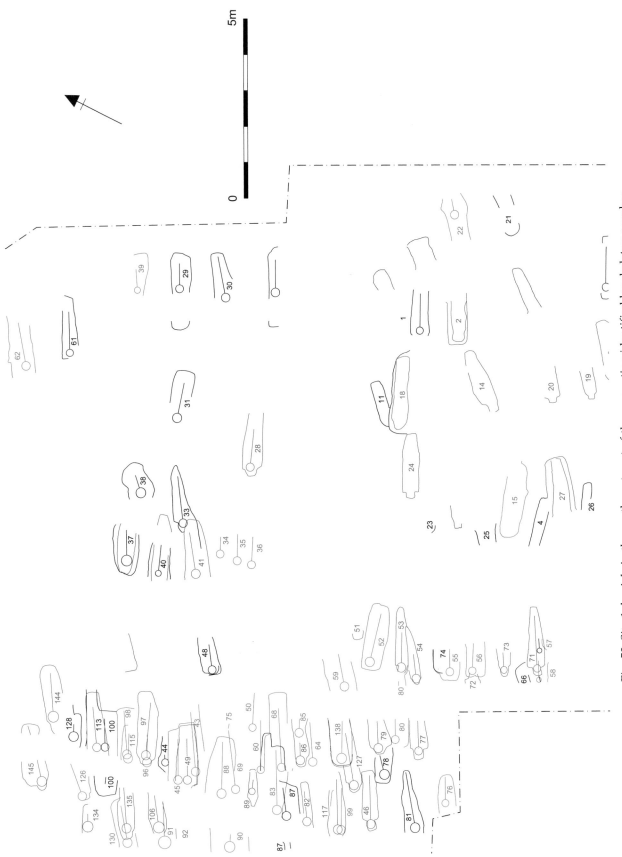

Fig. 53 Site 1: burials in the north-east part of the excavation identified by skeleton number

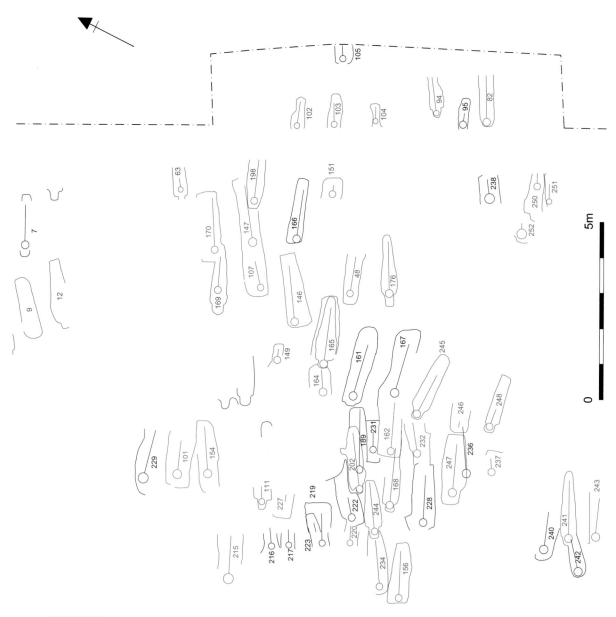

Fig. 54 Site 1: burials in the south-east part of the excavation identified by skeleton number

Fig. 55 Site 1: Sk. 110 showing skulls from earlier burials placed either side of the head and long bones around foot end of grave (½ metre scale)

Fig. 56 Site 1: Sk. 68 showing hands crossed on the chest (½ metre scale)

Fig. 57 Site 1: Sk. 125 showing 'ledge' in head-niche burial (½ metre scale)

Fig. 58 Site 1: Sk. 142 showing the remains of the pewter chalice resting on the abdomen (½ metre scale)

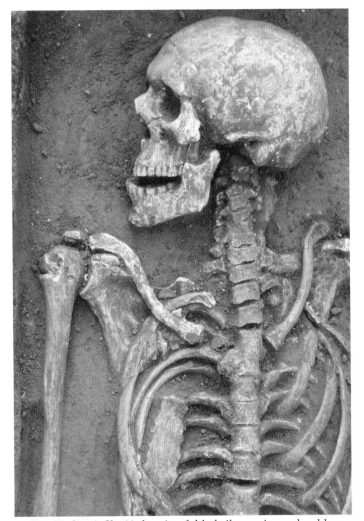

Fig. 59 Site 1: Sk. 64 showing folded silver coin on shoulder

Fig. 60 Site 1: Sk. 74 child burial on lead sheet (½ metre scale)

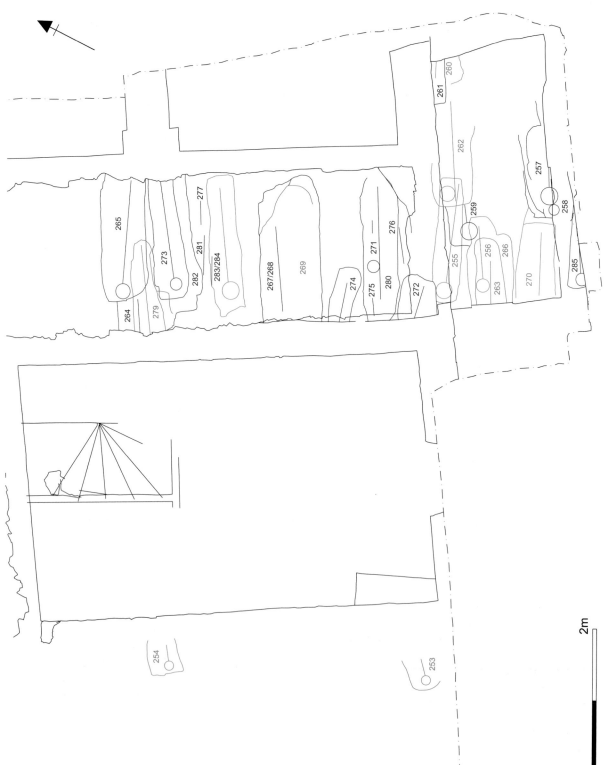

Fig. 61 Site 2: plan showing all burials and burial types identified by skeleton number

Burial Practice

A total of 244 skeletons form the basis of the following analyses and a detailed breakdown of their state of preservation, their stratigraphical relationship to each other, the finds from within their grave fills, the possible date of burial and the age and sex of the individual are given in Table 1. Most skeletons were not intact, subsequent burials and later disturbances having removed parts of the skeletons to varying degrees; in some cases only fragments of the skeleton remained, in others the majority of the skeleton survived with perhaps only the skull, feet or an arm missing. Thus any grouping by burial type or position cannot be precise and this must be taken into account when considering the following statistics.

Cemetery Layout, Burial Alignments and General Comments (Figs. 51 to 54, pages 87 to 90)

All the burials were facing east and were roughly aligned east/west. The majority of the graves followed the main axis of the priory church, rather than a true east/west orientation. However, some were skewed markedly to the general alignment, almost certainly due to careless digging of the graves rather than for any practical or religious reason.

The relative shallowness of the graves may seem surprising, some lying almost immediately below the present ground surface, even taking into account that the topsoil overlying the cemetery had obviously been reduced in level before the development of the area for housing in the mid 18th century and during the construction of the NFU building. However, the minimal depth of early medieval burials generally is well recorded. Late Saxon graves cut from a ground-surface excavated at the Holy Trinity Priory site in London were generally only 0.4m deep, adult burials in the late Saxon cemetery at Raunds averaged 0.44m in depth and graves in the medieval cemetery at Winchester Cathedral were only up to 1m deep (White 1988, 26 in note 7).

There was a marked concentration of burials near the east end of the priory church, although not immediately against its east wall, where several graves had been dug on a number of occasions on almost the same spot resulting in the disturbance of the earlier burials (Fig. 55, page 91). The heavy use of this part of the cemetery is to be expected on religious grounds as there was a desire to be buried as close as possible to the most sacred position within the church, the high altar. The area directly adjacent to the east end of the church may have been reserved for special use. There was a noticeable thinning out in the concentration of graves in the eastern portion of the cemetery and one area, a band running east/west to the north of burials Sk. 11, 18 and 24 where there were no graves, possibly marked the location of a pathway through the burial ground.

Within the apparent jumbled mass of graves the excavation plan of the cemetery appears to show that there were a number of north/south rows of burials. The layout of these rows seems to have been generally maintained throughout the life of the cemetery, although the positions of the graves within them wandered somewhat from the line of each row. This orderly layout suggests the use of a plan of the grave plots or some form of grave marker, although no archaeological trace of the latter was found. It does seem to show the controlled use of the cemetery over a long period of time.

While a number of different types of burial were present in the cemetery, the bodies, with one exception, were interred in a supine position. The only difference in the posture of the bodies were the positions of the arms and hands. The arms and hands were generally either placed crossed on the chest, abdomen or pelvis or laid straight beside the body. A number of combinations of these positions were observed with one hand on the pelvis, the other on the abdomen, and so on. There seems to be no particular reason for the different placing of the hands although an analysis shows that the majority had their hands crossed on their pelvis, followed by those with hands crossed on the abdomen. The sex or type of burial appears to be largely irrelevant to the positioning of the hands and arms, except in the case of those bodies with their hands crossed on their chest, as if in prayer, as they were exclusively male (Fig. 56, page 91). Similar observations concerning the position of the hands and arms of burials was noted at the cemetery of the Dominican Friary in Chester. There, the majority had their arms crossed on the pelvic region and there appeared to be no particular correspondence between position and date of burial or between position and sex (Ward 1990, 124). At Hull, a small number of burials in the area of the chancel, who were probably the priors of the Augustinian Friary, were buried with their hands on their chests (Daniell 1997, 118), seemingly confirming the religious and/or status significance of such a posture.

There was evidence for the reburial of the bones from earlier burials which had been disturbed by later graves. The long and other bones had generally been thrown back haphazardly in the fill of the later grave but the skulls were treated with some reverence and were often placed close to and, in one case, on either side of the head of the later burial (e.g. Sk. 110; Fig. 55, page 91).

Burial Types

Five distinct burial types were recognised. Each type and its occurrence within the burial ground is discussed below and listed in Table 1. Those burials which had some of the attributes of Type 1 burials but could not be ascribed to that category with certainty are given the sub-type 1A. The typology of forty-one burials could not be identified and these are recorded as an additional Type 6.

Type 1 – Head-niche Burials:

This type of grave has an anthropomorphic shape with a cut-out for the head, and from the shoulders a taper towards the feet, while the foot end is generally rounded. On the few occasions where a reasonable depth of grave-cut remained, it was noted that the grave was rectangular until it reached the natural sandstone bedrock and it was only at that point that it assumed the head-niche shape (*e.g.* Sk. 125; Fig. 57, page 92).

Head-niche burials have been recorded during the excavation of medieval cemeteries elsewhere. Seven were noted at Rivenhall where the vogue for this kind of burial was considered to date to the late 12th or early 13th centuries (Rodwell and Rodwell 1985, 101). Amongst the burials from Lewes Priory, cists with head-niches were the predominant type during the late 11th to 14th centuries (Lyne 1997, 74). At Wells Cathedral five head-niche graves were found in the Anglo-Saxon cemetery and were considered to have been more prestigious than other burials and perhaps associated with a distinct social class, one of the graves being lined with plaster and covered with a stone slab (Rodwell 2001, 65–68). In Bristol, a head-niche burial was found during the excavation of the church of St. Augustine the Less where it was sealed by 12th-century church foundations (Boore 1986, 211).

Head-niche burials were generally distributed throughout the cemetery, although there appear to have been concentrations in the southern part of the area excavated and in the north-west portion of the cemetery. This may indicate grouping around the east ends of the Lady Chapel and the priory church.

There were 59 cases of head-niche burials recognised which represent 24% of the total burials excavated. Of the burials which could be sexed there were 27 male (79%) and 7 female (21%) giving a ratio of 4 males to 1 female. Of the burials within this category which could be aged there were 57 adults, one juvenile and one child aged 10 to 15 years. The location of female and child burials show no concentration and were evenly distributed throughout the cemetery.

Within the general classification of head-niche burial a number of variations were noted in the mode of burial. Sk. 77, which was of a male aged 35 to 45 years, was in a grave cut considerably wider than normal. Sk. 156 had a pebble (SF 468B) near its jaw. Sk. 178, of a male aged 30 to 40, was lying in a posture suggesting the body had probably been tightly bound before burial. Another burial, Sk. 185, also appeared to have been tightly bound and the grave had been filled with clay, with a layer of mortar-like material at its base (see Burial Type 3). Sk. 205 had two upright stones against one edge of the grave cut.

Sherds of pottery were found in eight of the graves and these range in date from Romano-British to the early 13th century, with the majority being of the 12th century. One sherd from Sk. 178 dates to the mid 13th to the mid 14th centuries but may represent a possible contamination.

Other finds from these graves were lumps of iron slag from Sks. 19 and 46. A pewter object (SF 300B) on the abdomen of Sk. 142, a male aged 45+ years, was found on x-ray to be a chalice (Fig. 58, page 92).

Some coffin nails were ascribed to the fills of head-niche graves during excavation. Examination of the excavation archive shows that these were almost certainly contamination from later Type 2 coffin burials which had cut the head-niche graves, although it is just possible that they may indicate the presence of a wooden lid over the grave, the edges of which could have rested on the recessed sides. That was the interpretation put on nails found in some of the head-niche cist graves from Lewes Priory where the impression of a wooden lid was also found preserved in a layer of mortar covering one of the graves (Lyne 1997, 74–75).

Type 1A – Possible Head-niche Burials:

This classification has been ascribed where the most obvious diagnostic attribute of head-niche burials, a cut-out for the head, had been destroyed by later burials or disturbances but the remaining part of the grave cut exhibited features typical of head-niche burials, such as a tapering foot.

There were 32 Type 1A burials which represent 13% of the total burials excavated. Of the burials which could be sexed there were eight male (25%) and two female (6%) which, as with the Type 1 burials, gives a ratio of 4 males to 1 female. Due to the definition of possible head-niche burials, *i.e.* generally only the lower tapering end of the burials survived, over 50% of the burials could not be sexed.

Of those which could be aged, 26 were adults and there were five children (one juvenile, one aged 5 to 6 years, one aged 8 to 10 years, one aged 12 to 15 years and one aged 12 to 18 years).

Within this general classification a number of variations in the mode of burial were noted. Sk. 48 had a stone against the right side of the skull, Sk. 49 was in an abnormally wide grave, while the grave for Sk. 177 had been filled with clay (see also Burial Type 3).

One grave fill produced pottery and this was Romano-British in date, while a fragment of glass came from the fill of Sk. 106.

Type 2 – Coffin Burials:

Here the grave was rectangular or sub-rectangular in shape, sometimes with rounded corners. In order to be classified as a coffin burial the grave fill had to contain at least one iron coffin nail.

The coffin nails were generally jumbled in the grave fill, although in some cases their location at the bottom of the grave gave an indication of the position of the coffin. The coffins would all have been made of timber although generally no trace of this was found, except in the cases of Sk. 42 within the church where the outline stain of the coffin could be seen and four graves in the cemetery (Sks. 47, 112, 152 and 172) which contained fragments of wood.

There were 86 coffin burials which represent 35% of the total burials excavated. Of the burials which could be sexed 46 (81%) were male and 11 (19%) were female which gives a ratio of 4 males to 1 female. Of the burials in this category which could be aged, 73 were adults and there were 13 children ranging in age from 10 months to 15 years.

The coffin burials, and the female and child burials within this category, were relatively evenly distributed throughout the cemetery.

There were a number of variations to the straight forward coffin burial. Skeletons 34, 35 and 36 appeared to have been buried side by side in one large grave, Sk. 56 was lying on its right side, Sk. 118 had a stone by the right side of its skull and Sk. 214 was in an exceptionally wide grave.

The grave fills of 25 of the coffin burials produced sherds of pottery and floor and roof tiles ranging in date from Romano-British to the early 14th century. The majority of the grave fills contained pottery no later than early 13th-century in date.

A number of the grave fills contained pieces of folded lead associated with the skeletons (Sks. 42, 60 (see Chapter 6, Fig. 82.149), 159, 171 and 224) and in some cases this had been pierced by an iron nail (Sks. 43, 55 and 221) or contained rivets (Sk. 159).

Other finds consisted of a copper alloy pin (Sk. 101, SF 453B), a coiled length of copper alloy (Sk. 221, SF 388B) and fragments of a possible shale bracelet (Sk. 162, SF 607B). One burial, that of a male aged between 30 and 40 years (Sk. 64), contained two silver coins folded in half, one on each shoulder of the skeleton (SFs 193B and 194B) (Fig. 59, page 93). These were both short-cross pennies and one was certainly of Richard I and could therefore be dated between 1189 and 1199. Under the lower jaw of the same skeleton was a jet pendant inscribed with a simple cross and other symbols (SF 232B; see Chapter 6, Fig. 85.160). One burial (Sk. 224) had a pewter object (SF 389B) lying on its abdomen. This was in a poor condition but was probably a chalice.

Type 3 – Clay Filled Burials:
Four graves were filled with clay (Sks. 177, 185, 213 and 233) and one of these (Sk. 185) had a mortar-like material lining its base and the skeleton appeared to have been tightly bound before burial. One burial was in a head-niche grave (Sk. 185) while another was in a possible head-niche grave (Sk. 177).

Type 4 – Simple Burials:
The absence of coffin nails from grave fills does not necessarily imply that the burial was not in a wooden coffin. At the excavation at St Peter's Church, Barton-upon-Humber, the surviving coffins were secured with wooden pegs and very few of the Barton coffins antedating the 17th century employed a full complement of nails in their construction, although a few nails were employed to strengthen the joints between the sides and base. The coffin timbers were generally held with pegs and dowels, and where used nails were found to be subordinate and supplementary (Rodwell and Rodwell 1982, 301). A similar absence of coffin nails was noted at St Andrew Fishergate, York and in the cemetery of the 11th- to 12th-century church of St Benet, York where coffins were frequently of all wood construction and pegged rather than nailed together (Stroud and Kemp 1993, 153). For reasons of clarity, those graves from St James that did not have coffin nails in their fills but were rectangular or sub-rectangular in shape and therefore might have contained coffins have been classified separately as 'simple burials'. It is possible that these graves contained burials within shrouds, although no shroud pins were found in any of the grave fills.

There were 26 cases of simple burials which represent 11% of the total burials excavated. Of those that could be sexed, 12 (46%) were male, eight (31%) were female and six were unsexed, including a child aged between 10 and 12 years.

Within this classification the only slightly different mode of burial was where one body had its skull propped by a stone (Sk. 100) and where a skull rested on a stone (Sk. 204).

Seven grave fills produced pottery and tile sherds ranging in date from Romano-British to post-1400.

One skeleton of a male aged 45+ years (Sk. 142) had a pewter chalice (SF 300B) resting on its abdomen, while another (Sk. 167) had a fragment of glass in the grave fill (SF 562B).

Type 5 – Burial Laid on a Lead Sheet:
In one case the disarticulated bones of a child aged between 1 and 4 months (Sk. 74) had been laid on a fragment of lead sheet (SF 361B) (Fig. 60, page 93). It is possible that this burial had been cut by a later burial (Sk. 55) and the disarticulated bones reinterred after being gathered together and placed on the lead sheet.

Type 6 – Burials of Uncertain Type:
These are burials which could not be ascribed to Types 1 to 5, usually due to the shape of their grave cuts having been badly disturbed by later graves or other intrusions such as walls or drains.

There were 41 Type 6 burials, which represent 17% of the total burials excavated. Of those which could be sexed there were eight male and one female although due to the nature of this type of burial, which were generally fragmentary and badly disturbed, the majority could not be sexed. Amongst the burials were one foetus and five children ranging in age between 3 months and 8 years.

Four grave fills produced pottery and tile sherds ranging in date from the mid 12th to the early 13th centuries.

The fill of grave Sk. 121 contained two fragments of an unidentifiable copper alloy object (SF 320B and SF 353B) while the fill of Sk. 31 produced a copper alloy lace end (SF 80B) and a fragment of an iron object (SF 78B).

Discussion

The excavations have shown that there was an extensive cemetery to the east of the priory church, of which only the western and the northern boundaries have been defined. The burials appear to have been laid out in north/south rows although these had not always been respected. There was a concentration of graves in the area close to the east end of the priory church with a 'thinning out' of the graves further east.

The burials all belonged to the Period 2 use of the site, that is during the period of occupation of St James's Priory, extending from c.1129 to the Dissolution of the priory in 1540. The archaeological evidence for the date of the burials is limited to the type of burial, the presence of residual sherds of pottery within the backfill of the graves, the one occurrence of datable finds directly associated with a skeleton, and the relative position of the grave within the burial sequence. A radiocarbon date was obtained from one of the head-niche burials (Sk. 46).

The Romano-British pottery in the grave fills is residual and presumably derives from the Romano-British site known to be situated to the north-west, on the west side of Upper Maudlin Street (see Chapter 1).

The head-niche burials produced pottery dating mainly from the 12th through to the early 13th centuries, corresponding with the suggested date range for this type of grave at Rivenhall where they were dated by pottery in the grave fills to the late 12th/early 13th centuries. In every case where a relationship could be observed, head-niche burials were either cut by other head-niche burials or by Burial Types 2 to 6, indicating that the head-niche burials were the earliest in the cemetery. In no case were burials found to underlie the priory church so it seems certain that the head-niche burials post-date the foundation of the priory. The early date of the head-niche burials is supported by the result of a radiocarbon test on one of them (Sk. 46) carried out during the archaeological evaluation of the site. The work was undertaken by the Department of Scientific Research in the British Museum under their reference BM-2931. The calibrated result gave a 68% probability that the true date lay in the range AD 1050 to 1085 (15% probability) or AD 1120 to 1225 (53% probability). Their full report is held in the site archive.

The grave fills of Burial Types 2 to 6 produced pottery dating generally from the 13th century to post-1400. One individual, in a coffin burial, had been interred with two folded silver coins, one certainly minted during the period 1189 to 1199, showing a possible contemporary use of both head-niche and coffin type burials. Nevertheless it seems that the coffin and other types of burial generally post-date the head-niche burials and carried on through until the early 15th century. Such a transition from head-niche burials to coffin burials has been observed at Wells Cathedral, although there the head-niche generally formed part of cist (Rodwell 2001).

Apart from one grave containing 16th-century pottery, which was probably a contamination as the burial was very close to the surface, there is no archaeological evidence for the excavated portion of the cemetery continuing in use after the early 15th century.

A number of burials provided evidence of special burial practices or rituals.

Four clay filled graves (Burial Type 3) were found grouped in the north-west corner of the cemetery. At St Peter's Church, Barton-upon-Humber, one Saxo-Norman coffin burial was found to be completely filled with a stiff clay. It was considered that the clay had been poured into the coffin as a viscous liquid which had enveloped the corpse, and may have been intended to contain a dangerous disease (Rodwell and Rodwell 1982, 302). It is assumed that the clay in the graves at St James was intended to serve a similar function and it may be significant that these four graves were grouped together on the edge of the cemetery.

A few burials had stones set on one or both sides of the skull and, in one case at least, a stone seemed to have been placed under the skull in the form of a 'pillow'. The use of pillow or packing stones in graves has been recorded elsewhere. Their earliest appearance is in late 'pagan' Saxon cemeteries, a late Saxon cemetery in Norwich having burials where flints had been frequently used to support the skull as a pillow, and there were also occasional flints on either side of skulls (Ayers 1985, 19). Twenty-eight burials at St Oswald's Priory in Gloucester, including some coffin burials, had support stones placed on either side of the head, although they represented a minority burial rite dating from the late 10th century through to c.1230 (Heighway and Bryant 1999, 205). At St James's Priory there is evidence for the use of a packing stone inside a wooden coffin (Sk. 118). Cobbles holding the skull in position occurred at Barton-upon-Humber and according to the Rodwells (1982, 158) are apparently commonly found on other sites of 11th- to 12th-century date, their use fading out after the 13th century (Ayers 1985, 22). The standard archaeological explanation for these stones is that they kept the face up-right, so that on Judgement Day, when the body rose from the grave, the resurrected body would be looking east at the risen Christ. More recently Daniell

(1997, 7) has suggested that the inclusion of stones close to the head in a grave may well be a symbol of penance. When Henry, the eldest son of Henry II lay dying he was laid on sack-cloth and ashes, but also had stones placed under his head and feet, and the noose of a condemned criminal around his neck, in an extreme form of penance.

One burial of a male aged between 30 and 40 years (Sk. 64), had two silver coins placed in the region of each shoulder. These had been deliberately folded tightly in half and must have had some religious or symbolic significance. It has been noted elsewhere that there was a curious custom that seems to have derived from the ancient pagan practice of 'killing' an object to be devoted. Apparently, to the accompaniment of a prayer calling on the saint for help, a coin was bent above a sick person, usually by doubling it over across the middle. Silver pennies were most commonly used for this purpose (Merrifield 1987, 91). Daniell (1997, 151) has noted that there was a continuation of the practice of bending, folding or breaking objects throughout the Middle Ages to signify death, even though they were not always placed in graves. The same body which was associated with the folded coins also had a jet pendant around its neck. This took the form of a small, irregularly shaped piece of jet which was itself a piece of a larger object which had originally been decorated with incised dot and ring motifs and a number of incised lines extending around its edge. The top of this fragment had then been cut to provide a terminal to accommodate a suspension cord. A crude cross and four pi-like symbols were incised on one face of the pendant (see Chapter 6, Fig. 85.160). It is tempting to suggest that this pendant had been personally fashioned by its owner and that its association with the two folded coins may indicate that this was the grave of a particularly religious and penitent member of the monastic community.

Three burials contained lead alloy objects, one certainly a chalice and the others either chalices or pattens. These were associated with the skeletons of two males aged 45+ years and one male aged 50+ years. The most common status and belief symbol to be buried in graves was that of the priest's chalice and/or patten. They are found on many sites around the country, such as Wells Cathedral (Rodwell 2001, 523–529) and St Andrew Fishergate, York where one burial was found holding a lead chalice, whilst another held a lead patten (Stroud and Kemp 1993, 156–7). The role of the chalice or patten in the grave is not clear. In some instances they may have held consecrated wine or bread but it is now considered that they were not only a symbol of priestly office, but that the chalice symbolised Christ's tomb and the patten the stone before it (Daniell 1997, 169–70). In the 12th and 13th centuries various ordinances made a distinction between chalices made of precious metals to hold the consecrated wine, and those of base metal,

such as tin, pewter or lead, to bury with the priest (Daniell 1997, 170).

A number of graves contained small pieces of folded lead but these may have been residual material which went into the graves when they were backfilled and consequently have no particular significance. However, one burial of a woman aged between 25 and 35 years (Sk. 60) had a lead 'package' lying on its abdomen (see Chapter 6, Fig. 82.149). This was made out of a small sheet of lead which had been deliberately cut to enable it to be tightly folded into a rectangular container (SF 283B). On opening this package in the conservation laboratory it was found to contain a granular material, thought to be parchment.

It might be considered surprising that a monastic cemetery contained the burials of women and children in addition to the exclusively male members of the religious community. The majority of the skeletons were male but, amongst those that could be sexed, there was a ratio of one female to every three male burials. The monastic cemetery at St James is not unusual in containing female burials. That at Broseley Abbey in Shropshire had 56 burials which could be sexed and amongst them were three possible females and five children (Hirst and Wright 1989, 307). Some research has been carried out into the practice of burial within the precincts of Cistercian monasteries. The burial of lay-folk in Cistercian precincts, save for certain exceptions, was not sanctioned until 1217. Early injunctions of the Order only allowed sovereigns, prelates, founders, guests and hired workers dying within a monastery to be buried in its precincts. This policy was changed in 1217 to take account of what was by then a prevalent and lucrative practice; henceforth burial of seculars was permitted if their parish priest agreed (Williams 1991, 104–106). It is known that married servants lived within monastic precincts, that women were treated in the lay infirmary and that women worked within the precincts. In 1349 at Newnham there were only twenty monks and three novices in residence, but in addition the community comprised 88 layfolk of both sexes living within the walls (Williams 1991, 115–116). It seems most likely therefore that the female and child burials in the monastic cemetery of St James were those of benefactors of the priory, servants working in the priory, the relatives of benefactors and servants, or those who had died in the priory infirmary.

The Archaeology of the Lay/Parish Burial Ground (Sites 2 and 3)

Site 2: Adjacent to the West Front of the Church

The Condition of the Human Remains

While the state of preservation of the human bones

was good, only six of the 33 burials were undisturbed. The majority had been cut by the digging of sub-sequent graves within the cemetery and the con-struction of buildings during the medieval and post-medieval periods. The cellars below the 18th-century buildings had removed all the burials in those areas so that the majority of the surviving burials lay in a 2m wide strip between the cellars of nos. 13 and 14 St James's Parade and in the small area to the south of no. 13 St James's Parade.

The Cemetery Boundaries

The priory church had been built on a ridge of rock from which the ground sloped down towards the River Frome to the south. The bedrock was found just below the modern ground surface along the northern edge of the excavation and there were no graves in that area: either the presence of bedrock close the the surface prevented the excavation of graves or there had been a deliberate policy to keep the approach to the west front of the church free of burials. At an early date an east/west wall had been built which probably represented the northern boundary of the burial ground (see Chapter 4, Period 2A). The burials commenced some 1.6m south of the northern edge of the excavation and between there and the southern limit of the excavation the burial ground had been intensively used, the burials continuing outside the excavation to the south (Fig. 61, page 94). Figure 62 also shows the complex relationship between burials at just one level during the excavation of the burial ground.

The relationship between the church and the burials could not be determined as excavation did not take place within 2m of the standing walls of the church. However, to the west the extent of the cemetery was apparently restricted by the construction of a building in the late 13th century (see Chapter 4, Period 2B) although one coffin burial, Sk. 254, was found below the building and must pre-date it. A head-niche burial, Sk. 253, was situated just to the south of the building and, again, might pre-date its construction.

Burial Practice

The small number of burials recovered and their generally disturbed state prevented a detailed analysis of burial practice but some general comments can be made. A total of 33 skeletons form the basis of the following analyses and a detailed breakdown of their state of preservation, their stratigraphical relationship to each other, the finds from within their grave fills, the possible date of burial and the age and sex of the individual are given in Table 2.

All the burials were facing east and were roughly aligned east/west, although the graves appeared to follow the main axis of the priory church, rather than a true east/west orientation. The burials appeared to have been laid out next to each other in overlapping rows, with the east ends of some graves lying adjacent to the west ends of others. This could have been the originally intended layout of the cemetery or it might imply that the original burial plan of the cemetery had to be adapted due to overcrowding, with the insertion of later graves in the generous gaps left between earlier ones. However, some graves did not seem to have been laid out in any order or with respect for earlier graves and Sks. 256, 259, 260, 262 and 263 overlap along their lengths forming a continuous line of burials.

As at Site 1, all the bodies were interred in a supine position, the only difference between the postures of the bodies being the positions of the arms and hands. Where this could be determined there were three examples of the hands being crossed on the pelvis and one example each of the hands being laid across the abdomen or laid straight down by their sides. There were no bodies where the hands had been crossed on the chest as if in prayer, unlike the monastic cemetery (Site 1) where there were a number of examples, giving weight to the theory that the posture was reserved exclusively for members of the religious community.

The burials have been classified by the typology accorded to the burials found on Site 1 and described above.

Type 1 – Head-niche Burials:

Two examples of head-niche burials were recognised. One of these, Sk. 253, contained the body of a female aged 45+ years while the other, Sk. 269, held the body of a male again aged 45+ years.

No dating evidence was found in the graves. Sk. 253 had been cut by wall 71w of the 18th-century building (see Chapter 4, Period 4B). Sk. 269 had been cut by a later, undated, grave.

Type 1A – Possible Head-niche Burials:

There were three examples of possible head-niche burials. All of them contained the bodies of adults but the sex of only one could be determined and that was a female.

No dating evidence was found in the graves. However, they had all been cut by later graves and only one, Sk. 263, cut an earlier grave and that was another possible head-niche burial, Sk. 266.

Type 2 – Coffin Burials:

There were seven examples of coffin burials. The sex of the burials could only be determined in three cases of which two were female and one was male. Of the burials which could be aged, one was of a baby aged three to four weeks, another was of an infant aged 18 months to three years and the remaining five were adults under the age of 35 years.

Four of the coffin burials (Sks. 255, 260, 262 and 278) produced pottery ranging in date from the late 13th to the mid 14th centuries. One burial, Sk. 254, lay below the late 13th-century building and must pre-date it.

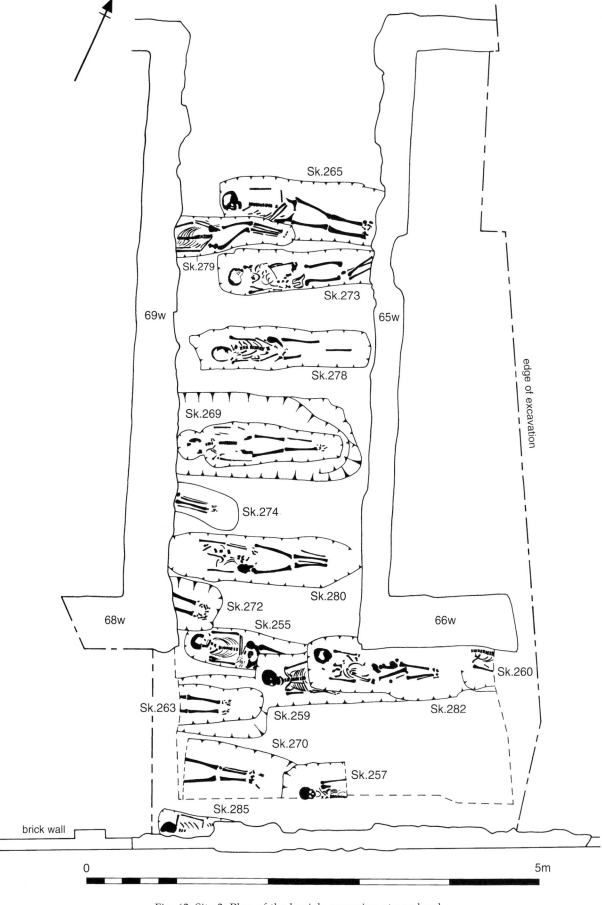

Fig. 62 Site 2: Plan of the burials occurring at one level

Table 2 Site 2: Analysis of burials from the lay/parish cemetery

Skeleton (Sk.) No.	Context Nos. Fill/Cut	Type of Burial	Sex: 1=M 2=F 0=?	Age	Disturbed Yes/No	Relationship to other Contexts	Finds	Small Find No.	Date of Finds, etc
253	123w/356w	1	2	45+	Y	Under 122w Cut by 71w			
254	273w/274w	2	0	18M-3YR	Y	Under 264w, 282w	Lead strip 2 coffin nails	SF 146C SF 145C	
255	292w/293w	2	1	25-30	N	Under 261w, 276w Cut by 330w (Sk. 272), 309w (Sk. 259)	Pottery Coffin nail Coffin nail Lead strip Lead strip	SF 123C SF 143C SF 138C SF 142C	early 14th century
256	299w/300w	2	0	3-4	N	Over 307w (Sk. 262), 309w (Sk. 259), 317w (Sk. 263), 317w (Sk. 266)	7 coffin nails	SF 154C	
257	303w/302w	6	1	45+	Y	Cut by 298w Cuts 306w (Sk. 258), 328w (Sk. 270)	Pottery		late 12th century
258	305w/306w	6	2	33-45	Y	Cut by 302w (Sk. 257)			
259	310w/309w	4	2	33-45	Y	Cut by 293w (Sk. 255), 308w (Sk. 262)			
260	312w/311w	2	0	A	Y	Cut by 66w, ?307w Cuts 313w (Sk. 261)	Pottery Coffin nail 7 coffin nails	SF 153C SF 156C	late 13th century
261	313w	6	0	A		Under 295w Cut by 66w, 308w (Sk. 262), 318w (Sk. 260)			
262	308w/307w	2	1	25-35	Y	Cuts 310w (Sk. 259), 313w (Sk. 261)	Pottery 6 coffin nails	SF 155C	late 13th/ early 14th century
263	316w/317w	1A	0	A	Y	Cut by 301w Cuts 319w (Sk. 266)			
264	318w/325w	6	0	A	Y	Under 295w Cut by 65w, 69w, 324w (Sk. 265) Cuts 355w (Sk. 279) Over 341w, 348w (Sk. 282), 350w	Pottery 3 coffin nails 15 coffin nails	SF 124C SF 158C	early 14th century
265	318w/324w	4	1	45+	Y	Cut by 65w Cuts 335w (Sk. 279), 325w (Sk. 264) Under 333w (Sk. 273)	see Sk. 264		see Sk. 264
266	319w/317w	1A	0	A	Only legs excavated	Under 300w (Sk. 256), 309w (Sk. 259) Cut by 316w (Sk. 263)			
267	323w/326w (Grave cuts for Sks. 267 & 268 indistinguish-able)	6	0	9M-1YR	Y	Under 295w Cuts 327w (Sk. 269)			
268	323w/326w (See Sk. 267)	6	1	A	Y	Cut by 69w Cuts 327w (Sk. 269)			
269	323w/327w	1	1	45+	N	Cut by 69w, 326w (Sk. 267), 326w (Sk. 268)			
270	322w/328w	2	0	A	Y	Cut by 298w, 301w, 302w (Sk. 257)	10 coffin nails	SF 151C	
271	331w/332w	6	1	33-45	Y	Under 295w Cut by 65w			
272	329w/330w	6	0	A	Y	Under 295w Cut by 69w Cuts 293w (Sk. 255)	Pottery		early 14th century
273	318w/333w	4	2	45+	Y	Under 295w Cut by 65w, 69w Over 335w (Sk. 279), 341w, 348w (Sk. 282), 350w, 324w (Sk. 265)			
274	336w/351w	6	0	A	Y	Under 295w Cut by 65w, 69w, 315w			

Table 2 Site 2: Analysis of burials from the lay/parish cemetery. Continued from opposite

275	336w/351w (Grave fills for Sks. 275, 276 & 280 indistinguishable)	6	0	Infant	Y				
276	336w/352w (See Sk. 275)	6	0	Neonate	Y	Cut by 315w, ?335w (Sk. 280)			
277	337w/338w	6	0	Neonate	Y	Under 295w Over 350w	Pottery		1120-1160s
278	339w/340w	2	2	25-35	N	Under 295w Cuts 344w (Sk. 281), 346w (Sk. 283)	Pottery 5 coffin nails 6 coffin nails	SF 125C SF 157C	?1300-1350
279	334w/335w	1A	2	A	Y	Under 333w (Sk. 273) Cut by 69w, 325w (Sk. 264			
280	336w/353w (See Sk. 275)	6	1	25-35	N	Cut by 65w, 69w Cuts ?352w (Sk. 276)	See Sk. 275	See Sk. 275	
281	343w/344w	6	0	25+	N	Under 295w Cut by 340w (Sk. 278) Cuts 346w (Sk. 283)			
282	347w/348w	6	0	Infant	Y	Under 295w, 318w (Sks. 264 & 265), 333w (Sk. 273)			
283	345w/346w (Grave cuts for Sks. 283 & 284 indistinguishable)	6	0	Infant	Y	Under 295w Cut by 340w (Sk. 278), 344w (Sk. 281), 326w (Sk. 268)	5 coffin nails (unclear which grave contained coffin nails)	SF 127C	
284	345w/346w (See Sk. 283)	6	0	Neonate	Y	Under 295w Cut by 340w (Sk. 278), 344w (Sk. 281)	See Sk. 283	See Sk. 283	
285	358w/359w	6	2	45+	Only partially excavated.	Noted in watching brief to south of main area of excavation.			

Two of the burials (Sks. 254 and 255) contained small strips of lead of unknown purpose.

Type 4 – Simple Burials:
There were three examples of simple burials. Two contained the bodies of adult females and one the body of an adult male. None of the burials contained dating evidence.

Type 5 – Burials of Uncertain Type:
The remaining 18 burials could not be classified. They contained 11 adults, three infants, one child aged between nine months and one year, and three neonates. Of the burials which could be sexed there were four males and two females.

Four of the graves produced pottery sherds ranging in date from the early/mid 12th century to the early 14th century.

Site 3: St James's Place

Introduction

The following information on the watching brief is taken from a client report prepared by Rod Burchill who carried out the work (BaRAS 1998). The site archive has been deposited with the Bristol City Museum and Art Gallery under accession number CMAG.1997.0041.

In the late summer of 1997, Bristol and Region Archaeological Services were commissioned by the Planning, Transport and Development Directorate of Bristol City Council to monitor contractor's groundworks associated with the construction of a new road layout and 'gateway' to Bristol's Broadmead shopping centre, known as St James's Place (Fig. 1; NGR ST 58967338). The site lay immediately south-west of a group of burials recovered in 1954 by Edward Mason (1957, 164–171) during the construction of the nearby department store (see Chapter 2).

Articulated human remains were exposed in three trenches cut by contractors for the foundations of boundary walls and a large ornamental structure. The skeletal material recovered comprised six articulated skeletons with a minimum of five other individuals represented by disarticulated bone. Five of the six articulated burials were removed after recording as they would have been destroyed by the foundations while the sixth burial (Sk. 288) lay a little below the contractor's foundation level and was left *in situ*.

State of Preservation of the Material

The bone was fairly well preserved although none of

the skeletons was complete; parts of the skeleton either lay beyond the excavated area or were truncated by later burials. The depth of the burials, some 0.5 to 0.7m below modern ground level, gave no indication of their original levels since it was obvious that the land surface had been considerably reduced by 19th-century and later development.

Burial Practice

All the burials were orientated east/west with their heads to the west. Grave cuts could not be detected and no burial sequence could be established, save that Sk. 288 lay immediately below Sk. 287. The bodies had been laid on their backs with the exception of Sk. 289 which appeared to have been interred face down. In only two cases could the positions of the hands be determined: Sk. 287 had its hands crossed at the pelvis and Sk. 291 had its arms folded across the abdomen. No remains of coffins or coffin furniture were found and the burials were mostly resting on the surface of the bedrock at between 8.59 to 9.2m above Ordnance Datum. Details of the burials are given in Table 3.

Dating

A sample from Sk. 289 was submitted to the University of Waikato in New Zealand for radiocarbon dating (laboratory code Wk 6139). This produced a conventional age result of 560± BP. The date has been calibrated to a two sigma age range (95% confidence) which has produced a date of AD 1290–1440. This compares well with the 14th-century date ascribed to the only burial from Mason's 1954 excavation which contained dating evidence in the form of two copper-alloy buckles.

Burials from Sites 2 and 3: Discussion

The excavations have shown that the area outside the west front of the church was probably kept clear of burials during the medieval period, an east/west boundary wall being used to define the northern limit of the lay burial ground. However, just to the south of the boundary wall, in the area closest to the church, the area had been intensively used for burials. There was evidence of order to the burial ground with graves in overlapping rows although others were laid out in a seemingly haphazard fashion.

Of the bodies that could be sexed from Site 2 there was an overall male to female ratio of 1:1 which is in keeping with the use of the area as a lay burial ground. This contrasts well with the overall male to female ratio of 3:1 from the monastic burial ground excavated on Site 1.

A number of grave fills contained residual sherds of pottery which date from the late 12th to the early 14th centuries and it seems likely that the burials close to the church at Site 2 ceased after the 14th century. It is not known why burials stopped but it was probably realised that the area had been too intensively used and there was no more space available. By that time the parish burial ground, covering a large area to the south of the church, was in use (see Chapter 2).

The 300 or so burials found in 1954 came from part of the parish burial ground, as did the six burials found during the watching brief on Site 3 in 1997. Those found in 1954 were laid out in parallel rows with a distance of about 1.2m or less between the bodies and the excavator noted the posture of the bodies: generally they had their arms crossed over the chest with the hands resting on opposite shoulders, although in a number of cases only one arm crossed the chest, the other lying horizontally across the abdomen. Interments in that part of the parish burial ground at least had been carried out in an orderly fashion implying that the graves had some kind of marker and/or that a plan of the graves was being kept.

The only dating evidence for the burials so far recovered from the parish burial ground comes from a pair of 14th-century buckles found in one grave in 1954 and a radiocarbon date of AD 1290–1440 from Sk. 288 found in 1997. It does seem likely that use of this part of the parish burial ground was restricted to

Table 3 Site 3: Analysis of burials from the lay/parish cemetery

Skeleton (Sk.) No.	Context Nos. Fill/Cut	Type of Burial	Sex: 1=M 2=F 0=?	Age	Position/ Special Features	Disturbed Yes/No	Relationship to other Contexts	Finds	Small Find No.	Date of Finds, etc
286		4	1	A		N				
287		4	1	A	Hands across pelvis	N	Over Sk. 288			
288		4			Not removed, left *in situ*	N	Under Sk. 287			
289		4	1	A	Interred face down	N				Radiocarbon date AD 1290–1440
290		4	1	25-35		N				
291		4	2	25-35	Arms across abdomen	N				

the medieval period and that no post-medieval interments took place there.

Analysis of the Human Bone from Sites 1 and 2 by Dr Louise Loe

Introduction

In total, 285 grave cuts were excavated from the burial grounds situated at the east and west ends of the priory church of St James (Sites 1 and 2). From these 278 skeletons were recovered and these were examined and reported on between 1995 and 1996. This is in addition to a quantity of disarticulated human bone excavated from various contexts, from both sites. This will be discussed in a separate section.

While excavation was in progress, the author was present to make observations on the skeletons *in situ*. In this way, the amount of information that is inevitably lost when lifting, washing, and packing human bone, was kept to a minimum.

Although the east and west ends of the priory are different sites, both types of burial (the head-niche and the coffin) occur at each end and they are all thought to date sometime between the foundation of the priory in the 11th century and its Dissolution in the 16th century. They therefore probably represent individuals from the same population. In order to maximise the results of the skeletal examination both sites have been examined together.

It has been somewhat difficult to attribute phasing to these burials. The head-niche are thought to predate the coffin burials and they could be as early as late Saxon. The coffin burials seem to be later, although both types of burial continue into the later centuries of the cemetery's use. In this report, all head-niche burials are treated as representing an earlier phase.

The aim of the skeletal examination was to establish a profile of this population sample in terms of age and sex distribution, stature, morphological variants, and evidence for disease. For this, the following questions were asked:

1. What is the proportion of males to females on both sites? Do they differ? Is there a difference between phases?

2. Is there any evidence to suggest that males and females are buried in different parts of the graveyard?

3. Does the average age at death vary over time, and between sexes?

4. How many children and juveniles are buried in the graveyard? Does this vary between both sites and does the number of children change with time?

5. What is the range of cranial and post-cranial traits present in the sample? Are there any unusual distributions within the graveyard of those traits thought to be genetically controlled?

6. What diseases are present on the skeletons? Do any of the disease frequencies change over time, or between sexes?

7. What is the average stature of the individuals from the different phases and how do they compare?

8. How does the sample from this site compare to other local sites, and to more distant, but contemporary collections of skeletal remains?

The Articulated Human Bone

Number of Individuals

Most of the sample was inhumed at the east end of the priory (Site 1), where there were 245 skeletons, while 33 individuals were recovered from Site 2.

Condition and Completeness

Based on the state of preservation of the bone, each skeleton was recorded as being good, fair or poor (Table 4).

The skeletons that were poorly preserved had suffered the most post-mortem damage. They had abraded joint ends and the surfaces of bones had undergone considerable post mortem damage. Damage was particularly extensive on skulls and vertebrae. 'Fair' skeletons were characterised by bones that had reasonably well preserved surfaces and relatively un-abraded joint ends, while 'Good' skeletons generally had un-abraded joint ends and bone surfaces that were in an excellent state of preservation. Breakage of bone was frequent across all categories. In general, there was a greater tendency for bone from Site 1 to be more friable and abraded than that from Site 2.

The skeletons ranged from being 2% to 95% complete. Skeletons from Site 1 were represented by a higher percentage of bones and in general more bone survived in coffin burials (Fig.63).

Sex

Provided that most of the skeleton is present, sex can

Table 4 Sites 1 and 2: Condition of skeletons

Location	Number of Skeletons	Number of Poor Skeletons (%)	Number of Fair Skeletons (%)	Number of Good Skeletons (%)
Site 1	245	148 (60.40%)	49 (20%)	48 (19.59%)
Site 2	33	14 (42.42%)	7 (21.21%)	12 (36.36%)

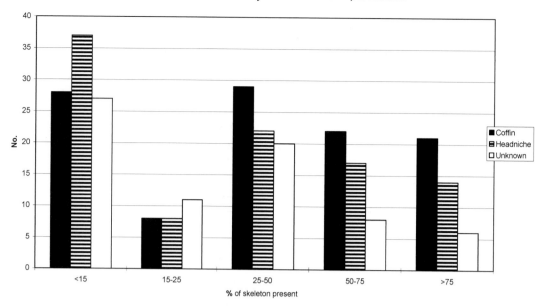

Fig. 63 Sites 1 and 2: The range of preservation between head-niche and coffin burials

be estimated with 80 to 90% accuracy. This is done by observing morphological traits of the pelvis and skull, and measuring the size of the femoral and humeral heads (Bass 1987; Brothwell 1981; Ferembach *et al.* 1980). Being more sexually dimorphic, the pelvis is more reliable with 90 to 95% accuracy. Sex differences between the skull and femoral and humeral heads tend to be less distinct and are therefore not as reliable (Ferembach *et al.* 1980). To date there are no standards that are considered acceptable among osteologists for determining the sex of non-adults (Buikstra and Ubelaker 1994). Therefore these techniques were applied to all adult skeletons only.

For those individuals where the sexing traits were borderline male or borderline female, they were recorded as possible males or possible females. However, for this analysis all possible males have been counted as male and all possible females have been counted as female giving a total of 112 males (104 from Site 1 and 8 from Site 2) and 37 females (30 from Site 1 and 7 from Site 2) (Table 5).

Although at least one of the aforementioned traits were present, 12 skeletons did not stand out as being either particularly male or particularly female and therefore no sex could be ascertained. In addition to this, a high proportion of the skeletons were too damaged for sex determination to be attempted and were therefore recorded as sex unattributable (78 individuals).

Sex attribution shows a ratio of 3 males to 1 female on Site 1 and a ratio of 1 male to 1 female on Site 2. The proportions of males to females remains constant in the east end for both phases. However, on Site 2, there is a higher ratio of males to females in the earlier phase (Table 6).

No relationship is suggested between sex distrib-

ution and the two types of burial employed on both sites. This is illustrated in Tables 7 and 8.

Age

Age was estimated for all non-adult skeletons by employing methods that relate to the ossification and eruption of deciduous and permanent teeth (Ubelaker 1978), diaphyseal length measurements (Ferembach *et al.* 1980) and epiphyseal union (Ferembach *et al.* 1980; Gray 1993). As growth can be affected by diet and disease to an unpredictable degree (Hoppa 1992), ages determined by teeth were preferential in cases where epiphyseal union and diaphyseal lengths presented different results.

Methods for estimating the age of adult skeletons involved observations of morphological changes at certain landmarks of the skull and pelvis. As the majority of skeletons had teeth, most ages were estimated based upon the degree of tooth attrition on the molars (Brothwell 1981). Changes to the morphology of the pubic symphysis is another method that was used, according to the criteria set out by Brooks and Suchey (1990). Auricular surface morphology and cranial suture closure, as described in Buikstra and Ubelaker (1994), were considered but less weight was afforded to them overall, the former being difficult to employ and the latter is generally regarded as unreliable among anthropologists (Hershkovitz *et al.* 1997; Saunders *et al.* 1992). The sternal rib end method (İşcan *et al.* 1984; 1985) could not be applied owing to poor preservation.

All current methods for ageing adults are considered far from accurate, particularly for older individuals (Bouquet-Appel and Massett 1982). For this reason, individuals were assigned to 10 year age brackets, or larger for those aged 45 years and over.

Table 5 Sites 1 and 2: Sex distribution

	Male	Female	Unsexed	Total
Site 1	104	30	111	245
Site 2	8	7	18	33
Total	**112**	**37**	**129**	**278**

Table 6 Sites 1 and 2: Ratio of males to females by phase

	Ratio of males to females overall	Ratio of males to females in head-niche phase	Ratio of males to females in coffin phase
Site 1	3:1	4:1	4:1
Site 2	1:1	3:1	1:1

Table 7 Site 1: Sex distribution among burial types

	Coffin	Head-niche	Unknown	Total
Male	48	39	17	104
Female	13	10	7	30
Unsexed	35	45	31	111

Table 8 Site 2: Sex distribution among burial types

	Coffin	Head-niche	Unknown	Total
Male	2	3	3	8
Female	2	1	4	7
Unsexed	8	0	10	18

Table 9 Sites 1 and 2: Distribution of ages and sexes

	0-5	6-15	16-25	26-35	36-45	45+	Adult	Total
Male			14	21	19	36	22	112
Female			8	5	3	8	13	37
Unknown	16	20	4	6	5	5	73	129
Total % of 278	16 6%	20 7%	26 9%	32 11%	27 10%	49 18%	108 39%	278

Table 10 Site 1: Distribution of ages and sexes

	0-5	6-15	16-25	26-35	36-45	45+	Adult	Total
Male			14	18	18	33	21	104
Female			8	4	1	5	12	30
Unknown	7	20	4	5	5	5	65	111
Total % of 245	7 3%	20 8%	26 11%	27 11%	24 10%	43 18%	98 40%	245

Table 11 Site 2: Distribution of ages and sexes

	0-5	6-15	16-25	26-35	36-45	45+	Adult	Total
Male				3	1	3	1	8
Female				1	2	3	1	7
Unknown	9			1			8	18
Total % of 33	9 28%	0 0%	0 0%	5 15%	3 9%	6 18%	10 30%	33

For the purposes of this analysis the following age categories have been employed:

Infant = 0–5 years
Juvenile = 6–15 years
Young Adult = 16–25 years

Adult = 26–35 and 36–45 years
Mature = 45+ years

Another group includes skeletons of individuals who had completed growth but, owing to incomplete preservation, could not be assigned to any of the adult age categories listed above. These individuals were described as 'Adult'.

The following tables show the distribution of ages for Sites 1 and 2 (Table 9, Fig. 64), Site 1 (Table 10, Fig. 65) and Site 2 (Table 11, Fig. 66). Figures 67 and 68 give the distribution of ages by phase.

Of the infants aged between 0–5, one of these was a foetus and three died at or around birth. Only the foetus was inhumed at Site 1 and the rest were buried at Site 2 where there was a higher proportion of children under 5 years of age (28% compared to 3%). The average age at death for males is 40 years and the average age at death for females is 36 years.

Stature

The maximum living stature has been estimated for all those individuals with complete longbones by using the appropriate regression equation as set out by Trotter and Gleser (1952, 1958), and revised by Trotter (1970). This does not apply to unsexed individuals and sub-adults, for which no stature could be estimated. However, all possible males and possible females were included and this must be taken into account when analysing the results as a different set of equations apply to males and females (Brothwell 1981).

Stature could be calculated for just 27 individuals, of which 22 are male and 5 are female. The range of heights for both sexes are given in Table 12 and Figs. 69 and 70 show the range of heights for both sexes over the two phases as represented by the head-niche and the coffin burials.

Overall, the average stature is 1.70m (5ft 5ins). The average male and female heights are 1.72m (5ft 6ins) and 1.59m (5ft 2ins) respectively.

Non-Metric Traits

Non-metrical or discontinuous morphological traits are discrete variants in the morphology of the skeleton. They occur both cranially, such as in the form of extra bones within the cranial sutures, and post cranially, such as an extra foramina in the humerus (referred to as a septal aperture). These are just two examples and many more have been described (for example, Berry and Berry 1967; Finnegan 1978).

Non-metric traits are of no apparent pathological significance and they vary in their frequency between populations. Some traits are found more commonly in one sex than the other, such as the septal aperture which is found more frequently in females (Saunders 1989). The presence of non-metric traits are thought to signify familial relationships, although it is not known as to what extent they are genetically and environmentally controlled (Brothwell 1981).

The material from St James has been examined for 14 cranial and 8 post cranial traits which are among the most common. Of these, 11 different cranial and 4 different post cranial traits were found and Tables 13

and 14 show the frequency of these traits. They give the number of individuals for which observations could be made, the number of those individuals where the trait was present, and the percentage.

Out of the skeletons for which an observation could be made, less than half had one or more traits present. The most common cranial trait is the parietal foramina and the most common post cranial trait is the septal aperture. Due to the fact that most of the numbers of traits are low, analysing them by side, would not be useful.

Dental Health

Of the adults, 133 had teeth surviving of which 81 were male, 27 were female and 25 were unsexed. Among them, 2,485 teeth were present; 224 teeth had been lost before death and 386 teeth had been lost after death. Also, 51 teeth were absent and in all cases this was the third mandibular or maxillary molar. Thus, 1,110 teeth cannot be accounted for due to missing jaws and teeth.

Signs of dental pathology found on these teeth include; caries, abscesses, ante-mortem loss (A/M loss), and calculus (Table 15).

The prevalence of dental disease was high, with 128 individuals (96% of individuals with teeth) showing evidence for one or more of the diseases. The majority of those affected are in the 36–45 and 45+ age categories. As Table 16 shows the number of individuals affected were found to increase with age. This accords well with the other medieval sites such as Taunton Priory, Somerset (Rogers 1984).

Out of 2,485 teeth that were present, 55 had a carious cavity (2.2% of all teeth present). Of the 33 individuals with caries, 12 are from the head-niche phase and 12 are from the coffin phase (Table 17).

Of the 2,682 tooth spaces that were present, 12 had abscess cavities (4.47%). This includes cavities in empty sockets where teeth had been lost ante-mortem. Skeleton 100 had an abscess situated on the inside (lingual surface) of the maxilla on the palate behind the right central and lateral incisors. All other abscesses occurred on the outside (buccal surface) of the maxillae and mandibles.

There was a high prevalence of ante-mortem loss among the individuals examined (45%). Of the 2,682 tooth spaces that were present 8.35 % had been lost antemortem. This is not unusual given that the majority of individuals are over 45 years of age and are therefore more likely to have lost teeth than a predominantly younger population.

Dental calculus, or tartar, which results from the build-up of plaque due to inadequate cleaning can give us an indication of an individual's oral health. In some cases it can lead to inflammation of the gums, and in severe cases, affect deeper tissues which may lead to peridontal disease. Calculus is easily flaked off during excavation and cleaning, making any record of

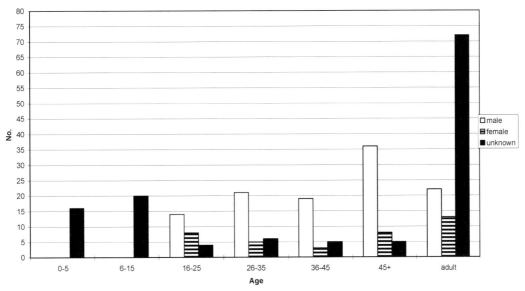

Fig. 64 Sites 1 and 2: Age/sex distribution

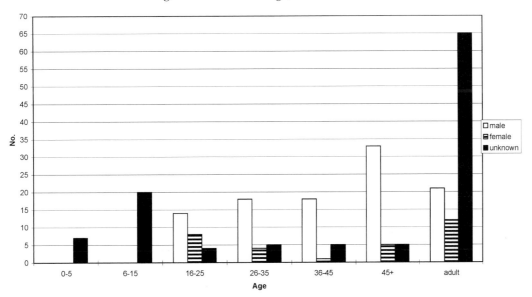

Fig. 65 Site 1: Age/sex distribution

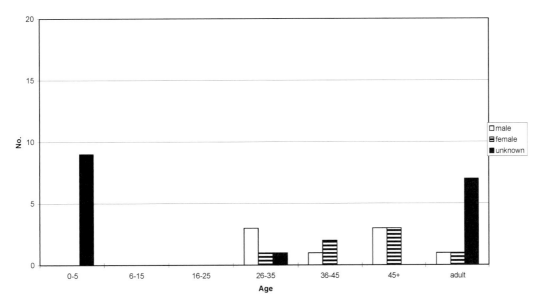

Fig. 66 Site 2: Age/sex distribution

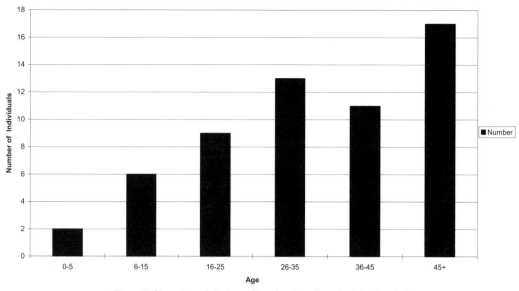

Fig. 67 Sites 1 and 2: Age distribution: head-niche burials

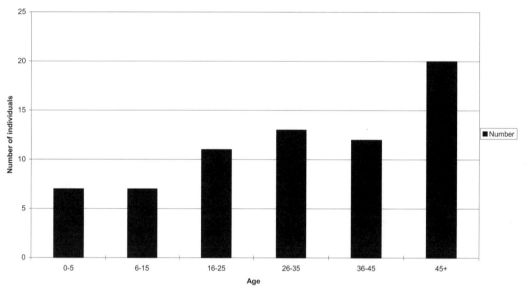

Fig. 68 Sites 1 and 2: Age distribution: coffin burials

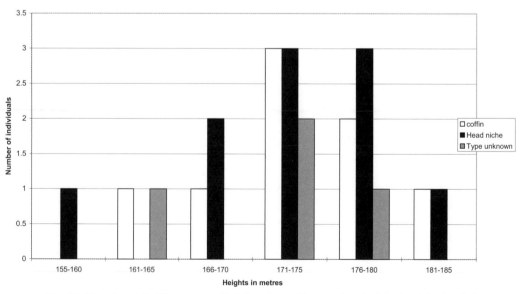

Fig. 69 Sites 1 and 2: The range of heights for coffin and head-niche burials (males)

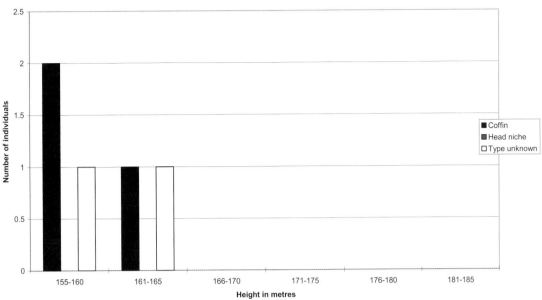

Fig. 70 Sites 1 and 2: The range of heights for coffin and head-niche burials (females)

Table 12 Range of heights for males and females

Height (m)	Male	Female	Total
1.55-1.60	1	3	4
1.61-1.65	2	2	4
1.66-1.70	3	0	3
1.71-1.75	7	0	7
1.76-1.80	7	0	7
1.81-1.85	2	0	2

Table 13 Frequency of cranial non-metric traits

Trait	Number of individuals	Number with traits	Percent
Metopism	63	3 (3M)	5
Bregmatic bone	59	1 (1?)	2
Lambda wormians	41	16 (11M, 3F, 2?)	39
Coronal wormians	52	1 (M)	2
Saggital wormians	48	1 (M)	2
Lamboid bone	50	7 (1F, 4M, 2?)	14
Supra orbital foramen	71	22 (4F,18M)	31
Parietal foramen	62	36 (6F, 1?, 29M)	58
Parietal notch	31	2 (2M)	6
Torus maxillaris	72	13 (3F, 10M)	18
Torus mandibularis	93	10 (2F, 8M)	11

Key:
M = male; F = female; ? = Unsexed

it somewhat unreliable. Therefore only the most definite deposits were recorded.

A total of 22 children had teeth. Fifteen of these had deciduous teeth (either with or without permanent teeth) which totalled 135. The number of permanent teeth totalled 256 and these were found in 18 individuals. A total of 65 tooth spaces were counted. Just 4 (18%) carious cavities were recorded on 3 individuals and no abscesses were observed.

One child (skeleton 190) had enamel hypoplasia present on the maxillary central incisors, and on the right first and second incisors and the right canine of the mandible. Enamel hypoplasia is a deficiency in enamel formation and results in grooves or pits on the crown of the tooth. These grooves or pits are taken to represent periods of stress during growth which could have been caused by disease, or nutritional deficiency. No other changes on this skeleton were observed post cranially.

Evidence for Bone Disease

Palaeopathology, the term used to describe the analysis of health in past populations, can be undertaken by examining changes on bones and joints of skeletal remains, and classifying them according to most probable cause. However, there are a number of

Table 14 Frequency of post cranial non-metric traits

Trait	Number of individuals	Number with traits	Percent
Lumbar sacralisation	70	1 (1M)	1
Vastus notch	61	3 (2M,1F)	5
Septal aperture	94	12 (6M,6F)	13
Os acrominale	62	1 (1F)	2

Key:
M = male; F = female; ? = Unsexed

Table 15 Number of individuals with dental pathology out of the 133 individuals with teeth examined

	Caries	Abscesses	A/M Loss	Calculus	Total out of 133 individuals (%)
Male	24	7	41	18	90 (67.6)
Female	4	1	15	6	26 (19.5)
Unknown	5	1	5	1	12 (9.0)
Total out of 133 individuals (%)	33 (24%)	9 (6.6%)	61 (45.1%)	25 (18.5%)	128 (96.2)

Table 16 Age distribution of individuals with dental pathology

	Caries	Abscesses	Calculus	A/M Loss	Total
16-25	5	1	2	3	11
26-35	6	3	7	8	24
36-45	2		6	11	19
45+	20	5	10	31	66
Adult				8	8
Total	33	9	25	61	128

Table 17 Numbers of individuals with caries from the head-niche and coffin phases

Phase	Number of individuals with teeth	Number of individuals with caries (%)
Head-niche	51	12 (23.5)
Coffin	52	12 (23.07)

limitations to this. While visual examination, backed up by radiology where necessary, demonstrate which diseases were present and thus act as an indicator of health, not all diseases leave indicators on bones and joints. It is rarely possible to find a cause of death and the amount of information about disability and discomfort is limited. It is the combination of a whole variety of morphological abnormalities that result in the bony changes that are observed on a skeleton and not all of these are assignable to a specific cause.

The bony lesions observed on the skeletons have been classified into five groups relating to joint disease, trauma, infection, metabolic disorders (for example, iron deficiency anaemia), and neoplastic diseases (for example, tumours).

Joint Disease: Joint disease is the most common type of pathological change to be found in a skeletal population, and the most common type of joint disease in both modern and archaeological populations is osteoarthritis (OA). OA is a disease that affects the synovial joints and it is found to increase in frequency with age. It is diagnosed in skeletal material by the presence of eburnation (polishing of bone) or the presence of at least two of the following: pitting on the joint surface, bony contour change, or marginal osteophyte and/or new bone on the joint surface (Rogers and Waldron 1995, 44). It can affect any synovial joint in the skeleton, the common sites of which have varied over time and among populations.

A total of 28 individuals, 25 from Site 1 (22 males, 1 female and 2 unsexed) and 3 from Site 2 (1 male and 2 females), showed changes characteristic of OA. Among them, 39 joints were affected (Table 18). Due to the small sample size it is not statistically possible to analyse the distribution of affected joints by age and sex. However, there are some general trends worth noting.

The commonest sites affected are the articular facets of the spine, with the hands being the next most frequent site (Table 19). Not included in the table is an

Table 18 Frequency of sites affected by OA by sex

Site	Number of Males	Number of Females
Knees	2	1
Spine	18	4
Wrists	3	0
Elbows	1	0
Ankles	1	0
Rib facet joints	1	0
Hands	3	1
Feet	2	0
Total	31 28% (of all males)	6 16% (of all females)

Table 19 Prevalence of sites affected by OA

Site	Number of Sites	Number with OA	Percent
Knees[1]	123	3	2%
Spine[2]	CV 106, TV 108, LV 106	18 CV, 6 TV, 2 LV	CV 17%, TV 6%, LV 2%
Wrists[3]	81	3	4%
Elbows[4]	111	2	2%
Ankles	101	1	0.9%
Rib facet joints	135	1	0.7%
Hip	112	0	0%
Shoulder[5]	124	1	0.8%
Hands[6]	81	4	5%
Feet[7]	88	2	2%

Key:
CV = Cervical vertebrae; TV = Thoracic vertebrae; LV = Lumbar vertebrae.
1. All compartments; 2. Articular facets; 3. All joints; 4. All compartments;
5. Gleno-humeral joint; 6. Any joint; 7. Any joint.

Table 20 Individuals with multiple site involvement of OA

Skeleton	Sex	Age	Joints affected by Osteoarthritis
83	M	45+	Ankles (R+L), Knees, (R+L), Wrists, (R+L)
48	M	45+	R. Gleno-humeral joint, cervical spine
99	?	A	R.fingers, elbow
177	M	45+	Cervical spine, bilateral fingers, bilateral toes
200	M	45+	R.hand, cervical and thoracic spine
284	F	45+	L. Knee(pfj), L. elbow, R.hand, Cervical spine

Table 21 Frequency of degenerative disc disease and Schmorl's nodes

Number of adult spines	Number with Degenerative Disc Disease (%)			Number with Schmorl's Nodes (%)	
	CV	TV	LV	TV	LV
141	5	5	6	12	6
	4%	4%	4%	9%	4%

Key:
CV = Cervical vertebrae; TV = Thoracic vertebrae; LV = Lumbar vertebrae.

individual who had bilateral tempero mandibular joint OA. This individual was male and was over 50 years of age.

Many patterns of OA have been described in the clinical literature and a number of these have distinct epidemiological features. For example, OA of the knee and the hand are positively associated with obesity (Waldron 1995). No hip OA was found on any of the 112 joints that were available for examination. The absence of hip OA is unusual for a skeletal population of this date (Rogers and Waldron 1995).

In six individuals, OA was present in more than one site and these are given in Table 20. OA of the ankle is usually associated with trauma either to the bones involved, or it may occur following fracture of the neighbouring bones. Although no signs could be seen either morphologically or on a radiograph, the involvement of both ankle joints on skeleton 83 suggests that the OA in this particular case is more than likely to have been secondary to trauma. These different patterns of joint involvement could be linked to a number of different activities and occupations in which the individual's age, sex and genetic pre-disposition will have played an important part.

Other Spinal Changes: In 29 individuals spinal changes other than osteoarthritis were also recorded.

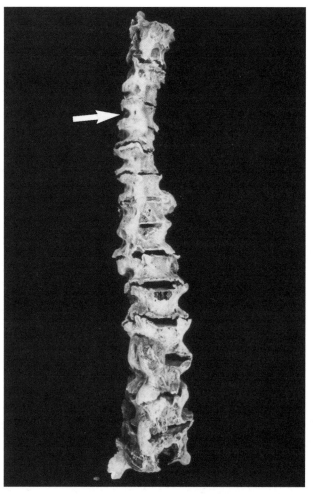

Fig. 71 An example of DISH (arrowed)

These are: Diffuse idiopathic skeletal hyperostosis (DISH), degenerative disc disease, Schmorl's nodes, and osteophytosis. Table 21 below shows the frequency of degenerative disc disease and Schmorl's nodes for cervical vertebrae (CV), thoracic vertebrae (TV), and lumbar vertebrae (LV). The frequency of DISH will be discussed separately.

Degenerative disc disease, or spondylosis, appears as coarse pitting and bone deposits on the surfaces of the vertebral bodies. Of the individuals affected, 73% are 45 years and over. This is not surprising since it is a phenomenon that is found to increase in frequency with age.

Schmorl's nodes are caused by intervertebral disc herniation into the vertebral body. They appear on dry bone as depressions either on the superior or inferior surface of the body. Although also associated with degenerative disease, Schmorl's nodes can also be caused by activity and trauma, especially in adolescence, or metabolic disorders (Rogers and Waldron 1995).

DISH is a disease of the ligament insertions or entheses. The characteristic site for this is the thoracic spine which becomes fused down the right hand side with bone that has the characteristic appearance of dripped candle-wax. The lumbar spine is also occasionally involved (Fig. 71).

This disease usually occurs in individuals over the age of 50, and is more frequent in males than females. It is known for its associations with obesity and metabolic disorders, but apart from some restricted movement and some spinal stiffness, it causes little discomfort or disability despite its spectacular appearance (Klippel and Dieppe 1994)

Altogether eight individuals showed changes characteristic of DISH on the thoracic vertebrae, that is 6% of the adult skeletons with spines. Seven of these are male and one is female. Except for one male who is in his thirties, all of the individuals are over 45 years of age. A further four individuals showed signs of early DISH where, although not fused, large 'beaks' of bone projected from the margins of thoracic vertebrae on the right hand side. In addition to this 31 individuals had bony out growths at other sites where tendons, ligaments and articular capsules insert into bone (the entheses).

Another spinal change that was found on the adult individuals is osteophytosis. On dry bone osteophytosis has the appearance of a rim of new bone around the edge of a joint. This was found on 9.2% of the superior and inferior margins of the adult vertebral bodies. It is a degenerative disease that is found to increase in frequency with age.

Trauma: Fractures were the most common lesions in this category. This includes 8 adult individuals, 6 from Site 1 (3 males and 3 unsexed) and 2 from Site 2 (2 males) with different elements being involved (Table 22).

Also included under this heading (but not in Table 22) is skeleton 140 who had a fused distal interphalangeal joint of the hand. This may have been due to a traumatic break, or it could be infective.

Infection and Inflammatory Change: The majority of cases included in this category were due to periostitis (Table 23). This is a non-specific change that affects the outer layer of bone (the periosteum). It can be associated with infection, although there may be many other causes. In typical cases it appears as a thin surface layer of finely laced bone, or sometimes it can be quite florid.

Thirty six of the skeletons, 27 males, 3 females and 6 unsexed, had periosteal changes. Of these, 34 (26 males, 3 females and 5 unsexed) are from Site 1 and 2 (1 male, 1 unsexed) are from Site 2. In most cases the changes were restricted to the tibiae and fibulae which are the most frequently observed sites for such lesions. Skeleton 257 had periosteal new bone situated on the alveolar margin of the right mandibular first molar due to an infection caused by an abscess at this site.

Four individuals had changes that are characteristic of osteomyelitis. This includes 3 males and 1 unsexed individual (all from Site 1), of which 3 also had

Table 22 Element distribution and frequency of fractures

	Site 1			Site 2			Total		
	n	N	%	n	N	%	n	N	%
Rib	1	1147	0.09	0	182	0	1	1329	0.08
Metacarpal	2	554	0.4	0	48	0	2	602	0.3
Ulna	1	245	0.4	0	26	0	1	271	0.4
Fibula	1	223	0.4	1	30	3.3	2	253	0.8
Femur	1	321	0.3	0	37	0	1	358	0.3
Tibia	2	283	0.7	1	35	2.9	3	318	0.9
Hand phalanges	2	884	0.2	2	131	1.5	4	1015	0.4

Key:
n = number of fractures; N = number of observable elements
(left sides and right sides have been combined)

Table 23 Frequency of periostitis and osteomyelitis

	Periostitis			Osteomyelitis		
	n	N	%	n	N	%
Mandible	1	2682*	0.04	0	0	0
Femur	2	358	0.6	0	0	0
Tibia	38	318	11.9	4	318	1.3
Fibula	23	253	9.1	1	253	0.4

Key:
n = number of elements with periostitis or osteomyelitis;
N = number of observable elements;
* = number of observable tooth spaces (left sides and
right sides have been combined) (Of the elements listed
here 1 tibia, 1 fibula and 1 mandible are from skeletons
buried in Site 2. The remainder are all from skeletons
buried in Site 1).

periositis involving additional elements (and are counted above).

Osteomyelitis is a bacterial infection where bone is simultaneously destroyed and repaired with pus formation that drains through sinuses known as cloacae. The appearance of infected bones can be quite spectacular with areas of irregularity, pitting and large plaques of new bone (Fig. 72). The most common bones to be affected are the femora and the tibiae. The different affected sites seen among the four individuals from St James are tibiae and fibulae only.

In addition to osteomyelitis, one of the individuals, skeleton 206, a 25–35 year old male, had deposits of layered, porous, new bone on the endocranial surface of several unidentified fragments of skull. This individual was poorly preserved and was less than 40% complete.

In addition to this, skeleton 117 had large punched out erosions involving the first tarso-metatarsal joint. The erosions covered both articular surfaces entirely and they had new bone growth around their margins. This is likely to be septic arthritis which is why it is discussed in this section.

Metabolic Disorders: These are triggered by either an excess or a deficiency in the body's dietary requirements and hormones, and results in specific changes to the skeleton such as in the form of increased or decreased bone turnover.

Cribra orbitalia is a phenomenon that is currently thought to be associated with iron deficiency anaemia

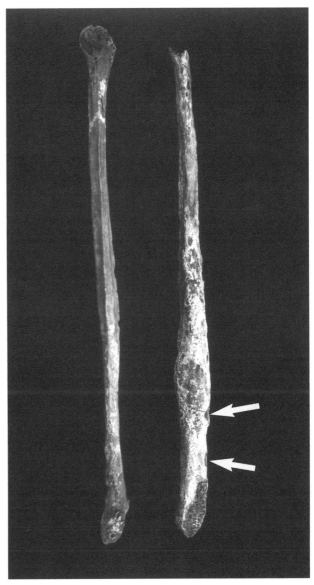

Fig. 72 An example of osteomyelitis involving the left fibula (arrowed)

(Stuart-Macadam 1985) and it is characterised by fine pitting on the roof of the orbits. Out of 194 orbits (left and right sides) examined, 9 (6 individuals) showed evidence for this disorder, that is 4.6% of all observable orbits. The ages and sexes of the individuals with cribra orbitalia are given in Table 24.

Anaemia tends not to leave traces on adult bone (Stuart-Macadam 1985) and therefore the above cases most probably relate back to a time during the individual's childhood, the only time when skeletal lesions relating to this disease are manifest.

A change that is found in the frontal bone known as Hyperostosis Frontalis Interna (HFI) is another metabolic disorder. This is new bone growth over the inside surface of the frontal bone which does not usually have any symptoms. Only four individuals (3.9% of all 103 adult skulls that could be examined) showed

Table 24 Individuals with cribra orbitalia

Skeleton	Age	Sex
123	25-35	M
152	45+	M
168	30-40	M
174	15-25	F
190	6 +/-24 months	?
212	10-12	?

Table 25 Individuals with HFI

Skeleton	Age	Sex
79	33-45	M
108	35-45	M
148	45+	M
206	25-35	M

evidence for this, these being skeletons 79, 148, 108 and 206 (Table 25). HFI is a phenomenon that has a high prevalence in post-menopausal women (Ortner and Putschar 1985). The low frequency at St James therefore may be due to the lack of females in the sample.

Rickets is characterised by the bowing of limb bones due to a deficiency in vitamin D. Skeleton 187 had very bowed tibiae at the midshaft, although no other changes in the other bones, including the fibulae, were found. Bowing of the fibulae would be expected if this was rickets. Differential diagnosis would include fractures although no evidence was found for this.

Pagets, or osteitis deformans, is due to an im-balance in the cells that break down old bone and make new bone. In this disease there is an excessive turn over of new bone which results in the thickening of the bone's cortex. The end result is an enlarged and distorted appearance. These changes were observed on the patellae, tibiae, fibulae and foot bones of skeleton 113. This individual was an unsexed adult.

Neoplastic Diseases: Skeleton 206 had a smooth ivory hard lump of about 20mm in maximum dia-meter situated ectocranially on the left parietal (impinging on the parietal foramina). Skeleton 108 also had an identical lump situated in the frontal sinus. These are probably an osteoma, which is a benign tumour. Osteomas mostly consist of dense lamellar bone with vascular channels and they are practically without marrow spaces (Ortner and Putschar 1991, 368). Due to their appearance they are referred to as button osteomas which are the most common type of osteoma and are most frequently found on the parietal.

Other evidence for benign neoplastic disease was found on the incompletely preserved spine of skeleton 132, an adult male. The posterior portion of the bodies of four lumbar vertebrae and the first sacral vertebra had scalloped erosions which measured between 4–15mm superior to inferior and 2–6mm medial to

lateral. There were no other apparent changes on the skeleton. Both visual and radiological examination have diagnosed a benign long standing intraspinal tumour as the most likely cause for these appearances. The site of the lesions are atypical for tuberculosis and infection is not a likely cause because of the lack of other reactive bony change.

Other Diseases and Abnormalities: Some bony changes which do not fit into the above categories will be discussed here. The first (skeleton 213) had the bodies of two (unidentified) cervical vertebrae fused, while the other (skeleton 185) had fusion occurring between the superior articular facets of C3 and the inferior articular facets of C2 with preserved joint space between the bodies. Congenital fusion between the cervical vertebrae usually occurs between the bodies and not the articular facet joints. As skeleton 185 also had new bone formation and pitting in association with the fused articular facets, it is possible that this is septic rather than congenital.

In addition to these skeleton 244 had clefting of the posterior arch of the atlas and the neural arch of CV3. Out of 7 cervical, 6 thoracic and 5 lumbar vertebrae that had survived, these were the only abnormalities observed in the spine of this skeleton.

The Disarticulated Human Bone

This includes all human bone that was not excavated from a discrete grave and cannot be assigned to a particular individual. It represents individuals that were disturbed by later burials or construction (of drains for example) during the later centuries of the site's history and were found in the fills of these features. The nature of this material means that it is mostly damaged and fragmented and therefore much less can be derived from it than the articulated remains.

Minimum Numbers

This was determined by the duplication of any bone, the size of the bone (*i.e.* if the bone was young or adult), and in some cases the presence of a pair of bones which obviously belonged to different indi-viduals. These methods determined at least 202 individuals.

Age and Sex

Where traits survived, ages and sexes were assigned using the same methods discussed for the articulated remains. Out of 202 individuals, 48 could be sexed, 36 being male, and 12 being female. The distribution of ages are given in Table 26 where the same age categories are used as before.

Stature

The height of individuals was calculated using the same method as discussed before. However, as the bones are

Table 26 Age distribution of disarticulated human bone

0-5	6-15	16-25	26-35	36-45	45+	Adult
19	22	7	10	8	4	132

Table 27 Range of heights

Context	Sex	Height (metres)
1271	M	1.82
1528	F	1.59
1154	M	1.68
1069	M	1.75
1263	M	1.79
1351	M	1.70

Table 28 Prevalence of non-metric traits, cranial and post cranial

Context	Parietal Foramen	Supra Orbital foramen	Lamboid bone	Lamboid Wormians	Occipital wormians	Torus Maxillarus	Sex
1483	R+L	-	-	-	-	-	?
1503	R+L	-	Y	-	-	-	?F
1263	R+L	-	-	-	-		M
1461	R+L	-	-	-	Y	-	M
1224	L	-	-	Y	-	-	?
339	-	L	-	-	-	-	?M
336	-	L	-	-	-	-	M
970	R+L	-	-	-	-	-	?
1341	R+L	-	-	-	-	-	M
1528	R	-	-	-	-	-	F
1528	-	-	-	-	-	-	?M
1271	-	-	-	-	-	R+L	?
1366	L	L	-	-	-	-	M
1478	Y (unsided)						M
1435	L	L	-	-	-	-	M
1069	L	-	-	-	-	-	?M

Key:

R = present on right side;

L = present on left side;

Y = present;

- = no data.

Table 29 Prevalence of disease

Joint Disease		Other Spinal Changes		Trauma		Periostitis		Metabolic Disorders	
Context	Bone	Context	Disorder	Context	Bone	Context	Bone	Context	Disorder
1271	Knee	322	Schmorl's Nodes	294	Broken Clavicle	1383	Tibia	1279	Cribra
		1131	Schmorl's Nodes			1027	Femur	607	Cribra
						1271	Tibia	1435	HFI
						1271	Tibia		
						336	Radius		
						1190	Humerus		
						1483	Tibia		
						1528	Tibia		

disarticulated, this was done using maximum femoral length only. This meant that for all femora used, sex could be estimated fairly accurately by measuring the maximum diameter of the femoral head.

The stature of six individuals from separate contexts could be estimated and are given in Table 27.

Non-Metric Traits

Where relevant, material from this group was exam-ined for the same traits as the articulated remains. Table 28 shows what traits were observed and where possible gives the sex of the individual. No post cranial traits were found.

Evidence for Bone Disease

The diseases that were found in this group of bones fall into the same categories as the articulated remains. Table 29 gives the condition and what bones were affected (where context numbers are repeated, the bones may belong to the same individual).

In addition to these diseases, osteophytosis and enthesopathies were also common. The former was found on the margins of joints and vertebral bodies, and the latter at sites where tendons, ligaments and articular capsules insert into bone (the entheses).

Since conclusions as to the severity and distribution of bony changes on an individual depend on the completeness of a skeleton, the fragmentary and disparate nature of disarticulated bone means that they are rarely reached. For this reason, it is not possible to compare the prevalence of the above bony changes with the rest of the skeletons from St. James.

Comment

The amount of information that we can expect a skeletal assemblage to yield is subject to its recovery rate. All anthropological techniques employed to determine age, sex and stature depend on the availability of certain bones and when there is evidence for disease, diagnosis is often dependent on the amount of the skeleton present and its condition. The majority of skeletons had suffered post-mortem damage to the extent that they were in a poor condition and very fragmented. Due to this it was not possible to give exact diagnoses for certain bony changes and nor was it possible to assign ages, sexes and statures in many cases. However, a large sample such as this means it is possible to examine the demographic and health attributes of this population both over time and across the site. It also presents the opportunity to place this information in a wider context by comparison with other medieval bone assemblages from monastic and parish burial grounds.

One hundred and forty-nine out of 278 individuals could be assigned a sex from this sample. An analysis of the distribution of male and female burials for each site shows a higher ratio of males to females in the east end (3:1) compared to the west end (1:1). This suggests that the east end was reserved primarily for the burial of monks and clerics while the west end was used as a lay cemetery.

A chi square test was carried out using an SPSS package (version 6.1) to see if this patterning could be supported. Results show that there is a significant difference in the distribution of male and female burials across the two sites (p = 0.05) and therefore the patterning is valid. Chi square tests also show that there is no significant difference in the distribution of male and female burials for each phase in the east end (p = 0.86531) and the west end (p = 0.46521). These tests only take into account those individuals who could be sexed but they suggest that geographical location and not spatial organisation nor time was important in determining where a person was buried.

The burial of females and children in the east end is not unusual despite the fact that it was probably the monastic burial ground. Monastic graveyards were popular places for burial among those of a higher social class and bequests of money or goods were frequently made by the lay community in return for a place to be buried (Stroud and Kemp 1993). Although the majority of skeletons buried in the eastern and southern sides of the east end were particularly poor and could not be sexed, a concentration of female burials may be suggested in the southern side.

In general, Sites 1 and 2 show greater numbers in the older age groups and, by contrast, few children and young adults. Children and young adults were also few in number among the skeletons from St Bartholomew's Hospital, Bristol (Stroud 1998) and comparison to the late medieval group from St Oswald's Priory, Gloucester (Rogers 1999) shows that this is not unusual.

The majority of the adults in this sample were aged using tooth attrition, a technique that does not enable individuals to be aged beyond 45 years. It is probable that many of the skeletons in the 45+ category are older and this is suggested by the high numbers of individuals in this group with changes that are associated with mature adults.

The peak of female deaths between the ages of 16 to 25 is interesting in that it falls at a time when childbirth would be most expected, although as females are so under-represented in this population, this cannot be statistically proven. In the earlier head-niche phase, there would seem to be significantly fewer children and there is a higher proportion of individuals aged over 45 years (35% compared to 29% for those buried in the coffin phase). This may reflect a change in the function of the burial ground over time or a rise in child deaths over time.

There does not appear to be any notable trend in the location of child and infant burials. The distribution of children under five years of age was found to be concentrated in the western part of the cemeteries of both Taunton Priory, Somerset and St Andrews Fishergate, York but no such treatment is suggested at St James.

Poor preservation of long bones has meant that only a small number of individuals could have their heights calculated and therefore the results cannot be taken to be representative of the whole sample. However, in general, the average male and female heights for this sample are similar to those at Spitalfields which is shorter than today, but similar to Romano-British and medieval populations (Molleson and Cox 1993). There is little variation in the range of heights for both sexes between the two phases.

Non-metric traits have been found both cranially and post cranially and these have been divided into groups according to sex. This does not reflect any pattern in their known tendency to be specific to either sex, although among females the septal aperture is more frequent than any other trait. This said, no real significance can be attached to these findings since the numbers are so small. Also, there would appear to be nothing unusual in the distribution of traits that are thought to be genetically controlled across the graveyard and there is no suggestion of family groupings.

In general, the common occurrence of parietal foramen and septal apertures is normal for a site of this date and type and this is similar to prevalences found among contemporary groups such as St Oswald's, Gloucester and St Peter's, Barton on Humber. However, the prevalence of mandibular and maxillary tori are slightly higher than expected.

Dental conditions were commonly observed throughout the sample. This was largely due to a high percentage of caries (24% of the individuals with teeth) and antemortem loss (45% of the individuals with teeth). This is not an unusual finding since the majority of cases concern older individuals. St Bartholomew's Hospital, which has a similar demographic profile, reflects the same trend while a slightly lower prevalence is seen among the younger population from the lay cemetery at Taunton Priory (Rogers 1984).

Figures for caries and ante-mortem loss among the younger groups at St James are typical for this period. However, the higher frequency of ante mortem loss in females (58%), compared to males (48%), is striking as it is a trend that is not typical for a medieval population of this type. The skeletal assemblages from Wells Cathedral, Jarrow and St Andrews all reflect a higher frequency in males. While this may suggest something significant, these results could be biased as this is a small sample size and most of the individuals are over 45 years of age.

The prevalence of caries between the two phases was examined to see if this reflects a difference in diet through time. However, the figures suggest no differences here. It is interesting that calculus was found on more females than males, and this may be indicative of a difference in diets.

Abscesses are among other dental conditions observed. They were found to be more frequent among males than females but their overall prevalence is within the normal range for an assemblage of this date.

Pathological lesions found on the sample are typical of those that are commonly found in skeletal assemblages. In general they are also ranked according to prevalence in an order that is similar to other sites of the same type and date (*e.g.* St Peter's, Barton on Humber; St Oswald's, Gloucester; Taunton Priory, Somerset; and St Bartholomew's Hospital, Bristol).

Osteoarthritis accounts for most of the diseases found and the most common sites are the same as those recorded on a modern population (Waldron 1993). Two exceptions are tempero-mandibular joint OA and shoulder OA, which are somewhat rarer sites for today and the past (Klippel and Dieppe 1994).

With the exception of one unaged adult, all of the individuals with multiple joint involvement are over 45 years of age. An investigation into the combination of shoulder, hands and spine OA at the 18th-century burial site of Spitalfields found that this was an age related phenomenon (Waldron 1993), and the same may be true at St James.

The patterns of OA found in this sample are different to those found today and this is a common finding in archaeological populations. This difference has often been attributed to a difference in activity. However, since the relationship between OA and activity is not clearly understood this should be viewed with caution. It is quite possible that these differences are a reflection more on the different methods employed by the palaeopathologist and the clinician when observing arthritic joints (Rogers and Waldron 1995)

Osteophytes found on joint margins were also common. These are frequently observed in archaeological and modern populations and they are known to be an age related phenomenon. Osteophytosis is found in common with many other joint diseases and it is of no particular significance in its own right.

On the whole, the prevalence of trauma at St James is low for a skeletal assemblage. Furthermore, the crude prevalence indicates that it may be lower than most other contemporary religious sites. At St Bartholomew's Hospital 23% (7 out of 30 individuals) of the population showed evidence for fractures (Stroud 1998, 178) compared to just 3% (8 out of 278 individuals) of the population from St James. This observation is despite the fact that a number of bones were examined radiologically in order that those injuries which do not always affect the morphological appearance of a bone, could be found. With the majority of this population having an age at death of over 45 years, this is unusual, since the longer one lives, the more one is likely to experience some form of traumatic injury.

An explanation for this may be sought in terms of occupation. This population is by definition a religious one and therefore one might assume that the activities they undertook did not put them at such a high degree of risk of injury as, for example, an agricultural population. It may also suggest a contrast in the type of activities that the population of St James undertook in comparison to other religious communities (*e.g.* St Bartholomew's Hospital, Bristol) of a similar date.

In a skeletal population, infection and inflammatory changes are generally less common than trauma (Rogers 1999). At St James there is a higher prevalence of the former, although attention must be drawn to the fact that the majority of cases from this group relate to periostitis, a non-specific infection which could be due to something as common as varicose veins, a condition which tends to affect older age groups.

Table 30 Medieval human bone assemblages excavated in Bristol

Site	Source	Total number of individuals examined	Males (? males)	Females (? females)	Unsexed
St James's Priory (Sites 1 and 2)		278	112	37	129
St Augustine the Less	O'Connell (1998)	119	46	28	25
St Bartholomew's	Stroud (1998)	30	12	11	7
Greyfriars	Stroud (forthcoming)	39	20	14	5

Note: All possible males are counted as male and all possible females are counted as female here

Conclusions

The human remains from St James's Priory not only represent the largest assemblage excavated and examined from Bristol to date, but they are also among the earliest to be recovered from this locality (Table 30)

This examination has afforded the opportunity to gain a greater understanding of Bristol's early religious communities and, by comparison to other contemporary burial sites, to place it in the wider context of medieval England.

The results of this examination show the assemblage to be typical of a religious community and, in particular, this is reflected in a bias in favour of male burials, a high life expectancy and evidence for certain diseases that one would expect to find in such a group. These results also suggest that, for its time, this population enjoyed a comfortable economic and social status. This is in contrast to the individuals from the lay cemetery at Taunton Priory where deaths are more common in the younger age groups and no bias is reflected in male and female burials (Rogers 1984).

Like other assemblages that have been examined from the same locality this is a relatively old population which in terms of stature, health, non-metric traits, age and sex distribution does not differ widely from other monastic sites of the same date.

This is the first human bone assemblage in Bristol to yield a sizeable amount of information about one of its medieval religious communities. There are several areas where further analysis would be most beneficial.

Although all of the standard techniques for sexing have been applied to this assemblage, just under half of the population remain unsexed. It may in future be possible to increase the numbers of sexed individuals by applying another method which involves comparing the maximum lengths of clavicles between the two sexes (Parsons 1916).

During analysis of the material, a new ageing technique was applied to the sample (Barber 1994) and the data generated from this is stored in the archive. Analysis of this data will not only increase the number of aged individuals, but it will also mean that the potential to estimate age at death will be increased beyond the age of 50. This will result in a more accurate age distribution for the population.

Spatial analysis of those skeletons in the assemblage with bony outgrowths on joint margins and at the sites of ligament insertions may reveal a pattern similar to those noted at Wells Camery where evidence suggested that these changes could be linked to socio-economic factors (Rogers et al. 1993).

Analysis of the Human Bone from Site 3 by Sophie Lamb

Introduction

The remains of five articulated skeletons and a relatively large amount of disarticulated bone was recovered from Site 3. Since these remains are believed to be of the same date and to come from the same lay / parish burial ground as the inhumations from the east end of St James's Church, they were examined as part of the same collection. They have not been included in the main report since they were excavated and examined by different specialists some time after its completion.

Examination was carried out to determine where possible ages, sexes, statures and for the disarticulated material, minimum numbers of individuals. In addition to this, the skeletons were examined for any evidence for disease or abnormality. The same methods that were used to examine the skeletons from the east and west ends of the church were applied to the examination of these remains.

Condition and Completeness

The condition of the skeletons ranged from poor to good. The skeletons which were in a fair condition had bones which had suffered some post mortem damage to their surfaces and had abraded joint ends but this was not extensive (Table 31).

All of the skeletons were fragmented and four out of five were less than 50% complete (Table 31).

Table 31 Site 3: Condition and amount of bone present for each skeleton

Skeleton (Sk.) Number	Condition	Amount Present (%)
286	Fair	5%
287	Fair	45%
289	Fair	35%
290	Good	15%
291	Poor	65%

Table 32 Site 3: Age and sex distribution

Skeleton (Sk.) Number	Age	Sex
286	Adult	Male
287	Adult	Male
289	Adult	Male
290	25-35	Male
291	25-35	Female

Table 33 Site 3: Calculated statures

Skeleton (Sk.) Number	Sex	Height (m)
289	Male	1.71
290	Male	1.74
291	Female	1.63

Table 34 Site 3: Distribution of dental conditions

Skeleton (Sk.) Number	Number of Teeth with Caries	Number of Abscesses	Number of Teeth Lost A/M	Enamel Hypoplasia
286	2	0	6	No
290	2	0	1	Yes
291	2	2	0	Yes

Age and Sex

All of the skeletons had at least one of the appropriate traits available with which to determine sex. From these it was concluded that they represent four males (skeletons 286, 287, 289 and 290) and one female (skeleton 291). Only two skeletons could be assigned to an age category based on the wear on their teeth. Indicators of age had not survived on the remaining individuals. From the size of their bones it was concluded that they all represent adults (Table 32).

Stature

Stature could be calculated for three of the individuals and these are given in Table 33. For each calculation, the long bone length with the lowest standard of error was used where possible.

Dental Health

Out of the five individuals, three (skeletons 286, 290 and 291) had dentitions surviving. Altogether 49 teeth were present out of a possible 96 (3x32). Seven teeth had been lost ante mortem, one third molar was erupted, five teeth had been lost post mortem and 34 teeth were unaccounted for due to missing jaws and teeth. Table 34 gives the dental conditions that were observed on these dentitions.

No evidence for calculus or peridontal disease was found on the teeth or jaws of any of these individuals.

Evidence for Bone Disease

Three individuals showed evidence for disease. Skeleton 289 had changes that are diagnostic of osteoarthritis of the hip (Rogers *et al.* 1997). Here the articular surface of the right femoral head and the acetabulum of the pelvis were eburnated and pitted and osteophytes were present on the articular margins. Skeleton 290 showed evidence for osteoarthritis (eburnation and joint surface pitting) of the patello-femoral joint of the left knee and the left ankle (tibio-talus joint). Osteoarthritis of the ankle is not as common as most other sites in the body, and is secondary to some other pathology, usually trauma. This skeleton is between 25 and 35 years of age. It is unusual to see osteoarthritis in such a young individual, unless it is caused by trauma. This individual also showed evidence of areas of bone necrosis on the left and right knees. Although its etiology is not completely understood, this bone necrosis, known as osteochrondritis dessicans (OCD), is believed to be caused in some cases by trauma during youth (Klippel and Dieppe 1994). Since OCD and OA are both present on this skeleton, trauma is a possible cause for these changes.

Substantial pathological changes to the right proximal femur and the acetabulum of the hip of skeleton 291 were also observed. These bones had the classic appearance of a dislocated hip and this was probably congenital in origin (Ortner and Putschar 1985). The femoral head was missing, leaving a smooth, flat stump. The articulating acetabulum of the hip was deformed, and osteophyte had grown over the original articular surface. A new secondary articular surface had been formed over it. There was no evidence for infection, nor fracture.

The Disarticulated Human Bone

The disarticulated bone comprised material from one context and probably derives from burials disturbed by a 19th-century drain. It was determined that a minimum of five individuals were represented: four adults and a sub-adult. Of the adults, two were male and two were female. One of the females was between the age of 17 to 25 years. It was not possible to assign ages to the remaining adults or the sub-adult. No pathology was noted on any of the fragments.

Comment and Conclusions

The sample that was examined from Site 3 comprises five articulated skeletons (four males and one female) and a minimum of five individuals (two males, two females and one sub-adult) within the disarticulated material. Only three could be aged with any accuracy, and an estimated stature calculated for three individuals. It is interesting to note the high frequency of pathology on these skeletons, although none of the pathologies are exceptionally rare. On the whole the results of this examination are consistent with the findings from the skeletons from the east and west ends of the church.

6 THE FINDS

This chapter deals mainly with the finds from Site 1, those from Site 2 having been fully assessed by specialists and, apart from the pre-Conquest pottery and the medieval floor tiles, thought not of sufficient interest to merit publication. The quantity of medieval finds from Site 2 was quite small and the ceramic finds in particular were generally duplicated by the finds from Site 1 which are reported in full below. The majority of the finds from Site 2 were post-medieval ceramics which occurred in either quite broadly dated contexts or residually in later contexts. In any event more complete forms of those vessels occurred amongst the material from the closely dated 17th- and 18th-century pit groups found on Site 1. The following assessment reports on the finds from Site 2 are available for study in the excavation archive:

The medieval and post-medieval pottery (by Rod Burchill), the ceramic, stone and slate roof tiles (Rod Burchill), the post-medieval wall tiles (Rod Burchill), the clay tobacco pipes (Reg Jackson), the glass (Rod Burchill), the coins and tokens (Rosie Clarke), the small finds including a note on their conservation and storage (Amanda Wallace), the stonework, brick, plaster and mortar samples (Reg Jackson) and the faunal remains (Geraldine Barber).

Apart from the medieval floor tiles and a few other objects, only the finds from the post-medieval pit groups are illustrated.

The letters SF before a number denote that the object has been recorded and identified in the site archive as a Small Find.

Abbreviations:
Approx: approximately
B: breadth
D: diameter
H: height
L: length
Max: maximum
Obv: the obverse side of a coin which normally shows the monarch's head
Rev: the reverse side of a coin
The letters BPT followed by a number refer to the Bristol Pottery Fabric Type series in the Bristol City Museum and Art Gallery.

The Pre-Conquest Pottery (Site 2) by Rod Burchill

The earliest pottery recovered from the excavations were four sherds from contexts 286w and 288w on Site 2. These probably represented a single vessel with a shallow curved rim, in a soft grey fabric with buff-brown surfaces containing very common to abundant clear and coloured quartz, moderate iron ores, rare mudstones and limestone, and very rare chert.

No clear local parallels were found for this fabric. However, it is similar to the late Saxon Bristol fabric BPT 309 which has been dated to between *c.*AD 950 and 1080. The presence of soft red iron ores and absence of sandstones distinguish it from that fabric. A possible Saxon date for the vessel is also suggested by the shallow curved rim which is typical of local pre-Conquest wares, *e.g.* BPT 2 (Ponsford 1998, 136).

The Medieval Pottery (Site 1) by Rod Burchill

The ceramic material recovered from excavated contexts was quantified by sherd count and weight. The fabrics were visually examined using a hand lens (x10 magnification) and, where necessary, a binocular microscope (x30) and identified by comparison with the Bristol Pottery Type Series (BPT).

This small assemblage of 238 sherds weighing 337 grams was allocated to two contextual groups. The first was a mostly unrelated group of features, layers, pits, etc; the second a series of grave fills.

Pottery from Contexts other than Burials

These mostly unrelated contexts contained pottery dating from the 12th to the early 17th centuries. The medieval wares included the 12th-century Ham Green 'A' type jugs and cookpots and the slightly later Ham Green 'B' jugs. From the late 13th and 14th centuries were the products of the Bristol/Redcliffe kilns, including the post-1350 late Redcliffe ware (BPT 118L). Fifteenth-century pottery included Malvernian wares, common from around 1400, and the so-called Tudor Green wares. These Surrey Whitewares are known to be in use in Bristol soon after 1420 as they were found sealed well below the mid 15th-century demolition deposits at Westbury College (Ponsford 1988, 125). Fragments of a black, or very dark green, glazed flared cup of East Somerset (Wanstrow) origin probably date to the early 17th century.

A small number of sherds of the later medieval, 1350–1500, partially glazed Saintonge jugs (BPT 160) were the only non-native imports.

An unusual fabric recovered from context 1423 was a smooth red earthenware with a streaky yellow-green internal glaze (BPT 222). This material was first recognised amongst pottery recovered from the excavations at Peter Street, Bristol in 1975. However, its source and date range is unclear.

From context 1589 came a sherd in a thick quartz gritted fabric with an external yellow-brown glaze (BPT 245). Ponsford (1979) dated this type between 1100–1200 at Bristol Castle. It must be residual in the present context.

Pottery Associated with the Burials

The burials have been assigned to three broad groups: head-niche, coffin and unclassified.

The pottery associated with the head-niche burials was mostly common mid to late 12th-century Ham Green wares and the ubiquitous flint tempered ware BPT 46. There was a single sherd of the Saxo-Norman ware BPT 309. The fill of grave 1184 (Sk. 97) contained a single sherd of BPT 63, a reduced, rough fabric with large flint inclusions and a crude, thumb-pinched hammer head rim. Possibly a variant of BPT 46, the material is currently unsourced but probably dates between 1100–1200. Six graves contained residual Romano-British pottery.

Pottery from the coffin burials, mostly common medieval wares, was generally later in date than the material associated with the head-niche graves. Mostly late 13th or early 14th century, with the exception of context 977 (Sk. 43), none was later than 1350 in date. Residual pottery, including 12th-century Ham Green wares and Romano-British material was recovered from a number of graves.

Context 977 (Sk. 43) contained sherds of Malvernian pottery (BPT 197), Falfield black-glazed ware (BPT 266) and Rhenish stoneware from Cologne (BPT 286). The presence of the Cologne vessel suggests that the back-filling of this grave must have taken place sometime after 1500.

The fills from the unclassifed group of burials all contained sherds of 12th- and early 13th-century Ham Green cookpot (BPT 32 and BPT 114). Graves 804 (Sk. 41), 1070 (Sk. 69), 1115 (Sk. 78), 1144 (Sk. 82), 1142 (Sk. 90), 1352 (Sk. 152), 1498 (Sk. 161), 1409 (Sk. 198), 1554 (Sk. 200) and 1486 (Sk. 203) contained residual

Romano-British pottery including a single sherd of Roman amphora.

Discussion

With the exception of the sherd of BPT 222 in context 1423 and BPT 245 in context 1589, none of the pottery recovered from the medieval contexts was unusual for a Bristol site.

None of the pottery associated with the head-niche burials is later than the end of the 12th century when, the ceramic evidence suggests, the first coffin burials make their appearance.

Grave 977 (Sk. 43) is clearly later than the others and could not have been back-filled earlier than 1500.

The presence of residual Romano-British pottery should not be considered unexpected, as most sites in Bristol produce the odd Roman sherd, and just to the north-west of St James's Priory is a known Romano-British site.

None of the medieval pottery was worthy of illustration.

The Medieval Floor Tiles (Sites 1 and 2 and Church House) by Bruce Williams

A total of 289 mostly incomplete tiles were found. The largest number (209) were retrieved from the excavation of Site 1 in 1995; from Site 2 at the west end of the church came 74 fragments; the others came from the 1988 excavation of Site 1 and from the evaluation of Site 2 in 1993.

The tiles are divided into three groups according to fabric, size, design and method of manufacture. All were from secondary contexts, including grave fills. About 30 tiles of Group 3 were found built into a courtyard wall at the rear of Church House which is adjacent to the north-west corner of the church. Four were removed for study and the others were left *in situ*.

Tile Group 1

There are twenty-seven tiles in this group, two of them undecorated. No tiles are complete; in thickness they vary from 15 to 27mm and the inward bevels on their sides from 0 to 9 degrees. The depth of the slip used in their patterns is up to 2mm, glazes are a rich brown, though in some it is pale-green. The backs of the tiles contain shallow scooped-out keys, though only two keys survive on one tile; probably they had all contained at least four keys originally.

Tiles with similar designs are known from other sites in Bristol, the castle being one of them (see Bristol City Museum and Art Gallery Accession No. Q614R). They are probably late 13th- to 14th-century in date.

Fabric

Grey with orange-brown surfaces, sometimes oxidised orange throughout. Contains abundant fine to medium quartz, rare red iron ores and occasionally rare fine to medium white grits. One tile contains a single fleck of gold mica. A small number of tiles exhibit a white marbling, possibly white firing clays as used in the decoration.

Fig. 73

1   Site 1, context 1202, fill of rob trench of church wall, Period 3.
2   Site 1, context 1361, fill of extraction pit, Period 3.
3   Site 1, context 125, general cleaning layer, Period 4B.
4   Site 2, context 276w, layer, Period 2D.
5   Site 1, context 1361, fill of extraction pit, Period 3.
6   Site 1, context 847, fill of drain, Period 4B.
7   Site 2, context 3w, flagstone floor, Period 4C.
8   Site 1, context 1161, fill of extraction pit, Period 3.
9   Site 1, context 1166, clearance layer, Period 4A.
10 Site 2, context 44t, layer, Period 2C.
11 Site 2, context 276w, layer, Period 3.
12 Site 2, context 136w, fill of foundation trench, Period 4B.
13 Site 2, context 1w, demolition debris, Period 4D.
14 Site 2, context 14w, mortar spread, Period 4C.

Tile Group 2

This group represents the largest number of tiles from the excavations at St James: two hundred and twenty-seven having been found. The tiles are larger than average and none are complete, the largest fragment measuring 184mm across. In thickness they vary between 21mm and 32mm, though one piece measures 34mm. They were formed on a flat, un-sanded surface. Most of the tiles' edges are square, though a few have inward bevels of between 1 and 10 degrees. One tile is a triangle cut from its parent tile while the clay was still soft.

Fifty-eight of the tiles are decorated, all in the incised technique using a blunt instrument which had penetrated up to 1mm into the surface of the soft clay quarry. The tile patterns are fairly crude, consisting of simple geometric forms comprising roundels or curved, often intersecting linear shapes, and occasionally infilled with pecked or stabbed decoration. The upper surface of the tiles was usually covered in rich, green glaze, much of which has now worn away, or they were left unglazed.

As well as the unusual method of manufacture the tiles are characterised by their keys, which were stabbed randomly into their reverse sides. Two joining fragments contain ten keys, each formed from a square-sectioned, tapering, pointed tool probably made of wood. The smallest outer dimension of the keys is 7mm by 8mm across, others measure 10mm square or have sides of 9mm by 12mm. Occasionally

the keys pierce the upper surface of the tiles which has allowed glaze to run down through the holes on to their undersides.

Discussion and Date

The floor tiles are crude alternatives to the two-colour floor tiles commonly found in Bristol. Examples of tiles decorated in the incised technique are not common in south-west England, though examples of this same type have occurred at other sites in the city – at Bristol Cathedral decorated fragments were found in the 1980s stored in a box in the undercroft, and specimens were also noted from an excavation at Peter Street in 1975.

The paucity of tiles of this type outside Bristol, the crude nature of their decoration and the close visual similarity between the Group 2 floor tiles and roof tiles in a similar fabric commonly found on archaeological sites in Bristol, led the writer to suspect they are of local origin. Two specimens of Group 2 floor tiles and three specimens of roof tile were subsequently submitted to Dr David Williams, at the University of Southampton, for thin section analysis. The full results of that study are given below.

The date of the manufacture of the floor tiles can only be given by analogy to the roof tiles in the same or a similar fabric, since no floor tiles of this group have been found *in situ*. At excavations at nos. 82–87 Redcliff Street, Bristol, roof tiles (Type 9) in the above fabric are dated to the 14th century and a similar date may be given for the floor tiles (Williams forthcoming a).

Fabric

For a detailed description of the petrology see the thin section analysis below.

Fig. 74

15 Site 2, context 254w, occupation layer, Period 2C.
16 Site 1, context 959, fill of grave Sk. 42 within the church, Period 2C.
17 Site 1, context 894, fill of linear feature, Period 3.
18 Site 1, context 1503, fill of ditch, Period 2C/2D.
19 Site 1, unstratified.
20 Site 1, context 1423, fill of ditch, Period 2C/2D.
21 Site 1, context 1423, fill of ditch, Period 2C/2D.

Fig. 75

22 Site 2, context 292w, layer, Period 3.
23 Site 1, context 754, fill of rob trench of church wall, Period 3.
24 Site 1, context 1423, fill of ditch, Period 2C/2D.
25 Site 2, context 154w, layer, Period 3.
26 Site 1, context 754, fill of rob trench of church wall, Period 3.
27 Site 1, context 744, fill of pit, Period 4A.
28 Site 1, context 1423, fill of ditch, Period 2C/2D.
29 Site 1, context 1202, fill of rob trench of church wall, Period 3.
30 Site 1, context 1423, fill of ditch, Period 2C/2D.

Fig. 73 Group 1 medieval floor tiles

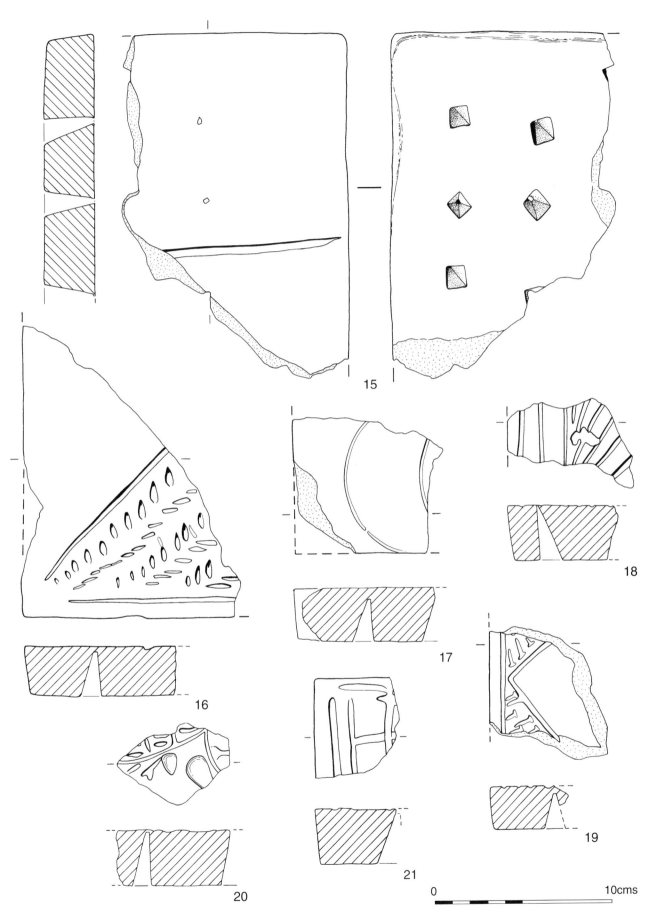

Fig. 74 Group 2 medieval floor tiles

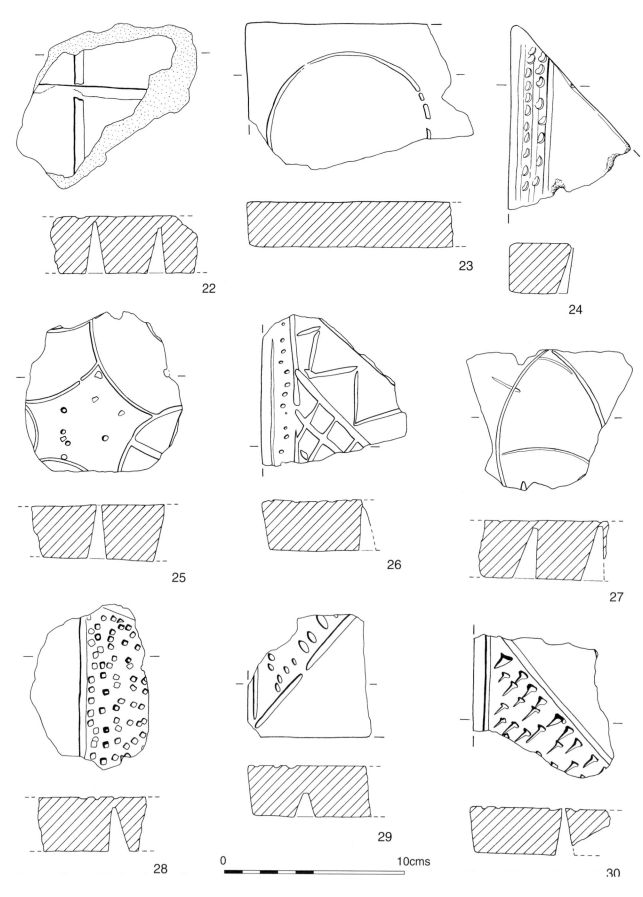

Fig. 75 Group 2 medieval floor tiles

Tile Group 3

Tiles in this group total thirty-five and form part of the well known Malvern/Canynges series (Eames 1980). They measure about 128mm square, with a thickness of between 20mm to 33mm and an inward bevel on their sides of 4 to 15 degrees. Twenty of the tiles are plain, with black glazed upper surfaces; one has a surface coating of slip beneath lead glaze, which has produced a yellow colour. Most of the tiles are square, but one is an oblong cut from the parent tile while soft, representing one-third of a complete tile; another is a triangle being half a tile.

Of the decorated tiles ten of the patterns are represented in the Canynges pavement, which came from a house in Redcliff Street, Bristol, in 1913, and these are included in the British Museum's catalogue of glazed earthenware tiles (Eames 1980). Not all the tiles in Group 3 from St James are present in the Canynges pavement (see Fig. 77.42). There are also a few differences between the St James and the Canynges pavement tiles. In Fig. 76 nos. 31 and 33, the patterns are similar to examples in Canynges pavement (Cat Brit Mus Design Nos. 2922, 2996) but clearly the same stamps were not used. In contrast Fig. 76 nos. 32 and 34 appear to have been formed using the same stamps as in the Canynges pavement (Cat Brit Mus Design Nos. 2921 and 2809).

Some of the designs used in the Group 3 tiles are similar to others found locally at Acton Court, South Gloucestershire, but the same stamps do not appear to have been used there either. For example, Fig. 76 no. 31 is a direct reversal of Poyntz 1b from Acton Court (Williams 1979). The designs in Fig. 77 nos. 38 and 43 are paralleled from Great Malvern in Worcestershire, Gloucester Cathedral and from Lenton Priory.

Discussion and Date

Tiles and variants of the Malvern/Canynges series are distributed widely throughout the Lower Severn Valley and it is beyond the scope of this report to list them all, suffice to say they occur at various sites in Bristol. Tiles in this group from St James are clearly related to the tiles that were manufactured in and around Great Malvern in Worcestershire in the mid 15th century and which probably supplied the tiles for Abbot Sebroke's pavement in Gloucester Cathedral (AD 1455). The St James's Priory tiles are similar to, but not the same as, a large group of tiles discovered in 1974 at Acton Court, Iron Acton, the former seat of the Poyntz family, a few miles to the north-east of Bristol (Williams 1979, 61–76). These tiles were almost certainly laid after 1471, when Sir Robert Poyntz came of age, and may possibly have been ordered in advance of Henry VII's visit to Acton Court in 1486 (Williams 2004, 226–235).

The tiles from St. James show a striking similarity to a complete floor of tiles that was removed from William Canynges's house in Redcliff Street, Bristol, earlier this century (Eames 1951, 33–46). William Canynges was a well-known Bristol merchant during the mid 15th century; he was five times mayor of the city and a Member of Parliament for Bristol in 1451 and 1455. In 1461 he entered the College of Canons at Westbury-on-Trym and remained there until his death in 1474.

The floor in question in Canynges's house is reputed to have been located behind the hall on the first floor, presumably in the solar or private chamber (Eames 1980, 240); however, this conflicts with the archaeological evidence gathered during excavations at the site in 1983. At that time a mortar floor of similar dimensions to the Canynges pavement was found on the ground floor above a stone vaulted cellar roof. The mortar contained the ghost impressions of floor tiles in its surface, and a fireplace on one side equates with that in the reconstructed pavement. There can be little doubt that this was the room that, until removed in 1913, contained the tiled pavement, preserved beneath a timber floor. That the tile pavement was actually in a room on the ground floor, not on the first floor is difficult to explain, unless antiquarians described it as 'above a cellar', in which case it may wrongly have been assumed to be above a ground floor cellar.

Some of the tiles from St James were manufactured using the same stamps as the Canynges examples. Eames (1980) considers the Canynges pavement was probably made between 1481 and 1515, after the death of William Canynges himself, and a similar date may be attributed to this group from St James's Priory.

Fabric

Hard red with common clear and rose quartz, moderate black iron ores and very rare soft white grits in a matrix containing fine crushed quartz.

Fig. 76
31	Church House
32	Church House
33	Church House
34	Church House

Fig. 77
35	Site 1, context 899, fill of linear feature, Period 3.
36	Site 1, context 899, fill of linear feature, Period 3.
37	Site 1, context 1212, fill of pit 1213, Period 4A.
38	Site 1, context 1212, fill of pit 1213, Period 4A.
39	Site 2, context 32t, fill of pit, Period 2D
40	Site 1, context 899, fill of linear feature, Period 3.
41	Site 1, context 899, fill of linear feature, Period 3.
42	Site 1, context 851, layer sealing pit, Period 4B.
43	Site 1, context 899, fill of linear feature, Period 3.

Fig. 76 Group 3 medieval floor tiles

A Note on the Petrology of Two Medieval Floor Tiles and Three Roof Tiles by Dr David Williams

Comments

A thin section examination was conducted on two samples of Group 2 floor tiles, one each recovered from the 1988 and 1995 excavations on Site 1. A previous hand-specimen study of these and other Group 2 floor tiles had suggested that they are in a similar fabric to Type 9 in the Bristol roof tile series (BRF 9; see the report on the ceramic roof tiles below), which is suspected of being made in the Redcliffe area of Bristol. A sample of a Bristol Type 9 roof tile was therefore included for comparative purposes, to see if the fabrics of the floor tiles and roof tiles matched at

Fig. 77 Group 3 medieval floor tiles

all. Also submitted were samples from the Bristol roof tile series Types 2 and 4 (BRF 2 and 4), to see if they also shared the same fabric as Bristol roof tile 9, and by implication have the same origin in the Redcliffe area.

Petrology

1. Group 2 Floor Tile (Site 1, Context 851)

The anisotropic clay matrix contains a ground mass of silt-sized quartz grains. Scattered throughout this are moderately frequent, subangular to angular, ill-sorted grains of quartz, ranging up to over 1mm in size. Some of the larger grains are polycrystalline. Also present are several small fragments of quartz-arenite, with some chert, siltstone and a little opaque iron oxide.

2. Group 2 Floor Tile (Site 1, Context 351, SF 628A)

A fairly clean anisotropic clay matrix, which is noticeably micaceous. Scattered throughout are moderately frequent, generally ill-sorted, subangular to subrounded quartz grains, reaching up to over 1mm at times. Some of the larger grains are polycrystalline. Also present are a few small pieces of quartz-arenite, mudstone and sparse chert, with some opaque iron ore.

3. Bristol Roof Tile Series – Type 9

An isotropic clay matrix containing frequent subangular to angular ill-sorted quartz grains, reaching up to 1mm in size. Some of the larger grains are polycrystalline. Also present are small pieces of quartz-arenite, chert and mudstone, with a little opaque iron oxide.

4. Bristol Roof Tile Series – Type 2

An isotropic clay matrix containing moderately frequent, subangular to subrounded, grains of well-sorted quartz, only occasionally reaching more than 0.40mm in size. Some of the grains are polycrystalline. Pieces of mudstone are common throughout the matrix. Also present are small pieces of chert, a few small fragments of cryptocrystalline limestone and a little opaque iron oxide.

5. Bristol Roof Tile Series – Type 4

In thin section a similar fabric to no. 4.

Comments

The general range and texture of the non-plastic inclusions present in the two samples of Group 2 floor tiles from St James's Priory and the Bristol Type 9 roof tile are fairly similar. This suggests the possibility that the roof tiles may also have been made in the Redcliffe area. There is, however, a noticeable difference in the clay matrix of sample no. 2, in which mica is commonly found, and samples nos. 1 and 3, which are comparatively free of mica. These two fabrics, one rich in mica and one lacking mica, have been noted previously in the suspected pottery and tile products of the Redcliffe kiln area and it would appear that both fabrics are common to the site (Vince 1983).

The two Bristol roof tile samples Types 2 and 4 appear to share a similar fabric, which is rich in mudstone fragments and also contains small pieces of limestone. This in turn is noticeably different to the fabrics of two samples of floor tile from St James's Priory and the Bristol Type 9 roof tile discussed above. However, a mudstone/limestone fabric also seems to be present amongst the tile fabrics thought to have been produced in the Redcliffe area (Vince 1983).

The Ceramic Roof Tiles (Site 1)
by Rod Burchill

The Roof Tile

The ceramic roof tile recovered from excavated contexts was quantified by sherd count and weight. The material was visually examined and identified by comparison to the Bristol Roof Tile Fabric series (BRF). The original type series (Williams and Ponsford 1988, 145) has been enlarged and a complete listing is included in this report.

The roof tile recovered from the excavation consisted of 316 sherds weighing 26.640kg. Some 55% of the material examined was pan-tile, and of the remainder locally made Bristol/Redcliffe tile accounted for 24.3% of the assemblage with a further 17.4% being tiles from the Malvern Chase area.

Fabrics BRF 1, 2, 4, 5 and 9 are petrologically similar to the Bristol/Redcliffe pottery fabric (BPT 118) and all date to the late 13th and 14th centuries. These fabrics are very common, usually forming the major part of the medieval component of roof tile assemblages from Bristol sites.

The Malvernian tiles (BRF 7; Vince 1977) are later, first making their appearance in the 15th century and continuing into the 16th century.

The assemblage included seven sherds of BRF 10, a pinky orange fabric with purple-brown glaze. The source of this type is not known. However, BRF 10 is possibly similar in date to the Mavernian tiles. Also present were two sherds in the North Devon gravel tempered fabric (BRF 11) and part of a single tile in a thin, very hard grey fabric with flint inclusions and a grey-green glaze, a type previously unseen in Bristol.

No complete tiles were found and none were worthy of illustration.

The Bristol Roof Tile Fabric Series

The Bristol Roof Tile Fabric series (BRF), based on the work of Williams and Ponsford (1988) and updated by the present writer, currently consists of 15 fabrics with an additional number, BRF 14, being used as a miscellaneous category for single previously unknown fabrics. A reference collection of typed sherds is held by Bristol and Region Archaeological Services.

BRF 1 Tiles in a grey/buff fabric containing common large lumps of unhomogenized clay (4–6mm). Green or yellow-green glaze. Knife cut crests, stab or wavy comb decoration. Made in Bristol. 14th century.

BRF 2 Grey fabric similar to BRF 1 with the addition of common lumps of mudstone. Green glaze. Knife cut crests sometimes with stabbed decoration. Bristol. 14th century.

BRF 3 Fabric similar to BPT 123, pink with a grey core. Yellowish green glaze. Bristol. 14th century.

BRF 4 Grey fabric containing abundant white quartz. Thin section analysis has shown this fabric to be petrologically identical to BRF 2 (see report by David Williams above). Green glaze. Low-profile crests. Bristol. 14th century.

BRF 5 Redcliffe fabric, grey core, common quartz, rare limestone. Green glaze. Low profile crest. Bristol. 14th century.

BRF 6 Deep pink iron-rich fabric. Occasional yellowish glaze. Flat tiles with peg holes. Bristol.

BRF 7 Malvern fabric. 15th to 16th centuries.

BRF 8 North-west Wiltshire (Minety) fabric. 14th/15th century.

BRF 9 Macroscopically similar to BRF 2. Thin section analysis has shown that BRF 9 is noticeably different from that fabric as it contains no limestone (see report by David Williams above). BRF 9 is similar to pottery type BPT 118. Tall, knife cut crests with thumbed applied strips. Bristol. 14th century.

BRF 10 A chaotic, poorly mixed, orange fabric with fine mica, iron ores and rare clay pellets. Purple-brown glaze.

BRF 11 North Devon gravel tempered roof tile. 17th century.

BRF 12 A quartz gritted fabric with orange surfaces and green tinged amber glaze. Thumb applied strips.

BRF 13 Pan-tile.

BRF 14 A category for miscellaneous types.

BRF 15 Pink/orange fabric with abundant rose quartz and sparse quartzite up to 4mm. Patchy yellow-green glaze.

BRF 16 Grey fabric with red surfaces. Inclusions of abundant clear fabric and rare limestone in a matrix of fine quartz sand, some reaction with hydrochloric acid. The glaze, where present, is a purplish greeny-brown.

The Clay Tobacco Pipes (Site 1) by Reg Jackson

The post-medieval contexts produced a large number of clay pipe stem fragments and pipe bowls dating from the 17th to the 19th centuries. The pipes from six of the 17th- and 18th-century pit groups are described in more detail, illustrated and quantified later in this chapter.

Those pipes which bore the names or initials of pipe makers were, with three exceptions, all made by known Bristol manufacturers while the unmarked bowls were typical of those known to have been made in Bristol. As Bristol was a major pipe manufacturing centre and the heart of that industry in the 17th and 18th centuries lay just to the south-west of the present site in the area around Lewin's Mead, there would have been no need for the inhabitants to have imported pipes from elsewhere.

The products of the Bristol pipe makers represented in the clay pipe assemblage are shown in Table 35. The information on the working dates of the pipe makers is taken from Jackson and Price (1974) and Price and Jackson (1979).

One bowl, marked with the name 'IEFFRY.HVNT' incuse on the heel (Fig. 86.162; context 1212, Period 4A) was made by the Wiltshire pipe maker Jeffrey Hunt who is known to have been working in the mid 17th century. Another mid 17th-century bowl was marked with what appears to be 'EDMVND HI...' incuse on the heel, although the maker's identity and place of work is unknown (Fig. 93.193; context 191, Period 4A).

Only two pipes appear to be of Continental European origin. One bowl, which is highly decorated and depicts a man on horseback, is probably Dutch and dates to the 18th century (context 159, Period 5A). Another stem is marked 'FIOLET' and refers to the French firm of Fiolet who were working in St Omer in the 19th century (context 956, Period 5B).

The Coins and Tokens (Site 1) by Rosie Clarke

(Coins and tokens from the major post-medieval pit groups appear later in this chapter).

None illustrated.
A total of 14 items (two being stuck together) are described below.

44. Silver short-cross penny folded in half. The obverse is the only side visible but enables the coin to be identified as Richard I (1189–99). Class 4b. The face is grotesque and of degraded style with one large curl on each side. The eyes are large annulets and the pearls of the crown run together. Obv: – NRICVS–. (SF 193B, Context 1101, Burial Type 2, Sk. 64).

45. Silver short-cross penny folded in half. The reverse is the only side visible, but the legend is illegible so it is impossible to assign the coin to any particular issue. Rev: Short Cross. (SF 194B, Context 1101, Burial Type 2, Sk. 64).

In 1180 a coinage of new type, known as the Short Cross coinage, replaced the earlier Tealby issue of pence. The coinage covers not only the latter part of

Table 35 The occurrence of marked clay tobacco pipes and the identity of their makers

Note: All are Bristol pipe makers. Free indicates the date when the pipe maker took his freedom to work in the city.

Pipe maker's Name	Working Dates	Mark and number of examples in assemblage in brackets
James Abott	Free 1677, dead by 1718	'IA' incuse on decorated stem (2 examples)
John Arthurs	Free 1707, died 1721	'IA' incuse on back of bowl (1) 'IA' in relief in cartouche on side of bowl (2) 'I.ARTHURS' in relief in cartouche on side of bowl with 'IA' incuse on back of bowl (1) 'I.ARTHURS' in relief in cartouche on side of bowl (2)
John Bladen I	Free 1657, to at least 1689	'IB' incuse on heel (1)
Richard Bourne	Free 1739, to at least 1762	'RB' in relief in cartouche on side of bowl (1)
Henry Edwards	Free 1699, to ?1739	'H.EDWARDS' in relief in cartouche on side of bowl (4)
Philip Edwards I	Free 1650, died 1683	'PE' incuse on heel (11)
Llewellin Evans	Free 1661, died 1688	'LE' incuse on heel (2) 'LE' incuse on back of bowl (?5) 'LE' incuse on decorated stem (1)
William Evans I or II	Free 1660, to at least 1713	'WE' incuse on back of bowl (2)
John Harvey I or II	Free 1706, to at least 1746	'I.HARVEY' in relief in cartouche on side of bowl (1)
Henry Hoar	Free 1699, died 1728	'HH' incuse on back of bowl (1)
James Jenkins	Free 1707, to at least 1739	'II' in relief in cartouche on side of bowl (1)
Devereux Jones I	Free 1691, died 1713	'D.JONES' in relief in cartouche on side of bowl (2)
Edward Lewis I	Free 1631, dead by 1652	'EL' incuse on heel (2)
Thomas Monkes	Working 1656 to at least 1670	'TM' incuse on heel (1)
William Naylor	Free 1722, died ?1736	'WN' incuse on back of bowl (1)
Richard Nunney	Free 1655, dead by 1713	'RN' incuse on heel (20)
John Pearce I	Free 1696, to at least 1738	'IP' incuse on rear of bowl (1)
Maurice Phillips	Free 1721, dead by 1740	'MP' incuse on rear of bowl (1) 'MP' in relief in cartouche on side of bowl (1)
William Phillips I	Free 1690	'WP' incuse on rear of bowl (7) 'WP' in relief in cartouche on side of bowl (1)
Jacob Prosser	Free 1663, to at least 1700	'IP' incuse on decorated stem (?3)
Edward Reed	Free 1706, to at least 1739	'ER' in relief in cartouche on side of bowl with 'ER' incuse on back of bowl (1)
Samuel Richards I or II	Free 1747, to at least 1812	'SR' in relief on either side of spur (1)
John Ring	1803 to 1818	'JR' in large scrolled letters in relief on side of bowl (1)
Francis Russell I	Free 1669, dead by 1714	'FR' incuse on heel (1)
William Scott	Free 1708, to at least 1715	'WS' in relief in cartouche on side of bowl (1)
John Sinderling	Free 1668, dead by 1699	'IS' incuse on back of bowl (1)
Thomas Smith I	Free 1651, dead by 1667	'TS' incuse on heel (2)
John Squibb	Free 1705, to at least 1739	'IS' in relief in cartouche on side of bowl (2)
Robert Tippet I	Free 1660, dead by 1687	'RT' incuse on heel (2)
John Tucker I	Free 1662, dead by 1690	'IT' incuse on heel (2)
Joel Williams or John Wilson	Free 1713, to at least 1729 Free 1707, to at least 1723	'IW' in relief in cartouche on the side of bowl with 'W' in relief on one side of heel (1) 'IW' in relief in cartouche on the side of the bowl with 'IW' in relief on either side of the base of the bowl (1)

the reign of Henry II but also the reigns of his sons Richard and John and the first part of the reign of his grandson Henry III. It continued up to 1247, when the Long Cross coinage was introduced, the new pennies having the reverse cross extended to the edge of the coin to help safeguard the coins against clipping. The entire Short Cross issue uses the king's name as 'HENRICVS' – there are no English coins with the names of Richard or John. The Short Cross coins can be divided chronologically into various classes: eleven or twelve mints were operating under Henry II, thirteen mints under Richard I, seventeen under John, but only six under Henry III.

46. Henry VI (first reign 1422–61) AR penny, York, Class A. Leaf-pellet coinage (1445–1454). Quatrefoil and pellet in centre of reverse, no extra pellets in quarters or by hair. Obv: Legend illegible. Rev: CIVI– —ACI (Civitas Eboraci). A similar coin was found in 1993 on the evaluation carried out at the west end of St James's church (BaRAS 1993, 15). (SF 544B, Context 1603, Period 3).

47. Billon Ceitil, Portugal (Lisbon), probably Alfonso V (1438–81). Obv: Castle, legend illegible. Rev: Shield, legend illegible. The Ceitil took its name from Ceuta, the fortress whose capture in 1415 marked the beginning of Portuguese expansion in Africa (Grierson 1991, 191). (SF 213B, Context 1166, clearance layer, Period 4A).

48. Lead token, dia. 15mm. Probably 14th-15th century. Similar to Mitchener and Skinner 1984, pl.10, no. 50. Obv: Cinquefoil. Rev: Illegible, ?uniface. (SF 126A, Context 166, fill of pit, Period 4A).

49. Lead disc, dia. 20mm. Probably an early Tudor token. Similar to Mitchener and Skinner 1985, pl. 6, no. 6. Obv: Plain cross. Rev: Illegible, ?uniface. (SF 410A, Context 260, fill of pit, Period 4A).

50. Lead token, dia. 20mm. Probably Elizabethan. Similar to Mitchener and Skinner 1985, pl. 14, no. 87. Obv: Field voided by triple cross. Rev: Illegible, ?uniface. (SF 409A, Context 260, fill of pit, Period 4A).

51. Æ Jetton. Nuremberg copy of a Savoy original. Obv: Cross pattée in shield with helmet above ornamented with ribbons, surmounted by a lion's muzzle ornamented with five tassels. Letters 'R' and 'S'. The whole is framed in garlanded scooped out crescents. No legend, decorated border. Rev: Two love-knots of Savoy ending in tassels, the whole framed in garlanded scooped out crescents. No legend. Dated to the first quarter of the 16th century. This is of an unusual type and not usually found on English excavations. (SF 326B, Context 1299, fill of extraction pit, Period 3).

52. Æ Jetton. Nuremberg. Obv: 3 open crowns and 3 lys arranged alternately round a rose within an inner circle of rope-pattern. Fictitious Lombardic lettering. Rev: The *Reichsapfel* within a double tressue of 3 curves and 3 angles set alternately all within an inner circle of rope-pattern. Fictitious Lombardic lettering. (SF 423B, Context 1206, fill of drain, Period 3).

53. Æ Jetton. Nuremberg. Obv: –NSSCHULT. 3 open crowns and 3 lys arranged alternately round a rose within an inner circle of rope-pattern. Rev: The *Reichsapfel* within a double tressue of 3 curves and 3 angles set alternately all within an inner circle of rope-pattern. Lettering illegible. There were three Hans Schultes producing Nuremberg jettons but this one would have to have been made between 1553 and 1612. (SF 315B, Context 1011, clearance layer, Period 4C).

54. Token. Copper alloy. Inscribed 'Bank/Token/1s 6d/1811'. D: 28mm. (SF 51A, Context 125, layer,

Period 4B).

55. Two coins found stuck together. AR Shilling and Sixpence, George III (1760–1820), last or 'new' coinage (1816–20). The shilling is illegible, the sixpence is dated 1819. (SF 52A, Context 125, layer, Period 4B).

56. AR Shilling, George III (1760–1820), last or 'new' coinage (1816–20). Obv: Illegible. Rev: Crowned shield in garter. (SF 56A, Context 125, layer, Period 4B).

Objects of Bone and Ivory (Site 1) by Rod Burchill

(Objects of bone and ivory from the major post-medieval pit groups appear later in this chapter).

Illustrated: 57 and 73.
The assemblage of bone and ivory objects comprised 94 items. Much of this material consisted of objects

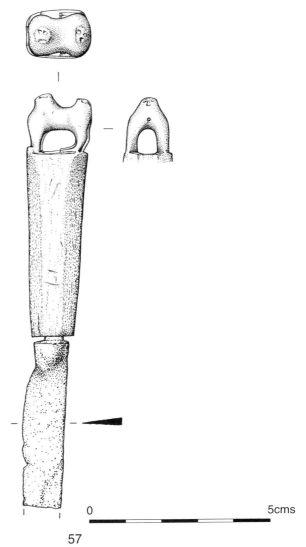

57

Fig. 78 Knife handle and blade

from late contexts or waste from bone working. Full details of the items not discussed here can be found in the archive.

57. Fig. 78. Handle of a small knife with iron blade. The handle is decorated with a free-standing zoomorphic figure, probably a dog. The head and tail appear to be missing, and there is evidence for possible attachment holes for them. A small hole seems to represent the anus of the animal. There are three toes on each back foot. The triangular blade is broken at its tip. Handle: 65mm x max. 20mm, blade: 45mm x 13mm. (SF 166B, Context 842, garden soil, Period 4B).

Nos. 58 to 62 probably represent toothbrushes. Three of the heads have longitudinal grooves on the upper surface. These grooves are to take retaining wires to hold the bristles in place (MacGregor 1985, 183). Several of the present examples are copper stained including one without retaining grooves. MacGregor suggests that copper-stained brush heads lacking grooves for retaining wires probably had tufts of fine copper wire. However, the lack of other evidence for wire bristles has led Crummy (1988, 24) to suggest that tufts of organic bristles may have been bound with copper wire.

58. Handle of a small brush, probably a toothbrush with four rows of holes to take the bristles. The round-sided rectangular section handle and head has a waisted neck. Handle stamped 'North ...' on upper face. L: of head 49mm, handle broken. (SF 96B, Context 718, garden soil, Period 4B).

59. Toothbrush. Head has three rows of bristle holes. Handle has a rectangular section and waist at neck. Patchy copper staining on head. 138mm x 12mm x 4mm. (SF 415B, Context 904, fill of drain, Period 4B).

60. Toothbrush head. Three rows of bristles with three grooves in upper surface of head to take retaining wires for bristles. Copper stained. 56mm x 12mm. (SF 62B, Context 575, make-up for floor of Scottish Presbyterian Church, Period 4C).

61. Toothbrush. Three rows of bristles with three grooves on reverse. 134mm x 15mm. (SF 152B, Context 937, fill of drain, Period 4B).

62. Part of a small brush (?toothbrush) with four rows of bristle holes. Four longitudinal grooves on reverse. Copper stained. 50mm x max. 12mm x 5mm. (SF 101B, Context 585, fill of ?drain, Period 4B).

Nos. 63 to 65 are four bone bobbins. All were probably lathe-turned and examples of similar bobbins have been described by MacGregor (1985, 183).

63. Swollen waisted ?bobbin with reed and cord decoration at end and faint grooves at base of shaft. L: 59mm. (SF 1B, Context 575, make-up for floor of Scottish Presbyterian Church, Period 4C).

64. Fragment of ?bobbin with double reed and cord decoration beneath a rounded knob. L: 14mm, D: 4mm. (SF 100B, Context 609, fill of pit, Period 4B).

65. Part of a lathe turned bobbin with reed and cord decoration and end boss with knob. (SF 158B,

Context 937, fill of drain, Period 4B).

66. Bone peg. Stepped shaft with rounded knob end. Hollow core. Split along longitudinal axis. Possibly a tuning peg. For other examples of tuning pegs see MacGregor (1985, fig. 77). (SF 157B, Context 1515, fill of pit, Period 4B).

67. Incomplete spatulate object. Possibly part of a spatulate spoon. The shaft tapers from 13 to 5mm with a semi-eliptical terminal. L: 61mm. Similar examples are described by Margeson (1993, 137, fig. 102.930). (SF 289B, Context 729, fill of construction trench for drain, Period 4B).

68. Spoon. Shallow eliptical bowl. The handle flaring from the bowl, has a rounded spatulate terminal. Bowl: 40mm x 19mm. Handle: 70mm x 6mm. Spatulate end D: 16mm. MacGregor (1985, 181, fig. 98.r) illustrates a spatulate spoon although that example has a rounded bowl. Such spoons usually copy the style of metallic spoons. (SF 231B, Context 1042, fill of drain, Period 4B).

69. Plain, double sided one-piece comb with curved end pieces. W: 44mm. Teeth L: 13mm. A full discussion on simple and compound combs may be found in MacGregor (1985, 73–95). (SF 18B, Context 655, lower fill of cellar, Period 4C).

70. Fragment of double comb. No decoration. W: of comb 46mm. (SF 276A, Context 248, layer, Period 4A).

71. Small decorative lid, domed in the Chinese style. Lathe turned with thread on underside. D: 21mm. (SF 85A, Context 126, layer of cess-like material, Period 4A).

72. Seal or lid for a small container. Grooved top, internal screw thread. D: 34mm. (SF 215B, Context 1042, fill of drain, Period 4B).

73. Fig. 79. Bone needle. Curved, polished bone shaped to form a point with large 'eye' at opposite end. Probably used for weaving or net-making and the regular striations on its lower end may have been caused by use. L: 185mm, D: of eye 7mm. Similar bone needles have been recovered from Exeter (Megaw 1984, 351, B17–19), Northampton (Williams 1979, 310) and King's Lynn (Clarke and Carter 1977). (SF 68B, Context 866, fill of quarry pit, Period 3).

74. Part of a hollow bone object with internal screw thread. L: 50mm x max. D: 17mm. Its function is unclear, although Margeson (1993, fig. 161.1758) tentatively suggests the object may be part of a musical instrument. (SF 495A, Context 187, fill of pit, Period 4B).

75. Lathe-turned object. Multiple reeds and cord decoration. Pointed terminal with perforated disc on the centre stem. Slot cut out of shaft in the manner of whistles. Hollow or part hollow shaft. Function unclear. (SF 335B, unstratified).

76. A group of eleven bone discs with a central perforation. They probably represent button blanks or formers. Diameter of the discs varies between 9mm and 26mm and the perforation between 1mm and 2mm. All are approximately 1mm thick. (SF 46A; SF 36A; SF 274A; SF 279A; SF 284A; SF 287A; SF 288A; SF 593A; SF 70B; SF 243B; SF 461B; SF 469B;

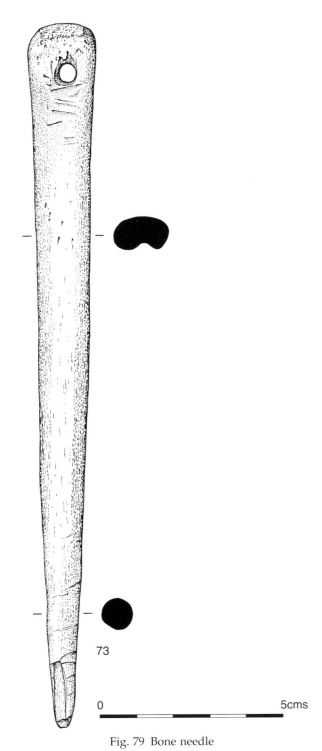

73

0   5cms

Fig. 79 Bone needle

from contexts 64, 109, 248, 338, 718, 938, 1026, 1042).

MacGregor (1985, 99–102) has described the process of making buttons from the long bones of cattle. He describes the method of producing the discs by the use of a centre-bit drill with a curving profile and projecting centre point. The bones were drilled from both sides using the centre point to align the drill. MacGregor lists a number of sites where similar material has been found, although a number of these

are medieval in date as are the previously excavated examples from Bristol (Williams forthcoming b).

Objects of Glass (Site 1) by Rod Burchill

(Objects of glass from the major post-medieval pit groups appear later in this chapter).

Illustrated: 111.

The assemblage of glass small finds, 128 pieces, consisted mostly of domestic utensils such as bottles and drinking glasses. A number of vessels had a probable medical function and these included flasks and phials. A glass tube (SF 467A) was probably part of an alembic, used for distillation, possibly of medicinal spirits.

Medieval window glass was recovered from seven contexts. All was in poor condition. A number of examples were decorated and in others it was possible that the decoration was obscured by degradation of the glass surface. Medieval window glass was likely to have been fitted only to high status buildings and the present examples were probably derived from the priory church.

77. Seven fragments of medieval window glass. Very poor condition. (SF 545B, Context 1224, primary fill of extraction pit, Period 3).

78. Fragments of smooth black surfaced medieval window glass with painted decoration. Conservation analysis suggests a dark blue glass with red and black decoration. (SF 316(a)B, Context 1160, fill of extraction pit, Period 3).

79. Fragments of medieval window glass. Green core, with dark surface weathering but white where protected by lead came. (SF 316(b)B, Context 1160, fill of extraction pit, Period 3).

80. Fragment of clear, slightly yellow, medieval glass. (SF 316(c)B, Context 1160, fill of extraction pit, Period 3).

81. Fragment of medieval glass. (SF 316(d)B, Context 1160, fill of extraction pit, Period 3).

82. Two fragments of opaque, heavily weathered, late medieval window glass with painted surface decoration. (SF 431B, Context 1202, fill of rob trench of church wall, Period 3).

83. Fragment of medieval window glass with painted surface decoration. (SF 321A, Context 294, layer, Period 3).

84. Fragments of medieval glass. Material very unstable and has deteriorated to a silica mass. (SF 321B, Context 759, layer sealing extraction pits, Period 4A).

85. Two very decayed fragments of medieval glass. (SF 398B, Context 1205, stone-lined drain, Period 3).

86. Decorated window glass. One with botanical motifs and bands, the other with simple coloured bands. (SF 547B, Context 580, layer, Period 4B).

87. Small sub-rectangular bottle with simple everted rim and dimpled sides. Green glass. Height 41mm

x 25mm x 25mm. See Margeson (1993, 1001, fig. 630) for a similar vessel. (SF 614A, Context 359, fill of pit, Period 4A).

88. Neck and shoulder of a straight-sided bottle with string rim. Green glass. See Charleston (1984, 227) for a similar example. (SF 465A, Context 278, fill of pit, Period 4A).

89. Flanged rim of a square-shouldered bottle. Green glass with heavy surface degradation. (SF 99A, Context 126, layer of cess-like material, Period 4A).

90. Complete straight-sided bottle with tall, narrow neck with string rim and deep punt. Brown glass with little surface degradation. (SF 73A, Context 126, layer of cess-like material, Period 4A).

91. Rim of narrow necked bottle. Dark green glass. (SF 92A, Context 126, layer of cess-like material, Period 4A).

92. Narrow necked bottle with string rim. Dark green glass. (SF 100A, Context 126, layer of cess-like material, Period 4A).

93. Glass bottle seal with letters 'I' and 'N' separated by a raised dot with three raised dots below and a stylised sun above. Bottle seals are described by Charleston (1975, 225; 1984, 276) and Oakley (1979, 301). (SF 200B, Context 851, layer sealing pit, Period 4B).

94. Fragment of scent bottle with moulded rib pattern. Smokey grey glass. A similar vessel is described by Charleston (1986, 48). (SF 25A, Context 75, make-up layer for floor of Scottish Presbyterian Church, Period 4C).

A number of glass phials were recovered from the excavations. These vessels, all very similar in form, are likely to have had a medical or pharmaceutical use, probably being used to hold medicines. Similar glass phials have been described by Margeson (1993, 102), Charleston (1984, 276; 1986) and Preston (1979, 121).

95. Phial with flange rim and shallow punt. Pale green glass with iridescent surface weathering. H: 76mm, D: of base 33mm. (SF 97B, Context 687, fill of linear feature, Period 4A).

96. Large cylindrical phial with narrow flange rim and shallow punt. Colourless glass. H: 130mm, D: of base 40mm. (SF 228A, Context 248, layer, Period 4A).

97. Rolled back flange rim of a phial. Colourless glass. (SF 6A, Context 145, fill of shallow rectangular feature, Period 4A).

98. Misshapen wide flanged rim of a small phial or bottle. Green glass. (SF 131A, Context 127, fill in top of gully, Period 4A).

99. Flanged rim and shoulder of a small phial. Green tinted glass. (SF 102A, Context 126, layer of cess-like material, Period 4A).

100. Flanged rim of a phial. Green glass. (SF 86A, Context 126, layer of cess-like material, Period 4A).

101. Small rectangular phial with flange rim and deep punt. Pale green glass. (SF 284B, Context 949, courtyard surface, Period 4B).

102. Small glass phial with flange rim. Weathered green glass. H: 55mm, D: of base 22mm. (SF 168B, Context

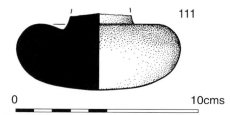

Fig. 80 Possible glass linen smoother

886, cultivation soil, Period 4A).

103. Neck of a small flask with vertical mould-blown ribs. Brownish-white translucent glass. (SF 293A, Context 248, layer, Period 4A).

104. Neck and shoulder of a small flask with simple rim and vertical mould-blown ribbing. (SF 273A, Context 248, layer, Period 4A).

105. Flanged rim and shoulder of a small flask with vertical mould-blown ribbing. Pale blue-green glass. Margeson (1993, 100) describes a similar vessel from Norwich. (SF 230A, Context 248, layer, Period 4A).

106. Shoulder of a ?flask with crudely applied grooves. Glass has become opaque as a result of heavy surface degradation. Charleston (1984, 148, figs. 66 and 67) describes similar vessels. (SF 340B, Context 1250, fill of quarry pit, Period 3).

107. Hollow stem and base of a conical bowl in colourless glass. The inverted baluster stem has a knob beneath the bowl. (SF 127A, Context 126, layer of cess-like material, Period 4A).

108. Stem and base of a conical bowled drinking glass. The hollow stem has top and bottom knobs. (SF 4B, Context 621, possible garden soil, Period 4A).

109. Wine glass. Stem with base of conical bowl. Twisted quatrefoil stem with small base knob. See Charleston (1986, 51) for a similar example. (SF 11B, Context 623, fill of pit or hollow, Period 4A).

110. Long, narrow glass tube, possibly from an alembic. Green glass. Similar tubes from alembics have been recovered from Norwich (Margeson 1993, 98, fig. 109). (SF 467A, Context 278, fill of pit, Period 4A).

111. Fig. 80. Large doughnut shaped object with broken ?stem. Similarly shaped objects from medieval contexts have been described as linen smoothers (Charleston 1984, 267; Oakley 1979, 297; Margeson, 1993, 137). However, the present example, at 88mm diameter, is somewhat larger than those. (SF 608B, Context 949, courtyard surface, Period 4B).

112. Small, decorative head (part of a larger object) in white opaque glass with painted facial features. Hair is applied millefiori cane in red, green and purple. (SF 281, Context 248, layer, Period 4A).

Objects of Iron (Site 1) by Rod Burchill

(Objects of iron from the major post-medieval pit groups appear later in this chapter).

None illustrated.

The iron assemblage was mainly composed of nails, the majority of which were coffin nails. Much of the material was unidentifiable being mostly corrosion products. Details of items not recorded here will be found in the site archive.

113. Key. Solid shaft with kidney-shaped bow and two section bit. L: 105mm. Medieval and post-medieval keys have been described by Crummy (1988, 82–83) and Margeson (1993, 160–161). (SF 87A, Context 126, layer of cess-like material, Period 4A).

114. Offset finger loop from a pair of scissors. See Margeson (1993, 136) for a similar example. (SF 286A, Context 248, layer, Period 4A).

115. Buckle frame lacking both pin and strap attachment. Approx. 45mm x max. 40mm. Similar buckles are described by Goodall *et al.* (1979, 274) and Margeson (1993, 33). (SF 630A, Context 351, fill of pit, Period 4A).

116. Part of the base of a cauldron with D-section foot. D: 220mm plus. L: of foot approx. 100mm. (SF 139B, Context 678, fill of water tank, Period 4B).

The small assemblage of knife blades contained both whittle-tang and scale-tang types. Whittle-tang knives, where the tang is inserted into a hollow or drilled handle, are common throughout the medieval period and the presence of a number of bone-handles of whittle-tang type of 17th- and 18th-century date demonstrates the whittle-tang's continued popularity for utility knives. Scale-tang knives, with a wider tang to which leaves or scales of wood, bone or metal were riveted to form the handle, first appeared in the 14th century (Cowgill *et al.* 1987, 51) and continue in use to the present day.

117. Whittle-tang knife. Narrow blade and slightly curved back, the edge curves towards the back, tip broken. The tang (broken) is set central to the blade on angular shoulders. Blade: 100mm x 17mm. Tang: 24+mm x 6mm (tapering). See Cowgill *et al.* 1987 (79, fig. 54.12) for a similar example. (SF 417B, Context 1299, fill of extraction pit, Period 3).

118. Incomplete knife blade. Rounded tip, edge curves up back. L: 50mm x 15mm. (SF 464B, Context 776, area of mortar, Period 4B).

119. Possible fragment of a knife blade. Orientation is unclear. However, the edge probably curves to meet the straight back. L: 80mm. (SF 90A, Context 126, layer of cess-like material, Period 4A).

120. Part of knife blade. Wide scale-tang with twin rivets. See Margeson (1993, 124–132) for a similar example. (SF 422B, Context 1299, fill of extraction pit, Period 3).

A small assemblage of structural ironwork was recovered from the excavations. The assemblage consisted principally of staples, wallhooks, looped-spikes and nails. The nails are not discussed here, but further details may be found in the site archive. Margeson (1993) provides a full discussion of the function of structural ironwork.

121. Part of a large staple with broken arms. L: 55+mm.

W: between arms 35mm. See Goodall *et al.* (1979, 145), Margeson (1993, 272) and Williams (1988, fig.26.8) for similar examples. (SF 317B, Context 1041, layer of grey mortar, Period 4B).

122. Incomplete looped-spike. Rectangular shaft with circular hole in head. L: 95mm. Margeson (1993, 146) describes a number of functions for looped-spikes. (SF 319B, Context 1250, fill of extraction pit, Period 3).

123. Looped-spike with flattened rectangular shaft and circular 'eye'. Shaft broken. L: 120mm. D: of hole 10mm. (SF 612B, Context 866, fill of extraction pit, Period 3).

124. Holdfast. Tapering spike with L-shaped head. Holdfasts were used to attach wood to masonry, brickwork or other timbers. They are principally post-medieval in date (Margeson 1993, 146). L: 135mm x max. 10mm. (SF 445A, Context 187, fill of pit, Period 4B).

125. Possible wallhook or holdfast. L: 105mm. (SF 105A, Context 128, fill of shallow feature, Period 4B).

126. Incomplete object. Rolled sheet with two small rivets. (SF 342(a)B, Context 1160, fill of extraction pit, Period 3).

Objects of Copper Alloy (Site 1) by Rod Burchill

(Objects of copper alloy from the major post-medieval pit groups appear later in this chapter).

Illustrated: 147.
The copper alloy assemblage consisted of 201 items. A number were unidentifiable scrap or waste, or were from late contexts. Details of material not recorded here will be found in the site archive.

127. Fragment of a key. Solid shaft with kidney-shaped bow. See Margeson (1993, 160–162) for a similar example. (SF 63A, Context 125, layer, Period 4B).

128. Plain disc. D: 25mm. (SF 54A, Context 125, layer, Period 4B).

129. Plain disc. D: 21mm. (SF 64A, Context 125, layer, Period 4B).

A group of thimbles were recovered from excavated contexts. Two date to the late 17th century and two from the late 18th century. Seventeenth-century copper alloy thimbles were usually imported from Holland. Those with machine made indentations are post-1620. All the types described here can be recognised in the examples from Colchester (Crummy 1988, 28–29). Crummy also describes the origins of many of these thimbles.

130. Fragment of rolled sheet. Decorated with a wide plain band beneath a band of circular indentations. Probably a thimble of open ring-shaped type although it is likely to have been a simple dome with the top now decayed (Crummy 1988, 29.104). (SF 59A, Context 125, layer, Period 4B).

131. Thimble. Plain band between base and area of

circular indentations. Narrow body. H: 24mm, D: 16mm. (SF 55A, Context 125, layer, Period 4B).

132. Small thimble. No obvious decoration but x-ray suggests presence of diamond pattern indentations. H: 21mm, D: 13mm. (SF 218A, Context 159, fill of construction trench for drain, Period 4B).

133. Shoe buckle. Single frame, rectangular with rounded corners. Central bar with double rotating forked pins: one simple, the other ornate with long backward sweeping terminals and short forward facing points. It is attached to the bar with an inverted fork. Frame has a simple moulded decoration. See Fairclough (1979, 125) and Burchill (forthcoming) for examples of twin pin shoe buckles. (SF 174B, Context 715, fill of rubbish pit, Period 4A).

134. Fragment of buckle frame, probably from a shoe. (SF 71A, Context 126, layer of cess-like material, Period 4A).

135. Small spatula with circular recessed area set within a rounded terminal. Incomplete. Possibly for medical or toilet use. (SF 68A, Context 126, layer of cess-like material, Period 4A).

The assemblage includes six lace chapes or points. Four of these are Oakley's Type 1 and two Type 2 (Oakley 1979, 262–3). Type 1 lace-ends are made from a tapering piece of sheet rolled around the end of the lace to form a butt-joint and then rivetted with one or two copper alloy (occasionally iron) rivets. Type 2 lace ends are formed by folding a piece of sheet metal in from one or both sides to grip the lace. Type 1 lace ends are considered to be medieval, dating between *c*.1375 and 1550/75, although examples are found in 17th-century contexts. Type 2 lace chapes date between 1550/75 and 1700+ (Crummy 1988, 12–13). A full discussion of the production and use of lace chapes can be found in Egan and Pritchard (1991, 281–290).

136. Lace chape with single rivet. Type 1. See Crummy (1988, 13, fig. 13.1425 and 1426) and Egan and Pritchard (1991, 284, fig. 184.1414 and 1428). (SF 612A, Context 354, fill of pit, Period 4B).

137. Lace chape. Oakley Type 1. Single rivet. L: 25mm. (SF 613A, Context 354, fill of pit, Period 4B).

138. Lace chape with twin rivets. Oakley Type 1. L: 30mm, D: 2mm. See Crummy (1988, 13, fig. 13.1535 and 1536). (SF 248B, Context 1202, fill of rob trench of church wall, Period 3).

139. Lace chape with single rivet. Oakley Type 1. L: 25mm. (SF 84B, Context 725, fill of scaffold hole, Period 4C).

140. Lace chape. Plain folded sheet. Oakley Type 2. See Crummy (1988, 13, fig. 14.1542, 1614) and Egan and Pritchard (1991, 288, fig. 188). (SF 453B, Context 1429, fill of possible grave, Period 2).

141. Lace chape. Plain folded sheet. Oakley Type 2. L: 18mm. (SF 80B, Context 713, fill of grave Sk. 31, Period 2).

142. Domed button with loop fixing. D: 20mm. See Crummy (1988, 15, no.1704) for a similar button in lead-alloy. (SF 181A, Context 159, fill of construction trench for drain, Period 4B).

143. Possible button. Decorated disc now detached from

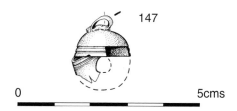

Fig. 81 Copper alloy rumbler bell

thin bone back plate with four attachment holes. D: 22mm. (SF 512A, Context 187, fill of pit, Period 4B).

144. Button. Concave face with four securing holes. D: 16mm. (SF 8B, Context 575, make-up layer for Scottish Presbyterian Church floor, Period 4C).

145. Plain button with fixing loop to rear. D: 28mm. (SF 105B, Context 678, fill of water tank, Period 4B).

146. Pendant-mount, possibly from a watch-chain. Circular central boss with engraved band around a dark red semi-precious stone. Bar attached to a suspending ring. Opposing terminal is a hollow socket, possibly to accommodate a metal tassel. Some evidence of gilding. L: 32mm. (SF 271B, Context 864, fill of linear feature, Period 4B).

147. Fig. 81. Rumbler bell. Made from two sheets of copper alloy beaten to shape on a former and then soldered together after the insertion of an iron pea. The suspension loop was created out of a thin strip of copper alloy sheeting. On the present example it is not clear how the loop was attached to the top of the bell. A typical dumb-bell shaped slot was cut into the lower hemisphere and the bell decorated with pairs of incised latitudinal grooves. D: 17mm. Similar bells have been found at Colchester (Crummy 1988, no. 3251[post-Roman]), Exeter (Goodall 1984, 339), Southampton (Harvey 1975, 262) and London (Egan and Pritchard 1991, 336–341) where the type described here is said to date between the 13th and 15th centuries. (SF 255B, Context 973, cut for service trench, Period 4D: redeposited medieval object).

148. Plain ring with rounded profile. There is a ridge on the external mid-point of the profile. D: 22mm. See Williams (1979, 261) and Platt and Coleman-Smith (1975, 1710 and 1765) for similar examples. (SF 482B, Context 1260, fill of cemetery boundary ditch, Period 2).

The assemblage includes a further ten, plain, rings varying in diameter from 15mm to 26mm. All are of late 17th-century or later date and probably represent curtain or harness rings.

Eleven contexts, all dated post-1700, contained fragments of fine copper wire, possibly waste from an industrial activity.

The excavations recovered a large number of complete and incomplete (broken) (?sewing) pins. The complete pins, mostly of fine wire with simple, slightly domed or flattened round heads, varied in length between 23mm and 55mm. Where identifiable all were Crummy Type 2 (Crummy 1988). Mostly from contexts dated post-1700, the largest group of pins was recovered from pit fill 248. The quantity recovered prevents their listing here. However, a full description and list of contexts producing pins may be found in the site archive.

Objects of Lead/Lead Alloy by Rod Burchill

(Objects of lead/lead alloy from the major post-medieval pit groups appear later in this chapter).

Illustrated: 149 and 151.
The burials of three males had lead alloy objects resting on their abdomens. One of these, on Sk. 142 (SF 300B), was sufficiently preserved to be certain that it was a chalice. The two others, on Sk. 165 (SF 383B) and Sk. 224 (SF 389B), were also probably chalices but were badly crushed and in poor condition.

It is not clear when the practice of burying a chalice

with a priest began; however, chalices of gold, silver, tin, pewter and glass were in use from Anglo-Saxon times, although by the end of the 12th century silver would appear to have been the preferred material (Oman 1990). The use of precious metal chalices to accompany priest burials was probably becoming expensive by the 13th century, as in 1229 William of Blois, Bishop of Worcester ordered every church to have two chalices, one of silver for celebration and another of pewter with which the priest might be buried (Oman 1990).

At Winchester, twenty of the 1,070 13th- to 15th-century burials excavated north of the nave contained chalices and seven of these were accompanied by patens (Biddle and Kjolbye-Biddle 1990). None of the chalices from St James were accompanied by a paten and it is possible that they were simply covered by a *pall*, a cloth used to cover the chalice at Eucharist. It is unlikely that evidence for a cloth pall would have survived at St James.

It is likely that the chalices were originally placed upright in the grave and had fallen over and been crushed when the grave was backfilled. Only one, that with Sk. 224, seemed to have been within a coffin burial.

149. Fig. 82. Folded sheet package, 58mm x 52mm, found associated with Sk. 60. The package lacks corners to facilitate folding. On opening the package was found to contain fragments of an organic material, possibly parchment or other skin material. The function of this object is not certain and no parallels are known. However, the folded sheet may have contained an indulgence, prayer, or simply the name of the grave's occupant (J. Cherry, pers. comm.). (SF 283B, Context 1052, on abdomen of Sk. 60, Period 2).

150. Sheet (folded). Sheet has been pierced by three iron

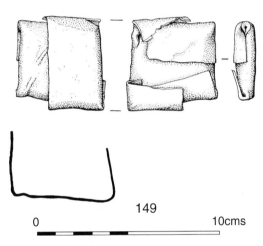

149

0   10cms

Fig. 82 Folded lead sheet package

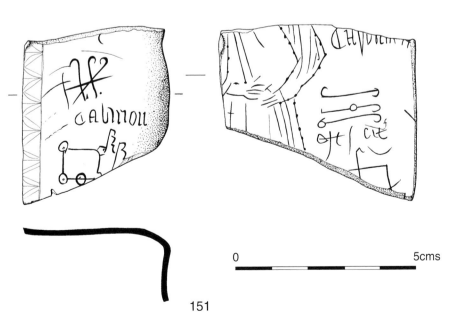

0   5cms

151

Fig. 83 Inscribed lead sheet

rivets or nails. The sheet had become folded after the insertion of the nails. At Northampton a similar lead sheet with iron nails was suggested to have been part of a U-shaped or curved channel (Oakley 1979). (SF 346B, Context 1483, fill of grave Sk. 159, Period 2).

151. Fig. 83. Fragment of sheet inscribed on both obverse and reverse with various scratched letters and geometric designs and part of a human figure, with the head, shoulders, legs and the left side of the body missing. Possibly a test piece. Max. dimensions 54mm x 43mm. (SF 568B, Context 1579, clearance deposit, Period 4A).

152. Three discs recessed on underside. D: 38mm, depth 7mm. Function is unclear but possibly a container cap or closure. Lead alloy bottle tops have been recovered at Northampton (Oakley 1979). However, the Northampton examples are of a more intricate design. (SF 5B, Context 621, layer, Period 4A).

153. Shaped, tapering strip, flat on back; upper edges chamfered. 67mm x 7mm x B: 3mm. (SF 581B, Context 1218, fill of possible robber trench, Period 3).

154. Window came. L: (bent) 54mm. See Crummy 1988, 72, fig. 73. (SF 622A, Context 119, make-up for Victorian church floor, Period 4C).

Objects of Stone and Fired Clay
by Rod Burchill

(Objects of stone and fired clay from the major post-medieval pit groups appear later in this chapter).

Illustrated: 159 and 160.

155. Fragment of fired clay cylinder, possibly part of a wig curler. L: 39mm. (SF 122B, Context 705, fill of scaffold hole, Period 4C).

156. Thirty-seven marbles, eight stone and twenty-nine fired clay, were recovered from the excavations. Two marbles were patterned. All were of 18th- and 19th-century date. D: varies between 13mm and 30mm.

157. Stone counter, one face divided into four quadrants by parallel 'tram-lines' scratched into the surface. A similar counter, but in slate, was found at Colchester (Crummy 1988, 45, no.2018). (SF 744A, unstratified).

158. Undecorated stone counter. D: 28mm, B: 12mm. (SF 446A, Context 187, fill of pit, Period 4B).

159. Fig. 84. Fragment of worked freestone although the rear face of it is left unworked possibly as it was not intended to be seen. Presumably part of a church monument. It takes the form of a torch, the flames of which are painted red and bear traces of gilding. There are red painted decorative motifs below the torch. (SF 121B, Context 866, fill of extraction pit, Period 3).

160. Fig. 85. Jet pendant. Re-used and cut piece of decorated jet. The original design consisted of ring

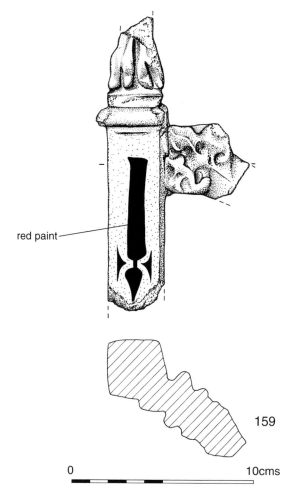

red paint

159

0   10cms

Fig. 84 Part of a stone church monument

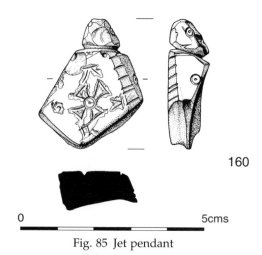

160

0   5cms

Fig. 85 Jet pendant

and dot motif which is visible on one side. The object had later been fashioned into a roughly pentagonal shape and decorated with a crude Maltese cross and pi-like symbols cut into its major flat surface. A series of grooves or notches had been cut into the upper edge. The top had been cut to provide a terminal to accommodate a suspension cord. Max. dimensions 33mm x 30mm. (SF 232B, Context 1101, associated with skeleton Sk. 64, Period 2).

The Post-Medieval Pit Groups (Site 1)

A number of rubbish pits were excavated spanning the 17th and 18th centuries (Periods 4A and 4B). The six dealt with in detail here have been selected for the quality and variety of the ceramics and other finds which they contained and also for the way in which together, with some overlapping, they span the period from the mid 17th to the late 18th centuries. The quality of the finds which include Chinese porcelains, tin-glazed earthenware tablewares, decorated drinking glasses and bone fans indicate the presence in the area of moderately well-off households in the post-medieval period. Some of the pits produced evidence for a local bone-working industry in the form of off-cuts and partly-worked items such as knife handles.

It has not been possible to provide an exhaustive description of all the ceramics and the other objects due to space and financial constraints. The intention has been to show which types of pottery, glass, small finds and clay tobacco pipes were in use together and the range and origin of, in particular, the pottery available to households in this part of St James's parish.

The faunal remains and the worked bones are dealt with in detail in the report by Geraldine Barber later in this chapter.

The finds reports have been prepared by: Peter Hardie (porcelain); Rod Burchill and Reg Jackson (pottery), Reg Jackson (clay tobacco pipes); Rod Burchill (glass, bone and ivory, fired clay, iron, copper alloy, lead/lead alloy and shell objects); Rosie Clarke (coins and tokens).

The Finds From Pit 1213

Date:
Late 17th century, probably *c*.1670 to 1680 (Period 4A).

Description:
A large rectangular pit measuring 3.4m east/west by at least the same distance north/south. It had vertical sides, was unlined and up to 0.66m deep. The fill

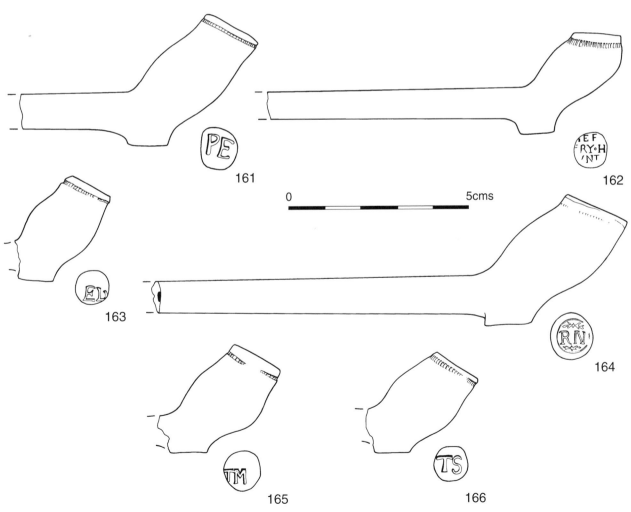

Fig. 86 Pit 1213, clay tobacco pipes

(1212) consisted of a number of interleaving bands of ash and cinder debris which had been dumped in from the north-east corner of the pit.

Clay Tobacco Pipes:

Five barrel-shaped bowls marked with the initials 'PE' incuse on the heel – Philip Edwards I took his freedom to work as a pipe maker in Bristol in 1650 and died in 1683 (Fig. 86.161); one forward projecting West Country style bowl with 'IEF/FRY.H/VNT' incuse on the heel – Jeffry Hunt was working in Wiltshire in the mid 17th century (Fig. 86.162); one small heeled bowl marked 'EL' incuse on the heel – Edward Lewis I, free 1631, dead by 1652 (Fig. 86.163); eleven heeled but forward projecting bowls with 'RN' incuse on the heel and two heel fragments with 'RN' incuse with decoration – Richard Nunney, free 1655, dead by 1713 (Fig. 86.164); one small heeled bowl marked 'TM' incuse on the heel – Thomas Monkes, working 1656 to at least 1670 (Fig. 86.165); two small heeled bowls marked 'TS' incuse on the heel – Thomas Smith I, free 1651, dead by 1667 (Fig. 86.166); ten small, heeled bowls – early/mid 17th century; two fragments of forward projecting West Country type heeled bowls – mid 17th century; eleven barrel-shaped heeled bowls – c.1660–80; two spurred bowls – c.1670–1700.

Pottery:

German stoneware: Brown salt-glazed Frechen jug with applied moulded medallion of flower (Fig. 87.167); Westerwald jug with applied moulded decoration coloured blue and purple.

English tin-glazed earthenware: Charger with foot-ring pierced for suspension and painted with a floral/geometric decoration predominantly in blue but with the circular motifs on border infilled with light green (Fig. 87.168); plate painted in blue with a rabbit sat on a rock surrounded by floral and geometric decoration, with blue under-rim decoration (Fig. 88.169); fragments of at least twelve other plates and dishes with decoration painted in blue, green and purple; bowl painted in blue externally with a Chinese-style figure in a landscape of trees, with Chinese-style calligraphic letter internally on base (Fig. 88.170); bowl with blue dash border, turquoise and purple decoration on sides and central ?floral design outlined in purple and infilled with turquoise (Fig. 88.171); base of goblet imitating a drinking glass (Fig. 88.172); two double handled globular vases on pedestal base (Fig. 89.173); cup with speckled purple decoration; straight sided ?tankard painted externally in blue with stylized trees; small drug jar.

Bristol/Staffordshire yellow slipware: Bases of three candlesticks with applied brown slip dots around upper edge of 'collar' (Fig. 89.174); base of candlestick with brown trailed slip; possible dish with external/internal dark and light brown trailed slip; two moulded plates with brown combed slip decoration; fragments of at least six cups with brown trailed and combed slip.

Brown salt-glazed stoneware: Jug with handle; sherd of bowl in Nottingham-style stoneware.

North Devon ware: Sgraffito dish with geometric/floral decoration (Fig. 89.175); two sgraffito bowls (Fig. 89.176); large gravel-tempered ware pancheon with horizontal handle on rim; gravel-tempered ware bowl with horizontal handle on body.

Somerset ware: Sgraffito jug with pulled spout, white slip cut through to red body with patches of copper green (Fig. 89.177); sgraffito dish with much green copper splashing overall; bowl with internal white slip glazed yellow but this changes to green where slip has been partly removed (Fig. 89.178); handled bowl with internal white slip (Fig. 89.179); another similar (Fig. 90.180); possible chamber pot with trailed white slip decoration and overall dark green glaze (Fig. 90.181); dish with trailed white slip decoration and medium brown glaze (Fig. 90.182); candlestick with trailed white slip decoration and dark brown glaze (Fig. 91.183).

Local redware: Fragment of garden urn with applied moulded decoration of swags and traces of red paint around decoration (Fig. 91.184); storage vessel with applied thumb impressed strip below rim (Fig. 91.185); five trailed slipware dishes and bowls with green or brown internal glaze; dish with incised wavy line decoration on rim and internal green glaze; bowl or dish with internal brown glaze, finger impressed rim and stamped decoration in the form of panels of small squares; storage vessel with internal speckled green-brown glaze (Fig.91.186); a number of storage vessels of various forms, some with internal green glaze.

Glass:

Long necked globular bottle with string rim and shallow punt in thick dark green-brown glass, with applied glass seal depicting an animal (possibly a unicorn) and the entwined initials 'T(?R)A' (Fig. 92.187). Neck and upper part of a rectangular bottle with shallow concave sides in green glass (Fig. 92.188).

Bone:

Lathe-turned bone knife handle and iron blade (Fig. 92.189). The handle is decorated with multiple reeds. A bone peg had been inserted into the end of the otherwise hollow handle. The whittle-tang blade is triangular in section. Handle 70mm. Blade 44mm x 13mm. A similar but less ornate pegged handle was found at Colchester (Crummy 1988, fig. 75.3087) (SF 331B).

Lathe-turned bone object, body decorated with spiral grooves (Fig. 92.190). Plain top with reed decoration and grooves at junction with the body. Probably a bobbin. Incomplete: L: 55mm x max. D: 10mm (SF 430B).

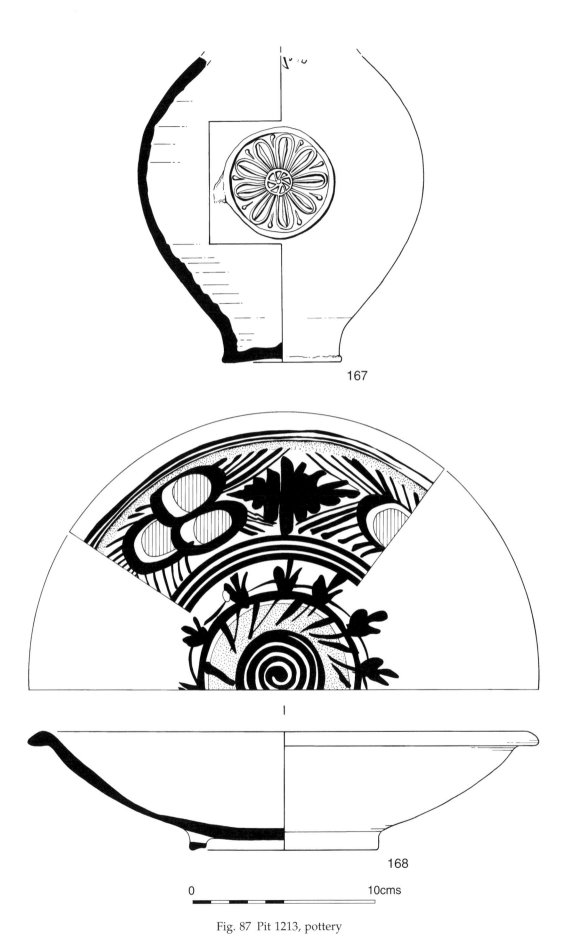

167

168

0   10cms

Fig. 87 Pit 1213, pottery

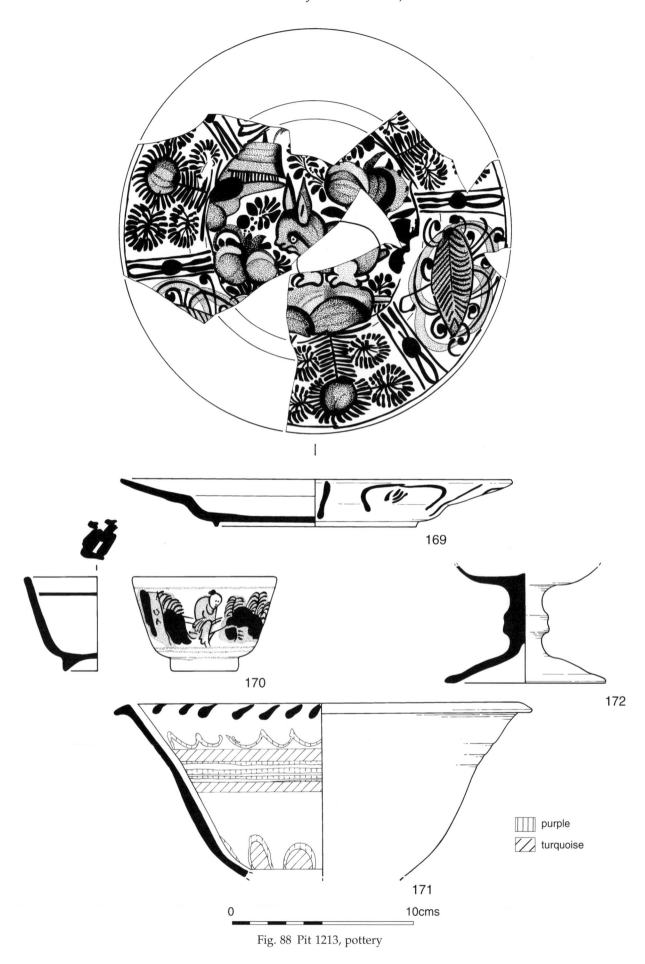

169

170

172

171

purple

turquoise

0   10cms

Fig. 88 Pit 1213, pottery

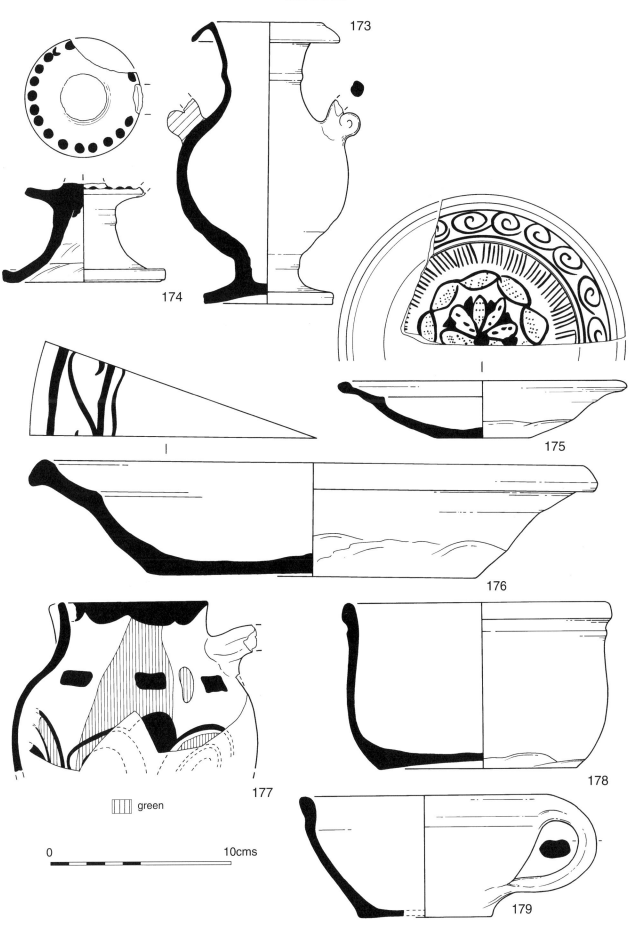

Fig. 89 Pit 1213, pottery

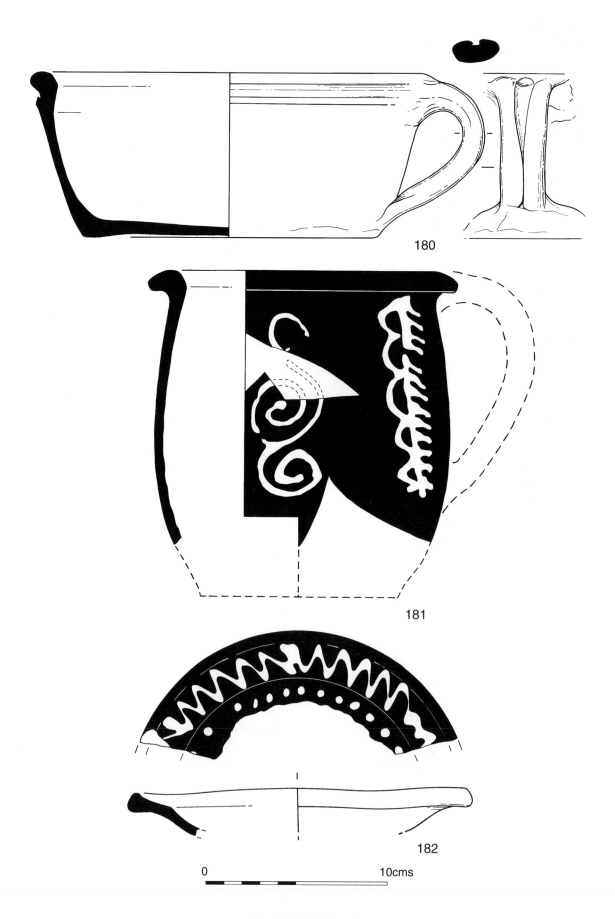

180

181

182

0   10cms

Fig. 90   Pit 1213, pottery

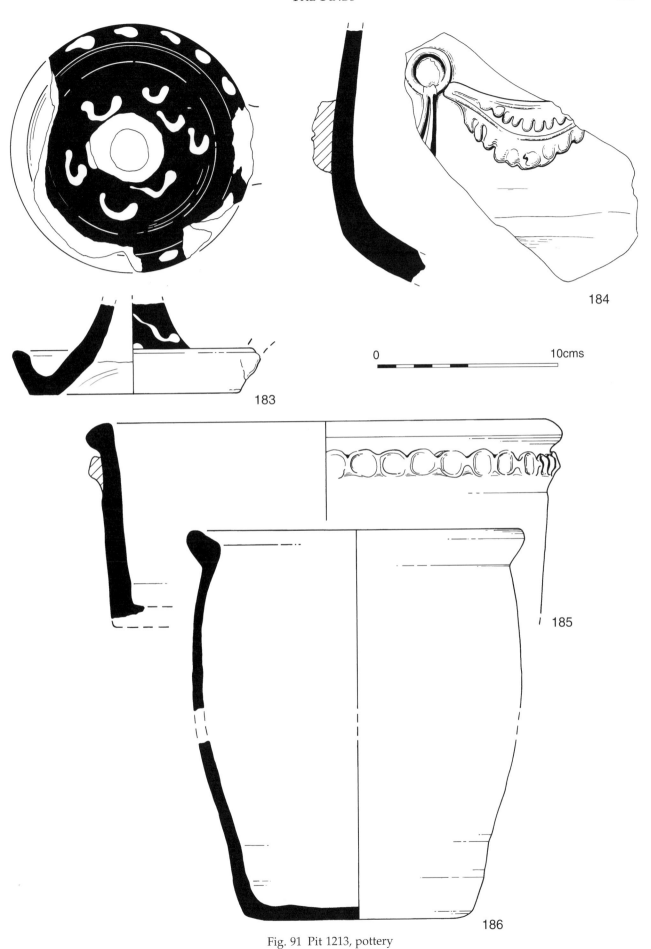

Fig. 91 Pit 1213, pottery

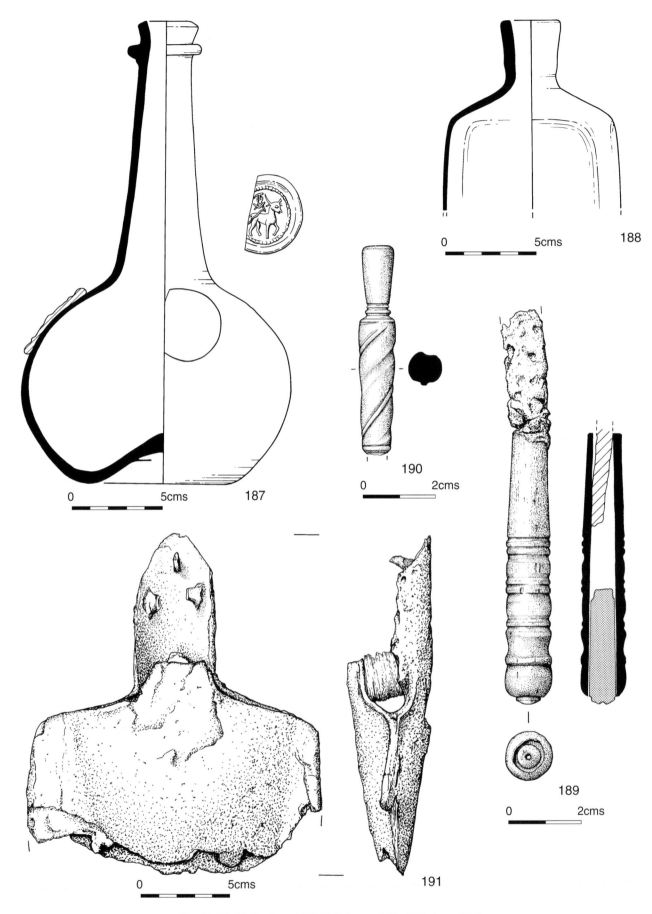

Fig. 92 Pit 1213, glass (187–188), bone (189–190), iron (191)

Iron:
Incomplete staple. Arms broken. L: 55+mm (SF 506B).
Possible spade (Fig. 92.191). Blade constructed of two sheets of iron with socket to take a ?wooden handle. Handle attached with three rivets. Blade 170mm x 100mm. Socket D: 50mm (SF 605B).
Curved sheet with rivet. Possibly part of a tool socket, *e.g.* spade (SF 403B).

Fired Clay:
Three pottery counters, all re-cut sherds of tin-glazed earthenware. Diameters: 18mm, 23mm and 30mm. (SFs 418B, 432B, 507(a)B).
Pottery counter. Re-cut sherd in a Somerset fabric. D: approx. 20mm. (SF 507(b)B).
Pottery counter. D: 27mm. (SF 596B).

Discussion:
The presence in the pit fill of thirteen clay tobacco pipes made by Richard Nunney, who did not obtain his freedom to work as a pipe maker in Bristol until 1655, gives the earliest date when the pit group could have been deposited. The occurrence of two spurred pipe bowls suggests a date somewhat later in the 17th century, although it is not known exactly when spurred bowls were first made in Bristol: a date around 1670 to 1675 seems likely. The earlier pipes, including those of Edward Lewis and Jeffry Hunt, must be residual. Thus the filling of the pit probably began around 1670 and, taking into account the consistency of the fill, may have been completed within a relatively short period.

The Finds From Pit 192

Date:
Late 17th century, probably *c*.1680 to 1700 (Period 4A).

Description:
Only a part of this sub-circular pit could be excavated.

It had sloping sides, was at least 1.8m across from north to south and was 1.7m deep. Its upper fill (166) was a dark brown ashy loam while the lower fill (191) was a brown loam with many large flecks of charcoal and mortar.

Clay Tobacco Pipes:
Two roulette decorated stems marked 'IA' – James Abbott, free 1677, dead by 1718 (Fig. 93.192); bowl with incuse heel mark 'EDM/VND/HI..' – maker unknown, mid 17th century (Fig. 93.193); four roulette decorated stems marked 'LE' – Llewellin Evans, free 1661, died 1688; two bowls with incuse heel mark 'PE' – Philip Edwards I, free 1650, died 1683; two roulette decorated stems marked 'IP' – John Pearce I, free 1696, working to at least 1738; small unmarked heeled bowl.

Pipe Clay Wig Curler:
Fired clay cylinder, possibly part of a wig curler, length 47mm (SF 142A).

Pottery:
German stoneware: Westerwald tankard with applied decoration, painted blue and mauve; Rhenish (probably Frechen) Bellarmine-style jug.
  Dutch tin-glazed earthenware: Sherd of plate glazed externally, probably Dutch.
  English tin-glazed earthenware: Plate with pastoral scene painted in blue showing a deer standing on its hind legs (Fig. 94.194); small fragments of at least four plates with blue or blue and mauve internal decoration; small fragments of at least four bowls with blue internal decoration; chamber pot (Fig. 94.195); cup with external mauve speckled decoration; drug jar (Fig. 94.196).
  Bristol/Staffordshire yellow slipware: Three cups and one press-moulded dish with brown combed slip decoration.
  North Devon wares: Four plates with internal

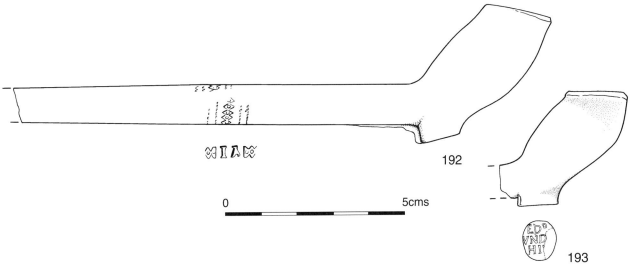

Fig. 93 Pit 192, clay tobacco pipes

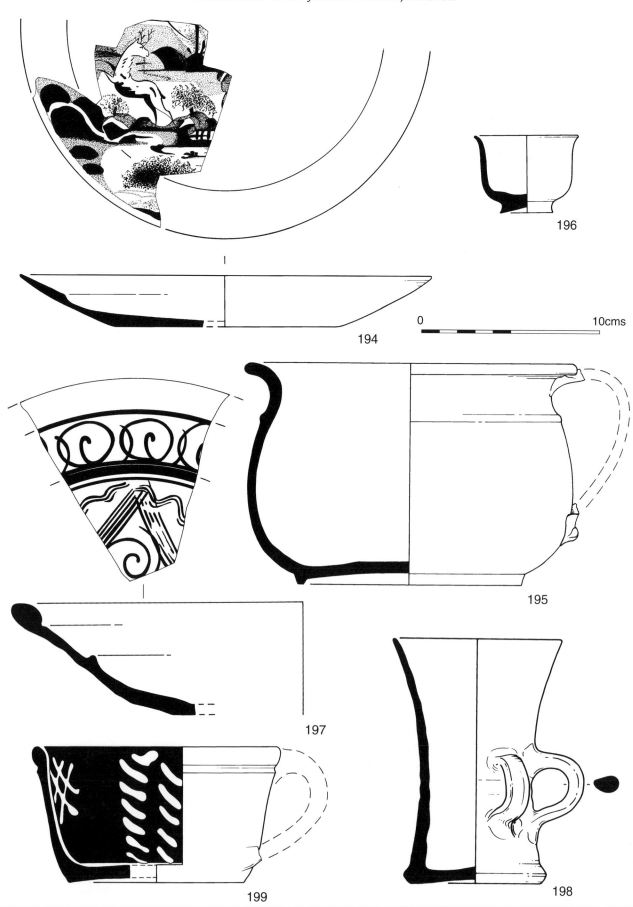

0   10cms

Fig. 94 Pit 192, pottery

sgraffito decoration (Fig. 94.197); various gravel-tempered ware storage vessels, chamber pots and skillets.

South Gloucestershire (Falfield) ware: Cistercian/ blackware two-handled tyg (Fig. 94.198); Cistercian/ blackware two-handled tall cup or tyg.

Somerset wares: Sgraffito decorated plate or bowl; two sgraffito decorated jugs; sgraffito decorated cup; three bowls with internal white trailed slip decoration; chamber pot with external white trailed slip decoration; handled bowl with internal white trailed slip decoration (Fig. 94.199).

Local redwares: Dish with white trailed slip decoration on rim and side and sgraffito decoration in base, patchy green internal glaze; bowl with internal white trailed slip decoration and green glaze; various redware bowls, plates and storage vessels.

Tile:
Fragment of tin-glazed earthenware tile with blue painted decoration, probably Bristol or London.

Glass:
Bottles: Wide mouth and string rim of a crudely formed bottle, very thick green glass (SF 161A); part of neck of bottle, weathered green glass (SF 158A); bottle neck with string ring square edged rim, weathered dark green glass (SF 160A).

Drinking glass: Fragment of drinking glass stem with knob decoration (SF 141A).

Miscellaneous: Fragment of thin flat glass (SF 136A).

Iron:
Scissors with external finger loops and central rivet, the blades have pointed terminals (Fig. 95.200), similar scissors have been reported from Norwich (Margeson 1993, 136 no.921) (SF 587A).
Fragment of knife blade, L: 80mm x 16mm (SF 143A).
Incomplete wallhook, L: 75mm (SF 139A).
Fragment of strip, 40mm x 15mm (SF 599A).
Four large pieces of sheet, no clear function (SF 135A).

Copper Alloy:
Pin, L: 32mm (SF 125A).

Token:
Lead token, D: 15mm. Obv: Cinquefoil. Rev: Illegible, ?uniface. Probably 14th/15th century. Similar to Mitchener and Skinner 1984, pl.10, no. 50. (SF 126A).

Discussion:
The presence of pipes made by Philip Edwards I in the assemblage shows that deposition of the material could not have begun before 1650, the date of his freedom. The pit must have continued in use until at least 1696 to have included pipes made by John Pearce I, who obtained his freedom in that year. Although some of the 'PE' marked pipes could have been made

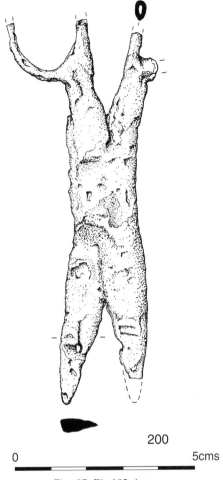

Fig. 95 Pit 192, iron

by Philip Edwards II, the pit must have been in use by 1688 to have included pipes made by Llewellin Evans, who died in that year, and assuming pipes made by him were not being sold for any length of time after his death. On the evidence of the clay tobacco pipes the rubbish pit was therefore in use during the second half of the 17th century and it is suggested that the period of use may be narrowed to *c.*1680 to 1700. The pottery such as the Westerwald tankard, Rhenish stoneware, tin-glazed earthenware, North Devon sgraffito ware and Bristol/Staffordshire yellow slipware would also fit well within that time period.

The Finds From Pit 259

Date:
Late 17th/very early 18th century (Period 4A).

Description:
The pit was roughly rectangular, 1.8m square and 0.2m deep, a large part of its fill having been removed by a modern pit. The upper fills (238 and 239) consisted of rich brown loam with charcoal flecks although 239 contained many lumps of pink mortar. The bottom layer of the pit (260) was a green cess-like

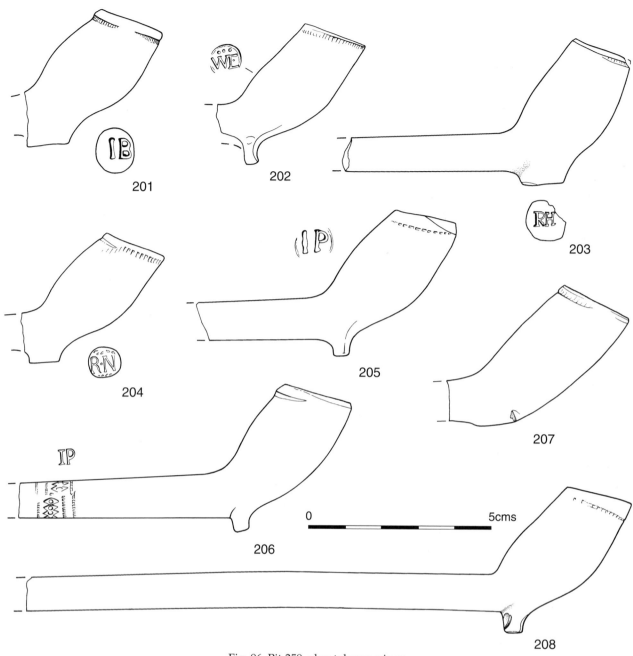

Fig. 96 Pit 259, clay tobacco pipes

material. Both 238 and 260 contained much bone-working waste.

Clay Tobacco Pipes:

One heeled bowl marked 'IB' incuse on the heel – probably John Bladen I, free 1657 and was still working in 1689 (Fig. 96.201); spurred bowl with 'WE' with decoration incuse on the back of the bowl – William Evans II, free 1667 and still alive in 1713 (Fig. 96.202); heeled bowl marked 'RH' incuse on the heel – Robert Hancock, free 1655 and working until at least 1693 (Fig. 96.203); heeled bowl with 'RN' and decoration incuse on the heel – Richard Nunney, free 1655, dead by 1713 (Fig. 96.204); spurred bowl with 'IP'

incuse on the rear of the bowl – John Pearce I, free 1696, working until at least 1713 (Fig. 96.205); spurred bowl, the stem with roulette decoration consisting of the initials 'IP' between milling and diamonds – John Pearce I, free 1696, working until at least 1713 (Fig. 96.206); bowl without heel or spur – late 17th century (Fig. 96.207); unmarked heeled bowl – c.1660–1680; two unmarked spurred bowls – late 17th/early 18th century (Fig. 96.208).

Pottery:

German stoneware: Westerwald tankard with blue and purple decoration (Fig. 97.209); Westerwald tankard with applied decoration of hearts and other motifs in

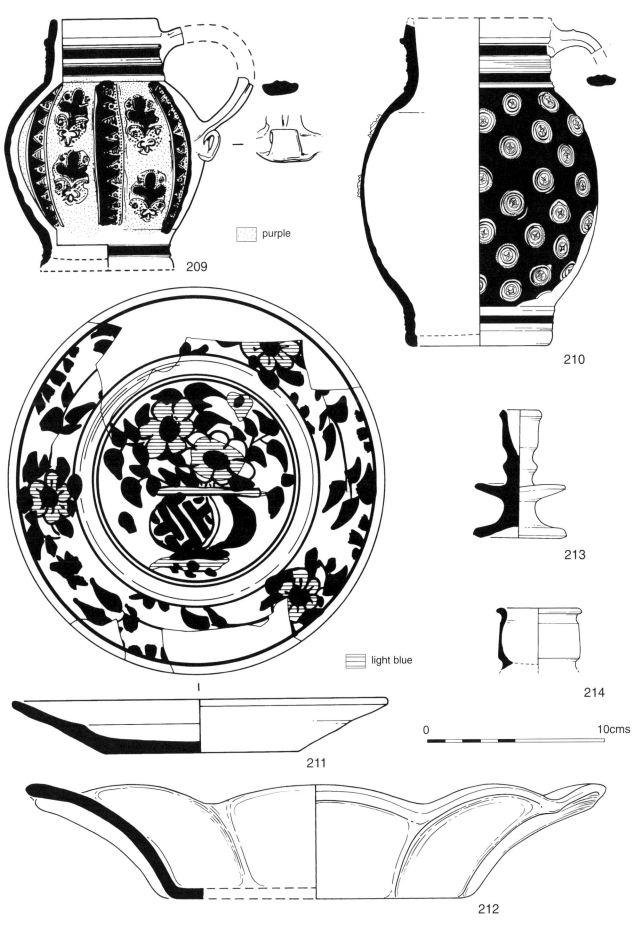

purple

209

210

light blue

213

211

214

0   10cms

212

Fig. 97 Pit 259, pottery

blue and purple; Westerwald jug with applied circular motifs against a blue ground (Fig. 97.210).

Dutch tin-glazed earthenware: Plate with floral decoration painted in blue and purple, probably Dutch (fragments of a similar, if not the same vessel, occur in pit 753); fragment of a jug finely painted with flowers and foliage in green, blue and orange, probably Dutch.

English tin-glazed earthenware: Plate with floral decoration on border and a vase of flowers as the central motif painted in dark and light blue (Fig. 97.211); large plate with concave segments and scalloped rim (Fig. 97.212); seven plates (single sherds only) with blue painted decoration and two with blue and purple decoration; charger (base only) with blue floral decoration and foot-ring pierced for suspension; bowl (base only) with blue flower decoration; plain white glazed candlestick (Fig. 97.213); plain white glazed drug jar (Fig. 97.214); drug jar decorated primarily in blue but with purple stems to 'flowers' and one area of turquoise, the decoration being much bubbled and run (Fig. 98.215); drug jar with blue decoration but the central panel has double diagonal lines in purple (Fig. 98.216); drug jar with blue decoration and pinkish glaze (Fig. 98.217); small ointment jar.

Bristol/Staffordshire yellow slipware: Cup with internal combed slip decoration (Fig. 98.218); four cups with external brown combed slip decoration; dish with internal brown combed slip decoration; chamber pot with single handle and external brown trailed slip, with dots of brown slip on rim (Fig. 98.219).

Slipware of unknown origin: Chamber pot with single handle, overall brown glaze with internal and external yellow trailed slip decoration (Fig. 98.220); cup with a medium brown overall glaze decorated externally with alternate stripes of dark brown and white trailed slip and in the same colours a slipped portrait of a king wearing a crown and ?wig (Fig. 99.221).

Brown stoneware: Neck of salt-glazed ?flask.

Somerset ware: Three chamber pots with sgraffito decoration cutting through white slip to red body and with patches of copper green (Fig. 99.222 and 223).

North Devon ware: Plate with sgraffito decoration; two gravel-tempered ware chamber pots; five gravel-tempered ware pancheons (two very large); rectangular dripping pan with horizontal handle and finger impressed decoration on outside edge of rim.

Local redware (all with red/brown glaze unless otherwise stated): Pancheon with applied thumbed strip below rim externally, horizontal handles and glazed internally (Fig. 100.224); two plates with internal glaze and white trailed slip decoration on rim; bowl with external glaze and white trailed slip decoration; storage vessels with external and internal dark green glaze and applied thumb impressed strip below rim externally (Fig. 100.225); three storage vessels or pancheons with internal glaze; three storage vessels with internal very dark brown/black glaze; shallow dish with external and internal green glaze; three storage vessels with internal mottled green glaze; shallow handled bowl with internal yellow glaze; handled pitcher with external dark green/black glaze; bowl glazed internally with finger impressed decoration around edge of rim; jug with external glaze.

Glass:

Bottles and flasks: Long neck with string rim, the top is poorly formed, brown-green glass (SF 466A); neck of a bottle with a string rim, green glass (SF 373A); shallow neck of bottle with string rim, raised scar above shoulder, green glass, heavy surface degradation (SF 405A); short-necked onion bottle with poorly applied string rim, dark green glass (Fig. 101.226) (SF 464A); short-necked onion bottle with well formed string rim, dark green glass (SF 402A); rim and neck of a bottle with crudely formed string rim, dark green glass (SF 377A); short neck of a bottle with string rim, weathered dark green glass (SF 395A); neck and simple everted rim of a flask, green glass, external D: 29mm (see Charleston 1984, 270 for a similar vessel) (SF 393A).

Drinking glasses: Part of the stem of a drinking glass, moulded glass with spiral twist, seven lobed ring and 'berry' pellets (Fig. 101.227) (SF 403A); stem and base of a conical bowl with a crude quatrefoil knob below the bowl, wide simple base, smokey grey glass (Fig. 101.228) (SF 432A); fragment of drinking glass stem with moulded decoration (SF 394A); fragment of moulded glass with 'raspberry' pellet decoration (SF 397A); fragment of white opaque glass with blue 'berry' decoration (SF 396A); two fragments of possible drinking glass of thin ?clear (now opaque surfaces) glass with ten horizontal ridges below rim (SF 401A).

Possible medical vessel: Wide simple base with hollow knob above, thin colourless glass, possibly from a medical vessel (SF 392A).

Jar: flange rim of a glass jar, much surface weathering, colour of glass uncertain, possibly pale green (Fig. 101.229) (Margeson 1993, 102–3) (SF 404A).

Bone and Ivory:

Medical nozzles: Tapering bone tube or nozzle, the hollow stem is bulbous at its narrow end, the opposite end is flared with reed and double cord decoration. Internally there is a series of grooves, possibly a non-spiral thread. L: 113mm x max. D: 15mm (Fig. 102.230) (SF 414A).

Tapering bone tube or nozzle, lathe turned plain hollow shaft, one end flared with wide external rebate and internal chamfer. L: 103mm x max. D: 13mm (Fig. 102.231) (SF 408A).

Carved ivory tube or nozzle, tube flares and is decorated with twin grooves, the end is parallel

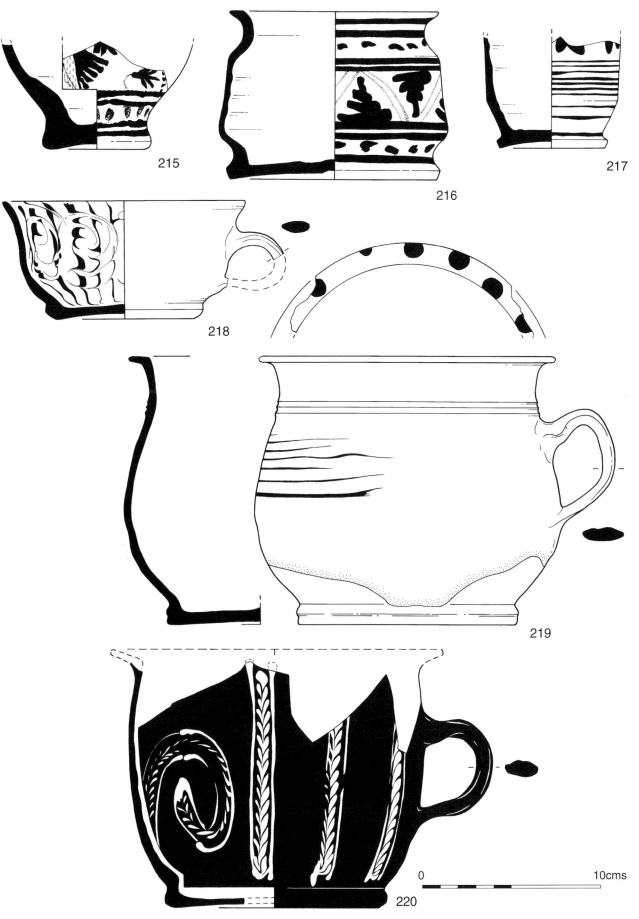

Fig. 98 Pit 259, pottery

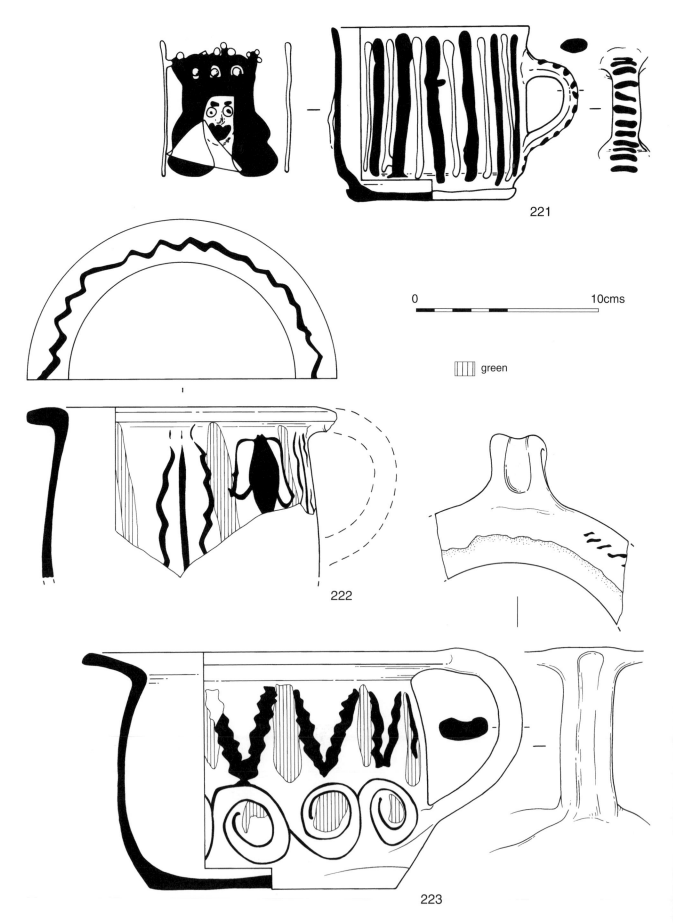

0   10cms

green

221

222

223

Fig. 99 Pit 259, pottery

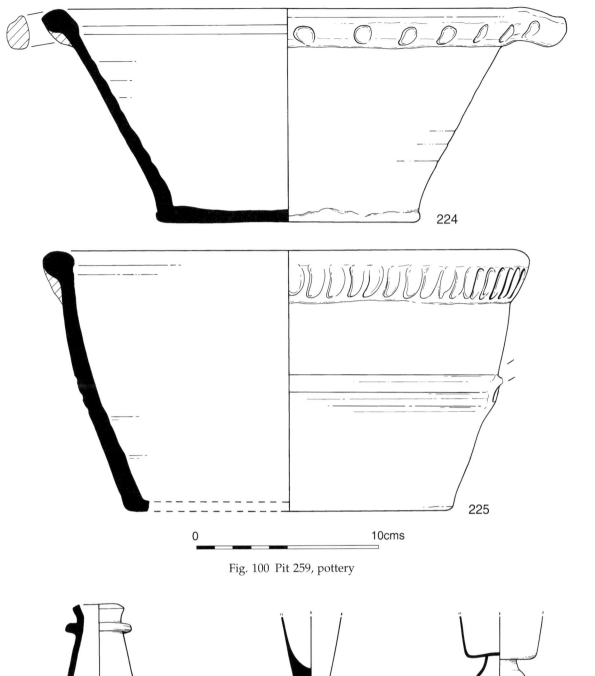

Fig. 100 Pit 259, pottery

0   10cms

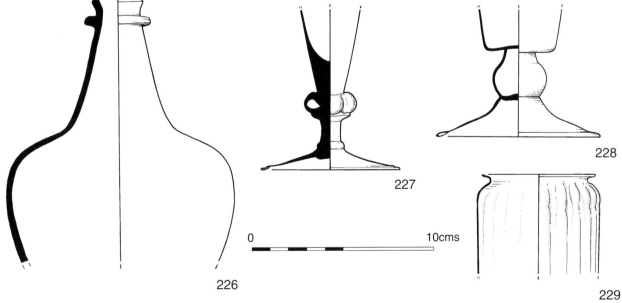

Fig. 101 Pit 259, glass

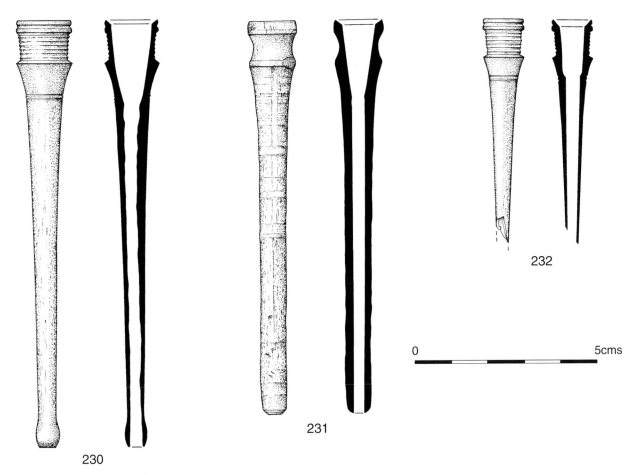

Fig. 102 Pit 259, bone and ivory

grooved externally and has an internal chamfer. L: 59mm x max. D: 11mm (Fig. 102.232) (SF 390A).

Similar objects found at Plymouth have been described as medical nozzles (Gaskell-Brown 1986, M/F8).

Fans: Eleven strips of whalebone – part of a fan – holes drilled through a bulbous end to take an iron rivet. Max. L: 208mm, W: 10mm. (see MacGregor 1985 for the use of baleen) (SF 381A).

Very thin strip possibly used as a veneer or fan. ?waste. L: 90mm (SF 380A).

Thin strip of bone possibly from a fan or veneer. L: 64mm x 9mm. (SF 383A).

Iron:

Purse frame: Iron frame mounted with leather riveted with iron rivets at 10mm centres. Surviving L: 52mm, W: 14mm (Fig. 103.233). Iron purse frames are not common. Margeson (1993, 43) describes an iron purse from Norwich. The Norwich example and two further frames cited by Margeson, one from London and another from Amsterdam, were quite ornate with decorative finials. The Norwich frame had a spring clasp enabling the purse to be locked. Margeson suggests that these purses were imported from the

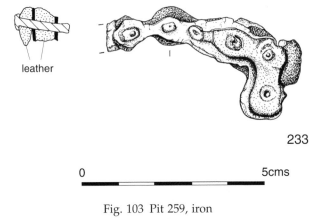

leather

233

Fig. 103 Pit 259, iron

Low Countries. The frames described by Margeson would appear to be earlier than the present example having been dated to the second half of the 15th century on the basis of parallels in paintings. The Norwich frame was recovered from fire deposits dated 1507. (SF 518A).

Miscellaneous: Hollow, tapering, socket: possibly to take a wooden shaft. The terminal is broken. Possibly military – an object of similar type is described by Goodall (1993, fig. 176.1863) as a long tapering arrow head dated 1650–1700 and Shoesmith (1985) describes similar objects as spear tips of medieval date. However, the possibility of a domestic function cannot be precluded (SF 371A).

Knife blade with tang, mostly corrosion products (SF 364A); part of hollow object, externally stepped at one end, (raised) studded band at other end, five studs present, internal D: 20mm (SF 566A); concreted mass mostly corrosion products, x-ray suggests the presence of wire or fine ?pins/nails within the matrix (SF 592A).

Circular object, form not clear but possibly head of a bolt or similar (SF 516A); bolt or spike, round headed, ?wood adhering to shaft, L: 138mm (SF 399A).

Iron sheets and strips: Fragment of folded sheet, the material appears to have been plated (SF 412A); fragment of folded sheet, plated, the sides have been folded to form a corner, 50mm x 40mm (SF 420A); folded sheet, plated, L: 45mm (SF 412A); fragment of strip, probably part of a blade but x-ray not clear, very degraded (SF 418A); six fragments of ?tinned iron (SF 416A); fragment of plate with plated edge (SF 560A); strip 35mm x 8mm (SF 370A); fragments including handle (D-shaped), all very corroded, W: between terminals 87mm (SF 413A).

Copper Alloy:
Fragment of wood/copper alloy split disc, covering end fixed with an iron nail/rivet, L: 25mm, D: of disc 20mm (SF 372A); three pin fragments (SFs 324A, 325A, 480A).

Lead:
Window came. Two pieces: L: (bent) 26mm and 38mm. (Crummy 1988, 72, fig. 73). (SF 479A).

Stone Moulds:
One valve of a bi-valve mould. Series of circular depressions with six petal floral design. Face very smooth, reverse rougher with crude incised circle with simple five-armed cross (Fig. 104.234). Probably a jetton or token mould. The form and function of stone moulds has been discussed by Allan (1984, 304) and Margeson (1993, 177). Most are considered to date to the 16th or 17th centuries. (SF 437A).

Fragment of limestone with crude inscribed circle containing eight crossed lines plus a second simple circle. There are two depressions in the back of stone (Fig. 104.235). Possibly a test-piece or unfinished mould (SF 438A).

Tokens:
Lead disc, D: 20mm. Obv: Plain cross. Rev: Illegible, ?uniface. Probably an early Tudor token. Similar to Mitchener and Skinner 1985, pl.6, no.6. (SF 410A).

Lead token, D: 20mm. Obv: Field voided by triple cross. Rev: Illegible, ?uniface. Probably Elizabethan. Similar to Mitchener and Skinner 1985, pl.14, no.87. (SF 409A).

Discussion:
The presence of pipes made by John Pearce I in the assemblage shows that deposition of the material could not have begun before 1696, the date of his freedom. The almost equal mixture of heeled and spurred bowls suggests that backfilling of the pit occurred at the end of the 17th century and during the early years of the 18th century. The presence of three tin-glazed earthenware drug jars and one small ointment jar, a fragment of what may be a glass medical vessel and three bone and ivory tubes which are almost certainly medical nozzles, suggest the use of the pit by a pharmacist or barber-surgeon who was living or practising in the locality. Dr Roger Price has kindly examined these nozzles and suggests that they may be *clyster-pipes*, a type of syringe used for injecting a clyster or enema into the rectum.

The Finds From Pit 753

Date:
Late 17th/early 18th century (Period 4A).

Description:
The rectangular pit was lined with a drystone wall of Pennant sandstone. It measured 1.3m east/west, at least 0.6m north/south and was 1.3m deep. The fill of the pit, which showed clear tip lines sloping down from east to west, consisted mainly of a brown clayey silt with much charcoal flecking and small stones (744), and with large pieces of stone rubble close to the base.

Clay Tobacco Pipes:
Bowl marked 'LE' incuse on the heel; spurred bowl marked 'LE' incuse on the back of the bowl (Fig. 105.236) – Llewellin Evans, free 1661, died 1688; bowl marked 'RN' incuse on the heel between swags – Richard Nunney, free 1655, dead by 1713; two roulette decorated stems with the initials 'IP' between milling and diamonds – John Pearce I, free 1696, working until at least 1713 (Fig. 105.237); spurred bowl with fragment of roulette decorated stem (Fig. 105.238); 142 spurred bowls of various forms – late 17th/early 18th century; twelve heeled bowls – c.1660–1680; eleven West Country style heeled bowls – third quarter of the 17th century (Fig. 105.239); small heeled bowl – early/mid 17th century.

Pottery:
German stoneware: Westerwald jug with applied geometric decoration coloured with blue and purple.

Dutch tin-glazed earthenware: Plate with floral decoration painted in blue and purple, probably

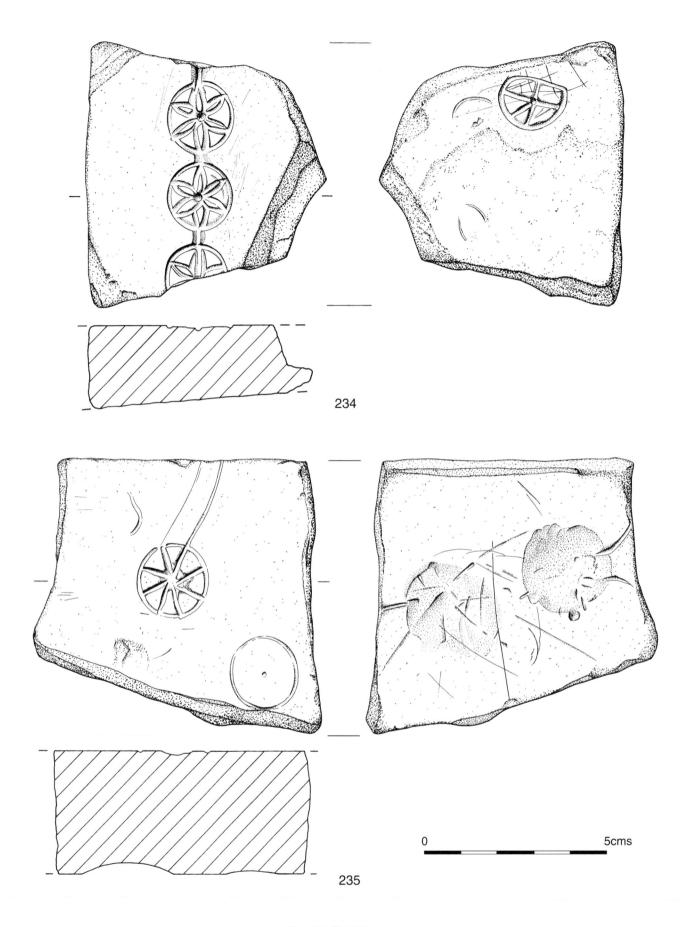

234

235

0   5cms

Fig. 104 Pit 259, stone

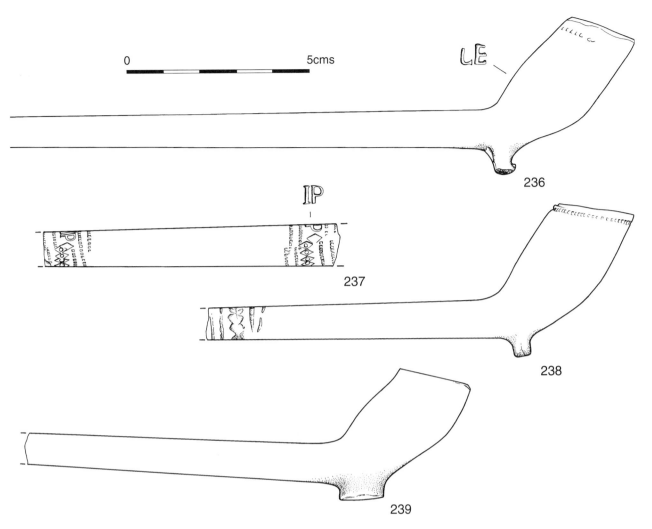

Fig. 105 Pit 753, clay tobacco pipes

Dutch (fragments of a similar, if not the same vessel, were found in pit 259).

English tin-glazed earthenware: Plate with overall light blue glaze painted with blue floral and ?geometric border; plate with light/dark blue stylized ?flower border and with stylized decoration as the central motif (Fig. 106.240); fragments of at least fourteen other plates or dishes painted mainly in blue but with some green, yellow and purple; decorated bowl with foliage outlined in blue and infilled with green and mauve, with a fragment of a flower painted in yellow (Fig. 106.241); bowl with blue painted geometric decoration and stylized flowers; handled mug or tankard with plain internal and external glaze (Fig. 106.242); five other mugs or tankards, one with a pink tinged glaze; cup with purple speckled decoration; small white glazed drug jar; fragment of blue painted pierced lobed handle of a bleeding bowl.

Brown stoneware: Salt-glazed jug.

Bristol/Staffordshire yellow slipware: Tall cup with combed brown slip decoration (Fig. 106.243); cup with 'jewelled' decoration (yellow spots over black/dark brown slip); cup with alternate lines of brown and yellow trailed slip; two combed slipware cups; two small press moulded dishes with combed brown slip decoration, one with a scalloped rim and one with a 'pie crust' rim.

Somerset ware: Jug with pulled spout and sgraffito decoration cut through white slip to red body and with patches of copper green (Fig. 107.244); base of a similar jug (Fig. 107.245); three chamber pots of different sizes and with different sgraffito decoration (white slip cut through to brown body with splashes of copper green externally) (Fig. 107.246); plate with sgraffito geometric decoration with possible central flower motif, olive green glaze cut through to dark green, possibly Somerset (Fig. 108.247); plate with sgraffito geometric decoration; sgraffito cup or bowl; plate undecorated but with internal olive green glaze heavily splashed with copper green.

North Devon ware: Plate with sgraffito decoration (Fig. 108.248); two sgraffito plates, one with a central motif of a large flower; two gravel-tempered ware pipkins (Fig. 109.249); two gravel-tempered ware

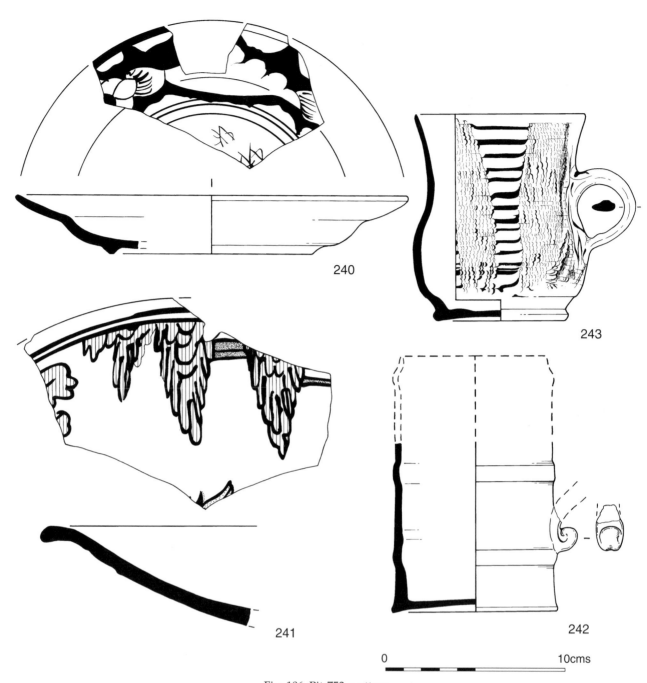

240

243

241

242

0   10cms

Fig. 106 Pit 753, pottery

chamber pots (Fig. 109.250 and 251); gravel-tempered ware storage vessel (Fig. 110.252); gravel-tempered ware dripping pan (Fig. 110.253); various other gravel-tempered ware pancheons, storage vessels (one with a spigot hole) and chamber pots.

Black or Cistercian ware: Cup.

Local redware: Bucket-handled vessel with patchy green glaze externally and internally around upper part of body (Fig. 110.254); handled bowl with internal yellow glaze (Fig. 110.255); storage vessel with internal dark brown glaze (Fig. 110.256); money pot, single slit in upper body for coins, plain knob finial at top, light green glaze; chamber pot with trailed slip decoration externally consisting of vertical bands of two wavy lines each with vertical band of crosses between and an overall red-brown glaze; two dishes or bowls (one handled) with internal geometric white trailed slip decoration and dark green glaze; fragment of plate with white trailed slip decoration and green glaze; fragment of white trailed slip bowl with internal red-brown glaze; three plates with internal geometric white trailed slip decoration and patchy light brown and green glaze; bowl with internal geometric white trailed slip and patchy brown glaze; various storage vessels and pancheons with either a red-brown or green glaze internally.

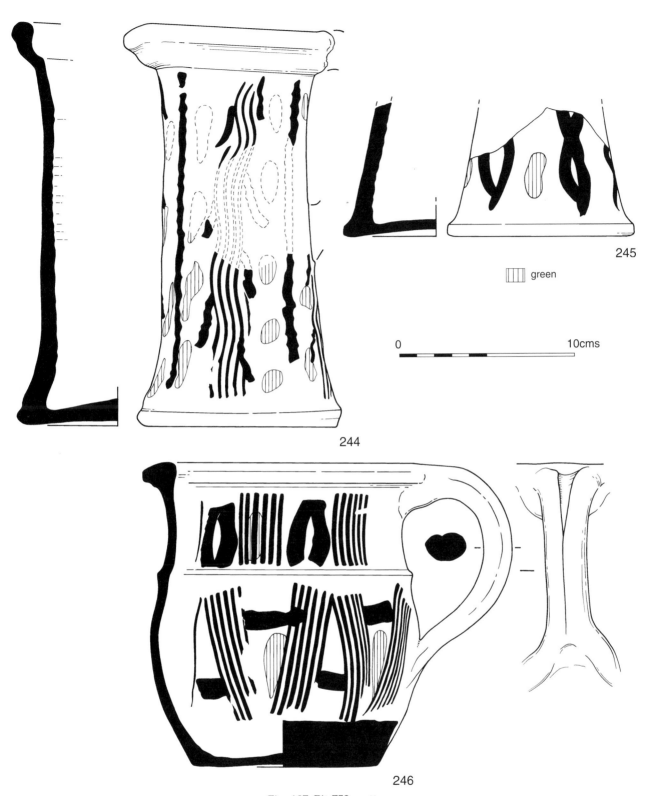

green

0   10cms

Fig. 107 Pit 753, pottery

Glass:
Base of a beaker with rounded splay and shallow punt, brownish-green glass (Fig. 111.257) (SF 472B); ornate handle of a jug or tankard with turned back base and winged top, moulded green glass (see Charleston 1986, 52 for similar handles) (SF 123B); handle, heavily weathered, single fixing point (SF 98B); two short necked onion bottles with string rims, dark green glass (Fig. 111.258 and 259) and one similar but with longer neck (Fig. 111.260); flanged neck and rim of possible beaker, light green glass (Fig. 111.261); rim of tall drinking glass, light green glass (Fig.

sgraffito decoration (Fig. 94.197); various gravel-tempered ware storage vessels, chamber pots and skillets.

South Gloucestershire (Falfield) ware: Cistercian/blackware two-handled tyg (Fig. 94.198); Cistercian/blackware two-handled tall cup or tyg.

Somerset wares: Sgraffito decorated plate or bowl; two sgraffito decorated jugs; sgraffito decorated cup; three bowls with internal white trailed slip decoration; chamber pot with external white trailed slip decoration; handled bowl with internal white trailed slip decoration (Fig. 94.199).

Local redwares: Dish with white trailed slip decoration on rim and side and sgraffito decoration in base, patchy green internal glaze; bowl with internal white trailed slip decoration and green glaze; various redware bowls, plates and storage vessels.

Tile:
Fragment of tin-glazed earthenware tile with blue painted decoration, probably Bristol or London.

Glass:
Bottles: Wide mouth and string rim of a crudely formed bottle, very thick green glass (SF 161A); part of neck of bottle, weathered green glass (SF 158A); bottle neck with string ring square edged rim, weathered dark green glass (SF 160A).

Drinking glass: Fragment of drinking glass stem with knob decoration (SF 141A).

Miscellaneous: Fragment of thin flat glass (SF 136A).

Iron:
Scissors with external finger loops and central rivet, the blades have pointed terminals (Fig. 95.200), similar scissors have been reported from Norwich (Margeson 1993, 136 no.921) (SF 587A).
Fragment of knife blade, L: 80mm x 16mm (SF 143A).
Incomplete wallhook, L: 75mm (SF 139A).
Fragment of strip, 40mm x 15mm (SF 599A).
Four large pieces of sheet, no clear function (SF 135A).

Copper Alloy:
Pin, L: 32mm (SF 125A).

Token:
Lead token, D: 15mm. Obv: Cinquefoil. Rev: Illegible, ?uniface. Probably 14th/15th century. Similar to Mitchener and Skinner 1984, pl.10, no. 50. (SF 126A).

Discussion:
The presence of pipes made by Philip Edwards I in the assemblage shows that deposition of the material could not have begun before 1650, the date of his freedom. The pit must have continued in use until at least 1696 to have included pipes made by John Pearce I, who obtained his freedom in that year. Although some of the 'PE' marked pipes could have been made

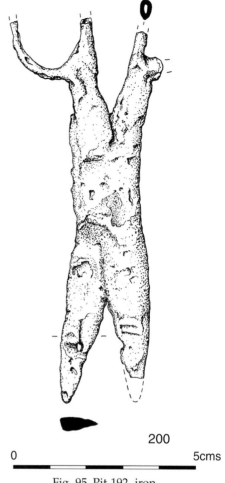

Fig. 95 Pit 192, iron

by Philip Edwards II, the pit must have been in use by 1688 to have included pipes made by Llewellin Evans, who died in that year, and assuming pipes made by him were not being sold for any length of time after his death. On the evidence of the clay tobacco pipes the rubbish pit was therefore in use during the second half of the 17th century and it is suggested that the period of use may be narrowed to *c*.1680 to 1700. The pottery such as the Westerwald tankard, Rhenish stoneware, tin-glazed earthenware, North Devon sgraffito ware and Bristol/Staffordshire yellow slip-ware would also fit well within that time period.

The Finds From Pit 259

Date:
Late 17th/very early 18th century (Period 4A).

Description:
The pit was roughly rectangular, 1.8m square and 0.2m deep, a large part of its fill having been removed by a modern pit. The upper fills (238 and 239) consisted of rich brown loam with charcoal flecks although 239 contained many lumps of pink mortar. The bottom layer of the pit (260) was a green cess-like

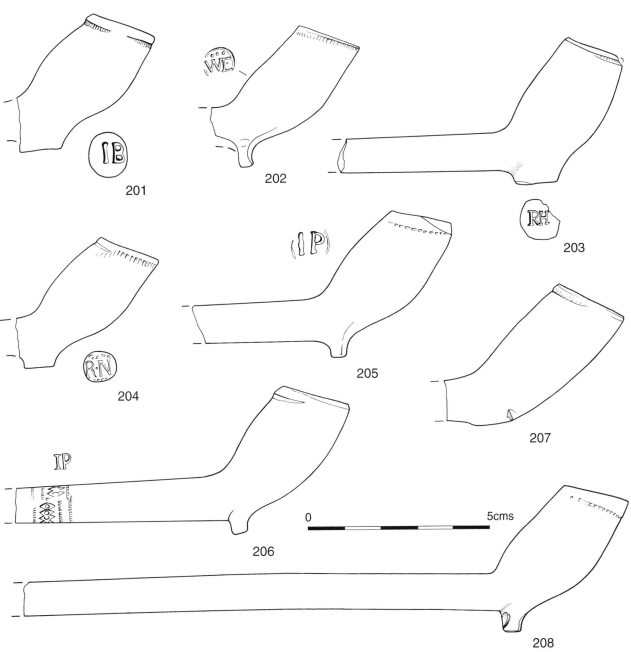

Fig. 96 Pit 259, clay tobacco pipes

material. Both 238 and 260 contained much bone-working waste.

Clay Tobacco Pipes:
One heeled bowl marked 'IB' incuse on the heel – probably John Bladen I, free 1657 and was still working in 1689 (Fig. 96.201); spurred bowl with 'WE' with decoration incuse on the back of the bowl – William Evans II, free 1667 and still alive in 1713 (Fig. 96.202); heeled bowl marked 'RH' incuse on the heel – Robert Hancock, free 1655 and working until at least 1693 (Fig. 96.203); heeled bowl with 'RN' and decoration incuse on the heel – Richard Nunney, free 1655, dead by 1713 (Fig. 96.204); spurred bowl with 'IP'

incuse on the rear of the bowl – John Pearce I, free 1696, working until at least 1713 (Fig. 96.205); spurred bowl, the stem with roulette decoration consisting of the initials 'IP' between milling and diamonds – John Pearce I, free 1696, working until at least 1713 (Fig. 96.206); bowl without heel or spur – late 17th century (Fig. 96.207); unmarked heeled bowl – c.1660–1680; two unmarked spurred bowls – late 17th/early 18th century (Fig. 96.208).

Pottery:
German stoneware: Westerwald tankard with blue and purple decoration (Fig. 97.209); Westerwald tankard with applied decoration of hearts and other motifs in

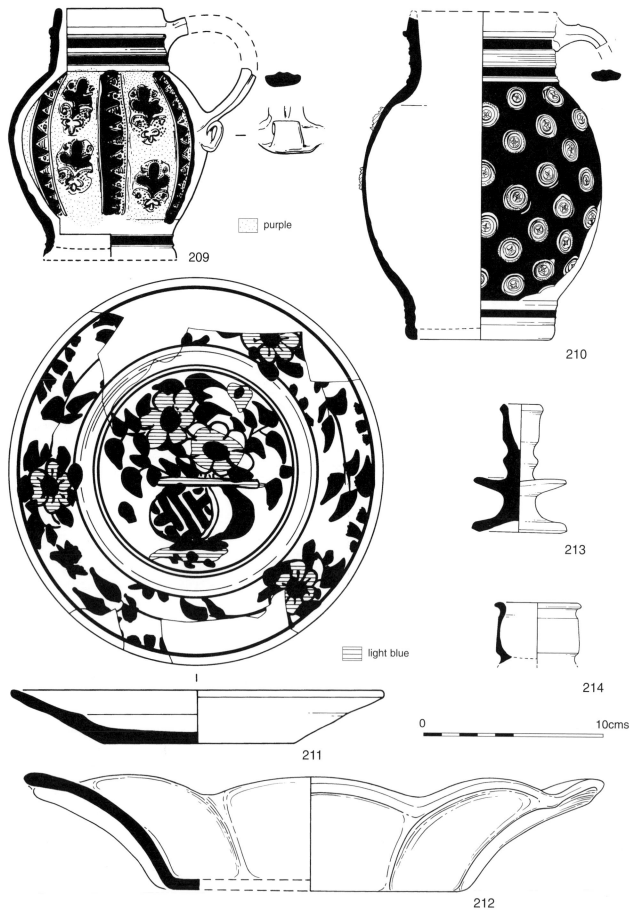

purple

209

210

213

light blue

214

0   10cms

211

212

Fig. 97 Pit 259, pottery

blue and purple; Westerwald jug with applied circular motifs against a blue ground (Fig. 97.210).

Dutch tin-glazed earthenware: Plate with floral decoration painted in blue and purple, probably Dutch (fragments of a similar, if not the same vessel, occur in pit 753); fragment of a jug finely painted with flowers and foliage in green, blue and orange, probably Dutch.

English tin-glazed earthenware: Plate with floral decoration on border and a vase of flowers as the central motif painted in dark and light blue (Fig. 97.211); large plate with concave segments and scalloped rim (Fig. 97.212); seven plates (single sherds only) with blue painted decoration and two with blue and purple decoration; charger (base only) with blue floral decoration and foot-ring pierced for suspension; bowl (base only) with blue flower decoration; plain white glazed candlestick (Fig. 97.213); plain white glazed drug jar (Fig. 97.214); drug jar decorated primarily in blue but with purple stems to 'flowers' and one area of turquoise, the decoration being much bubbled and run (Fig. 98.215); drug jar with blue decoration but the central panel has double diagonal lines in purple (Fig. 98.216); drug jar with blue decoration and pinkish glaze (Fig. 98.217); small ointment jar.

Bristol/Staffordshire yellow slipware: Cup with internal combed slip decoration (Fig. 98.218); four cups with external brown combed slip decoration; dish with internal brown combed slip decoration; chamber pot with single handle and external brown trailed slip, with dots of brown slip on rim (Fig. 98.219).

Slipware of unknown origin: Chamber pot with single handle, overall brown glaze with internal and external yellow trailed slip decoration (Fig. 98.220); cup with a medium brown overall glaze decorated externally with alternate stripes of dark brown and white trailed slip and in the same colours a slipped portrait of a king wearing a crown and ?wig (Fig. 99.221).

Brown stoneware: Neck of saltglazed ?flask.

Somerset ware: Three chamber pots with sgraffito decoration cutting through white slip to red body and with patches of copper green (Fig. 99.222 and 223).

North Devon ware: Plate with sgraffito decoration; two gravel-tempered ware chamber pots; five gravel-tempered ware pancheons (two very large); rectangular dripping pan with horizontal handle and finger impressed decoration on outside edge of rim.

Local redware (all with red/brown glaze unless otherwise stated): Pancheon with applied thumbed strip below rim externally, horizontal handles and glazed internally (Fig. 100.224); two plates with internal glaze and white trailed slip decoration on rim; bowl with external glaze and white trailed slip decoration; storage vessels with external and internal dark green glaze and applied thumb impressed strip below rim externally (Fig. 100.225); three storage vessels or pancheons with internal glaze; three storage vessels with internal very dark brown/black glaze; shallow dish with external and internal green glaze; three storage vessels with internal mottled green glaze; shallow handled bowl with internal yellow glaze; handled pitcher with external dark green/black glaze; bowl glazed internally with finger impressed decoration around edge of rim; jug with external glaze.

Glass:
Bottles and flasks: Long neck with string rim, the top is poorly formed, brown-green glass (SF 466A); neck of a bottle with a string rim, green glass (SF 373A); shallow neck of bottle with string rim, raised scar above shoulder, green glass, heavy surface degradation (SF 405A); short-necked onion bottle with poorly applied string rim, dark green glass (Fig. 101.226) (SF 464A); short-necked onion bottle with well formed string rim, dark green glass (SF 402A); rim and neck of a bottle with crudely formed string rim, dark green glass (SF 377A); short neck of a bottle with string rim, weathered dark green glass (SF 395A); neck and simple everted rim of a flask, green glass, external D: 29mm (see Charleston 1984, 270 for a similar vessel) (SF 393A).

Drinking glasses: Part of the stem of a drinking glass, moulded glass with spiral twist, seven lobed ring and 'berry' pellets (Fig. 101.227) (SF 403A); stem and base of a conical bowl with a crude quatrefoil knob below the bowl, wide simple base, smokey grey glass (Fig. 101.228) (SF 432A); fragment of drinking glass stem with moulded decoration (SF 394A); fragment of moulded glass with 'raspberry' pellet decoration (SF 397A); fragment of white opaque glass with blue 'berry' decoration (SF 396A); two fragments of possible drinking glass of thin ?clear (now opaque surfaces) glass with ten horizontal ridges below rim (SF 401A).

Possible medical vessel: Wide simple base with hollow knob above, thin colourless glass, possibly from a medical vessel (SF 392A).

Jar: flange rim of a glass jar, much surface weathering, colour of glass uncertain, possibly pale green (Fig. 101.229) (Margeson 1993, 102–3) (SF 404A).

Bone and Ivory:
Medical nozzles: Tapering bone tube or nozzle, the hollow stem is bulbous at its narrow end, the opposite end is flared with reed and double cord decoration. Internally there is a series of grooves, possibly a non-spiral thread. L: 113mm x max. D: 15mm (Fig. 102.230) (SF 414A).

Tapering bone tube or nozzle, lathe turned plain hollow shaft, one end flared with wide external rebate and internal chamfer. L: 103mm x max. D: 13mm (Fig. 102.231) (SF 408A).

Carved ivory tube or nozzle, tube flares and is decorated with twin grooves, the end is parallel

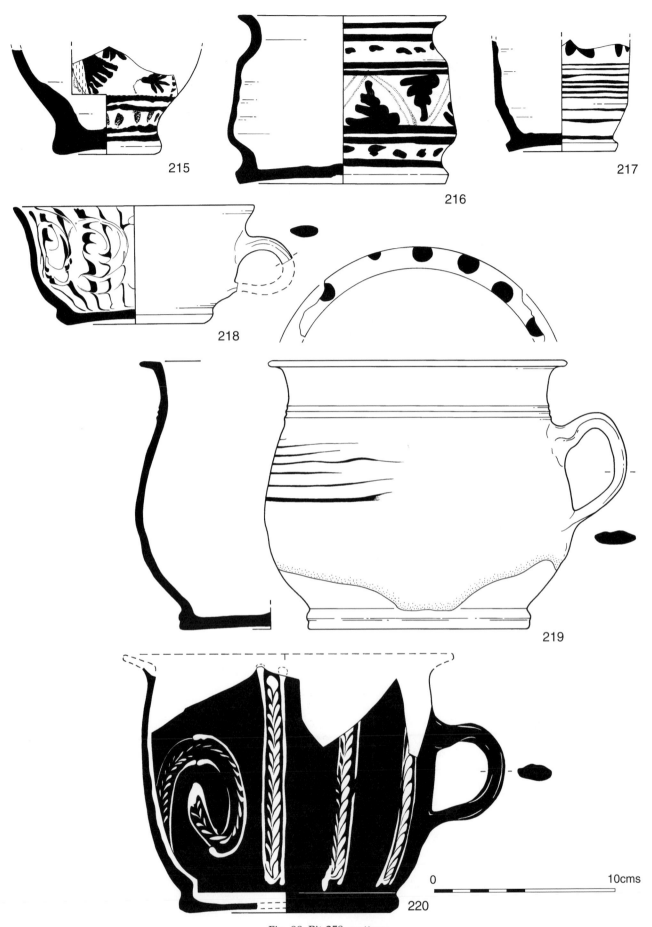

Fig. 98 Pit 259, pottery

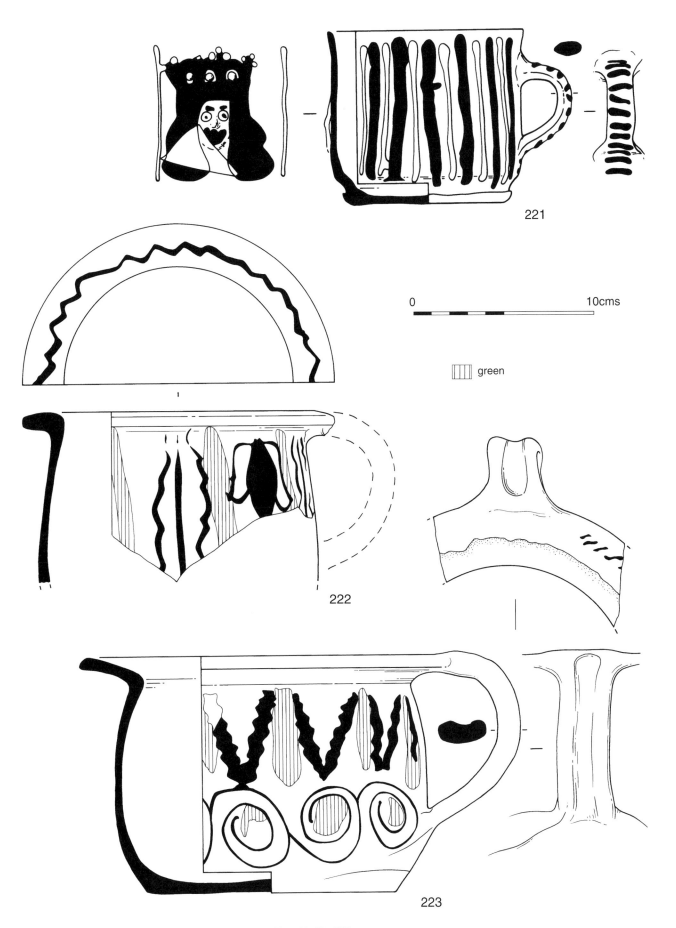

221

222

223

green

0   10cms

Fig. 99 Pit 259, pottery

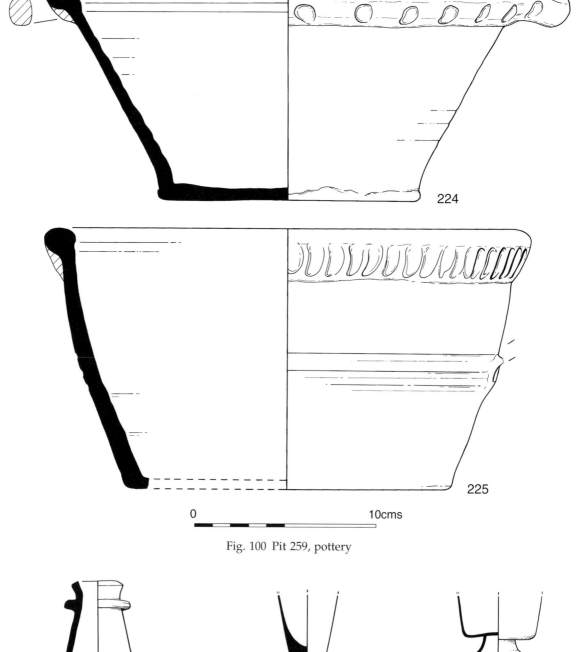

Fig. 100 Pit 259, pottery

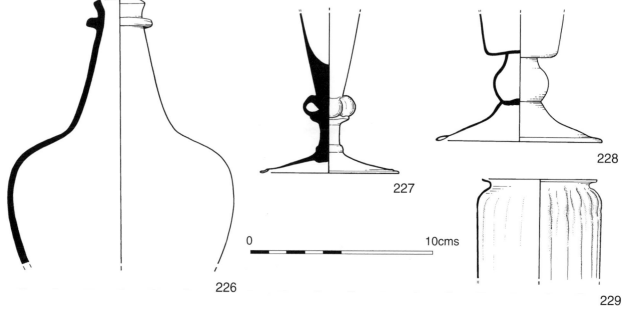

Fig. 101 Pit 259, glass

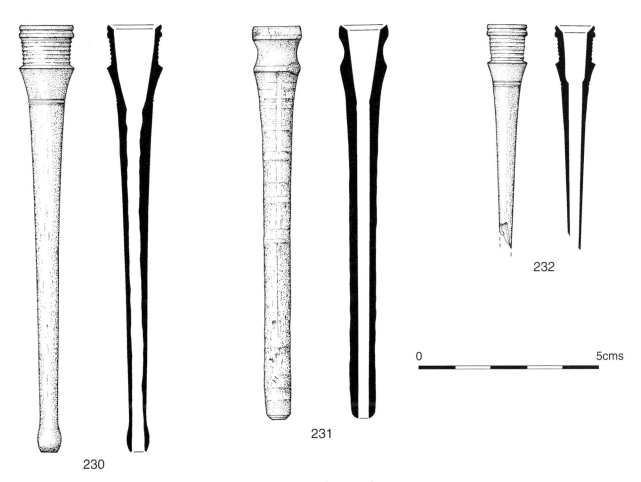

Fig. 102 Pit 259, bone and ivory

grooved externally and has an internal chamfer. L:
59mm x max. D: 11mm (Fig. 102.232) (SF 390A).

Similar objects found at Plymouth have been
described as medical nozzles (Gaskell-Brown 1986,
M/F8).

Fans: Eleven strips of whalebone – part of a fan –
holes drilled through a bulbous end to take an iron
rivet. Max. L: 208mm, W: 10mm. (see MacGregor 1985
for the use of baleen) (SF 381A).

Very thin strip possibly used as a veneer or fan.
?waste. L: 90mm (SF 380A).

Thin strip of bone possibly from a fan or veneer. L:
64mm x 9mm. (SF 383A).

Iron:

Purse frame: Iron frame mounted with leather riveted
with iron rivets at 10mm centres. Surviving L: 52mm,
W: 14mm (Fig. 103.233). Iron purse frames are not
common. Margeson (1993, 43) describes an iron purse
from Norwich. The Norwich example and two further
frames cited by Margeson, one from London and
another from Amsterdam, were quite ornate with
decorative finials. The Norwich frame had a spring
clasp enabling the purse to be locked. Margeson
suggests that these purses were imported from the

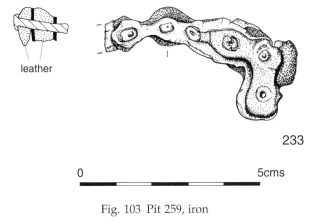

leather

233

Fig. 103 Pit 259, iron

Low Countries. The frames described by Margeson
would appear to be earlier than the present example
having been dated to the second half of the 15th
century on the basis of parallels in paintings. The
Norwich frame was recovered from fire deposits
dated 1507. (SF 518A).

Miscellaneous: Hollow, tapering, socket: possibly to
take a wooden shaft. The terminal is broken. Possibly

military – an object of similar type is described by Goodall (1993, fig. 176.1863) as a long tapering arrow head dated 1650–1700 and Shoesmith (1985) describes similar objects as spear tips of medieval date. However, the possibility of a domestic function cannot be precluded (SF 371A).

Knife blade with tang, mostly corrosion products (SF 364A); part of hollow object, externally stepped at one end, (raised) studded band at other end, five studs present, internal D: 20mm (SF 566A); concreted mass mostly corrosion products, x-ray suggests the presence of wire or fine ?pins/nails within the matrix (SF 592A).

Circular object, form not clear but possibly head of a bolt or similar (SF 516A); bolt or spike, round headed, ?wood adhering to shaft, L: 138mm (SF 399A).

Iron sheets and strips: Fragment of folded sheet, the material appears to have been plated (SF 412A); fragment of folded sheet, plated, the sides have been folded to form a corner, 50mm x 40mm (SF 420A); folded sheet, plated, L: 45mm (SF 412A); fragment of strip, probably part of a blade but x-ray not clear, very degraded (SF 418A); six fragments of ?tinned iron (SF 416A); fragment of plate with plated edge (SF 560A); strip 35mm x 8mm (SF 370A); fragments including handle (D-shaped), all very corroded, W: between terminals 87mm (SF 413A).

Copper Alloy:

Fragment of wood/copper alloy split disc, covering end fixed with an iron nail/rivet, L: 25mm, D: of disc 20mm (SF 372A); three pin fragments (SFs 324A, 325A, 480A).

Lead:

Window came. Two pieces: L: (bent) 26mm and 38mm. (Crummy 1988, 72, fig. 73). (SF 479A).

Stone Moulds:

One valve of a bi-valve mould. Series of circular depressions with six petal floral design. Face very smooth, reverse rougher with crude incised circle with simple five-armed cross (Fig. 104.234). Probably a jetton or token mould. The form and function of stone moulds has been discussed by Allan (1984, 304) and Margeson (1993, 177). Most are considered to date to the 16th or 17th centuries. (SF 437A).

Fragment of limestone with crude inscribed circle containing eight crossed lines plus a second simple circle. There are two depressions in the back of stone (Fig. 104.235). Possibly a test-piece or unfinished mould (SF 438A).

Tokens:

Lead disc, D: 20mm. Obv: Plain cross. Rev: Illegible, ?uniface. Probably an early Tudor token. Similar to Mitchener and Skinner 1985, pl.6, no.6. (SF 410A).

Lead token, D: 20mm. Obv: Field voided by triple cross. Rev: Illegible, ?uniface. Probably Elizabethan. Similar to Mitchener and Skinner 1985, pl.14, no.87. (SF 409A).

Discussion:

The presence of pipes made by John Pearce I in the assemblage shows that deposition of the material could not have begun before 1696, the date of his freedom. The almost equal mixture of heeled and spurred bowls suggests that backfilling of the pit occurred at the end of the 17th century and during the early years of the 18th century. The presence of three tin-glazed earthenware drug jars and one small ointment jar, a fragment of what may be a glass medical vessel and three bone and ivory tubes which are almost certainly medical nozzles, suggest the use of the pit by a pharmacist or barber-surgeon who was living or practising in the locality. Dr Roger Price has kindly examined these nozzles and suggests that they may be *clyster-pipes,* a type of syringe used for injecting a clyster or enema into the rectum.

The Finds From Pit 753

Date:

Late 17th/early 18th century (Period 4A).

Description:

The rectangular pit was lined with a drystone wall of Pennant sandstone. It measured 1.3m east/west, at least 0.6m north/south and was 1.3m deep. The fill of the pit, which showed clear tip lines sloping down from east to west, consisted mainly of a brown clayey silt with much charcoal flecking and small stones (744), and with large pieces of stone rubble close to the base.

Clay Tobacco Pipes:

Bowl marked 'LE' incuse on the heel; spurred bowl marked 'LE' incuse on the back of the bowl (Fig. 105.236) – Llewellin Evans, free 1661, died 1688; bowl marked 'RN' incuse on the heel between swags – Richard Nunney, free 1655, dead by 1713; two roulette decorated stems with the initials 'IP' between milling and diamonds – John Pearce I, free 1696, working until at least 1713 (Fig. 105.237); spurred bowl with fragment of roulette decorated stem (Fig. 105.238); 142 spurred bowls of various forms – late 17th/early 18th century; twelve heeled bowls – *c.*1660–1680; eleven West Country style heeled bowls – third quarter of the 17th century (Fig. 105.239); small heeled bowl – early/mid 17th century.

Pottery:

German stoneware: Westerwald jug with applied geometric decoration coloured with blue and purple.

Dutch tin-glazed earthenware: Plate with floral decoration painted in blue and purple, probably

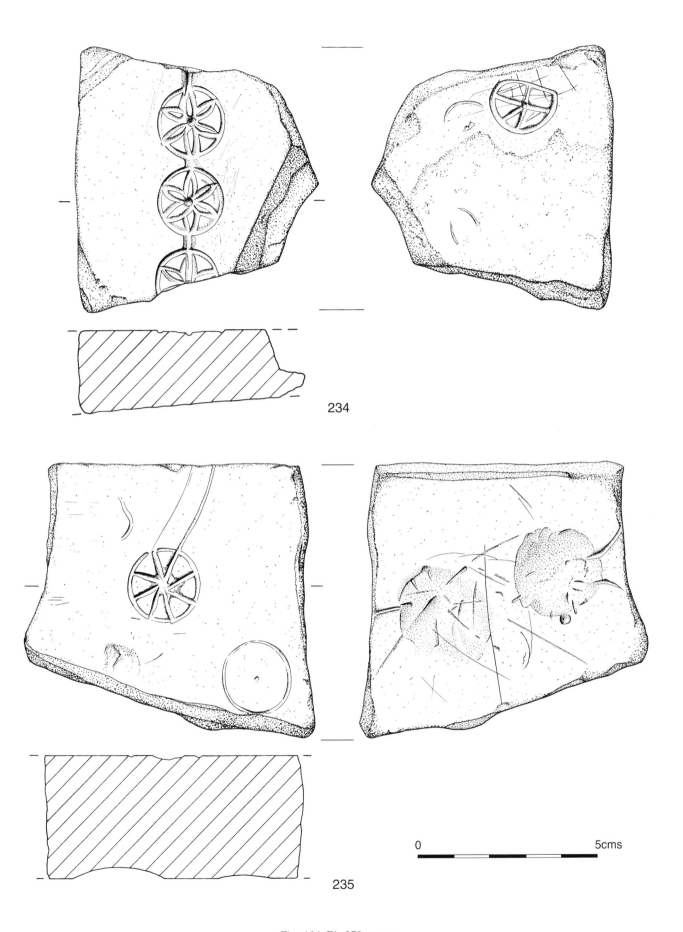

234

235

Fig. 104 Pit 259, stone

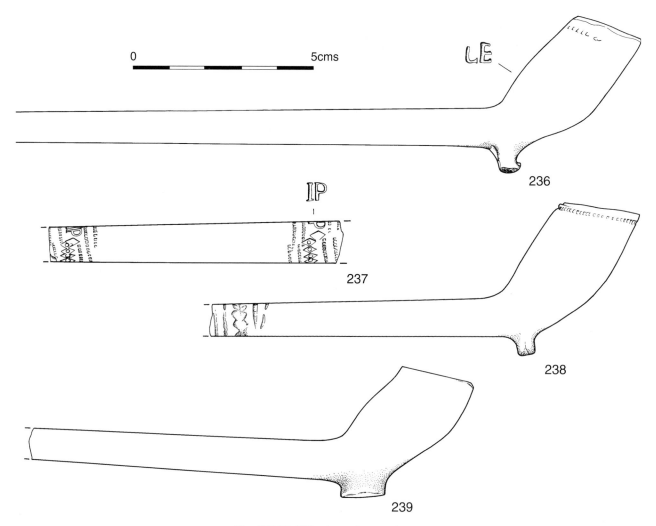

Fig. 105 Pit 753, clay tobacco pipes

Dutch (fragments of a similar, if not the same vessel, were found in pit 259).

English tin-glazed earthenware: Plate with overall light blue glaze painted with blue floral and ?geometric border; plate with light/dark blue stylized ?flower border and with stylized decoration as the central motif (Fig. 106.240); fragments of at least fourteen other plates or dishes painted mainly in blue but with some green, yellow and purple; decorated bowl with foliage outlined in blue and infilled with green and mauve, with a fragment of a flower painted in yellow (Fig. 106.241); bowl with blue painted geometric decoration and stylized flowers; handled mug or tankard with plain internal and external glaze (Fig. 106.242); five other mugs or tankards, one with a pink tinged glaze; cup with purple speckled decoration; small white glazed drug jar; fragment of blue painted pierced lobed handle of a bleeding bowl.

Brown stoneware: Salt-glazed jug.

Bristol/Staffordshire yellow slipware: Tall cup with combed brown slip decoration (Fig. 106.243); cup with 'jewelled' decoration (yellow spots over black/dark brown slip); cup with alternate lines of brown and yellow trailed slip; two combed slipware cups; two small press moulded dishes with combed brown slip decoration, one with a scalloped rim and one with a 'pie crust' rim.

Somerset ware: Jug with pulled spout and sgraffito decoration cut through white slip to red body and with patches of copper green (Fig. 107.244); base of a similar jug (Fig. 107.245); three chamber pots of different sizes and with different sgraffito decoration (white slip cut through to brown body with splashes of copper green externally) (Fig. 107.246); plate with sgraffito geometric decoration with possible central flower motif, olive green glaze cut through to dark green, possibly Somerset (Fig. 108.247); plate with sgraffito geometric decoration; sgraffito cup or bowl; plate undecorated but with internal olive green glaze heavily splashed with copper green.

North Devon ware: Plate with sgraffito decoration (Fig. 108.248); two sgraffito plates, one with a central motif of a large flower; two gravel-tempered ware pipkins (Fig. 109.249); two gravel-tempered ware

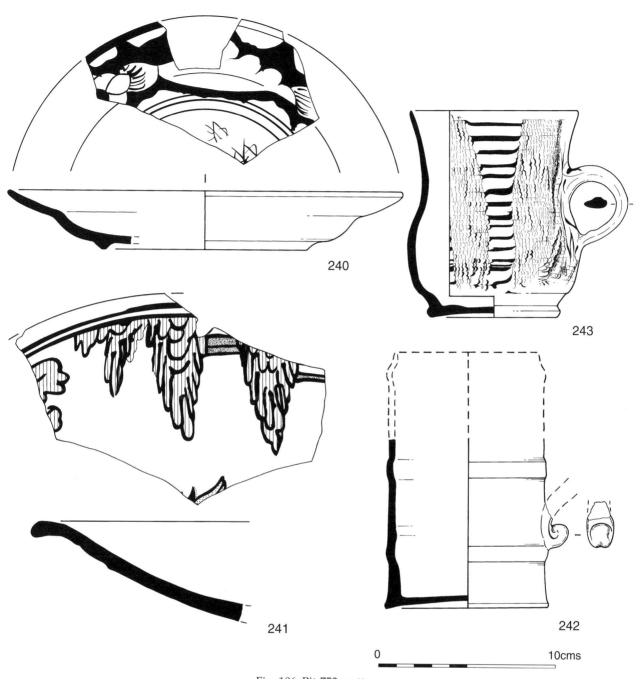

Fig. 106 Pit 753, pottery

chamber pots (Fig. 109.250 and 251); gravel-tempered ware storage vessel (Fig. 110.252); gravel-tempered ware dripping pan (Fig. 110.253); various other gravel-tempered ware pancheons, storage vessels (one with a spigot hole) and chamber pots.

Black or Cistercian ware: Cup.

Local redware: Bucket-handled vessel with patchy green glaze externally and internally around upper part of body (Fig. 110.254); handled bowl with internal yellow glaze (Fig. 110.255); storage vessel with internal dark brown glaze (Fig. 110.256); money pot, single slit in upper body for coins, plain knob finial at top, light green glaze; chamber pot with trailed slip decoration externally consisting of vertical bands of two wavy lines each with vertical band of crosses between and an overall red-brown glaze; two dishes or bowls (one handled) with internal geometric white trailed slip decoration and dark green glaze; fragment of plate with white trailed slip decoration and green glaze; fragment of white trailed slip bowl with internal red-brown glaze; three plates with internal geometric white trailed slip decoration and patchy light brown and green glaze; bowl with internal geometric white trailed slip and patchy brown glaze; various storage vessels and pancheons with either a red-brown or green glaze internally.

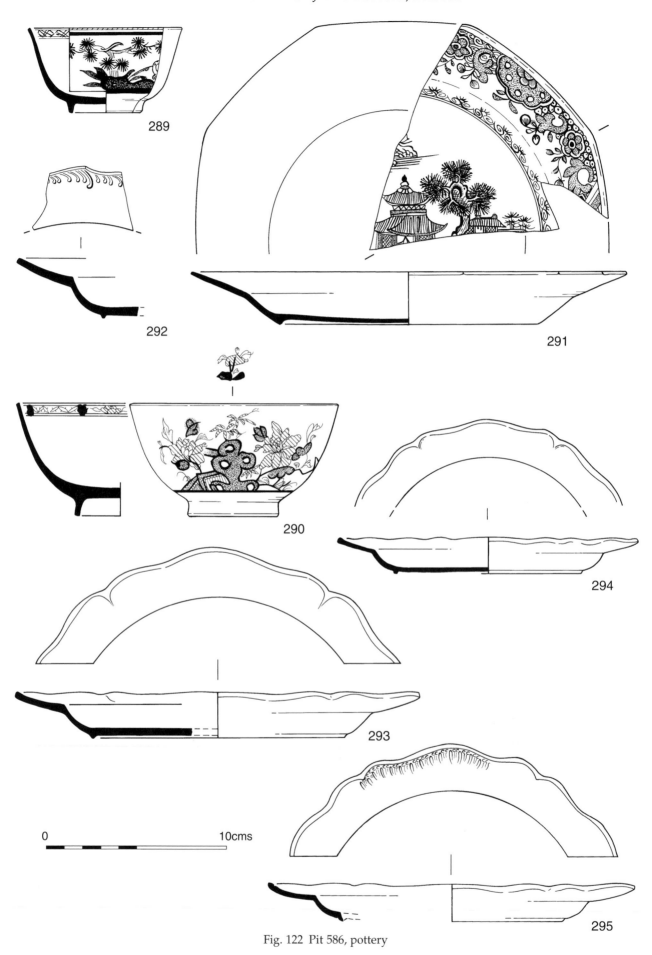

Fig. 122 Pit 586, pottery

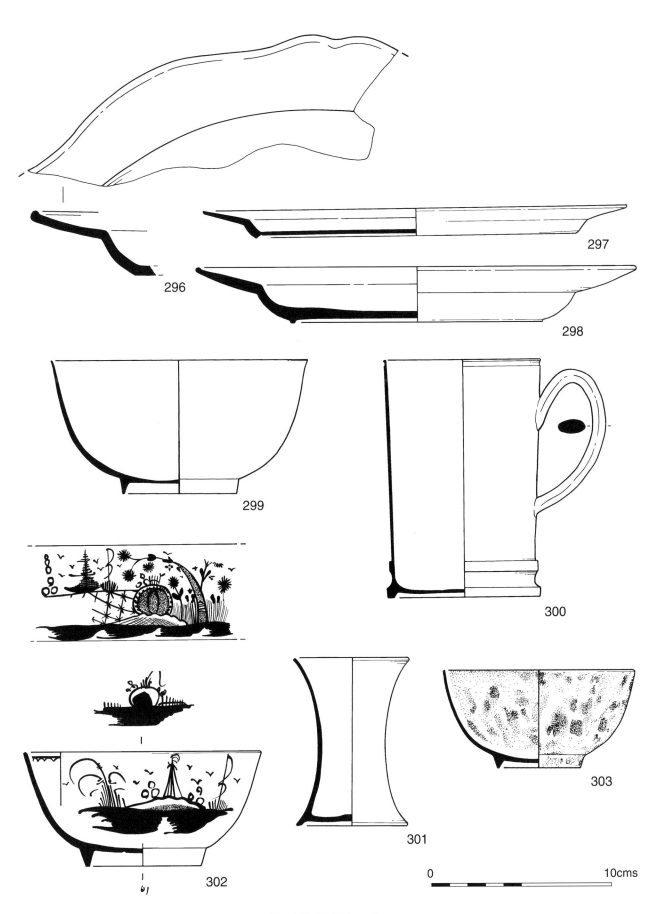

Fig. 123 Pit 586, pottery

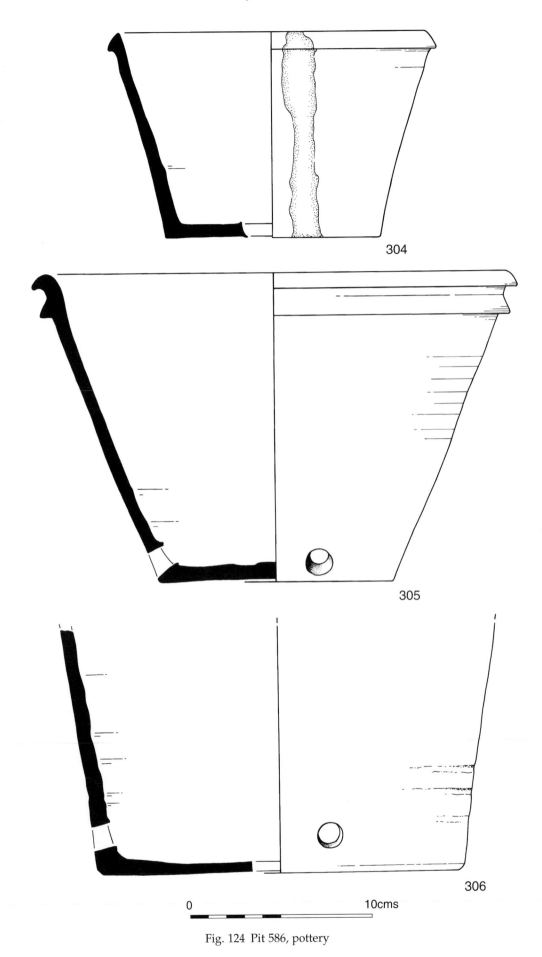

0 10cms

Fig. 124 Pit 586, pottery

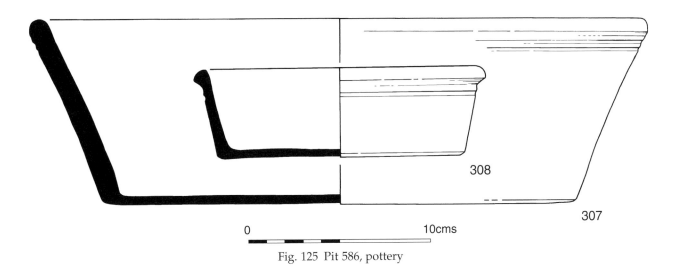

0   10cms

Fig. 125 Pit 586, pottery

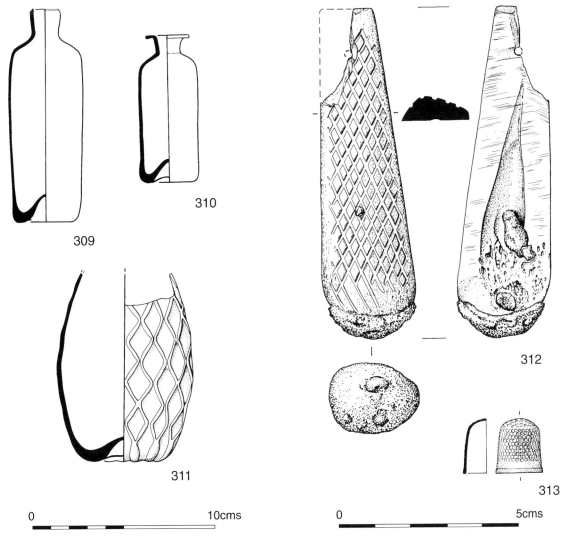

0   10cms   0   5cms

Fig. 126 Pit 586, glass (309–311), bone (312), copper alloy (313)

Lead:
Two lead alloy shallow spoon bowls: bowl 1: L: 75mm x 40mm x approx. 10mm; bowl 2: L: 75mm x 43mm. (SF 381B).

Discussion:
The presence of a large collection of Bristol/Staffordshire creamwares and the almost total absence of transfer-printed ware (one sherd) indicates a date for the pit in the latter quarter of the 18th century, before the production of transfer-printed wares generally, and especially in the Water Lane Pottery in Bristol, became predominant. This would correspond with the date range of the two clay tobacco pipe bowls, one of which was made by Samuel Richards I or II and therefore cannot pre-date 1747. Their bowl forms suggest a date of manufacture towards the end of the 18th century. The redware flowerpots, with drainage holes around the sides close to the base or with a single central drainage hole in the base, fit in well with Currie's typology for the development of flowerpot design (Currie 1993) and correspond with a late 18th-century date for the pit.

The Faunal Remains (Site 1)
by Geraldine Barber

Introduction

The excavation of St James's Priory, Bristol during 1988 and 1995 produced a large quantity of animal bones (over fifteen thousand) in addition to the human remains recovered. The site itself is made up of the priory, its adjacent graveyard and subsequent post-medieval occupation, with continuous use from the 12th century through to the 20th century.

Parts of the site were truncated by subsequent building and much of the animal bone recovered came from reworked deposits and grave cuts. These could not be dated with any accuracy. The post-excavation strategy was to concentrate on the best contexts, which could answer specific archaeological questions posed by the site. Only dated contexts were examined. Contexts which had been disturbed or which had few fragments were discarded before analysis, as were contexts that had a date range greater than one period. The bones studied came from 304 contexts, ranging in nature from drains and gullies to graves and postholes. Most of the material came from large pits that were dominant features of this site. It appeared from the pottery and small finds that the pits present on the site were mainly domestic in nature although some contained industrial waste.

The site can be divided into five main phases that contained animal bone – Medieval, Dissolution, 16th, 17th and 18th centuries. These phases have been further sub-divided in the main report. However, any further sub-division of these phases for the analysis of the faunal remains would produce samples too small to permit interpretation.

The Sample

Almost seven thousand fragments were selected for analysis. Of these, nearly three and a half thousand (51%) were identified to species. The material was in fair to good condition. The bones were well preserved, but in a fragmentary state.

Very few small mammal, bird and fish remains were present. There was no sieving strategy on site; all bones analysed were hand recovered. It must be assumed that this will have biased the sample towards larger types of species and skeletal element.

Aims

A sample size of three and a half thousand identified bones spread over five main phases is too small a sample to support lengthy statistical analysis. However, it is large enough to begin to answer several questions about the site and animal husbandry practices in the area. After discussion with the archaeologists the aims of the post excavation analysis were agreed as follows:
1. To assess the range of species represented on the site.
2. To determine if there is any change in relative proportions of species over time.
3. To look for evidence of changing animal husbandry over time in terms of the age of death, butchery practices and size of the major food species.
4. To compare the results from this site with those of contemporary urban sites locally and across the country.
5. To look at the animal remains from the large pits with a view to determining the occupations of the local businesses which created them.

Methods
Recording
The methods by which the fragments are identified and counted can bias results. It must be always borne in mind that the majority of any animal bone excavated is only a fragment of the original assemblage of bones from a site, and a biased one at that (Levitan 1989). Certain bones often preserve better than others, *i.e.* teeth and phalanges as opposed to the spongy epiphyses (Payne 1975). Other bones can often be difficult to assign to species such as ribs, vertebrae and some of the less diagnostic skull fragments.

All bones were identified as accurately as possible. For some fragments it was only possible to identify body part, but not species. These are all recorded in the database but they are not used for the analysis.

A selected number of skeletal parts were chosen for

analysis. The skeletal elements chosen were: horn-cores, individual teeth, mandibles, maxilla, proximal and distal humerus, proximal and distal radius, proximal ulna, first and second cervical vertebrae, proximal and distal tibia, proximal and distal femur, astragalus, calcaneum, proximal and distal meta-podials, and phalanges. These were chosen as they represented different parts of the body, are frequently occurring and are easily identifiable.

Meaurements

Measurements of the identifiable bones were taken where possible. These followed the criteria of von den Dreisch (1976) and are listed in the site archive.

Ageing

Ageing animals can be a problem when they are alive and complete. It is much more difficult if one has only a fragment of bone to assess. Two methods were used to estimate age. State of fusion of epiphyses of the long bones was recorded (as unfused, fusing and fused). These were compared to known fusion ages of modern animals (Silver 1969). One problem with this method is that different breeds can fuse their epiphyses at different ages, so sometimes average or range of ages is given.

The second method of ageing is by tooth eruption and tooth wear patterns. Tooth eruption ages and grades of wear after Grant (1982) for cows and pigs, and Payne (1973) for sheep and goats, have been used.

Sexing

It is very difficult to determine the sex of individual animal bones. The most accurate part of the body is usually the pelvis. Unfortunately this bone is usually fragmented or butchered. With pigs, the shape and size of the canine can also be used (Schmid 1976). Sexual dimorphism, the differences in size between the male and female of a species is another way of estimating sex. This can be a problem when castrates are involved as they may not reach the same size as males of the same breed.

Minimum Number of Individuals (MNI)

Minimum numbers of individuals (MNIs) were calculated for each of the main food species using the simple method of counting the most frequently occurring body part (*e.g.* left proximal femur, odontoid process or right distal radius). However, MNIs can be a difficult concept to use on urban sites (Levitan 1989) as meat was most likely to have been brought to this site as joints as well as or instead of whole animals.

Butchery/Bone Working

Cut marks and other signs of butchery were recorded, with relevant comments on jointing or use of meat or offal. Several pits containing large numbers of meta-podial fragments that appeared to be industrial off-cuts were excavated.

Pathology

Where a bone showed some form of pathology it was photographed, x-rayed and described. It was not always possible to arrive at a definite diagnosis, but the probable diagnosis and a list of differentials are given where possible.

The Archive

Publication constraints mean that there is not enough space to publish all data. Measurements are given in Appendices 1 – 5 which, together with copies of the database containing these and all other recorded information, are contained in the site archive.

Results

Species Represented

Fig. 127 shows a list of all the species identified from this site (NISP), and their relative frequencies for each of the main phases.

Mammal:

cow *Bos taurus*
sheep *Ovis aries*
goat *Capra hircus*
pig *Sus domesticus*
horse *Equus caballus*
red deer *Cervus elephas*
rabbit *Oryctolagus cuniculus*
cat *Felis catus*
dog *Canis familiaris*
mouse *Mus musculus*

Bird:

goose *Anser anser*
domestic fowl *Gallus gallus*
mallard/teal *Anas* sp.

Most of the identified fragments are of the three major food species – cow, sheep/goat and pig. Together, they represent 84% of the sample. Cattle were the most common species identified, but it is likely that this species is over represented as a food source. Many of the fragments of bone in the 17th- and 18th-century phases appear to be waste from bone working (see below for further details), and not from domestic refuse.

Sheep and goat bones are hard to separate to species. Where possible they were separated using the criteria of Boessneck (1969). In most cases the species could not be distinguished and are discussed as sheep/goat. Of the 38 bones that could be identified to species, all were sheep. It is highly likely that the bones identified as sheep/goat are in reality sheep.

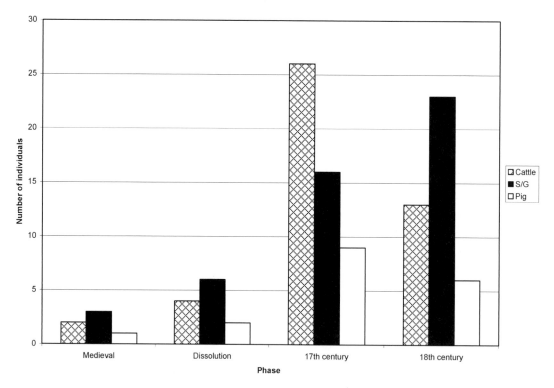

Fig. 127 MNIs for the major food species: all phases

This has been suggested at other contemporary sites including Exeter (Maltby 1979).

Most of the bird bones identified are from the domestic chicken. These account for 8% of the total fragments identified. Goose and duck were also present, in much smaller numbers. In addition nine fragments from other species of bird were recorded. The bones were fragmentary, so it was not possible to identify them to species.

Deer are rare in urban sites (Grant 1984), and St James's Priory is no exception. A small number of red and roe deer were identified; inspection of the measurements suggests that fallow deer may also be present. Only four fragments of horse were present. Horse were also found to be uncommon on sites of the same date in nearby Exeter.

Other species identified include a small number of rabbit bones, a large number of cat bones – though these are from only four individuals – and a few of dog.

Only one fragment of small mammal, mouse, was identified. No fish bones were present in the selected sample. The lack of specimens from these and other small taxa are a result of studying a hand-retrieved sample.

Frequencies of Species Through Time

There is a considerable difference in the numbers of identified bones of the medieval, Dissolution and 16th-century phases and the large samples of the 17th and 18th century. It has not always been possible to compare all five phases. This has produced some inconclusive results. Table 36 and Fig. 127 show the frequencies of the species in terms of NISP and MNI respectively. From Table 36 it can be seen that cattle is the most commonly represented species in terms of numbers of fragments. In the medieval and 18th-century phases cattle are slightly outnumbered by sheep/goat. The MNI calculations are very low, representing just over 100 animals. Sheep outnumber the other species. In terms of meat weight, however, cattle are the most important food species.

Part Representation

Figs. 128 to 130 show the distribution of the parts of the skeleton for the four phases (the 16th century had not enough data to merit analysis).

Cattle

There is a marked change in the part representation between the medieval and Dissolution phases and the 17th and 18th centuries. It can be seen that in the later phases the greatest number of identified fragments are metapodials. These are the remains of the bone-working industry (discussed below). In addition it can be seen that some of the remains are domestic food waste. All body parts including skull fragments, long bones and feet are present.

Table 36 Numbers of identified fragments of each species per phase

	Medieval	Dissolution	16th Century	17th Century	18th Century	Total
Sheep/Goat	33	50	3	738	241	1065
Cow	24	60		1253	187	1524
Pig	11	7		240	30	288
Horse		1		3		4
Deer	1	5		3	9	18
Rabbit	1	8		28	26	63
Dog	1	1		9	2	18
Cat		106		15	7	128
Mouse					1	1
Domestic Fowl	5	9		116	127	257
Goose	2	2		19	13	36
Mallard				2	2	4
Other Bird		2		2	2	6
Total	78	251	3	2428	647	3407

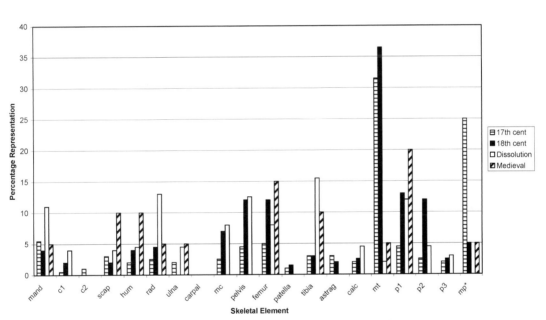

Fig. 128 Percentage representation of cow skeletal elements

Sheep/Goat

Comparisons of the 17th and 18th centuries show a profile of skeletal elements that are very similar. All body parts are represented. However, the earlier medieval phase shows a lack of skull, mandible and neck vertebrae. There are relatively few lower limb bones present. The numbers involved are small but this may be a change from bringing in joints to whole animals in the area. It may be that more of the animal is being utilised in the later phases – there is evidence from the butchery marks to show that in the 17th and 18th centuries sheep skulls were sawn open to remove the brains. One interesting finding is the absence of both sheep and cattle horn cores from this site. Skulls were recovered but the horn cores had been removed from them. It is likely they were used off site in some type of horn-working industry.

Pig

There are data only for the 17th and 18th centuries – the other phases have too few identified fragments. Both phases are similar in body part representation. Most of the skeleton is represented, indicating that the animals came to or near the site whole. The bones identified here appear to be butchery waste. This finding is in contrast to some sites of the same date,

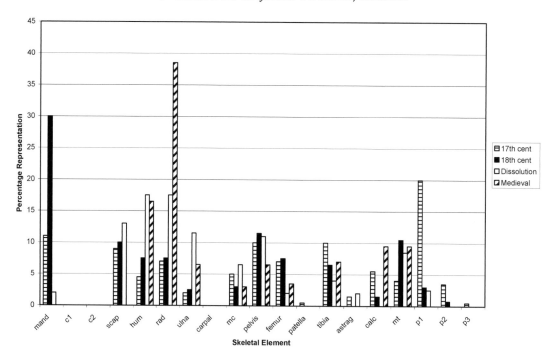

Fig. 129 Percentage representation of sheep/goat skeletal elements

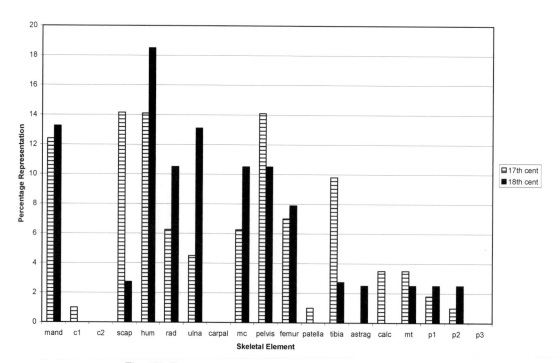

Fig. 130 Percentage representation of pig skeletal elements

e.g. Launceston Castle (Albarella and Davis 1996), where much larger numbers of skull and teeth were recovered in relation to postcranial skeletal elements.

Ages of the Major Food Species

Cattle

The material from the 17th and 18th centuries are very similar. The few mandibles present are mostly from younger animals (see Table 37). The epiphysial fusion data from these phases also suggest that most of the animals recovered from these phases are of immature or sub-adult individuals. These findings are consistent with those of Noddle (1985) from the nearby parish of St Mary-le-Port.

The numbers of fragments are much smaller from the two earliest phases. However, the age at slaughter appears to differ from that defined for the 17th/18th

Table 37 Ages of cattle by mandibular tooth eruption and attrition

	Deciduous teeth only	M1 erupting	M2 erupting	M3 erupting	M3 in wear	M3 well worn
Medieval						
Dissolution	1			1		
17th century	11	3	1		1	
18th century	1					1

Table 38 Ages of sheep/goat by mandibular tooth eruption and attrition

	Deciduous teeth only	M1 erupting	M2 erupting	M3 erupting	M3 in wear – Paynes score							
					A	B	C	D	E	F	G	H
Medieval												
Dissolution							1					
17th century				2	1	1	1	1	2	6	2	
18th century		1		5	1	1	2	1	8	7	2	

Table 39 Ages of pig by mandibular tooth eruption and attrition

	Deciduous teeth only	M1 erupting	M2 erupting	M3 erupting	M3 in wear
Medieval					
Dissolution					
17th century	3	2	2	2	
18th century				2	

centuries. Approximately half of the bones from the earliest phases are from adult animals. This pattern is similar to that found at Exeter (Maltby 1979).

Sheep/Goat
In contrast to the cattle and pig data, most sheep/goat mandibles were from adult animals. Only three of the five phases had mandibles that were complete enough to estimate age. Table 38 shows that the 17th- and 18th-century phases were dominated by older adult animals – over half of the individuals present were at wear stages F and older (aged over four years). It was not possible to compare the two later phases with the others as no data were available.

Pig
The pig teeth and bones identified were mostly of young and sub-adult individuals in all phases (see Table 39). This is a very common finding on most urban sites.

Sex
Cattle
Very few of the fragments could be assigned a sex. The only skeletal element that had any number of whole adult bones were the metatarsals. For this group there were still only thirteen bones from two phases. Fig. 131 shows a scattergraph of greatest length against distal breadth. The numbers involved are small and it is not possible to speculate on sex groupings.

Sheep/Goat
It was not possible to estimate sex for any of the fragments present.

Pig
The estimate of sex of the pigs was based entirely on the size of the canines. The numbers which could be assigned a sex were very small (N = 7) and only from the 17th- and 18th-century phases. All individuals except one were classed as male. Given the small numbers involved it is impossible to interpret these data.

Measurements
Cattle
As discussed previously, most of the bones recovered were from young animals, which could not be measured. Those long bones that were from adult animals were usually fragmented.

Sheep/Goat
There were very few complete bones from any phase that could be studied. However, the single measurements that could be obtained in the 17th and 18th centuries were very similar. It was not possible to compare these to the earlier phases due to lack of data.

Pig
Only eleven fragments of bone were measureable from all five phases. This is too small a sample to draw any conclusions.

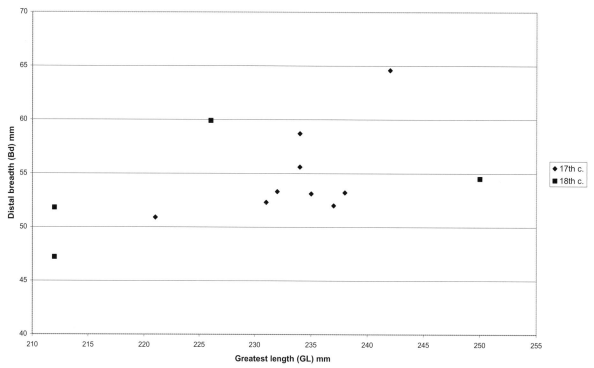

Fig. 131 Cattle metatarsals: Scattergram of Bd plotted against GL

Pathology

Few bones showed any evidence for pathology. Those that did are noted here, by phase.

Medieval

There were no pathological bones from this phase.

Dissolution

Three bones showed some degree of pathology. A fragment of a deer proximal metatarsal has an oval-shaped swelling on the antero-lateral part of the shaft approximately 24mm long and 16mm wide. On x-ray a radio-opaque area is seen on the surface of the bone. The internal surface of the bone is unaffected. No evidence for infection can be seen, and the cause of this pathology is probably traumatic in origin. A left calcaneum from a sub-adult animal (which may be from the same individual as the above metatarsal) also showed evidence for abnormality. The surface of the distal point has a periosteal reaction. On x-ray the bone looks poorly circumscribed ('fluffy'). This type of appearance may be associated with infection. Both of these bones may be from the same individual.

The third pathological bone is a cow mandible, which has ante-mortem loss of the second and third molars. Three pathological bones out of the 476 from this phase is quite a high proportion (0.6% of all bones affected compared to an overall site prevalence of 0.1%). It is interesting to note that this pattern is similar to that found at the site of Minster House, Bristol (Barber forthcoming) which saw an increased prevalence of pathology during and just after the Dissolution phase.

16th Century

No pathological bones were present in this phase. This is probably due to the small size of the sample.

17th Century

A right sheep maxilla shows evidence of ante-mortem tooth loss of the first molar. An abscess cavity is also present over the partially resorbed socket. Given the mild amount of socket resorption that is present the tooth was lost only shortly before death.

Three fragments of bone showed a small amount of periosteal reaction – a chicken tarso-metatarsus, a rib, and a pig tibia. Periosteal reactions have a multiple aetiology including trauma, infection or the presence of ulcers. These reactions can occur on bone with little effect on the individual, and are probably inconsequential.

18th Century

Three fragments of bone displayed pathological changes. There was evidence of a fracture from a rib fragment of a large animal, probably a cow. The fracture had callus formation and at the time of death was well healed with no sign of infection.

A sheep maxilla showed some dental abnormality. The upper fourth premolar is only partially erupted in an adult maxilla. The tooth is rotated and erupting at an angle.

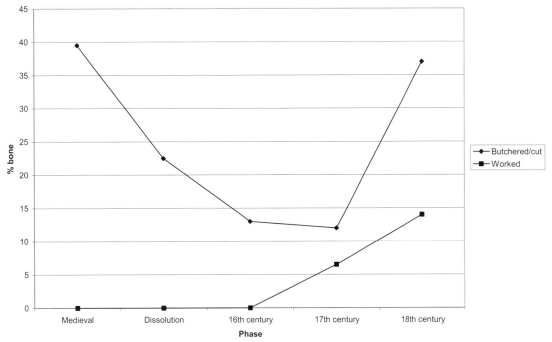

Fig. 132 Percentage of bones butchered and worked: all phases

Butchery

Most of the fragments of bone from all phases showed evidence of butchery. An average of 36% of all fragments of bone (including vertebrae and un-identifiable fragments) has some kind of cut or butchery mark (including the worked bone). Fig. 132 summarises the percentage of all fragments of bone that had been either butchered or worked.

It is clear that the animals whose remains are represented here have been extensively butchered. The earlier phases show cut marks on long bones and flat bones. There is evidence that skulls and mandibles were removed. Several of the tarsal bones had cut marks at the ligament insertions. These would be severed to remove the lower limbs.

There are two major differences between the earlier and late phases. Firstly, there is a change in the way that the vertebrae are butchered. In the later phases vertebrae at all levels were cut in half dorso-ventrally. This would indicate that carcasses were being butchered into sides of beef and mutton. Maltby (1979) found a similar change at Exeter. He dates the change from the sixteenth century. There is not enough data from the 16th-century levels at St James's Priory to see if it is the same.

Secondly, there is evidence of butchery of the skulls to utilise the brains which was not apparent before. All of the sheep skulls in the two later phases that

could be studied had been sawn open sagittally. This would have been the favoured method for obtaining the brain from which to make brawn, a popular food. This practice has also been noted at the contemporary site of St Bartholomew's Hospital (Barber 1998) which was located only a few hundred metres away. In addition all of the horn cores of these individuals had been removed post-mortem. They were most likely used elsewhere.

Bone Working

The most striking feature of the faunal remains from this site were the large numbers of worked bone. The worked bone was concentrated in the two later phases – the 17th and 18th centuries.

The majority of the bone identified were worked cow metapodials, mostly metatarsals (see Table 40). The worked bone appears to have been sawn into four types of shape: (1) short quarter sections of metapodial shaft, approximately 40mm long on average, (2) longer quarter sections – 90mm on average. The third type are bone rings made from centre metapodial shafts, smoothed to a circular shape from 5 to 40mm thick. The fourth type of sawn bone is the proximal metatarsal joints – these appear to be the off-cuts to get to the shaft of the metapodial. Fig. 133 illustrates bone types 1 to 3 and Table 40 shows the relative amounts of each type of worked bone present. The off-cuts are very similar to those described by Mac-Gregor (1989) from the 8th-century site at Münster.

From the shape of the cut fragments the most likely use of these bones is to create handles for domestic items such as hairbrushes, toothbrushes and cutlery. No completed items were found, although four pieces of bone handle were found which were worked to quite an advanced stage.

Pit 259 is typical of those contexts that produced industrial waste, although the relatively minor amounts would indicate small-scale activity. Most of the pieces were discarded at a relatively early stage. The small number of pieces found, as well as lack of more advanced pieces, would imply that the workshop was not very close to the site. It may be that this pit was just one local rubbish dump for local industries and was used for only a short time or one or two visits. The fact that other unusual objects (medical instruments and glass phials) came from the pit would support the argument that this was a general rubbish pit used by several local industries instead of an on-site rubbish pit.

Further Discussion and Comparisons With Other Sites

It is difficult to come to many conclusions from the faunal remains recovered from this site. The sample size overall is relatively small, and covers a long period of time. Uneven sample sizes make comparisons across phases difficult, sometimes impossible. It is important to avoid over-interpretation of the data, and although some interesting results have been noted, they usually involve sample sizes that are too small for statistical analysis. However, from the remains presented for analysis the site of St James's

Priory, while providing little information about the priory itself, does give some evidence about domestic and industrial activities in the locality.

After the Dissolution, the area around St James's Priory was open ground until the 18th century. At that time a few houses were built in the area. During its time as wasteland, the area was obviously a site for the dumping of both domestic and industrial refuse. It cannot be certain what houses used this area, nor for what length of time, but the nearby Brayne mansion (see the rest of the report for further information) may have been one.

St James's Priory has a similar profile of domestic animal remains to many contemporary excavations both locally and across the country. Locally, St Bartholomew's Hospital and St Mary-le-Port have the same relative proportions of species, as does the nearby city of Exeter.

There is also evidence that butchery practices were similar across many sites, and that the practices changed over time. At St Bartholomew's Hospital there were high numbers of sheep skulls sawn in half to remove the brains – this would have been a cheap food source and is backed up by documentary references on the site as to the poverty of the occupants. This practice is also noted at St James's Priory, though in not such great numbers. At Exeter Maltby had a much larger sample size from several sites, but his results are very similar. He notes the changes in butchery patterns over time with a trend towards butchering sides of meat.

There also appears to be some evidence from this site that there is a change in age at slaughter of cattle over time. The 17th-century phase shows a marked increase in the number of juvenile animals on site. The numbers involved are extremely small and on their own do not provide a strong case for this phenomenon. However, this data compares favourably with that of other sites of similar date across the country. Data from Launceston Castle shows an increase in juvenile animals in periods 8 and 9 (15th to 16th century). This, the authors suggest, is due to

Table 40 Relative amounts of each type of bone off-cuts identified

Bone type	Relative frequency
Short quarter sections	37
Long quarter sections	17
Worked rings	27
Sawn proximal metatarsal heads	19

Fig. 133 Types of worked bone (scale 1:2)

increased specialisation in the cattle industry. Beef and veal are appearing by demand, not solely as a by-product of milk production. They discuss other sites showing a similar countrywide pattern in their report – a contemporary increase in juvenile numbers is noted in Exeter by Maltby (1979), at Sandal Castle by Griffiths *et al.* (1983) and at St Andrew's Priory by O'Connor (1993). Grant (1988, 156) also notes the phenomena of increasing numbers of juveniles 'in later deposits at some sites' in her survey of animal resources – she suggests this is due to an increasing importance of cattle as suppliers of meat, not just milk.

One of the most interesting findings from this site is that some of the many 17th- and 18th-century pits on the site show evidence of specialised use, including some degree of small-scale industrialised bone working. No evidence for any bone-working industry was noted in any samples from the earlier periods of the site (medieval, Dissolution and 16th-century phases), although the numbers of fragments in these samples was considerably smaller than those of later dates. This is similar to the site of St Mary-le-Port, Bristol. Here, Noddle (1985) found large numbers of metapodials on site of a contemporary date. She notes that these are the bone workers' 'favourite' material but none of the metapodials on the site were worked. However, the site did contain a large number of horn-cores which may have been worked. Noddle suggests that the material from St Mary-le-Port was derived from slaughterhouses and butchers waste more than domestic refuse. The comparison with the contents of some of the pits on the St James's Priory site suggests a similar mix of domestic and industrial waste.

In summary, the remains from St James's Priory are difficult to interpret. This is partly due to the small numbers of fragments that are involved, but also due to the fact that the site appears to contain debris from many different aspects of urban life in Bristol over time. There are obviously remains from the occupation of the priory, though these are scant and are largely disturbed by later activity on the site. There is some evidence of changes over time in the urban economy of Bristol city – perhaps a change to using younger cattle more for meat (veal, even) in the 17th and 18th centuries which can be seen in other areas around the country. There is also some evidence for localised industries – bone working and tanneries perhaps. Though this site cannot on its own answer many of the aims which it set out to complete, when seen in conjunction with other larger sites both locally and nationally, it can help add a few more pieces to the 'jigsaw'.

Conclusions

The major conclusions of this report are:

1. The majority of species identified were from the three major food species – cow, sheep/goat and pig. Smaller numbers of other species were also present. No unusual or 'exotic' species were identified.

2. There is little change in the relative number of species across all phases, however different body parts are represented over time. A wider variety of skeletal elements are present in the later phases.

3. There is a change in age at slaughter of cattle towards younger animals in the later centuries. Sheep were mostly slaughtered as adults across all phases. Pigs were killed as immature or sub-adults in all phases.

4. Butchery practices change between the Dissolution and the 17th-century phases. These findings are similar to contemporary urban sites both in Bristol and in the nearby city of Exeter.

5. The site has several pits that produced evidence for small-scale bone working in the 17th and 18th centuries. Remains of skulls with horn cores removed suggests a local horn industry, though not on this site.

7 DISCUSSION

The broad aims of the two excavations at St James's Priory were set out in Chapter 1 and, despite the destruction caused to the medieval archaeology by later interventions on both sites, those aims were largely achieved.

It was our intention to establish the extent and date of the U-shaped gullies, located during the 1989 excavation on Site 1, which pre-dated the monastic burials and thus may have pre-dated the 12th-century priory. In fact, the area of Site 1 excavated in 1995 had been so intensively used for burials and post-medieval housing that no trace of any pre-burial features remained. The gullies excavated in 1989 contained no dating evidence and although the backfill of six of the medieval graves produced residual and much abraded sherds of Romano-British pottery, it seems unlikely that the gullies date to that period, the pottery almost certainly coming from a settlement some 300m to the north-west of the priory. An interpretation of the purpose of the gullies is difficult as the nature of their fills did not show signs of gradual silting or a build-up of organic material as might be expected in ditches used for drainage or as land divisions.

An indication of the date of the gullies is perhaps provided by the three shallow features found on Site 2 which, again, pre-dated the medieval activity on the site and contained a few small sherds of late Saxon pottery. These finds hint at a late Saxon date for the establishment of a religious community on the site of St James's Priory and may lend support to the somewhat obscure and possibly unreliable documentary sources referred to by the 18th- and 19th-century antiquarians, Barrett and Seyer. However, in the absence of a more substantial body of archaeological or documentary evidence a pre-Norman date for the foundation of the priory must remain conjectural.

Whatever the possible Saxon origins of the religious settlement, we know that the Normans established a Benedictine priory here sometime around 1129. The reason this location was chosen by the earliest known monastic community in Bristol is apparent when the area can be imagined without the trappings of a modern city. Here was a plateau of Triassic sandstone lying just above the flood plain of the River Frome and with a southerly aspect overlooking, but safely

removed from, the walled medieval town, the river forming a natural barrier between the two. The topography of the site made it necessary for the cloisters and conventual buildings to be located on the north, rather than the more usual south, side of the church although that layout is paralleled elsewhere. This plan had the advantage of making the priory church the most prominent building visible from the town, standing immediately at the top of the hillslope above the river. The river provided food and also water power for the priory mill, while the land around, particularly the south facing slopes of Kingsdown, were ideally situated for orchards and vineyards. The priory's extensive landholdings included areas of woodland which provided timber for use in the construction and repair of the priory buildings, the agricultural activity centring on the priory farm with its great tithe barn situated to the east at St James's Barton.

It is possible that the earliest religious structure on the site was the Lady Chapel, the construction of that chapel in advance of the main programme of church building having been argued by F. W. Potto Hick, an hypothesis supported by discoveries made at other monastic sites. Unfortunately, this can never be put to the test archaeologically as the site of the Lady Chapel was destroyed by office building in the 1960s.

Only ephemeral structural remains of the east end of the priory church survived on Site 1 and those largely consisted of spreads of mortar or, at the most, one or two courses of stone foundations, the floors and any internal structures of the church having been generally removed during a reduction in ground level after the Dissolution. The position of the east end wall of the church located by excavation compares favourably with its supposed position identified from the measurements given by William Worcestre after his visit in 1478. During the 14th century a wall was built which, had it stood to any height, would have blocked the south transept and this may have been connected with the re-ordering of the church after 1374. Only two burials survived within the east end of the church, of which only one could be fully excavated. That was of a male aged between 35 and 45 years who, judging by the size and quantity of the coffin nails in the grave fill, had been buried in a substantial wooden coffin. That burial, presumably by its proximity to the position of the high altar, would have been of a person of some importance either within, or as a benefactor to, the religious community.

Although no archaeological dating evidence was found for the construction of the church, the walls appeared to have been of one build, employing a distinctive yellow sandy mortar. The building work on the church was presumably completed within a short time after the foundation of the priory and it is significant that no head-niche burials, the earliest type of burial found in the monastic burial ground, underlie or were cut by the foundations of the church.

The area outside the east end of the church was used solely as a burial ground from the earliest days of the priory until at least the 16th century. The northern limit of the burial ground was marked by a shallow ditch but none of its other boundaries were found. The burials appeared to have been set out in rows indicating the use of grave markers, although none survived, or a burial plan or possibly both. Over the centuries, and through intensive use of the burial ground, these rows became less well defined. In the absence of any other dating evidence associated with the bodies, the burials can only be dated by their relationship to each other, by the pottery found within their fills and, to a limited extent, by the burial type. The prolonged use of the burial ground, which led to overcrowding and the removal of any stratification by which burials could be linked, made phasing of the burials virtually impossible, although the head-niche type were clearly the earliest.

A number of different forms of burial were present of which the three main types were: head-niche burials where the shape of the grave had been cut to take the head and shoulders and then tapered towards the feet; coffin burials where the presence of iron nails points to the use of a wooden coffin; and simple burials where the absence of coffin nails or shroud pins could imply the use of wooden coffins held together by wooden dowels or pegs, the use of shrouds which were not fastened by pins or the absence of wooden coffins or shrouds. A few burials were packed with clay or mortar perhaps to seal in disease. The archaic use of stone pillows for the head was noted with a number of burials. There was a general absence of finds associated with the burials although three each had a pewter object, probably a chalice – and were almost certainly the burials of priests – and one had two folded silver coins in the region of the shoulders and a jet pendant, decorated with an incised cross and other symbols, below the chin. A folded lead package, possibly containing parchment, was found with the burial of an adult female.

The three to one ratio of male to female burials on Site 1 indicates that the area around the east end of the church was indeed mainly reserved for the burial of the all male religious community and follows the pattern noted on other monastic sites for the location of the community's burial ground. However, the presence of female and child burials within that burial ground is not unusual and has been noted elsewhere: these were almost certainly the burials of layfolk either working as servants of the community themselves or the wives and children of servants. In addition to defining the sex and age at death of the individuals the analysis of the skeletal material identified various types of diseases and, perhaps significantly, a lower proportion of trauma injuries than generally occurs in a contemporary non-monastic community.

Site 2, to the south-west of the priory church, was also partly used as a burial ground, its northern extent being defined by an east/west boundary wall apparently dating from the 12th century. This boundary wall probably divided the monastic community from the lay burial ground from the earliest period of the priory's existence, the presence of head-niche burials again suggesting an early date for some of the interments. The use of some form of grave markers or a plan of the burial plots is suggested by the orderly, overlapping nature of, at least, the earlier burials. An examination of the skeletal remains gives a ratio of male to female burials of one to one, as would be expected in a parish or lay burial ground, and this corresponds with the known use of the nave of the priory church by parishioners from an early period. The burials excavated were part of a much larger lay or parish cemetery used throughout the medieval period and continuing in use until the 20th century, other groups of medieval burials having been recovered during a watching brief in another part of the cemetery in 1997 and as a result of rescue excavations in 1954. The orderly layout of all the graves found does not support the popular local story of the discovery of 'plague pits' arising from the public interest in the 1954 excavation.

The most westerly area of Site 2 never seems to have been part of the lay burial ground. A building occupied the site from the late 13th century, but even before that there was no evidence of burials having taken place there. A wall found in an evaluation trench suggests that the building also extended further to the west. The building went out of use in the 15th century but was then reoccupied in the early 17th century, continuing in use in a modified form until its demolition in the 1950s. It is possible that this building was connected with the lay use of this area of the priory precinct but its purpose is unknown. Little archaeological work has been carried out on such areas of monastic complexes and there appear to be no parallels for a building of this type and in this location elsewhere. Close to the west front of St. Augustine's abbey in Bristol, an excavation in 1992 uncovered a building identified as the abbot's house and the guest-house of the abbey, but there the building was adjacent to cloisters and other conventual buildings rather than on the opposite side of the church from them.

The Dissolution of the priory took place in 1540 and, while the nave of the church survived because of its use by the parish, the east end quickly became ruinous, the walls and foundations being comprehensively robbed away presumably for use as building materials elsewhere, probably in the conversion of the cloisters and conventual buildings to the mansion house owned by Henry Brayne, a conversion and re-use typical of other urban monastic sites. The Lady Chapel almost certainly survived in a ruinous state into the 18th century when it was incorporated into the houses built on the north side of St James's Parade, only being demolished in the 1960s.

Shortly after the Dissolution pits were dug within the monastic cemetery, possibly to extract sand for industrial purposes, and their backfill included debris from the priory such as decorated floor tiles, roof tiles and a few fragments of decorated window glass.

Much archaeological evidence was found for the post-medieval development of the areas to the west and east of the church for housing. Millerd's map of 1673 depicts buildings to the west of the church and evidence for these was found, including the re-use of the late 13th-century building. No 17th-century structures were found to the east of the church and it is assumed that those shown by Millerd in that area lay just outside the excavation. Instead there were a number of rubbish pits, some stone-lined, which were presumably within the garden areas or common ground adjacent to the properties. The pottery and other finds from the rubbish pits provide clues as to the status of the occupants in this area of St James's parish during the 17th and early 18th centuries. As might be expected in an area of urban expansion outside the confines of the medieval city and adjoining Brayne's mansion house, the ceramics, glass, and small finds indicate the presence of moderately high status households using imported ceramics and high quality local wares – the contents of their tables at least suggesting they were keeping abreast of contemporary fashions. The occurrence in one pit of tin-glazed earthenware drug jars, syringes and glass medical equipment may indicate that an apothecary or barber-surgeon resided in one of the adjoining houses. A small scale bone-working industry operating locally is suggested by the inclusion of bone working waste in a number of the pits.

During the 18th century the narrow thoroughfare known initially as The Churchyard and later as St James's Parade was laid out from east to west across the parish churchyard to the south of the church. Development took place along the north side of this thoroughfare and then to the east and south of Cannon Street. The existing medieval and 17th-century buildings to the west of the church and the remains of the Lady Chapel were incorporated into this development, the shell of the Lady Chapel being converted into two tenements. The remains of two of these 18th-century houses, mainly their cellars and gardens, were excavated to the west of the church while on Site 1 the rear of at least two properties fronting St James's Parade and other houses fronting Cannon Street were uncovered together with ancillary structures. The development of these houses is recorded in documents and on maps and plans but the excavations provided more detailed information about the houses and their households, ranging from the size and position of water tanks, the nature and position of the boundaries separating the back gardens and courtyards and the complex nature of the stone-lined drainage systems, to the nature of the tablewares, cooking utensils, clay smoking pipes and other everyday objects collected from their rubbish pits.

Although demolition of some of the houses fronting St James's Parade occurred in the mid 19th century to make way for the construction of the Scottish Presbyterian Church, the area did not see large-scale change until the decades following the Second World War. During that period all the 18th-century houses fronting St James's Parade and Cannon Street in the areas of Sites 1 and 2 were systematically demolished, either to allow the development of the area for office buildings or simply to clear the ground for car parking. In turn, the 1960s offices have been demolished and replaced by a larger office block, this time with a basement car park, whose construction necessitated the archaeological excavation carried out in 1995. On Site 2, the car park has been replaced by a drug rehabilitation unit and hostel run by the Little Brothers of Nazareth, a monastic order based in St James's Church who are dedicated to helping the homeless and needy. After its use as a parish church, and following a period of redundancy, the presence of a monastic community has enabled the fortunes of the church to come full circle since its establishment as a religious centre in the 12th century.

And what of the future? Due to its location on the edge of the city centre the area around St James's Church will be subject to constant rebuilding due to the high value of the land and the changing needs of the city's commercial sector. Although the church itself and the surviving remains of its parish burial ground, now a public park, should be safe from development, there is still a great deal of potential for archaeological work on St James's Priory. To the north of the church, on the site of the cloisters and conventual buildings, lies the Bristol Bus and Coach Station which, by the nature of its construction, has probably caused minimal damage to the archaeological resource. Any future development in that area must be preceded by archaeological excavation which should not only take account of the medieval structures, but the substantial alterations made to them in the post-medieval period to produce the elaborate urban mansion house initially owned by Brayne. The site of the priory farm and tithe barn has probably been largely destroyed by the modern office block formerly known as Avon House, now the Premier Travel Inn, and the sunken roundabout adjoining, but any building work in that area should be monitored archaeologically. Indeed, every opportunity should be taken to excavate, observe and record the remains of the priory in the future in order that its extent and history may be more fully understood.

BIBLIOGRAPHY AND REFERENCES

Primary Sources

Bristol Record Office (BRO)

P/St J/F/28/13
P/St J/F/28/15
P/St J/HM/4(a–h)
P/St J/HM/7
P/St J/V/12/4
P/St J/V/12/4/1
P/St J/V/12/4/3
P/St J/V/12/4/6
St James's Parish Lamp Rate
St. John's Parish Deeds No. 99
Building Plan Book A. folio 264
Building Plan Book 4, folio 176
17563, folio 129
35709 Box 1
5139(175)

Gloucestershire Record Office (GRO)

D293/2
D1799/T34
D1799/T7

The National Archives (PRO)

E315/214 folio 106
E318/164

Bristol City Museum and Art Gallery

Watercolour by T. L. S. Rowbotham 1826, Accession No.
M.2839

Bristol City Valuer's Office

Bristol City Survey, c.1855

Secondary Sources

Addyman, P. and Black, V. (eds.) (1984) *Archaeological papers from York presented to M. W. Barley*. York: York Archaeological Trust.
Albarella, U. and Davies, S. (1996) Mammals and birds from Launceston Castle, Cornwall: decline in status and the rise of agriculture. *Circaea* 12.1, 1–156.
Allan, J. P. (1984) Medieval and post-medieval finds from Exeter, 1971–1980. *Exeter Archaeological Reports* 3.
Arthur, B. V. (1962) St James's Priory site, Bristol. *Bristol Archaeological Research Group Bulletin* 1(3), 36–37.
Astill, G. and Grant, A. (eds.) (1988) *The countryside of medieval England*. Oxford, Blackwell.
Aston, M. and Iles, R. (eds.) (undated) *The archaeology of Avon: a review from the Neolithic to the Middle Ages*. Bristol, Avon County Council.
Ayers, B. (1985) Excavations within the north-east bailey of Norwich Castle, 1979. *East Anglian Archaeology Report* 28.
BaRAS (1993) *Archaeological evaluation at St James's Church*. Bristol and Region Archaeological Services unpublished client report no. BA/BO17 (author: J. Bryant).
BaRAS (1994a) *Desktop assessment of the former NFU Insurance Office site, St James Parade/Cannon Street, Bristol*. Bristol and Region Archaeological Services unpublished client report no. BA/C075 (author: R. Burchill).
BaRAS (1994b) *Archaeological evaluation of St James Parade, Cannon Street, Bristol*. Bristol and Region Archaeological Services unpublished client report no. BA/C088 (author: E. Boore).
BaRAS (1998) *Archaeological watching brief at St James's Place, Bristol*. Bristol and Region Archaeological Services unpublished client report no. 294/1998 (author: R. Burchill).
BaRAS (2002) *Archaeological evaluation at Quakers Friars, Broadmead, Bristol*. Bristol and Region Archaeological Services unpublished client report no. 926/2002 (author: R. Jackson).
Barber, G. (1994) *Arachnoid granulations and age: a possible correlation?* Paper presented to the tenth European Members' Meeting of the Palaeopathology Association, Gottingen, Germany.
Barber, G. (1998) Animal bones. In R. Price and M. Ponsford, St Bartholomew's Hospital, Bristol. The excavation of a medieval hospital: 1976–8. *Council for British Archaeology Research Report* 110, 181–192.
Barber, G. (forthcoming) The animal bones. In E. Boore *Excavations at Minster House, Bristol Cathedral, 1992*.
Barrett, W. (1789). *The history and antiquities of the city of Bristol*. Bristol.
Baskerville, G. (1927) The dispossessed religious of Gloucestershire. *Transactions of the Bristol and Gloucestershire Archaeological Society* 49, 63–122.
Bass, W. M. (1987) *Human osteology: a laboratory and field manual of the human skeleton*. Missouri Archaeological Society Special Publication 2.
Berry, A. C. and Berry, R. J. (1967) Epigenetic variation in the human cranuim. *Journal of Anatomy* 125, 23–37.
Bickley, F. B. (ed.) (1900) *The Little Red Book of Bristol, Volume 1*. Bristol, Crofton Hemmons.
Biddle, M. (1990) *Artefacts from medieval Winchester. Part II: Object*

and economy in medieval Winchester, 789–791. Winchester Studies 7.ii. Oxford, Clarendon Press.

Biddle, M. and Kjolbye-Biddle, B. (1990) Chalices and patens in burials. In M. Biddle *Artefacts from medieval Winchester. Part II: Object and economy in medieval Winchester*, 791–799. Winchester Studies 7.ii. Oxford, Clarendon Press.

Blockley, K. (forthcoming) *Excavations at Welsh Back, Bristol, 1995*.

Boessneck, J. (1969) Osteological differences between sheep and goats. In D. Brothwell and E. Higgs (eds.) *Science in archaeology*. London, Thames and Hudson.

Bond, C. J. (1993) Water management in the urban monastery. In R. Gilchrist and H. Mytum (eds.) Advances in monastic archaeology. *British Archaeological Reports, British Series* 227, 43–78.

Boore, E. (1984) *Excavations at Tower Lane, Bristol*. Bristol, City of Bristol Museum and Bristol Threatened History Society.

Boore, E. (1986) The church of St Augustine the Less, Bristol: an interim statement. *Transactions of the Bristol and Gloucestershire Archaeological Society* 104, 211–214.

Boore, E. (1989) The Lesser Cloister and a medieval drain at St. Augustine's Abbey, Bristol. *Transactions of the Bristol and Gloucestershire Archaeological Society* 107, 217–222.

Boore, E. (1990) Lower Maudlin Street, City. In M. Ponsford, R. Jones, B. Williams, E. Boore, J. Bryant and A. Linge (eds.) Archaeology in Bristol 1989. *Transactions of the Bristol and Gloucestershire Archaeological Society* 108, 181–182.

Boore, E. (forthcoming) *Excavations at Minster House, Bristol Cathedral, 1992*.

Bouquet-Appel, J. P. and Masset, C. (1982) Farewell to palaeo-demography. *Journal of Human Evolution* 11, 321–333.

Brooks, S. T. and Suchey, J. M. (1990) Skeletal age determination based on the Os pubis: a comparison of the Ascádi-Nemeskéri and Suchey-Brooks methods. *Human Evolution* 5, 227–238.

Brothwell, D. R. (1981) *Digging up bones*. 3rd edn. Oxford, Oxford University Press.

Bryant, J. (1993) Architectural recording at St James's Priory, Bristol. *Bristol and Avon Archaeology* 11, 18–34.

Buikstra, J. and Ubelaker, D. (eds.) (1994) Standards for data collection from human skeletal remains. *Arkansas Archaeological Survey Research Series* 44.

Burchill, R. (forthcoming) The small finds. In K. Blockley *Excavations at Welsh Back, Bristol, 1995*.

Butler, L. A. S. (1984) The Houses of the Mendicant Order in Britain: recent archaeological work. In P. Addyman and V. Black (eds.) *Archaeological papers from York presented to M. W. Barley*, 123–136. York: York Archaeological Trust.

Butler, L. A. S. (1993) The archaeology of urban monasteries in Britain. In R. Gilchrist and H. Mytum (eds.) Advances in monastic archaeology. *British Archaeological Reports, British Series* 227, 79–86.

Charleston, R. J. (1975) The glass. In C. Platt and R. Coleman-Smith *Excavations in medieval Southampton 1953–1969. Vol.2 The Finds*, 204–226. Leicester, Leicester University Press.

Charleston, R. J. (1984) The glass. In J. P. Allan, Medieval and post-medieval finds from Exeter 1971–1980. *Exeter Archaeological Reports* 3, 258–278.

Charleston, R. J. (1986) Glass from Plymouth. In C. Gaskell-Brown, Plymouth excavations: the medieval waterfront, Woolster Street, Castle Street, Finds Catalogues. *Plymouth Museum Archaeology Series* 3, 36–52.

Clark, G. T. (1850) *Report to the general Board of Health, on a preliminary inquiry into the sewerage, drainage and supply of water and the sanitary condition of the inhabitants of the city and county of Bristol*. Bristol.

Clarke, H. and Carter, A. (1977) Excavations in medieval King's Lynn 1963–70. *Society for Medieval Archaeology Monograph* 7.

Clason, A. T. (ed.) (1975) *Archaeozoological Studies*. Amsterdam, Elsevier.

Coppack, G. (1990) *Abbeys and priories*. London, Batsford/English Heritage.

Corfield, M., Hinton, P., Nixon, T. and Pollard, M. (eds.) (1998) *Preserving archaeological remains* in situ. London, Museum of London Archaeology Service.

Cowgill, J., de Neergaard, M. and Griffiths, N. (1987) *Knives and scabbards. Medieval finds from excavations in London: 1*. London, HMSO.

Crummy, N. (1988) The post-Roman small finds from excavations in Colchester 1971–85. *Colchester Archaeological Reports* 5.

Currie, C. K. (1993) The archaeology of the flowerpot in England and Wales, *circa* 1650–1950. *Garden History* 21(2), 227–246.

Dallaway, J. (1834) *Antiquities of Bristow in the middle centuries, including the topography by William Wycestre and the life of William Canynges*. Bristol, Mirror Office.

Daniell, C. (1997) *Death and burial in medieval England*. London, Routledge.

Dawson, D. (1974) *Excavations at Bristol, St. James, Horsefair*. Unpublished typescript, Bristol City Museum and Art Gallery Archive.

Dawson, D. (1981) Archaeology and the medieval churches of Bristol, Abbots Leigh and Whitchurch. *Bristol Archaeological Research Group Review* 2, 9–24.

Dickinson, J. C. (1976) The origins of St. Augustine's, Bristol. In P. McGrath and J. Cannon (eds.) *Essays in Bristol and Gloucestershire history*, 109–126. Bristol, Bristol and Gloucestershire Archaeological Society.

Donne, B. (1826) *A plan of Bristoll, Clifton, the Hotwells and from an actual survey by B. Donne*. Bristol: Donne.

Driesch, A. von den (1976) A guide to the measurement of animal bones from archaeological sites. *Peabody Museums Bulletin* 1. Peabody Museum of Archaeology and Ethnology, Harvard University, Cambridge (Mass).

Dugdale, W. (1823) *Monasticon Angliacanum: A history of the abbies and other monasteries, hospitals, frieries and cathedral and collegiate churches, with their dependencies, in England and Wales ... Vol. IV*. London.

Eames, E. S. (1951) The Canynges Pavement. *Journal of the British Archaeological Association* 14, 33–36.

Eames, E. S. (1980) *Catalogue of medieval lead-glazed earthenware tiles in the Department of Medieval and Later Antiquities*. London, British Museum.

Egan, G. and Pritchard, F. (1991) *Dress accessories c.1150–c.1450. Medieval finds from excavations in London: 3*. London, HMSO.

Evans, J. (1816) *History of Bristol, civil and ecclesiastical including biographical notices of eminent and distinquished natives. Vol. II*. Bristol, M. Bryan.

Fairclough, G. (1979) St Andrews Street, Plymouth. *Plymouth Museum Archaeology Series* 2.

Ferembach, D., Schwidetsky, I. and Stloukal, M. (1980) Recommendations for age and sex diagnoses of skeletons. *Journal of Human Evolution* 9, 517–549.

Finnegan, M. (1978) Non metric variation of the infracranial skeleton. *Journal of Anatomy* 125, 23–37.

Gaimster, D. R. M., Margeson, S. and Hurley, M. (1990) Medieval Britain and Ireland in 1989. *Journal of the Society for Medieval Archaeology* 34, 168–169.

Gaskell-Brown, C. (1986) Plymouth excavations: the medieval waterfront, Woolster Street, Castle Street, Finds Catalogues. *Plymouth Museum Archaeology Series* 3.

Gilchrist, R. (1994) *Gender and material culture. The archaeology of religious women*. London and New York, Routledge.

Gilchrist, R. and Mytum, H. (eds.) (1993) Advances in monastic archaeology. *British Archaeological Reports, British Series* 227.

Gomme, A., Jenner, M. and Little, B. (1979) *Bristol – an architectural history*. London, Lund Humphries.

Goodall, I., Ellis, B. and Oakley, G.E. (1979) The iron objects. In J. H. Williams *St. Peter's Street, Northampton excavations, 1973–1976*, 268–277. Northampton, Northampton Development Corporation.

Goodall, I. H. (1984) Iron objects. In J. P. Allan, Medieval and post-medieval finds from Exeter, 1971–1980. *Exeter Archaeological Reports* 3, 337.

Goodall, I. H. (1984) Objects of non-ferrous metal. In J. P. Allan, Medieval and post-medieval finds from Exeter, 1971–1980. *Exeter Archaeological Reports* 3, 337–348.

Goodall, I. H. (1993) Iron weapons and armour. In S. Margeson, Norwich households: the medieval and post-medieval finds from the Norwich Survey excavations 1971–1978. *East Anglian Archaeology Report* 58, 229.

Graham, R. (1907) The religious houses of Gloucestershire. In W. Page (ed.) *The Victoria History of the Counties of England: Gloucestershire, vol 2*, 113–26. London, Constable.

Grant, A. (1982) The use of tooth wear as a guide to the age of domestic ungulates. In B. Wilson, C. Grigson and S. Payne, Ageing and sexing animal bone from archaeological sites. *British Archaeological Reports, British Series* 109, 91–108 .

Grant, A. (1984) Medieval animal husbandry: the archaeozoological evidence. In C. Grigson and J. Clutton-Brock, Animals and archaeology: 4 husbandry in Europe. *British Archaeological Reports, International Series* 227, 179–86.

Grant, A. (1988) Animal resources. In G. Astill and A. Grant (eds.) *The countryside of medieval England*. Oxford, Blackwell.

Gray, H. F. R. S. (1993) *Anatomy descriptive and surgical*. London, Magpie Books Ltd.

Greene, J. P. (1992) *Medieval monasteries*. Leicester, Leicester University Press.

Grierson, P. (1991) *Coins of medieval Europe*. London, Seaby.

Griffiths, N. J. L., Halstead, P. L. J., MacLean, A. and Rowley-Conwy, P. A. (1983) Faunal remains and economy. In P. Mayes and L. A. S. Butler. *Sandal Castle excavations 1964–1973*. Wakefield, Wakefield Historical Publications.

Grinsell, L. V. (1986) *The history and coinage of the Bristol mint*. Bristol, Bristol City Museum and Art Gallery.

Hall, I. V. (1944) Whitson Court sugar house, Bristol, 1665–1824. *Transactions of the Bristol and Gloucestershire Archaeological Society* 65, 1–97.

Harding, N. D. (ed.) (1930) Bristol charters 1155–1373. *Bristol Record Society* 1.

Harvey, B. (1993) *Living and dying in England 1100–1540: The Monastic Experience*. Oxford, Clarendon Press.

Harvey, J. H. (ed.) (1969) *William Worcestre: Itineraries*. Oxford, Clarendon Press.

Harvey, Y. (1975) Catalogue: the bronze. In C. Platt and R. Coleman–Smith *Excavations in medieval Southampton 1953–1969. Vol.2 The Finds*, 254–268. Leicester, Leicester University Press.

Haslam, J. (ed.) (1984) *Anglo-Saxon towns in Southern England*. Chichester, Phillimore.

Heighway, C. and Bryant, R. (1999) The Golden Minster: The Anglo-Saxon and later medieval priory of St Oswald at Gloucester. *Council for British Archaeology Research Report* 117.

Herbert, N. M. (ed.) (1988) *The Victoria County History of the County of Gloucester. Vol. IV: The City of Gloucester*. Oxford: Oxford University Press.

Hershkovitz, I., Latimer, B., Dutour, O., Jellema, L. M., Wish-Baratz, S., Rothschild, C. and Rothschild, B. M. (1997) Why do we fail in aging the skull from the sagittal suture? *American Journal of Physical Anthropology* 103, 393–399.

Hinton, D. A. (1984) The towns of Hampshire. In J. Haslam (ed.) *Anglo-Saxon towns in Southern England*, 149–165. Chichester, Phillimore.

Hirst, S. M. and Wright, S. (1989) Bordesley Abbey Church: a long-term research excavation. In R. Gilchrist, R. and H. Mytum (eds.) The archaeology of rural monasteries. *British Archaeological Reports, British Series* 203, 295–311.

Hobley, B. (1971) Excavations at the Cathedral and Benedictine Priory of St. Mary, Coventry. *Transactions of the Birmingham and Warwickshire Archaeological Society* 84, 45–139.

Hoppa, R. D. (1992) Evaluating human skeletal growth: an Anglo-Saxon example. *International Journal of Human Osteoarchaeology*. December 1994, 275–289.

İşcan, M. Y., Loth, S. R. and Wright, R. K. (1984) Age estimation from the rib by phase analysis: white males. *Journal of Forensic Sciences* 29, 1094–1104.

İşcan, M. Y., Loth, S. R. and Wright, R. K. (1985) Age estimation from the rib by phase analysis: white females. *Journal of Forensic Sciences* 30, 853–863.

Jackson, R. (2000) Archaeological excavations at Upper Maudlin Street, Bristol, in 1973, 1976 and 1999. *Bristol and Avon Archaeology* 17, 29–110.

Jackson, R. (forthcoming) *Excavations at Union Street, Bristol, 2000*.

Jackson, R. G. and Price, R. H. (1974) Bristol clay pipes: a study of makers and their marks. *City of Bristol Museum and Art Gallery Research Monograph* 1.

Jones, R. H. (1988a) *Trial excavations at the Welsh Congregational Chapel, Aug/Sept 1988*. Unpublished typescript, Bristol City Museum and Art Gallery Archive.

Jones, R. H. (1988b) Archaeology in Bristol 1988–89: St James Parade. *Bristol and Avon Archaeology* 7, 33.

Jones, R. H. (1989) Excavations at St James's Priory, Bristol, 1988–9. *Bristol and Avon Archaeology* 8, 2–7.

Klippel, J. H. and Dieppe, P. A. (1994) *Rheumatology*. New York, Mosby.

Lambert, M. W. (1971) The history of the Benedictine Priory of St Mary, Coventry. In B. Hobley, Excavations at the Cathedral and Benedictine Priory of St. Mary, Coventry. *Transactions of the Birmingham and Warwickshire Archaeological Society* 84, 50–78.

Latimer, J. (1887) *The annals of Bristol in the nineteenth century*. Bristol, Morgan.

Leach, P. (ed.) (1984) The archaeology of Taunton: excavations and fieldwork to 1980. *Western Archaeological Trust Excavation Monograph* 8.

Leighton, W. (1933) The Black Friars, now Quaker's Friars, Bristol. *Transactions of the Bristol and Gloucestershire Archaeological Society* 55, 151–190.

Levitan, B. (1989) Bone analysis and urban economy: example of selectivity and a case for comparison. In D. Serjeantson and T. Waldron, Diet and craft in towns. *British Archaeological Reports, British Series* 199.

Loades, J. (ed.) (1991) *Monastic Studies II*. Bangor, Headstart History.

Lobel, M. D. and Carus-Wilson, E. M. (1975) *Bristol. The atlas of historic towns 2*, 1–27. London, Scolar Press.

Longman, T. (2003) Excavations on the site of the priory of St Mary Magdalen, Upper Maudlin Street, Bristol, 2000. *Bristol and Avon Archaeology* 18, 3–29.

Loyn, H. R. (1962) *Anglo-Saxon England and the Norman Conquest*. London, Longman.

Lyne, M. (1997) *Lewes Priory. Excavations by Richard Lewis 1969–82*. Lewes, Lewes Priory Trust.

MacGregor, A. (1985) *Bone, antler, ivory and horn: the technology of skeletal materials since the Roman period*. London.

MacGregor, A. (1989) Bone, antler and horn industries in the urban context. In D. Serjeantson and T. Waldron, Diet and crafts in towns. *British Archaeological Reports, British Series* 199.

Maltby, M. (1979) Faunal studies on urban sites: the animal bones from Exeter 1971–1975. *Exeter Archaeological Reports* 2.

Margeson, S. (1993) Norwich households: medieval and post-medieval finds from Norwich Survey excavations 1971–1978. *East Anglian Archaeology Report* 58.

Mason, E. J. (1957) The Horsefair Cemetery, Bristol. *Transactions of the Bristol and Gloucestershire Archaeological Society* 76, 164–171.

Mayes, P. and Butler, L. A. S. (1983) *Sandal Castle excavations 1964–1973*. Wakefield, Wakefield Historical Publications.

McAleavy, T. (1996) *Life in a medieval abbey*. London, English Heritage.

McCann, J. (translator) (1976) *The Rule of St. Benedict*. London, Sheed and Ward.

McGrath, P. and Cannon, J. (eds.) (1976) *Essays in Bristol and Gloucestershire history*, 109–126. Bristol, Bristol and Gloucestershire Archaeological Society.

Megaw, J. V. (1984) The bone objects. In J. P. Allan, Medieval and post-medieval finds from Exeter 1971–80. *Exeter Archaeological Reports* 3, 349–351.

Merrifield, R. (1987) *The archaeology of ritual and magic*. London, B.T. Batsford Ltd.

Millard, A. (1998) Bone in the burial environment. In M. Corfield, P. Hinton, T. Nixon and M. Pollard (eds.) *Preserving archaeological remains in situ*, 93–102. London, Museum of London Archaeology Service.

Millerd, J. (1673) *An exact delineation of the famous Citty of Bristoll and Suburbs*. Bristol.

Mitchiner, M. and Skinner, A. (1984) English tokens c.1200 to 1425. *The British Numismatic Journal* 53.

Mitchener, M. and Skinner, A. (1985) English tokens c.1425 to 1672. *The British Numismatic Journal* 54.

Molleson, T. and Cox, M. (1993) The Spitalfields Project, Volume 2: The anthropology. The middling sort. *Council for British Archaeology Research Report* 86.

Moore, J. S. (ed.) (1982) *Domesday Book 15: Gloucestershire*. Chichester, Phillimore.

Noddle, B. (1985) Some of the faunal remains from Mary-le-Port, Bristol. In L. Watts and P. Rahtz, Mary-le-Port, Bristol: excavations 1962/3. *City of Bristol Museum and Art Gallery Research Monograph*, 7, 177–179.

Oakley, G. E. (1979) The glass; the copper alloy objects; the lead alloy objects. In J. H. Williams *St Peter's Street, Northampton excavations, 1973–1976*, 296–302; 248–264; 265–267. Northampton, Northampton Development Corporation.

O'Connell, L. (1998) *The articulated human skeletal remains from St Augustine the Less, Bristol*. Unpublished skeletal report, Bournemouth University.

O'Connor, T. (1993) Bone assemblages from monastic sites: many questions but few data. In R. Gilchrist and H. Mytum (eds.) Advances in monastic archaeology. *British Archaeological Reports, British Series* 227, 107–111.

Oman, C. (1990) Chalices and patens: background and typology. In M. Biddle *Artefacts from medieval Winchester. Part II: Object and economy in medieval Winchester*, 789–791. Winchester Studies 7.ii. Oxford, Clarendon Press.

Ortner, D. J. and Putschar, W. J. (1985) *Identification of pathological conditions in human skeletal remains*. Washington DC, Smithsonian Institution Press.

Page, W. (ed.) (1907) *The Victoria History of the Counties of England: Gloucestershire, vol 2*. London, Constable.

Parsons, F. G. (1916) On the proportions and characteristics of the modern English clavicle. *Journal of Anatomy* 51, 71.

Patterson, R. B. (1973) *Earldom of Gloucester Charters, the Charters and Scribes of the Earls and Countesses of Gloucester to A.D. 1217*. Oxford: Clarendon Press.

Payne, S. (1973) Kill-off patterns in sheep and goats: the mandibles from Asvan Kale. *Anatolian Studies* 23, 281–303.

Payne, S. (1975) Partial recovery and sampling bias. In A. T. Clason (ed.) *Archaeozoological Studies*. Amsterdam, Elsevier.

Peacock, D. P. S. (ed.) (1977) *Pottery and early commerce: characterisation and trade in Roman and later ceramics*. London: Academic Press.

Platt, C. and Coleman-Smith, R. (1975) *Excavations in medieval Southampton 1953–1969. Vol.2 The Finds*. Leicester, Leicester University Press.

Plumley, J. and Ashmead, G. (1828) *Plan of the City of Bristol and its suburbs (6 sheets)*. Bristol, Ashmead.

Ponsford, M. W. (1975) *Excavations at Greyfriars, Bristol*. Bristol, City of Bristol Museum and Art Gallery and Bristol Threatened History Society.

Ponsford, M. W. (1979) *Bristol Castle: archaeology and the history of a royal fortress*. Unpublished MLitt thesis, University of Bristol.

Ponsford, M. W. (1988) Pottery. In B. Williams, The excavation of medieval and post-medieval tenements at 94–102 Temple Street, Bristol, 1975. *Transactions of the Bristol and Gloucestershire Archaeological Society* 106, 124–145.

Ponsford, M. W. (1998) Pottery. In R. H. Price with M. Ponsford, St Bartholomew's Hospital, Bristol. The excavation of a medieval hospital: 1976–8. *Council for British Archaeology Research Report* 110, 136–156.

Ponsford, M. W. (undated) Bristol. In M. Aston and R. Iles (eds.) *The archaeology of Avon: a review from the Neolithic to the Middle Ages*, 145–159. Bristol, Avon County Council.

Ponsford, M., Jones, R., Williams, B. Boore, E., Bryant, J. and Linge, A. (eds.) (1990) Archaeology in Bristol 1989. *Transactions of the Bristol and Gloucestershire Archaeological Society* 108, 175–183.

Potter, K. R. (ed.) (1955) *Gesta Stephani. The deeds of Stephen*. London, Thomas Nelson.

Potto Hick, F. W. (1932) *Medieval history of St James, Bristol*. Unpublished MA dissertation. Bristol Record Office P/St. J/ HM/4(a–h).

Preston, A. (1979) The glass. In G. Fairclough, St Andrews Street, Plymouth. *Plymouth Museum Archaeology Series* 2, 120–124.

Price, R. H., Jackson, R. G. and Jackson, P. (1979) *Bristol clay pipe makers: a revised and enlarged edition*. Bristol, privately published by the authors.

Price, R. H. with Ponsford, M. (1998) St Bartholomew's Hospital, Bristol. The excavation of a medieval hospital: 1976–8. *Council for British Archaeology Research Report* 110.

Pritchard, J. E. (1898) Archaeological notes for 1898. *Proceedings of the Clifton Antiquarian Club* 4, 158.

Pritchard, J. E. (1906) Bristol archaeological notes for 1904. *Transactions of the Bristol and Gloucestershire Archaeological Society* 29, 133–141.

Pryce, G. (1861) *A popular history of Bristol*. Bristol, W. Mack.

Rawes, B. (1993) Archaeological review 1992. *Transactions of the Bristol and Gloucestershire Archaeological Society* 111, 216–217.

Rocque, J. (1743) *A plan of the city of Bristol. Survey'd and drawn by John Rocque. Engrav'd by John Pine 1742*. Bristol, Hickey.

Rodwell, K. and Bell, R. (2004) *Acton Court: the evolution of an early Tudor courtier's house*. London, English Heritage.

Rodwell, W. (2001) Wells Cathedral: excavations and structural studies, 1978–93. *English Heritage Archaeological Report* 21.

Rodwell, W. and Rodwell, K. (1982) St Peter's Church, Barton-upon-Humber: excavation and structural survey 1978–81. *Antiquaries Journal* 62, 283–315.

Rodwell, W. and Rodwell, K. (1985) Rivenhall: investigation of a villa, church and village, 1950–1977. *Council for British Archaeology Research Report* 55.

Rogers, J. (1984) Skeletons from the lay cemetery at Taunton Priory. In P. Leach (ed.) The archaeology of Taunton: excavations and fieldwork to 1980. *Western Archaeological Trust Excavation Monograph* 8, 194–199.

Rogers, J. (1999) Burials: the human skeletons. In C. Heighway and R. Bryant, The Golden Minster: The Anglo-Saxon and later medieval priory of St. Oswald at Gloucester. *Council for British Archaeology Research Report* 117, 229–246.

Rogers, J. and Waldron, T. (1995) *A field guide to joint disease in archaeology.* London, John Wiley and Sons.

Rogers, J., Waldron, T. and Dieppe, P. (1987) Arthropathies in palaeopathology: the basis of classification according to the most probable cause. *Journal of Archaeological Science* 14(2), 179–193.

Rogers, J., Young, P. and Dieppe, P. (1993) 'Bone formers' – positive correlations between osteophyte and enthesophyte formation. *British Journal of Rheumatology* 32 (suppl. 2), 51.

Saunders, S. R. (1989) Nonmetric skeletal variation. In M. Y. İşcan and K. A. R. Kennedy (eds.) *Reconstruction of life from the skeleton,* 95–108. New York, Wiley-Liss.

Saunders, S.R., Fitzgerald, C., Rogers, T., Dudar, C. and McKillop, H. (1992) A test of several methods of skeletal age estimation using a documented archaeological sample. *Canadian Society Forensic Science Journal* 25(2), 97–118.

Schmid, E. (1976) *Atlas of animal bones for prehistorians, archaeologists and Quaternary geologists.* Amsterdam, Elsevier.

Schofield, J. (1993) Building in religious precincts in London at the Dissolution and after. In R. Gilchrist and H. Mytum (eds.) *Advances in monastic archaeology. British Archaeological Reports, British Series* 227, 29–41.

Serjeantson, D. and Waldron, T. (1989) Diet and crafts in towns. *British Archaeological Reports, British Series* 199.

Seyer, S. (1821) *Memoirs historical and topographical of Bristol and its neighbourhood, from the earliest period down to the present time.* Vols 1 and 2. Bristol.

Shoesmith, R. (1985) Hereford City excavations. Vol. 3: the finds. *Council for British Archaeology Research Report* 56.

Silver, I. (1969) The ageing of domestic animals. In D. Brothwell and E. Higgs (eds.) *Science in Archaeology,* 283–302. London, Thames and Hudson.

Skeeters, M. C. (1993) *Community and clergy. Bristol and the Reformation c.1530–c.1570.* Oxford, Clarendon Press.

Stewart, T. D. (ed.) (1970) *Personal identification and mass disasters.* Washington DC, Smithsonian Institution.

Stroud, G. (1998) Human bone. In R. Price with M. Ponsford, St Bartholomew's Hospital, Bristol. The excavation of a medieval hospital: 1976–8. *Council for British Archaeology Research Report* 110, 175–181.

Stroud, G. (forthcoming) *The human bones from Greyfriars, Bristol.*

Stroud, G. and Kemp, R. L. (1993) *Cemeteries of St. Andrew Fishergate.* London, Council for British Archaeology for York Archaeological Trust (Fascicule AY 12/2).

Stuart-Macadam, P. (1985) Porotic hyperostosis: representative of a childhood condition. *American Journal of Physical Anthropology* 66, 391–398.

Suchey, J. M. (1985) *Ageing the male os pubis.* Paper presented at the 37th Annual Meeting of the American Academy of Forensic Sciences, Las Vegas.

Taylor, J. (1878) The Hospital of St. Mark, commonly called Billeswicke, or Gaunt's Hospital. *Transactions of the Bristol and Gloucestershire Archaeological Society* 3, 241–245.

Toulmin Smith, L. (ed.) (1910) *The itinerary of John Leland in or about the years 1535–1543.* Vol. 4. London, Bell and Sons.

Trotter, M. (1970) Estimation of stature from intact limb bones. In T. D. Stewart (ed.) *Personal identification and mass disasters,* 71–83. Washington DC, Smithsonian Institution.

Trotter, M. and Gleser, G. C. (1952) Estimation of stature from long bones of American white Negroes. *American Journal of Physical Anthropology* 10, 463–514.

Trotter, M. and Gleser, G. C. (1958) A re-evaluation of estimation of stature based on measurements of stature taken during life and long bones after death. *American Journal of Physical Anthropology* 16, 79–123.

Ubelaker, D. H. (1978) *Human skeletal remains: excavation, analysis, interpretation.* 2nd edn. Chicago, Aldine.

Vince, A. G. (1977) The medieval and post-medieval ceramic industry of the Malvern region: the study of a ware and its distribution. In D. P. S. Peacock (ed.) *Pottery and early commerce: characterisation and trade in Roman and later ceramics,* 257–305. London: Academic Press.

Vince, A. G. (1983) *The medieval ceramic industry of the Severn Valley.* Unpublished Ph.D. thesis, University of Southampton.

Waldron, T. (1993) The health of the adults. In T. Molleson and M. Cox, The Spitalfields Project Vol. 2: the anthropology. The middling sort. *Council for British Archaeology Research Report* 86, 67–89.

Waldron, T. (1995) Changes in the distribution of osteoarthritis over historical time. *International Journal of Osteoarchaeology* 5, 385–390.

Ward, S. W. (1990) Excavations at Chester: The lesser medieval religious houses. *Grosvenor Museum Archaeological Excavation Survey Report* 6.

Warren, R. H. (1896) On some encaustic tiles recently found in Bristol. *Proceedings of the Clifton Antiquarian Club* 3, 95–98.

Warren, R. H. (1907) The medieval chapels of Bristol. *Transactions of the Bristol and Gloucestershire Archaeological Society* 30, 181–211.

Watts, L. and Rahtz, P. (1985) Mary-le-Port, Bristol: excavations 1962/3. *City of Bristol Museum and Art Gallery Research Monograph* 7.

White, W. J. (1988) Skeletal remains from the cemetery of St. Nicholas Shambles, City of London. *London and Middlesex Archaeological Society Special Paper* 9.

Whitelock, D. (ed.) (1961) *The Anglo-Saxon Chronicle: a revised translation.* Rutger University Press.

Williams, B. (1979) Late medieval floor tiles from Acton Court, Iron Acton, Avon, 1974. *City of Bristol Museum and Art Gallery Research Monograph* 2, 61–76.

Williams, B. (1988) The excavation of medieval and post-medieval tenements at 94–102 Temple Street, Bristol, 1975. *Transactions of the Bristol and Gloucestershire Archaeological Society* 106, 107–168.

Williams, B. (2004) Medieval floor tiles. In K. Rodwell and R. Bell *Acton Court: the evolution of an early Tudor courtier's house,* 226–235. London, English Heritage.

Williams, B. (forthcoming a) *Excavations at 82–87 Redcliff Street, Bristol, 1980.*

Williams, B. (forthcoming b) *Excavations at Bristol Bridge, Bristol 1981.*

Williams, B. and Ponsford, M. W. (1988) Clay roof-tiles. In B. Williams, The excavation of medieval and post-medieval tenements at 94–102 Temple Street, Bristol, 1975. *Transactions of the Bristol and Gloucestershire Archaeological Society* 106, 145–149.

Williams, D. H. (1991) Layfolk within Cistercian precincts. In J. Loades (ed.) *Monastic Studies II,* 87–117. Bangor, Headstart History.

Williams, J. H. (1979) *St. Peter's Street, Northampton excavations, 1973–1976.* Northampton, Northampton Development Corporation.

Wilson, B., Grigson, C. and Payne, S. (1982) Ageing and sexing animal bones from archaeological sites. *British Archaeological Reports, British Series* 109.

Winstone, R. (1970) *Bristol in the 1940s.* 2nd edn. Bristol.

Winstone, R. (1979) *Bristol as it was, 1928–33.* Bristol.